BY JANICE REYNOLDS

Logistics
and
Fulfillment
FOR
e-business

A Practical Guide to Mastering
Back Office Functions for
Online Commerce

LOGISTICS & FULFILLMENT FOR E-BUSINESS

Published by CMP Books
An Imprint of CMP Media Inc.
Converging Communications Group
12 West 21 Street
New York, NY 10010

ISBN 1-57820-074-1

For individual orders, and for information on special discounts
for quantity orders, please contact:

CMP Books
6600 Silacci Way
Gilroy, CA 95020
Tel: 800-500-6875 or 408-848-3854
Fax: 408-848-5784
Email: cmp@rushorder.com

Distributed to the book trade in the U.S.and Canada by
Publishers Group West
1700 Fourth St., Berkeley, CA 94710

Manufactured in the United States of America

Table of Contents

Acknowledgment

I MUST EXPRESS . . .

My tremendous gratitude to Phil and Nat (you know who you are) for forgoing much needed time and attention while Deborah worked with me on this book. As always, I give much of the credit for the readability of this book to my editor, Deborah — thank you.

I also want to thank the staff at CMP — Robbie Alterio for the wonderful cover and the speedy and artistic layout of the book; Saul Roldan who took over from Robbie so the book could get to the printers on time. Then, of course, many thanks go to the staff of the CMP Book Division who have exhibited enormous patience in dealing with my peccadilloes — Christine Kern, Lisa Giaquinto and Frank Brogan.

Special thanks also to Richard Grigonis who was always ready to lend support and also Madeleine (this time spelled right) Delrow and Cliff Perciavalle for always being there.

Preface

ALTHOUGH THE WEB HAS quickly evolved from a browser-based information tool to an e-business enabler, the virtual world of e-business is increasingly blending with the realities of commerce: supply chain management, procurement, inventory management, order fulfillment and delivery of products to customers.

I've seen the confusion and frustration in e-business executive suites and IT departments, especially when it comes to implementing a viable logistics and fulfillment management system (LFMS). The necessity for a practical logistics and fulfillment solution can't be downplayed. The "duct tape" systems in place today must be re-engineered for an e-business to thrive. In this day and age, failures in an e-business's infrastructure result in problems, difficulties and outages that can not only turn away customers, but also garner negative global media attention.

I wrote <u>Logistics and Fulfillment for E-Business</u>, explicitly, to guide the non-technical executive through the ways and means of implementing an architectured infrastructure incorporating the correct tools to achieve a fail-safe LFMS. This includes walking the reader through the labyrinth of technical and outsourcing choices and helping them to understand the complex and comprehensive services that good partner relationships can provide. A robust, fail-safe LFMS is the only way for an e-business to be successful in this new competitive landscape. A best-of-breed LFMS is not only a means for increasing customer satisfaction and, therefore, retention; it also introduces efficiencies and cost savings throughout an enterprise.

If your business deals with e-businesses, is planning to adopt an e-business model in the near future, or is having trouble with its existing logistics and fulfillment system — whether it's B2B or e-tail — this book is written for you.

— Janice Reynolds

New York, NY

Introduction

THE MAJOR PORTION OF e-business is logistics. The Council of Logistics Management defines logistics as the process of planning, implementing, and controlling the efficient, effective flow and storage of goods, services, and related information from point of origin to point of consumption for the purpose of conforming to customer requirements.

Let's not forget the partner of logistics, fulfillment, which also plays a major role in many e-business models. Fulfillment comprises the back-office systems. For e-business sites, it's the systems that provide the link between the customer experience and the actual physical delivery of goods to the customer, which include inventory management, order capture and management and reconciliation.

As the year 2000 ended, several e-businesses, even pure-plays, began to turn the corner toward profitability. For example, Boston Consulting Group research in early 2000 indicated that about one-third of pure-play e-tailers that have been selling online for a year or more are now making money. And guess what, many of these stockholder-pleasing e-businesses are crediting their investment in a stable, scalable IT infrastructure (not marketing or branding or pretty pictures) for the glad tidings.

Although there are different factors at work in the B2B arena than there are in the e-tail area, infrastructure plays an important role in the success of both e-business models. Two of the key factors that separate the successful e-businesses from the failures are an efficient infrastructure and the integration of the e-business's value chain on the back-end.

The ascendancy of traditional bricks-and-mortar enterprises in the e-business community means that pure-play e-business models will have to match the well-built back-end systems and processes that the more established enterprises already have in place. As numerous industry experts

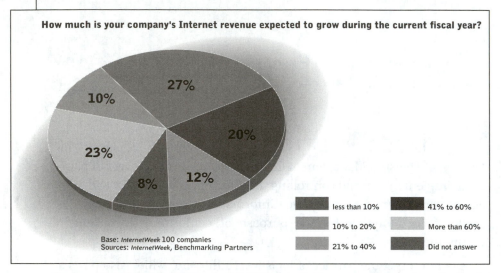

How much is your company's Internet revenue expected to grow during the current fiscal year?

27%
10%
20%
23%
8% 12%

less than 10%   41% to 60%
10% to 20%   More than 60%
21% to 40%   Did not answer

Base: *InternetWeek* 100 companies
Sources: *InternetWeek*, Benchmarking Partners

have pointed out, logistics and fulfillment is the area where a lot of e-businesses, pure-plays in particular, fail.

What the established e-business must realize is that *repeat* customers are the leading driver toward profitability. However, if an e-business is to earn the "bookmark," it must invest more time and resources in improving the customer experience. For many this means eliminating or re-working the processes that cause shopping cart abandonment.

Out of every ten shopping carts taken for a ride down cyber aisles, only three make it through the checkout process. While unexpected shipping costs or taxes put off some online shoppers, others are frustrated by logistics-and-fulfillment-related delays that slow their buying experience.

A first class LFMS could solve the problems of how to retain the customer, get the bookmark and get those overflowing shopping carts through the checkout procedures.

What most e-businesses are unprepared for, and all e-businesses must quickly get under control, is logistics and fulfillment management (LFM)

— the management of the flow of goods, services and information throughout the value chain.

The phenomenal growth of e-business brought the logistics and fulfillment issue to a head. When e-businesses first opened their sites to customers, the back-office systems could easily handle the relatively small number of daily orders regardless of how inefficient they might have been. But when online ordering and communications took off, mounting logistics and fulfillment problems, exacerbated by the customer's increasing demand for immediate delivery, resulted in chaos and disappointment.

It would appear that the shining promise of the Internet will soon be overshadowed by the failure of many "e-preneurs" — pure-plays and click-and-mortars, alike — whose demise will have been hastened by an inadequate logistics and fulfillment management system (LFMS).

Running a sophisticated e-business requires management that attends to day-to-day operations while constantly updating the business plan with input from the value chain. Ongoing operations include managing the inventory, packing product for shipment, coordinating the service of a shipping firm and tracking orders until they arrive at their destination. Post-sales issues, such as returned products, warranties and technical support, require additional functionality. An e-business must implement an LFMS in order to establish the systems that can carry out all these functions successfully.

There are many ways in which an e-business can implement an LFMS, but every e-business should begin with a strategy to assess its logistics and fulfillment requirements. Then once the requirements are outlined, the e-business can plan the most efficient and cost-effective manner in which to meet the requirements. This might mean entering into strategic partnerships to gain the technical, physical and staffing resources necessary, or it could entail building an in-house solution. Alternatively, a business can take a middle course defining what is feasible and cost-effective to handle in-house, and outsourcing the remainder through managed partnerships.

With the proper LFMS, which can include logistics and fulfillment partner(s), any enterprise can provide the "three Rs" of e-business — the *right* product at the *right* place at the *right* time. Although the Web can give e-businesses an advantage over most traditional businesses in terms of product, location, and price, many e-businesses have failed to realize this advantage. It's as if e-businesses have forgotten that the Web is a channel for commerce, to which most of the traditional business rules still apply, including those of logistics and fulfillment.

The challenge of e-business is to get the product quickly and cost-effectively to the customer. If not handled carefully, poor logistics and fulfillment will prove a decisive barrier to gaining and keeping online customers. Logistics and Fulfillment for E-business is a guide to inspire nontechnical executives to discover and utilize the correct tools and/or outsourcing solutions to achieve a fail-safe LFMS (with the same enthusiasm and energy as they embraced the Web). The technology necessary for a world-class LFMS is dense. I have sought to provide a book that is an easy read for the non-technical person and yet doesn't stint on the necessary business practices and technical issues involved in attaining the right logistics and fulfillment solution for your e-business model.

Initiating an LFMS project with straightforward targets requires dealing with "messyware" and a dizzying array of technical challenges. Completion of the project on time requires careful planning, commitment from the enterprise's executives and staff, and a cooperative value chain.

Logistics and Fulfillment for E-business will help any e-business to briskly apply the models of logistics and order fulfillment and adapt them to meet their own business needs. It will give the confidence to meet the demands of the value chain and show the steps necessary to begin to *immediately* develop a viable LFMS, which, in all probability, will include outsourcing through strategic partnerships.

Whether you're with a small start-up business or a large enterprise, an LFMS is both the source of competitive advantage and the lever for a positive profit margin. If you're not good at LFM, somebody else will be. That is the advantage that this book offers you.

Jon Ricker, president and CIO of Limited Technology Services, the technology division of The Limited Inc., (which owns Victoria's Secret and Victoria's Online), makes the author's point very clear. "You can have great graphics, but if you don't have a fulfillment system on the back-end to live up to the customer's expectations, you're not going to get the bookmark."

Setting the Stage

LOGISTICS AND FULFILLMENT, once considered a dirty back-office function, has acquired a new cachet in the e-business community. Businesses are finding that their current logistics and fulfillment infrastructures are unable to cope with the rapid growth in orders that comes with the implementation of a top-notch Web site. The heightened expectations of the online customer must be met if an e-business is to remain *in* business.

"A Web site is like an iceberg. What you see looks small and simple, but below it you have infrastructure integration issues with may be 40 or 50 databases. So building a Web infrastructure can be a pretty serious risk for older companies," says Delta Air Lines CIO Charles Feld.

Kyle Shannon, co-founder and chief people officer of Agency.com, a global Internet solutions provider, agrees. He states that the most common problem an enterprise must cope with upon adopting an e-business model is that of comprehending the impact of the move on the enterprise. He explains that although there is certainly a technological impact, the back-end systems that are necessary to any large enterprise clearly need to be integrated. "That, I think, is the most obvious one," says Shannon.

He goes on to comment on the cultural and structural business issues that have a dramatic impact as well. For example, in pre-Web practice a company usually responds to customer inquiries on a two-week schedule. On the Web, however, their online customers are probably going to expect a one-day or even a two-hour turnaround on their inquiries because that's what they get from Amazon.

"A lot of times, there is an impact in terms of how businesses are run — what things are happening from a cultural perspective," continues Shannon. "Division A hasn't talked to Division B in 40 years but on the Internet those two divisions have to talk to one another to provide the customer with a seamless experience. So sometimes the issues are cultural, and then sometimes they're really more about governing. Who makes the decision? Is the Web site an IT function, is it a marketing function, is it a business function? Should the CEO be involved? If the CEO should be involved, how involved should he be?"

BUSINESS MODEL

A business model integrates three activities. It formally identifies a path toward profitability; keeps that path clear and well paved; and installs enablers along the way to aid in the journey to the destination.

E-BUSINESS MODEL

The term "E-business Model" refers to the methodology enabling the conversion of activities throughout an enterprise into an electronic-based system. Such a model provides means of communication and a framework for the gathering, storing and sharing of data that facilitates an expedient and cost-effective mode for day-to-day business operations. The result of such methodology is a fully functional e-business, which provides support for physical entities such as warehouses, distribution centers, stores, transportation systems,etc.

Shannon cites the need to overcome the misleading notion of the relative simplicity of transferring processes to the Web. Instead, the Web is one of the greatest challenges an e-businesses faces. In reality this transition is quite complex, just as e-business is complex. Therefore, an enterprise that is contemplating the adoption of an e-business model must first lay out an e-business strategy. This usually requires bringing in a consultant well versed in e-business models.

The Internet and the resulting economic globalization have changed the face of business forever. Too many enterprises have made a considerable investment in developing Internet capabilities without full consideration of both the customer-centric and economic implications of their decision. Logistics and fulfillment falls within this realm. Logistics and fulfillment provide a structure and systems by which the e-business (whether it's B2B or e-tail) can:

1. Obtain the necessary product.

2. Position the product in a strategic location.

3. Offer the product at a competitive price.

4. Have the product available when needed.

5. Deliver the product to the customer at the right time.

That is the essence of an e-business logistics and fulfillment plan. However, it takes strategizing, planning, partnerships and technology to fulfill these five requirements.

Jane Gould of e-com-advisor.com recently interviewed Henry Bruce, vice president of corporate marketing for Optum (www.optum.com), a leading provider of configurable end-to-end fulfillment solutions for pure-plays, traditional, and transitional companies — B2B and e-tail alike. In that interview, Bruce pointed out that, "everything beyond order entry is logistics and fulfillment. It doesn't matter how the order comes in — EDI, Web site, white mail, or telephone, it still requires logistics and fulfillment processes to reach the customer." Optum has a star-studded list of clients including W.W. Grainger, Inc. (www.grainger.com), the Home Shopping Network (www.hsn.com) and Webvan.com, to name a few.

Customer questions, such as "Where is my order?," "When can I have it?," "When can you deliver it?" and "If I want it tomorrow, how much will that cost?," have all transformed how an e-business's value chain communicates. Everyone throughout the value chain wants to be 100% sure that what has been stated and promised is a virtual-delivery guarantee that can be met. However, if the front-end system is not properly integrated with the back-end system (and this holds true throughout the value chain), you have an information disconnect. You don't have a comprehensive logistics and fulfillment management system (LFMS) in place, and therefore, in reality, you can't offer guaranteed delivery.

Throughout the 20th Century, businesses evolved from small family-operated shops (usually serving a limited niche market in a small geographical area) to department stores (still serving a small geographical area, but a larger market) to mail order catalogs (overall expansion of the marketplace and its geographical reach). During the late decades of the 20th Century, businesses moved to expand their entire marketplace by moving first into discount stores (using demographics to reach a different market), then into the "chain store" model (again expanding the marketplace and its geographical reach through demographics and psychographics). However, during this evolution the ability of a business model to meet the essential components of the business remained constant.

As the 21st Century was born, a presence on the Internet had already become a must for a business to remain competitive, moving everyone into a global marketplace. The business community viewed the Internet as an opportunity to establish a new global channel for commerce, and some began to move their daily business tasks online. However, in the rush to adopt the new e-business model, the essential components seem to have been forgotten as three new factors worked to exert pressure on an e-business and its order fulfillment systems:

- An increasing expansion of product lines offered.

- Moving large volumes of packages at breakneck speed.

- Meeting growing value chain expectations.

The e-business model has brought with it a shift toward real-time markets that inherently changes how value chains interact. For example, with regard to inventory management: e-businesses will soon find it's common practice to automatically inform suppliers about what their customers are buying at any specific time, and about what isn't moving off the shelves. This real-time communication allows the e-business and its supply chain to make informed decisions and react in real-time — to adjust inventory levels, change production schedules, remove an item from stock (if not selling), or from the Web site (if inventory is depleted).

"Real-time" is an adjective pertaining to computers or processes that operate in real time versus "batch" processing. Real time describes a human rather than a machine sense of time. Batch processing allows a program to run automatically at a certain time without further user interaction.

For the online customer e-business means no back-orders, no out-of-stock notifications; if it's offered for sale, it's available.

There are many potential pitfalls that await the business traveling the complex path that is the transition to e-business. Failure to take the utmost care in constructing any one of the sophisticated elements in the e-business model can lead the hopeful pioneer into a quagmire.

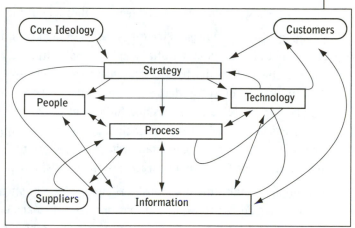

A common e-business model.

Corporate culture, business process systems and technology must be brought together. A powerful infrastructure must be erected, with the value chain connected at the system level and the technology and processes in place to translate data into real-time information. As if these design tasks are not daunting enough, things really become sticky when the multi-channel and other hybrid e-business models and sub-models are brought into play. But the goal, namely, a real-time seamless communication and sharing of data, more than justifies the effort. The key element in the e-business model is a robust LFMS that can handle the 3Rs across all channels simultaneously and, thereby, deliver first-class logistics and fulfillment.

The successful e-business model requires faultless integration

IMPLEMENTING LFM — A THREE STEP PROCESS

The e-business community knows it must get a handle on logistics and fulfillment. Although most executives are confused about what it takes to implement a robust LFMS — you can't just go out and buy one — an LFMS is a variety of systems, processes,technology and people that mesh together into a cohesive unit.It's complicated and requires:

Strategy - Understand the e-business customers' expectations and how to meet them. Once that is well in hand, decide what the e-business wants to accomplish with its LFMS, which requires strategizing throughout the value chain.

Planning - The strategy gives the e-business a map of what the end result should be, but not how to go about attaining it. To do that, an e-business needs to lay out the chain of events from procurement to receipt of the customer's order through delivery of the product and through the post-sale processes.It should be a guide upon which all logistics and fulfillment decisions are based. The e-business needs to work with its value chain partners to map this logistics and fulfillment path. Then it must understand what is necessary to fulfill customer orders in a narrow time frame and improve customer satisfaction.

Execution - Finally, the plan must be implemented in stages. This is where the decision is made as to what solutions are needed to achieve optimum logistics and fulfillment results — in-house, outsourcing,or others.At the same time, the e-business will utilize technology and channels to enhance its LFMS,enabling its value chain to share production, scheduling, inventory, forecasting and logistics information in real-time.Customer pull (i.e., goods that are supplied to meet the individual customer's specification) will be the norm in most e-businesses, not the exception.

between customer-facing applications and the supply chain so the entire value chain knows in real-time what's available and specific dates of availability. This allows pre-planning by all — the suppliers, the e-business, the strategic partners, the customer and the shipping companies. With the proper planning, the right technology and taut integration (whether provided in-house or through partnership(s)) everyone can avoid the potential bottlenecks lurking in procurement, credit approval, inventory management, order processing or shipping. The 3Rs will become the battle cry of the successful e-business.

End-to-end integration requires mammoth coordination between technology and the efforts of in-house IT personnel, consultants, vendors and integrators throughout the value chain. This is a serious challenge for any enterprise, but not insurmountable — IF there exists a clear and defined set of goals and objectives, a proper e-business strategy with structured

THE THREE STAGES OF E-BUSINESS

The most efficient, cost-effective and least disruptive way to implement an LFMS is in three stages:

Stage One - Adoption: The e-business, although online, hasn't optimized the procurement, movement and storage of materials and/or merchandise internally or through its supply chain. To do this entails implementing new technology to bring about real-time data sharing. Once the systems necessary to move into Stage One are in place, an e-business (and its value chain) will leave behind the gridlock that hampered productivity and negated the promised benefits that e-business was to have wrought.

Stage Two - Automation: When an e-business is ready to move to the second stage, it applies cutting edge logistical concepts to its processes. Eliminating unnecessary waste brings about improved customer service through inventory accuracy and elimination of stock-outs. The final outcome is increased sales and lower operating costs, due to smaller inventory stock, reduction in cycle times and smaller, decentralized distribution centers with real-time inventory control.

Stage Three - Transformation: In its race to achieve the necessary efficiencies so that it can respond to customer pull, the e-business expands its value chain to include additional suppliers and trading partners. There is a one-on-one relationship throughout the value chain. Integration of Web-based supply chain tools allows the value chain to share critical production, scheduling, inventory, forecasting and logistics information in real-time. Technology enables this process by providing a communication stream that allows value chains to collaborate in real-time, or by letting sales reps tap into permission-based systems so they can keep customers apprised of order status.

prioritization, and proper attention to detail.

Emerson Electric Co. (www.emersonelectric.com) is well on the way. In its chairman and CEO, Charles F. Knight's, Letter to the Investors giving the 1999 fiscal year report, Knight laid out a good e-business strategy plan:

> "E-Business presents many opportunities as Emerson evolves from using the Internet as an information medium [Stage One], to automating customer and supplier transactions [Stage Two], to ultimately transforming the way we do business [Stage Three].

> "We are moving beyond the information level and focusing on higher level applications of the Internet [i.e., Emerson is in Stage Two of its e-business strategy plan]. For example, in our electronics business, Liebert conducts virtually all sales transactions electronically, including product configuration, order entry and delivery update. In process control, Fisher-Rosemount has developed an innovative site, www.test-driveplantweb.com, to communicate the substantial benefits of PlantWeb in an intuitive and user-friendly manner that could not be achieved through printed documents.

> "In my opinion, we are just beginning to recognize the potential of Internet technology to transform our businesses. We are moving quickly in this area, and over the next year each of our divisions will identify E-Business models to further strengthen our competitiveness."

Emerson is making the move and doing it right. And to prove it, Emerson Electric is the recipient of numerous awards, such as making the year 2000 lists of: *Industry Week World's* 100 Best-Managed Companies, *InternetWeek* 100, *eWeek* Top 100 Innovators in e-Business Networking, *Fortune 500*, Fortune America's Most Admired Companies, and *Forbes* Platinum 400, to name a few.

Market	1997	1998	1999	2000	2001	2002
E-tail	$2.4 B	$8 B	$20.2 B	$38 B	$64 B	$108 B
B2B	$8 B	$43 B	$109 B	$250 B	$425 B	$1.331 T

Actual and projected growth of online sales. Powerful stuff ... are you convinced?

Still hesitating? Then consider this, Forrester (www.forrester.com), a leading independent research firm that analyzes the future of technology and its impact, estimates that over $1.5 trillion in goods and services will be purchased over the Web by the year 2003, with B2B commerce significantly outpacing e-tail commerce.

The complexity and cost of implementation of an LFMS is significant; but e-businesses will soon come to realize that their customers' satisfaction (or dissatisfaction) is explicitly linked to the performance of their LFMS. Other benefits from an LFMS: it can enable the integration of just-in-time, zero-stock inventory management and customer relationship management initiatives into the e-business processes, allowing for a credible return on investment (ROI).

DEFINING E-BUSINESS

There is enormous confusion in the terms used to describe Internet-based business. Buzzwords abound. Although I know the following may seem pedantic, it will help everyone to understand *my* usage of specific terminology for various business models.

Many experts would agree that the standard definition of *business* is that of a commercial or mercantile activity, an industrial enterprise; and that a group of such enterprises may compose a business district. Taking this one step further, "commerce" is one of the synonyms for "business." *Commerce* is the exchange or buying and selling of commodities on a large scale involving transportation from place to place.

Turning to our good friend, Merriam-Webster (www.m-w.com), you will find *retail* defined as "to sell in small quantities directly to the ultimate consumer."

I use *e-tail* for the business-to-consumer portion of e-business. A retailer or an electronic retailer (e-tailer) sells in small quantities which presents different fulfillment needs from those of the business or commerce provider (B2B) that buy and sell commodities on a large scale.

What I am getting at is that e-business (electronic business) and e-commerce (electronic commerce) are basically interchangeable. They are "the [electronic] exchange or buying and selling of commodities on a large scale involving transportation from place to place." It's just a personal preference.

E-business expresses the general concept of the overall "space." Webster's definition for business is "a commercial or an industrial enterprise; also such enterprises (the business district)."

The author isn't the only one trying to make sense out of the various "buzzwords." In a July 21, 2000 article, *The Standard's* (www.thestandard.com) Jonathan Webb, comments on the problem involved in trying to categorize e-business models like B2C and B2B. According to Webb, "B-to-c, which really means retailing, is now tainted — but to say that retailing will not be important in the future doesn't make a lot of sense. B-to-b, for its part, means different things to different people: some use it to refer specifically to online marketplaces, while for others it means any business that sells primarily to other businesses. To say that a company is a b-to-b company says nothing about its merits or prospects."

Webb mirrors the author's thoughts on buzzwords. He says that rhyming terms, especially, are often marketing devices for e-businesses trying to define themselves — *B2B-B2C-B2E* or *bricks-clicks-slicks* (for the uninitiated slicks=catalogs). "And investors, who frequently travel in packs, play into this as they try to read the fashions of the moment and deploy their money accordingly."

Roya Mofazali, VP of Business Development for Savvion Inc. (www.savvion.com), a leading global provider of automated business management solutions, had this to say about the definition of e-business: "The way we [Savvion] and IBM, among others, define e-business is that it's encompassing e-commerce. E-business means running your business online, which means you have to automate and bring to the Web all your operations, whether they are customer-facing (e-commerce), partner-facing (B2B), employee-facing (B2E) or operational. So e-commerce as the sell side of a business is only a subset of the e-business. Also, there are some people out there who don't think companies like Amazon are e-business."

Although Mofazali takes a while to make her point, she does confirm what the author is trying to impart by continuing, "It doesn't matter whether a business is an old economy, new economy or mix: *"As long as they automate their business processes and bring them to the Web, they are an e-business."*

E-BUSINESS FULFILLMENT

Although lately Wall Street has rained on their parade, e-businesses have achieved a most-envied status in the business world due to riches gained from initial public offerings, to unbelievable marketing budgets and to news articles that laud them as pioneers of an industrial transformation.

As with any business, an e-business is dependent upon the good will and purchasing power of the customer to keep its profit margin healthy. If it can successfully instill customer confidence in its e-business model, it will have an opportunity to become one of the top players in its category. However, the adoption of a logistics and fulfillment model that includes a value chain — the e-business's warehouse(s), a variety of suppliers of varying sizes, third party distribution centers, and retail stores — poses hard challenges for the e-business yearning to deliver an exceptional customer experience and build a loyal customer base. If care isn't taken, the problems in dealing with the varying technologies of a diverse supply chain ups the chance that possible slip-shod integration methodology will not scale to meet a high-volume demand.

The Internet community has suddenly awakened to the realization that the key to any e-business's success is not only getting the customer to the Web site, but also providing efficient order processing, sound logistics and fulfillment, and quality customer service. Along with the yelling, wringing of hands, and scurrying from vendors to consultants to integrators, e-businesses have suddenly started to court outsourcers, scrounge for competency in-house (such as a small catalog division), and/or rush to purchase a small business with the necessary competency and systems in place. There have even been mergers made specifically to effect a solution to an e-business's logistics and fulfillment problems.

Take a look at the February 1999 Federated Department Stores Inc.'s purchase of catalog and fulfillment house Fingerhut Cos. or at the April 1999 Toys R Us Inc.'s takeover of one of Proteam.com's fulfillment centers. Proteam.com is a direct-sales company that was once known as Genesis Direct Catalog.

Do you think these takeovers were born out of a need for in-house logistics and fulfillment competency?

Then in May 1999, Guitar Center, the world's largest musical-instrument retailer, announced that it had acquired catalog and Internet retailer Musician's Friend (www.musiciansfriend.com). Two distribution centers were an important part of the acquisition agreement.

No one is more surprised about this turn of events than the fulfillment industry itself. According to John Buck, president of Fingerhut Business Services, "We used to be those guys in the dirty suits out there. Would you believe that fulfillment is the darling of the day? It's actually stunning to me." It's a shocker to the e-business world also.

You Built It, They Came — Now What?

It's relatively easy to design and build a Web site and put it on the Web. But once you begin selling products, how do you actually fill the orders? B2Bs and e-tailers, whether they are manufacturers, trading partners, or pure-plays (i.e., the Web site is the business), are all wrestling with that problem, the magnitude of which is indicated by the new records continually being set in the online commerce space. Although most front-end solutions perform well under the pressure of heavy traffic, problems do occur; and more often than not, the difficulties are the result of an insufficient logistics and fulfillment infrastructure. Without a practical LFMS an e-business must deal with unavailable inventory, late or never delivered orders or deliveries to the wrong location, and incorrect billing issues. The results: unhappy customers and a declining customer-base.

Throughout this book I stress the fact that e-business must be more than a Web site that can take orders, but it's true. It needs integrated back-end facilities and systems that can fulfill any onslaught of orders the site might receive. Take Borders.com as an example. It's fulfilling its orders with 99.9% accuracy in all areas through its 187,000 square foot fulfillment center. After much research the Borders staff realized that although its typical warehouse contains about 200,000 SKUs of books, music, and videos, its e-business facility would need a much larger inventory and therefore built a facility to hold more than 750,000 items. This is an e-business that developed sophisticated strategy and planning *prior* to adopting its e-business and logistics and fulfillment models, giving it an undeniable advantage in the e-business realm.

Take a look at Brooksbrothers.com. The once staid, traditional Brooks Brothers' techno-savvy executive suite led the venerable retailer into the ranks of the e-tailers in 1998. But although Brooks Brothers was prepared for the logistics and fulfillment issues of an e-tail operation (it has a well-established catalog business), it did face some serious surprises. It found out that the maxim, "know thy customer," holds true no matter what venue. Brooks Brothers slowly reached the realization that its inventory for its Web site needed adjustment — it didn't expect customers wanting to buy tailored clothing through its Web site — suits and sport coats weren't among the initial product offering. Once Brooks Brothers woke up and expanded its online catalog to include tailored clothing, it began to sell thousands of these items in all sizes.

AN UNBEATABLE PARTNERSHIP

Logistics, fulfillment and customer service can constitute an unbeatable partnership. E-business fulfillment requires not only a complete-

Activity	The Partnership Required		
	Logistics	Fullfillment	Customer Service
Having product available; and if not, giving accurate information about availability and keeping to it	Yes	Yes	
Providing the right shipping options to the right customer	Yes	Yes	
Timely and accurate delivery	Yes	Yes	
Allowing order changes		Yes	
Dealing with returns and other post sale issues	Yes	Yes	Yes
Communication with the customer			Yes
Dealing with failure			Yes

ly integrated solution with real-time communications throughout the value chain, but also support for all back-office services. When looking for a logistics, fulfillment and customer service solution, consider the relationship between order and payment processing, warehousing, transportation and distribution, management of returns, repairs and customer service.

Cherish the reality that logistics and fulfillment go hand-in-hand with customer service.

Remember the 3Rs — the right product at the right place at the right time? Having product available and/or providing accurate information requires real-time access to data which, in turn, demands that the entire value chain be integrated ensuring 24 x 7 access when and where it's needed.

The "back-office" systems of most e-businesses — systems that provide the link between the customer's order and the physical delivery of the products to the customer — represent an ongoing challenge. Yet these are the very systems that allow an e-business to communicate in real-time throughout its value chain, allowing it to provide accurate inventory and shipping information including tracking numbers and estimated delivery dates and, therefore, can't be overlooked.

David Rucker, director of business development at TBM Institute (www.tbminstitute.com), a manufacturing consulting firm, advises, "People are looking at the entire value chain and want to see how the entire chain works." He goes on to speculate "companies that can develop a lean manufacturing process and tie it into the Internet will be the winners."

A successful e-business's goal is to provide perfect service throughout the customer experience; yet, there's always the chance of a snafu. The question is: How does the e-business handle a mistake? The customer must be assured that you care and that your enterprise is capable of dealing with any issue that arises. If you provide that assurance, at the end of the day that customer has the confidence to "come again, soon," no matter what the slipup may have been. Customers want and appreciate prompt information throughout the purchasing experience, including being informed about problems. Forewarned is forearmed;

thus, give the customer the chance to act upon any problems your mix-up may cause.

Customers may want to change an order after submission and that capability, too, must be built into the systems. For all of this to work the entire value chain needs a 360-degree view, i.e., total integration. Currently, most e-businesses fall short.

The problem of returns comes as quite a surprise for many e-pre-neurs. Many failed to factor into their processes the fact that when customers buy products without the ability to examine them, sometimes they are disappointed. Or the product may have been damaged during shipment. In either event, they will want an easy way to return the product. A stated return policy on the Web site is vital and, of course, easy methods of return should be offered, along with a system for fast refunds and/or replacements. But there is also a need to automate the processes an e-business uses to handle the returns internally (restocking, inventory updates, credit from supplier, etc.), so it can reduce the cost of such returns.

Every e-business will find out that customers want and demand information and that it must be provided. Customers want accurate data on such items as order acknowledgement, shipping confirmation, immediate notification of problems, order status tracking, and so forth. Then there is the need for an intelligent, sympathetic ear when things go wrong. That is when your customer service department really earns its money; but these services must be integrated into the e-business's systems so as to have a 360-degree view of the customers' profiles, which should include not only the current orders but the customers' past ordering and contact histories.

A positive profit and loss statement is dependent upon (1) how well an e-business can develop new capabilities and value chain integration on top of their existing technology and/or (2) how intelligently they can outsource solutions that are outside their core competency and/or their current budget. Ironically, it turns out that the most important issue facing e-business is the one with the least prestige in the executive suite: logistics and fulfillment. The majority of e-businesses can't respond to these issues solely by relying on their existing systems.

B2B

B2B can be as basic as an enterprise putting up a simple Web site for its business customers to securely order a handful of products. Or it can be an enterprise offering all of its trading partners customer-specific pricing and content, complex product configurators and real-time access to inventory levels for its entire product line. And it can be as elaborate as a corporate portal integrated with a virtual private network (VPN), thus enabling an extranet to provide full service to an e-business's entire value chain.

Beyond the strategic confusion that can stand in the way of a B2B effort, there are the serious technological hurdles, chief among them, legacy system integration. For example, the sales department may be segmented by what products they sell, with the automobile sales department using one legacy system, truck sales using another, and the European group on an altogether different system. Many e-businesses don't even attempt to integrate these home-grown, back-end systems; instead orders entered online generate e-mail forms that go to the sales department, where they get re-keyed into the appropriate system — not very efficient and ripe for human error.

As stated previously, before it can try to bring an entire value chain online, an e-business must get its own house in order. Once that is done, the infrastructure upgrade should include, at a minimum, an Internet-ready system to link to its supply chain partners. For example, by allowing a trading partner to see what inventory is available, the partner's sales department has the information necessary to enable it to sell off the excess inventory in the B2B's warehouse.

For the typical B2B operation, the largest return on investment will come from instituting business processes that attack the hard stuff — pre-production design and collaboration, parts rationalization, order fulfillment and inventory reduction. The successful B2B will translate its deep industry knowledge into an LFMS that will benefit its entire value chain.

This is illustrated in part by Boise Cascade's online business-supply catalog (www.bc.com), which offers its customers an easy way to make purchases. In doing so, Boise Cascade has already saved millions by economies brought about through adoption of its e-business model, while at the same time offering its customers faster, cheaper service.

One of the champions of the e-business model, Wal-Mart has established networked applications with its supplier Proctor & Gamble, among many others in its value chain. Every time Wal-Mart sells an item, the sale automatically triggers a replenishment request at P&G. The result is a dramatic improvement in customer service because inventory is always fully stocked. But for this to come about, both enterprises needed to have their e-business model fully integrated with their back-office systems and processes.

And finally, look at the technology giant, Cisco Systems (www.cisco.com). Through its use of the Internet in fashioning an extended enterprise of channel partners, Cisco can deliver products to its customers with delivery lead time cut in half because its suppliers can ship directly to Cisco's customers. It makes perfect sense that Cisco Systems, Inc. would build its entire e-business model around the Internet; Cisco is the world's largest seller of routers and switches for data networking.

Like the three models above, the e-business that understands its customer-buy scenario, and then optimizes its value chain to address the same, will find it has a truly valuable enterprise. An e-business's success requires real-time value chain visibility and the proper tools to enable strategic decision-making, collaboration and cooperation across the entire value chain resulting in a relatively fast positive return on investment. If you can't create that sort of a relationship with your value chain, you can't implement an LFMS or build a successful e-business.

E-TAIL

"What many of the newly created e-tailers have learned too late is that retailing is a customer service business on the front-end and a customer logistics and distribution business in the back," notes Carl Steidtmann, chief retail economist for PricewaterhouseCoopers (www.pwcglobal.com). "E-tailers who failed did so because they thought they were technology companies."

According to a recent survey, close to 70% of e-tailers state that they don't expect to be profitable by the end of 2001, and a little over one-third said profitability will elude them until the end of 2002. However, this same survey found that most e-tailers with a click-and-mortar model will find the black ink before the end of 2001, mainly due to the presence of apparel e-tailers that manufacture their own products. These enterprises will see a high gross margin (what's left after paying the cost of the product and getting it to the seller's warehouse). But when you drill down to the "contribution margin" (what's left from the gross margin after factoring in logistics and fulfillment costs), only two mainstream e-tail categories — apparel and booksellers — currently show a "positive contribution margin" (still not to the *profit margin* but getting closer).

For Some E-tailers it was Easy

According to a study by Shop.org, the trade association for e-tailers, catalog-based e-tailers are outperforming their click-and-mortar and pure-play counterparts in the logistics and fulfillment area. Catalog-based e-tailers have the lowest fulfillment costs, 18% lower than pure-plays and 43% less than click-and-mortars; they also have the highest on-time shipping rate at 91%, compared to 86% for both pure-play and store-based retailers. Catalogers are also the most responsive, shipping merchandise an average of 1.5 days after an order is placed. Pure-plays and click-and-mortars take 1.8 and 1.9 days, respectively.

One example of a catalog-based e-business achieving success out of the starting gate is Williams-sonoma.com; although Williams-Sonoma does have bricks-and-mortar stores, it's probably best known for its direct mail catalog business. Its the perfect example of a multi-channel logistics and fulfillment model — the brick-click-slick. Its catalog experience and infrastructure has allowed it to achieve consistent high ratings for successful fulfillment of its e-commerce orders. Williams-Sonoma's catalog and Web sales are supported out of the same distribution center and back-end logistics and fulfillment system. The proud parent, Williams-Sonoma, announced in late 2000 that Williams-sonoma.com has always outperformed expectations. The Web site has garnered industry recognition by setting the standard in overall sales, order fulfillment, conversion rates, customer acquisition and customer service.

An In-House LFMS

A good example of a faultless in-house LFMS is Gateway, Inc. (www.gateway.com). Gateway has optimized its manufacturing, logistics and fulfillment infrastructure to ensure that its customers receive their made-to-order computer within about a week, delivered right to their door. To demonstrate the confidence Gateway has in its LFMS, during one year Gateway instituted an outrageous, but successful, promotion wherein it promised customers that they could order a custom-built computer by noon on December 23rd and receive the cow-painted box by Christmas!

Gateway, which has adopted the "click-to-bricks" e-business model, operates out of facilities located in South Dakota where it manufactures and distributes the majority of its online orders. It also processes the receipt of returned goods and the fulfillment of add-on and replacement parts in-house.

Gateway and its shipper, UPS (www.ups.com), have worked together to provide real-time online shipping information. For example, the UPS OnLine Tools integrate shipment information throughout the entire supply chain — from customer service to accounts receivable and procurement. This allows Gateway to provide increased visibility throughout its value chain. UPS and Gateway have conspired to enhance Gateway's ability to reduce its inventory costs and cycle time, improve routing and networking, and provide virtual warehouse capability and superior inventory management. However, Gateway does outsource some of its delivery system functions to UPS, which includes managing hardware diagnostics and quality checking prior to delivery.

Never losing sight of the fact that the time needed to process the order is still critical to its customer's satisfaction, Gateway has fine-tuned its LFMS so it's a sight to behold, technically, physically and personnel-wise. Consider what's being done to process orders at this adaptable manufacturer's facilities: while computers are being built at one location to fit a specific customer's specifications, monitors and other peripherals that require no customization are simultaneously being allocated for that same order at a distant distribution center. When the time is right, all components needed to fulfill a specific order are merged at the fulfillment center and UPS is ready to swing by and pick up the order for shipment to the customer.

As demonstrated by Gateway (notwithstanding the demise of e-tailers such as furniture.com, pets.com and garden.com — all struggled with products that were difficult or expensive to deliver by courier service), the great advantage that pure-plays have over click-and-mortars is that they don't have a legacy system. Pure-plays have an infrastructure built from the ground up with an LFMS integrated from the get-go (or at least the ability to implement an LFMS without the expense of customization). Therefore, according to numerous analysts, the average pure-play spends only about $11.00 per order on fulfillment versus click-and-mortars that spend an average of $17.00.

Click-and-mortars have many implementation issues within their order fulfillment and customer service systems. Some try to tackle a portion of these problems by having employees pick items for shipment in their traditional retail storefronts or out of distribution centers that are set up for pallets or for bulk shipment. Such inefficient and cash gobbling methods won't ever produce that elusive positive contribution margin, much less a positive profit margin.

If an e-tailer intends to keep its Web site current with every item in its inventory (and it should), it needs to guard against breakdowns in the links between its inventory and the Web site. This requires everything (from inventory forecasting to Web technology that will withstand a tidal wave of traffic) to have been planned, mapped and implemented.

For example, a well-known click-and-mortar (that shall remain nameless) went live without having its back-office processes connected in real-time, nor was it online with its suppliers, distributors and shippers. Therefore, when customers clicked the "buy" button, entered their credit card information and then sat back to wait for the delivery of their white cotton shirts, they were disappointed to be told 24 hours later that the white shirts were out of stock. These white shirts were so popular that orders just flew from the Web site to the click-and-mortar's back-office, but the click-and-mortar couldn't keep up because of the way the orders were handled in the back-office systems and throughout the supply chain. The count that the e-tailer thought it had in its warehouse was different than what the data in the mainframe indicated was on hand. According to a spokesperson, the cause was human error. Think what the proper integration of the e-tailer's e-business processes could have done to ameliorate this situation.

That same click-and-mortar waited more than a year to begin integration of its business processes with its Web site. As in most click-and-mortar implementations, prior to implementation of a real-time LFMS, it had data manually pulled out of one system and manually re-entered into another system. Few click-and-mortars attempt to integrate their business processes until they've reached critical mass. Although launching a Web site can initially expand a business's customer base, the lack of integration gradually causes erosion in that customer base and also eliminates any overhead savings that could be achieved with an e-business model. So why build the Web site?

The successful implementation of the proper tools for managing suppliers, order fulfillment, distribution and shipping can result in up to a 25% reduction in staff, and a marked reduction in overhead through better inventory management, while significantly reducing the chance that a Web site will unexpectedly run out of product. It also brings about more efficient order processing and shipping through real-time integration of the entire supply chain enabling greater customer satisfaction. All of this paves the way toward the pot of gold at the end of the rainbow — the elusive positive profit margin.

Sound good? I will show you how to begin your march toward the positive profit margin. Then hopefully you too can achieve the real payoffs that will come with balancing the demands of cyberspace with warehouse space.

Outsourcing LFM

There is a misconception that taking the outsourcing route will ease much of an e-business's back-end integration woes. It won't — it just provides a different set of integration issues. Integrating an e-business's back-end with a fulfillment partner takes a horde of people on both sides working day and night. Many e-businesses, especially pureplays, never thought they would confront data-integration issues, especially when outsourcing their logistics and fulfillment. But even when an e-business brings on-board a first rate fulfillment service provider, the question remains: How will all the systems communicate with each other and share data? The answer is to build interfaces between the systems — a complex process even when there's no legacy systems involved on either end.

To help the reader understand the need for a tight integration of systems, even when outsourcing logistics and fulfillment, listen to what Louis Zambello, senior vice president of the beleaguered eToys.com, which in 1999 shipped a portion of their customer orders from Fingerhut's Utah warehouse, told the *New York Times*. "For every order, we have to pass information to their system, the warehouse then has to pass it back to us for confirmation. When the item ships, that information goes to us for confirmation. When they get inventory in stock, that also has to go to our system, and if you do anything special for the customer, it has to flow from you to the outsourcer, back to you for confirmation." Although struggling to stay afloat, eToys.com is one of the early adopters of the online commerce channel, and as such lit a fire under quite a few bricks-and-mortar toy retailers who are still playing catch-up. eToys decision to move all of its logistics and fulfillment in-house is discussed later in the book.

Another early adopter is Buy.com. Although Buy.com has been criticized for its LFM, board member David Ingram still thinks that Buy.com's LFM outsourcing strategy is superior to handling the duties in-house. By outsourcing fulfillment and inventory management, the e-business can better control its gross margins. Ingram explains, "Buy.com has one hand on the margin dial and another on the growth dial, which gives them both a short-term and long-term advantage by being able to tweak the margins to achieve the best results."

Buy.com's chairman and CEO Gregory Hawkins told CNBC in February 2000, "What we've done in this model really relied on world class distribution partners with enormous scale today and, frankly, shipping products for a long time to fulfill the portion of the business. So we are very comfortable the consumer gets a great experience every time they order from us."

In response to some of the criticism of its logistics and fulfillment practices, Buy.com did partner with Ingram Micro Inc.'s end-to-end logistics services division, IM-Logistics (www.im-logistics.com), to provide order management and logistics and transportation management for its consumer electronics product sales.

A click-and-mortar that's taking a page out of the pure-play's book is The Children's Place (www.childrensplace.com) — it outsources everything. The e-business tapped Fingerhut to handle its fulfillment and customer service duties.

According to Debra Bummer, director of e-commerce, "We wanted to stay focused on what we do best — children's merchandise and our customers."

An e-business trying to determine the right strategy must keep in mind that flawless logistics and fulfillment is a key driver of customer retention and long-term profitability. At this moment, due to inadequate logistics and fulfillment, there are not many e-businesses drawing in customers with their LFMS. All e-businesses need to get their corporate mind set straight: the e-business is all about the customer and a positive profit margin. The customers want the 3Rs and post-sale support, such as ease of returns, technical support, and the availability of a friendly and intelligent individual to deal with warranty issues; the e-business wants a profit. The challenge is to deliver both.

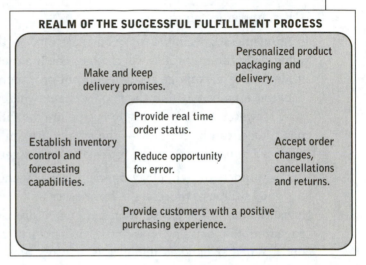

REALM OF THE SUCCESSFUL FULFILLMENT PROCESS

Make and keep delivery promises.

Personalized product packaging and delivery.

Provide real time order status.

Establish inventory control and forecasting capabilities.

Reduce opportunity for error.

Accept order changes, cancellations and returns.

Provide customers with a positive purchasing experience.

TECHNOLOGY

Today, the majority of e-businesses are entering into the fray with quick fixes, such as regional fulfillment partners, SKU limitations, and standard shipment pricing. But as volume increases, order-to-receipt cycle times shorten, and global delivery proliferates, the entire e-business community will need to ramp up or revamp their LFMS capability to incorporate technology with open architecture that provides:

- Easy integration with existing systems and applications.
- Multiple workflows.
- Flexible business rules.
- Web-based technology.
- Fast implementation.

As businesses begin to adopt e-business models, the mode in which the value chain communicates will change. The Internet has made it possible to develop a one-on-one relationship not only with customers, but also between members within the supply chain, wherever located, whatever size. However, there is a price to pay before the full benefit of an e-business model can be realized — the adoption of an infrastructure that is designed to handle the complexities of an e-business model.

The wonders of technology can help any e-business optimize its logistics and fulfillment processes. E-businesses in their search for the perfect logistics and fulfillment solution have taken diverse routes borrowing a page from the past, staying with the tried and true or inventing new solutions. Whether handled in-house (Gateway), provided through partnership(s) (Buy.com), letting the customer doing the walking (shop online, pick up at store), via extended enterprise (Cisco), or done in-store (local retail store's staff picks-packs-ships), the e-business community is in there pitching, trying to find the "right" combination.

GLOBALIZATION

The real power of the Internet and its e-businesses will be felt when everyone gets the courage to start hawking their products in the global market. When that day comes, however, the same e-businesses that thought domestic logistics and fulfillment was a nightmare will have an entirely new set of logistics and fulfillment issues.

As New Year 2001 came and we *really did* enter the new millennium, more than two-thirds of the businesses online couldn't fill international orders. There are just too many complexities in shipping across international borders. Many of the brave souls that are attempting to expand their reach into the global market are doing so through local warehouses. This, of course, limits the number of markets they can service.

The two-thirds of e-businesses that are "globally challenged" admit that their back-end systems suffer with the same malady. It's difficult for the majority of the LFM tools available today to register international addresses accurately or price total delivery cost. The taxes and tariffs make it hard for an e-business to post accurate product cost data (which also must compute the formula for shipping, VAT, customs, etc.) to customers from disparate nations. From the time the "buy button" is clicked to the time the product is received, the price of a product can change due to monetary fluctuations and other charges for which the buyer wasn't prepared.

Many e-businesses state flat out: We don't ship globally today, and we have no future plans to do so — period, end of discussion. They will soon change their minds.

Making the Move: E-Business Infrastructure

IN GENERAL, AN E-BUSINESS'S infrastructure demands more scalability, availability and security than a traditional business's infrastructure. When discussing the e-business infrastructure in this book, the author is referring to all the enterprise's system components — hardware-software-services — that enable the e-business to operate. The e-business infrastructure is more outward-facing than traditional business infrastructures, allowing the e-business's systems to communicate and exchange data with systems outside the enterprise and beyond the e-business's control — its supply chain, partners and customers.

Today, e-business, by its very nature, is not "business as usual" and in industry after industry, corporate America is becoming more anxious. As I read a year or so ago (and it's probably still true), the executive suites are drowning in antacids due to the stomach-churning mixture of technology envy, resentment, and increasingly, just plain fear.

John A. Byrne's feature, "The Corporation of the Future," appeared on www.businessweek.com in August 1998. Within that article he stated, "Few companies have grasped the far-reaching importance of the new technologies for management better than Cisco Systems. Cisco could well provide one of the best road maps to a new model of management." The author totally agrees.

Graphics courtesy of Cisco.

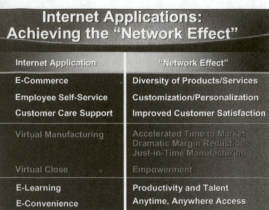

Internet Application	"Network Effect"
E-Commerce	Diversity of Products/Services
Employee Self-Service	Customization/Personalization
Customer Care Support	Improved Customer Satisfaction
Virtual Manufacturing	Accelerated Time to Market Dramatic Margin Reductions Just-in-Time Manufacturing
Virtual Close	Empowerment
E-Learning	Productivity and Talent
E-Convenience	Anytime, Anywhere Access

Pete Solvik, Cisco's senior vice president and CIO, in a keynote speech he gave at Cisco's Worldwide Partner Summit 2000 in Las Vegas addressed the issues that arise when an enterprise decides to adopt an e-business model.

According to Solvik, the biggest difficulty facing the traditional enterprise as it tries to capitalize on the Internet economy is developing, managing, and measuring an Internet strategy. He went on to say that most large enterprises, rather than demolish the walls of their bricks-and-mortar physical location to become a pure e-business, will instead develop an Internet presence and attempt to incorporate that into their existing bricks-and-mortar business processes.

Some enterprises actually try to put on what Solvik calls a "dot-com veneer," i.e., to launch a Web site without tying it to their back-end infrastructure and processes, much less laying out a material e-business strategy.

Solvik went on to point out that getting past the veneer to become a viable e-business requires giving the value chain unimpeded access via the Internet to the e-business's information. "Becoming an Internet corporation is about turning the company inside out, from the inside out. It's about providing ubiquitous access to information inside the company."

Solvik outlined four areas that distinguish whether an enterprise is ready for an e-business model:

- Leadership — an enterprise's decision to adopt an e-business model is driven by senior management. Solvik also added that an enterprise's e-business strategy needs to be a top initiative that has been well thought out and executed.

- Governance — the roles, responsibilities, and accountabilities of an e-business strategy must be clearly defined; a funding model needs to be put in place; and the strategy must be organized.

- Technology — a successful e-business model needs to implement the right technology (no Band-Aids). Also, a scalable infrastructure must be in place well in advance of integration of any planned e-business-enabling applications and/or existing business systems and processes.

- Competency — an enterprise contemplating the adoption of an e-business model needs to recruit and develop competent people and establish an e-business culture.

Solvik gave the example of a safe, although not innovative, step of Internet-enabling non-critical business processes and practices (i.e., HR processes and employee processes). In doing so an enterprise can achieve cost savings, improve productivity and gain confidence among the naysayers. He further gave the example of a higher-risk strategy with more payoff (which is what this book is addressing), i.e., to go online with mission-critical processes such as logistics and fulfillment and manufacturing processes.

"The network [i.e., the Internet] has become the center of computing," Solvik said. "Look at the network as an enabling infrastructure for new applications that will help [you] gain a competitive advantage."

Even before Solvik's rousing keynote speech, many board meetings had "Web Strategy" on their agenda.

Here is what Jack Welch, CEO of General Electric (www.ge.com), an enterprise that was late in its adoption of an e-business model and the ensuing move to the Internet, told *Forbes* (www.forbes.com) in June 2000: "I was afraid of it, because I couldn't type." That changed around the beginning of 1999 after he spent a weekend at the keyboard.

At a March 1999 meeting Welch issued a challenge to GE's more than

20 big businesses — "Destroyyourbusiness.com" became the GE battle cry — reinvent your business before some upstart does it for you. Neither General Electric nor the e-business community has been the same since. One of the benefits of this effort is that General Electric was the honoree among the general manufacturing group in the *InternetWeek* 100 list for the year 2000. GE was also among *eWeek* magazine's Fast Track 100 listing of e-business networking innovators.

GE's CEO isn't the only GE executive high on the Internet initiative. Its CIO, Gary Reiner told *InternetWeek* (www.internetweek.com) that he doesn't "think we've touched the surface on what it can do. But I think there are some things that are very productive as is, and the Internet won't change it. There are very complex sales that will go on the same way for a long time. The Internet can add some efficiencies around them, but there are some products that won't be sold over the Internet for a very, very long period of time. It's unlikely that we'll sell an engine over the Internet anytime soon. It's unlikely we're going to auction very strategic components on the buy side anytime soon."

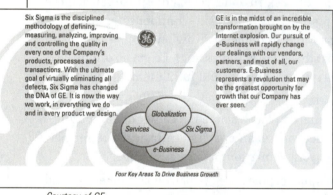

Six Sigma is the disciplined methodology of defining, measuring, analyzing, improving and controlling the quality in every one of the Company's products, processes and transactions. With the ultimate goal of virtually eliminating all defects, Six Sigma has changed the DNA of GE. It is now the way we work, in everything we do and in every product we design.

GE is in the midst of an incredible transformation brought on by the Internet explosion. Our pursuit of e-Business will rapidly change our dealings with our vendors, partners, and most of all, our customers. E-Business represents a revolution that may be the greatest opportunity for growth that our Company has ever seen.

Globalization
Services
Six Sigma
e-Business

Four Key Areas To Drive Business Growth

Courtesy of GE.

When asked if he considered GE an e-business, Reiner replied, "The Internet is a tool. It's a technology. We're leveraging it on all three dimensions: sell, buy and make. But GE is a company that has great physical fulfillment, a great brand in many product lines, and the Internet is going to make our customers more productive and us more productive. You can call it whatever you want. We think that some of the things that distinguish us from a dotcom company are our ability to fulfill and the fact that we have an established brand that we can leverage."

Although the old guard have begun to worry about those new kids on the block and reluctantly realize that they must do something or risk eventual extinction, most of corporate America is still dragging its feet when it comes to adoption of an e-business model. GE is a glowing exception. But even Welch admits GE made mistakes in its rush to the Internet. He told *Forbes* that in retrospect, separate e-business groups weren't right for GE and most have since been reabsorbed into GE's mainstream businesses. "It got everyone's attention," Welch said, "but the Internet is all about 'growyourbusiness.com,' not about destruction. In the end it's everyone's job."

Even Gartner Group's (www.gartner.com) analysts warn that while technologically aggressive businesses face failure from immature technology, an unready market and poor e-business strategies, more conservative enterprises who seek to avoid all risk by ignoring the Internet's compelling growth are also doomed to failure.

The same Gartner Group analysts suggest that despite the huge awareness of a need to adopt an e-business model, many companies will tumble into e-business disillusionment by 2001 with 75% of projects failing to deliver on their promise. Or they will do like GE, re-examine their strategy, regroup and move forward.

Gartner Group vice president of e-business transformation, Alexander Drobik, is quick to emphasize that the predicted e-business failures will not be because the adoption of an e-business model was wrong, but because the model, strategies and implementation failed. Furthermore, Drobik is optimistic that, in the long term, businesses will learn from other enterprises who take the time to get it right. "There is no doubt that the next few years will be tough on businesses making the 'e' transition and we expect to see a high level of disillusionment. However, by 2004 we will see a steady 'slope of enlightenment' as the true e-businesses begin to emerge. By 2006, many businesses will have made the transition, most likely to a 'Bricks and Click' mix, and e-business itself will cease to exist. At this point e-business will be completely embedded into an organization's business process."

Drobik also points out the need for astute business practices combined with an enterprise-wide vision that can serve to cut between the hype and the reality surrounding e-business. He goes on to state that it will be essential for enterprises to strike the balance between e-business aspirations and rushing headlong into an unready market with unproven business models and technology.

But don't wait too long, the Internet is also an environment where the "brand" counts, and if an established traditional "brand" loses the "first-mover advantage" to a Web "upstart," it has a big handicap.

That's the lesson that Barnes & Noble Inc. learned when an upstart, Amazon.com, managed to block its every move. Although, BarnesandNoble.com (www.bn.com), a spin-off of Barnes & Noble, Inc., did move quickly, it has continually had to play "catch up." Thanks to the capital backing of its parent company, since launching its online business in March 1997, BarnesandNoble.com has been able to pour a huge amount of money into marketing and advertising in its effort to keep apace with Amazon.com. And, although it has become one of the world's largest retailers and the fourth largest e-tailer, according to Media Metrix (www.mediametrix.com), it still finds itself dwarfed by Amazon (www.amazon.com).

BarnesandNoble.com hasn't given up the battle against Amazon, but Amazon, at the moment has the upper hand. "There are a lot of very anxious cyber and bricks-and-mortar retailers out there," observed Tony Levitan, vice chairman of Shop.org, an Internet retailing trade group. "[Amazon has] been successful at everything they've done, and they've got an enormous transaction-oriented customer base and a very, very strong customer service and fulfillment capability."

In late 2000 BarnesandNoble.com announced plans for three major integration initiatives that will provide new levels of service and convenience to the tens of millions of customers who shop in Barnes & Noble stores and at BarnesandNoble.com. These initiatives represent the acceleration of the companies' strategy of building an extensive click-and-mortar network, linking more than 550 retail stores with the popular e-tail site, through advanced proprietary technology.

BarnesandNoble.com does have one trick up its sleeve — the Barnes & Noble bricks-and-mortar retail stores. They give the e-business a tremendous advantage in delivery, pickup and after sales support, and the better an e-tailer can service its customer, the more successful the site will be.

THE CASE FOR E-BUSINESS

The technology that comes with the adoption of an e-business model provides an enterprise ready access to timely, accurate information on suppliers, customers, sales, fulfillment, inventory, accounting, and... (you get the idea). With Web-enabled software you can access your enterprise's information any time and anywhere — from timely responses to customer demands to minimizing inventory costs (i.e., a well-tuned LFMS) — this information can help you manage your enterprise more efficiently and more profitably.

Likewise, an e-business's customers can access its products, technical support, sales material and even customer service on a 24 x 7 basis. An e-business can have worldwide exposure without the expense of branch offices and constant travel. Small businesses that formerly could not afford to participate in international trade can now do so. An e-business model allows these same small businesses to compete with "The Big Guys" on an equal basis.

On the Internet, customers may shop around the clock without waiting for a bricks-and-mortar to open. If one wishes to purchase a gross of paper (as the author frequently needs), comparison shopping is as easy as the click of the mouse, without spending time and money driving to a local office supply store. If the e-business has everything in place (as suggested in this book), a purchase is as simple as clicking the "buy" button and the goods are delivered right to the customer's door. When it works, it's fast, efficient and seemingly effortless.

A properly designed e-business integrates an enterprise's existing processes and legacy systems with whatever is required to implement an e-business initiative. By integrating the Internet components into the existing business, information can be input to a single database and therefore, data integrity is maintained and productivity enhanced.

The cost of customer support can be greatly reduced, once the LFMS is in place, such as providing customers access to their order status, linking to carrier sites so customers can track shipment of their order without the need for intervention by the customer service staff.

The benefits of e-business are irrefutable. The enterprises that adopt the e-business model early will derive the greatest return on their investment. The Internet is changing the way the worldwide citizenry transacts business.

THE OTHER SIDE OF THE COIN

A mid-2000 global research study, "The E-business Value Chain: Winning Strategies in Seven Global Industries," conducted by The Economist Intelligence Unit (www.eiu.com) in co-operation with KPMG (www.kpmg.com) (the EIU/KPMG study), found that "57% of executives surveyed say e-business is transforming their company's role within their industry. E-business is changing nearly all that companies do, from the procurement of supplies to the delivery of products and services. New industry (e)- entrants, value-added services and delivery channels are shifting the boundaries within and between industries, greatly altering existing value chains."

Businesses that have adopted an e-business model must take into consideration that along with the newly implemented technology and electronic transactions comes an expectation of instantaneous attainment. Everyone — executives, managers, partners, vendors, customers, suppliers — truly believe that "all the information is in the computer" and, consequently, expect immediate gratification, be it a product, merchandise, materials, status report, accounting reconciliation, white paper, technical support, or information from a knowledge base. This occurs, in part, because of the promises made to obtain the capital necessary to implement the touted technology, and to gain everyone's cooperation as they live through the inconvenience and heartache of integration and implementation. Add to that the hype about the electronic environment being a "real-time environment" and what many e-business advocates end up with is a limited timeframe to produce and measure the success or failure of their e-business initiative.

Most entrepreneurs and successful traditional businesses rush into e-business without adequately considering and understanding the technology and processes that must be in place for a successful e-business venture. Some e-tailing sites (built to automate the consumer purchase transaction) have failed because they ignored two elements that need to be met before products can be sold online — *product availability* and *pricing standardization*. These two elements apply — no matter who is the customer.

Admittedly, these two elements may not be a factor for some B2B sites (built to automate the transactions between business entities). However, you still have B2B and e-tailers dealing in commodity goods and manufactured items, along with products, such as airplanes, automobiles, computers, and high-tech equipment, for example, that must be built to order. Some of these enterprises will allow their sales people to set product specification and pricing so as to get the order. How will they fit all of these scenarios into a product availability and pricing standardization model? A business dealing with this type of product mix requires a bit of re-engineering prior to making any move to take its entire business processes to the Internet.

As traditional businesses adjust to new technology, adopt an e-business model, and learn what it takes to exploit the strengths of an Internet-based business, many will capitalize on their formidable strengths. General Electric chairman, John F. Welch, told *Business Week*, "There are advantages for existing companies: They have the business processes, they have the fulfillment capabilities, they have the brand recognition, and they often have the technology." He is entirely right, the traditional businesses just have to get their house in order, lay out their e-business strategy and the stage will be set for a show down with the pure-plays that have, thus far, been operating with a free hand. However, no one should think it will be easy, the pure-plays are young and hungry, they have a head start and experience with the "new order" that the traditionalists will have to counter.

E-BUSINESS STRATEGY

The EIU/KPMG study showed that the majority of the executives interviewed found that the Internet played a major role in improving both internal and external collaboration between their business partners.

The greatest barriers to e-business lie within the corporation, according to the previously mentioned EIU/KPMG study. The need to redesign business processes, the lack of e-business skills and the lack of integration between front- and back-end systems are the three most formidable barriers to implementing an e-business strategy.

Before an enterprise or entrepreneur makes the move to an e-business model, ask these questions:

- What are the priorities of the e-business and what are their justifications?
- What are the expectations of the e-business initiative?
- What type of e-business processes are necessary and what are the enabling applications?
- What are the options and challenges for implementing and integrating the necessary applications through its value chain?
- What is the long-term plan and timeline for integration and implementation of the business processes and the enabling applications to an e-business model?

With your answers in hand, you can begin to develop an *e-business strategy* — step one in the adoption of an e-business model.

The Logistics and Fulfillment Challenge

Logistics and Fulfillment Management (LFM) presents an e-business with the constant challenge of trying to meet and exceed its customers expectation at a reasonable cost. Today, the trend is to attempt to dramatically reduce inventory costs and order cycle times, while conforming to customer requirements for labeling, shipping, gift-wrapping, and other "easy" fulfillment issues. To meet these high expectations, an e-business needs an infrastructure specifically tuned to manage interactions between sellers, suppliers, manufacturers, distribution centers, dropshippers, logistics providers, shipping companies and customers. There is also a need for the introduction of the widespread use of e-business processes that can effect an overall reduction in logistics and fulfillment costs by automation throughout the value chain.

The Logistics and Fulfillment Models

In this book the author has broken e-business into three basic models: B2B, e-tail and a converged model, which can mean a B2B with one or more e-tail sites, such as VF Corporation (www.vfc.com). These three models also have sub-models (pure-play, click-and-mortar, catalogs), and normally adopt the following logistics and fulfillment solutions: outsource, in-house or a hybrid solution (in-house and outsource). As we get deeper into the logistics and fulfillment maze you will find that even the basic logistics and fulfillment solutions have models (and sub-sets) that are, in effect, submodels of the e-business model, such as, extended enterprise, B2B buy-sell, in-store, kiosk, same day delivery, drop-ship, to name a few. Chapter 7 is devoted to the ways and means of the various logistics and fulfillment models and their sub-sets.

E-tailers, whether click-and-mortars, catalogers, or pure-plays have definitely jumped on the LFM bandwagon. In April 2000, *Catalog Age Weekly* (www.catalogagemag.com) reported the industry leaders such as Fingerhut, Lands' End, QVC, Kmart, and Omaha Steaks all felt that brand alone could not ensure online success. Instead, they all stated that the "less glamorous" side — delivery and retaining customer relationships — is where they would be concentrating their immediate efforts. "A solid infrastructure will make all the difference in the coming year as the shift from traditional retailing to e-commerce continues," said David Dyer, president and CEO of Lands' End (www.landsend.com). The author notes that Landsend.com is one of the few profitable e-tail sites today.

But you also have to consider the gap between perception and reality. While 96% of retailers are sharing information with customers/suppliers, 79% are using outdated modes of communication, such as paper or fax as part of that communication. The ones that use some type of electronic communication, such as electronic data interchange (EDI) are not using it to its fullest potential. More than half of the respondents place purchase orders via fax, and very few are using Internet-based technologies that could allow them to streamline and optimize their e-business processes.

Efficient manufacturing practices, such as just-in-time (JIT) manufacturing are essential to accurate inventory levels, but according to a KPMG study, they are largely absent from retailing and e-tailing businesses. "Although many of these companies realize the benefits of 'lean practices' in the supply chain, few have implemented the frameworks, processes or technology necessary to achieve them," states James G. Welty, KPMG Consulting's national director, consumer markets consulting. He goes on to say that "despite some widely publicized success in made-to-order manufacturing, it's a long way from being commonplace."

E-tail Model

The e-tail model has received the most attention during the past couple of years. Through the use of compelling technology, retail enterprises and their customers can successfully conduct value-based business online. However, find out before going "hog wild" over e-tailing and its technology if it will improve *your* customer's experience and, if so, how and what additional markets can be reached by taking an online approach?

Jeffrey F. Rayport, an associate professor at Harvard Business School, praised (in a *Business Week* article) QVC and its Web site iQVC (www.iqvc.com) as a case study in hybrid business models. He stated that "They stood back and said, 'What is it we can do uniquely for our customers offline and online?' and then built its e-business model around that." They must be doing something right, they're among the small elite group of profitable e-tail businesses.

Ask yourself the same question: What is it my business can do uniquely for our customers offline and online? Once you have the answer, get moving!

B2B Model

Although e-tailers were the media darlings at the beginning of the Internet craze, B2B is beginning to give e-tailers a run for their money. Oliver Kent of PricewaterhouseCoopers (www.pwcglobal.com) says, "B2B e-commerce has always outpaced on-line retailing, but it's only in recent months that people have been starting to see through the fog and recognize what's really happening."

"Business-to-business is hot," says Jim Hale, general partner at Financial Technology Ventures (www.ftventures.com), a venture capital firm. "Business-to-business is the most under-hyped trend in the Internet business today." A customer that's a business entity spends exponentially more money on each transaction than the individual customer and is also more amenable to new technologies.

Just look at the enterprises adopting the e-business model in the "old guard" industries — auto manufacturing, steel, building materials — ramping up so as to adjust and take advantage of what the Internet and the e-business model has to offer. Of course, there are also the e-preneurs looking for any sign of weakness so they can pull a "rear guard action" (sorry, couldn't help myself) to dislodge the old order.

The goal of most B2B models is to automate the value chain and its transactions. But again, look at *your* value chain, and ask yourself — how can technology and the Internet improve its business processes? Keep in mind that B2B transactions require that each participant in the value chain have the technical infrastructure to enable full automation. Yet, automating the value chain, believe it or not, is the easy part for *some* businesses. There are enterprises that will find their biggest challenge comes when they have to remake the very essence of their business processes, down to the level of lot-sizing and bar-coding.

According to the EIU/KPMG study, by 2002, the executives surveyed expect dramatic improvement in the Web- or Internet-based features that they offer suppliers and partners. For example, as of mid-2000, only 11% of those interviewed reported that their suppliers could access their inventory systems, but 46% stated that by 2002 their e-businesses will grant access to a majority of their supply chain.

Internal Operations

Incorporate your internal operation processes into your e-business initiative. For example, you might want to consider:

- What current business processes hinder your staff, divisions and subsidiaries in their daily endeavors to support the enterprise's goals and objectives?

- Could you automate, through your e-business initiative, internal operations — employee timekeeping, employee expense tracking and other HR processes such as self-management of employee benefits?

- Could you automate internal supply processes that fall outside the supply chain?

Taking internal business processes to the e-business level are usually somewhat difficult to justify because there is no "in your face" ROI figures an e-business advocate can wave in front of the decision-makers. Nonetheless, in the long run it's a cost saving move because of the efficiencies that will be obtained.

Technology Caveats

When implementing your e-business strategy keep in mind that the latest and greatest technology wonder may not be the answer. Many times management and the major value chain players need a walk-through demonstration of what is actually possible with a specific technological solution. However, it bears mentioning that technology is evolving at an unbelievable pace so what isn't feasible today may be feasible in six months or a year, the e-business just has to decide whether it has the time to wait for (or take the chance on) the "new wonder" to mature.

It's imperative that everyone, including the Powers that Be are made aware of what I call *vapor ware*. There is a lot of hype out there, some of it's pure snake oil and some of it's wishful thinking. Then there is the almost-there-but-still-in-beta product where it's anyone's guess as to when the product will actually be ready for installation in a working environment. Just be careful, do your due diligence and your enterprise won't get sucked into the black hole of someone's pipe dream. Sometimes it's better to go with the tried and true, rather than putting the new e-business model's bankroll on an untried "industry-changing" technology.

Don't forget as you build out the enterprise's infrastructure, and even after you have everything up and running, to systematically re-visit and re-evaluate the e-business strategy so as to not lose focus. It's easy to get so wrapped up in the technology that everyone neglects to take a breather and evaluate: what is being planned, what is actually being accomplished, how it's being accomplished and whether everything is meeting the enterprise's overall needs.

Finally, once you have everything built-out don't let all of your strategizing go to waste or become a forgotten tome that becomes shrouded in a layer of dust. It should be a continuing strategy, which is updated like a business plan — as the business grows, expands and changes, so will your e-business strategy. Bring it out, dust it off and re-evaluate on a regular basis, you will be glad you did.

ADOPTING A LOGISTICS AND FULFILLMENT MODEL

Logistics and fulfillment is a large part of any practical e-business model. An e-business needs a solid well thought out blueprint of its hardware, systems, business processes and services before considering its logistic and fulfillment issues. Before I drag you kicking and screaming into the briar patch of logistics and fulfillment, there are a few thoughts I want to share with you.

I hold out to you as a positive example of one type of multi-channel fulfillment model: QVC's Web site, iQVC, which from the very beginning was able to show a healthy profit/loss statement by piggybacking on QVC's existing order fulfillment and customer service systems. QVC operates its entire enterprise as a converged model and as such iQVC.com allows the entire enterprise to sell many more products than it could showcase in a 24-hour period on television.

QVC clearly treasures the partnership between logistics and fulfillment and customer service, because it knows that customer service is the best marketing tool any business can have on its workbench. And as such, for an e-business to guarantee the best customer service, it can't separate its warehouse from its order management. This is true regardless of size and whether you're operating an e-tail or B2B business model.

A small e-preneurial startup may have little experience with logistics and fulfillment. A larger e-preneurial click-and-mortar through its counterpart (the bricks-and-mortar) has an infrastructure that is, in all probability, geared toward shipping palettes or cases to distributors or stores — not quantities of ones and twos which most e-tailers have to deal with. Some enterprises will adopt a B2B model that also allows it to service the smaller customers that may have been dropped because it was an economic burden to service them through the traditional enterprise. An example of this e-business model is Healthtex (www.healthtex.com).

VF Corporation, the world's largest publicly held apparel company, was among the first large apparel enterprises to embrace the Web with its Healthtex Web site. An effort to find a way to better support retailers (especially the small retailer that had been dropped due to costs of offline servicing of their small orders) became the primary impetus for developing the Healthtex site. According to VF Gary Simmons, president of VF Playwear, "VF has always had strong relationships with retailers and selling online should only enhance those relationships. This will save our customers time and money while increasing their product selection."

Through the Healthtex B2B site, which went live in July 1999, the "trade" can view and select the entire line of seasonal products early and at their leisure as a way to extend their buying options instead of only working through a sales representative or participating in a market show. The site is also expected to offer an advantage over the traditional sales channel for apparel by enabling buyers to order replenishment items easily and cost-effectively when needed. Paving the way for the apparel industry, VF Corporation took its Healthtex brand direct to the consumer with its e-tail site that also launched in mid-1999.

Invacare (www.invacare.com), an $800 million medical equipment manufacturer, put in a new warehouse management system and created a frame relay network to link its corporate offices to its various warehouses and distribution centers located throughout the US. The project, which took three years to complete, has dramatically cut shipping times and costs along with giving Invacare inventory management flexibility so that in the long run it can effortlessly provide the 3Rs.

Carrie Messer, Invacare's corporate transportation manager, told Networkworld.com, "We have been able to handle 8% more carton volume [in the distribution centers], with only a 3% increase in costs."

The Networkworld.com article goes on to state that with the new system, customers around the world can get their orders shipped the same day if they place the order by 3:30 p.m. That kind of service would have required Invacare to pay employees overtime under the old labor-intensive system where inventory wasn't always in the right place at the right time and it also was difficult to alter shipping schedules to meet changing demands.

Don't forget GE, mentioned earlier in this chapter. It found that putting online the unglamorous tasks of internal operations saves money, provides faster answers for customers and partners and offers more interesting assignments for employees. Welsh told *Forbes* that customers of GE's plastics group now use the Web to track orders, sometimes right to the location of a delivery van, instantly getting details that once took a dozen phone calls. Pretty impressive, don't you agree?

Cardboard Boxes vs Pallets

The e-tailer and the B2B process an increasing number of products that are shipped via cardboard boxes for delivery to specific small businesses or individuals, instead of pallets where thousands of identical units at a time are delivered to factories and warehouses.

A VF Corp. spokesperson told the author that one of the benefits of moving its Healthtex division to an e-business model was its ability to once again serve the small retail stores that it had dropped as customers because of the cost of doing business with them. However, once it's online B2B Healthtex site began offering its products to the small local retail stores it had to deal with the fulfillment issue — 10 pair of boys corduroys in varying sizes rather than 1,000 pair. Healthtex had to change the way it picked, packed and shipped to these small retailers versus the pallet shipments it uses to fulfill its chain store customers.

An outstanding example of a successful B2B is Cisco Systems, who claims that more than 80% of its total sales of routers and networking tools are handled online. However, it's Cisco's suppliers who must deal with the ones and twos shipment puzzle since Cisco has adopted the drop-ship fulfillment model for many of its products. Today, rather than shipping a gross of a product to Cisco, these suppliers are drop shipping individual orders to Cisco's customers.

The 3Rs and Then Some

E-businesses should always keep in mind that they have customers, partners, a supply chain, management and employees each with high expectations, and all wanting everything delivered in a fast and accurate manner.

If you operate an e-tail model, your customer expects instantaneous shipment of all ordered products, flawlessly delivered to whatever address(s) are provided and the ability to obtain instant credit for returns, quality technical support and quick resolution to warranty issues. To provide these in a consistently accurate manner requires a robust infrastructure with proper integration throughout the entire value chain.

Staples.com knows the 3Rs provide the formula for success. That is one of the reasons that in mid-2000 Staples.com formed an alliance with CommercialWare (www.commercialware.com), a retail fulfillment software maker that targets multi-channel, e-tail businesses. According to Shira Goodman, senior vice president of Direct for Staples, "At Staples, our goal is to provide our customers with the best shopping experience, whether they shop with us in our retail stores, through our catalog or online. Fully integrating our call center and fulfillment operations across the multiple sales channels allows us to be even more responsive to our customers and provide an even better shopping experience. With CommercialWare's comprehensive solutions, domain expertise, and proven track record in e-commerce solutions, we have a solution that can scale to meet the growing market needs, as well as the flexibility to change with the new economy."

After all, Staples.com publicly announced that its goal was to achieve $350 million in Internet-based sales in 2000; its alliance with CommercialWare was a big step in that direction. The alliance allows Staples.com to seamlessly integrate customer order information delivered online, via catalogs, through call centers and/or its bricks-and-mortars.

Implementation of logistical business processes and solutions throughout the value chain allows an e-business to provide the right product at the right place at the right time. For an e-business to become more efficient and, therefore, profitable, it must be able to reduce its inventory, order fulfillment and logistics costs.

Just ask the executives at W.W. Grainger Inc., the world's largest B2B distributor of maintenance, repair and operating (MRO) supplies. Its B2B Web site, Grainger.com has online revenues that's creeping up on the one billion dollar mark, for the 200,000 products offered online (out of the 600,000 products it offers worldwide). According to a spokesperson this was due mainly to understanding how the Web increases the efficiency of Grainger's distribution process so as to provide impeccable logistics and fulfillment.

Grainger is methodically working its way toward a complete e-business model (it currently offers 24 x 7 online ordering), and recorded $200 million in sales or 5% of its business through its Web site and heralded its first million-dollar Web site sales day during the *first quarter* of 2000. Grainger expects the online sales to grow to between 20% and 25% within the next couple of years. Grainger is extremely cognizant of the fact that it must make LFM a major factor in growing its online business.

THE TIME IS NOW

Most traditional businesses can't tarry, they must move now. The only certainty: The earlier you get in on the game, the greater your chances of winning. For many, it will soon be too late.

Talk of implementing LFMS and the ensuing value chain makes many businesses and their IT managers nervous — but bear in mind that you don't implement, automate and integrate these sys-

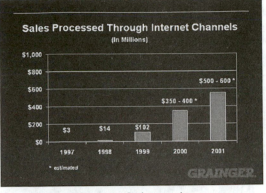

This graph shows how even Grainger under-estimated the power of its Web sales channel. *Courtesy of W.W. Grainger, Inc.*

tems overnight. It takes time and with that time, hopefully, everyone has a chance to adjust to the "new way" of doing business. And keep in mind that once you have chosen to adopt an e-business model, speed to market shouldn't become so important that systems testing suffers.

Last year, online shoppers became especially aggravated with e-tailers who ran out of items and then didn't notify them of the backorder status until days after they had placed the order. This leads to a high level of negative "word-of-mouse," with dissatisfied customers telling twice as many people about their experience (both online and offline) than satisfied online customers. This reflects the truism that bad news travels faster than good news, all because online ordering systems were not linked to warehouse inventories.

One executive that "gets it" is Mackey J. McDonald, chairman, president and CEO of VF Corporation. In one of his letters to the stockholders, McDonald wrote, "We know we face a complex and rapidly changing landscape. To be successful will require a seamless sharing of real-time information among consumers, retailers, manufacturers and suppliers. VF's knowledge-based business model of the future will be our competitive advantage."

With the proper e-business strategy you can keep everyone focused on the enterprise's overall business goals. You just need to maintain a good understanding of all existing business processes so as to ensure the

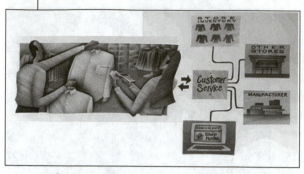

Courtesy of VF Corporation.

infrastructure is ready for the changes an e-business model necessitates.

Without an e-business strategy, you cannot implement a fail-safe LFMS. The approach an enterprise or e-business takes is driven by the unique needs that reside in every enterprise. The e-business strategy plan can take a couple of months or more because it requires that everyone involved participate in conceptualizing and memorializing a clearly defined statement of goals and objectives. If possible, invite the participation of major players throughout the value chain. Without clear goals and objectives it will be impossible to deliver an appropriate e-business strategy. An e-business strategy is an essential component of a practical LFMS

Adopting a B2B Model

B2B TRANSACTIONS FORM THE crest that e-business will ride to complete the technological revolution. Various research firms estimate that B2B transactions alone will top at more than $2 trillion by 2004. The move to adopt an e-business B2B model is driven by the desire to serve customers, eliminate inefficiency and spark new growth. In a July 24, 2000 *Forbes* article, General Electric's CEO Jack Welch euphorically proclaimed, "The big, old guys are going to beat the daylights out of the pure-play dot-commers. The existing business already has sales and expenses. Digitize it and costs fall. Sales climb. Instantly [the established company] gets to break even. Then the margins just pour in."

The e-tailers left standing at the end of the day will be those that have developed a solid relationship with the B2B partners within their value chain, thus allowing them to quickly ramp up to meet customer demand. Therefore, a lot of what is written herein also applies to e-tail models, especially since fulfillment is the decisive crossroad between the retailer (online and offline) and B2Bs.

As *InternetWeek* (www.internetweek.com) editor-in-chief, Robert Preston, wrote, "Some bricks-and-mortars will benefit much more by leveraging the Web to optimize fulfillment — moving inventory to where it's in demand — than by establishing an online-retailing presence."

The promise of supply chain management efficiencies is driving B2B demand in enterprises that want to reduce costs while accelerating the supply chain processes. However, the move to an e-business B2B model involves integrating a myriad of transactions throughout a value chain — B2B is far more diverse than a typical e-tail transaction. The products are more complex, ranging from raw materials to industrial equipment to specialty materials such as fabric or pharmaceutical supplies that require expertise to specify and configure properly. Also, the complexity of the business process itself involves multiple stages of requests for information (RFI), requests for quote (RFQ), competitive bidding, contract negotiation, purchase orders, shipping and financing.

Moving these multiple processes to an automated self-service environment, and replacing the labor-intensive manual interactions conducted via phone, snail mail and white mail (fax and e-mail) with instantaneous electronic interactions, using intelligence and process management built into the infrastructure itself is not easy. What I'm talking about could be a version of an extranet, a private network that uses the Internet protocol and the public telecommunication system to securely communicate and share an e-business's data or operations within a value chain.

I read somewhere that an "extranet is the state of mind" through which the Internet is viewed as the communication highway on which e-businesses can do business with other enterprises as well as sell products to their customers. This is exemplified by Cisco, Wal-Mart and Dell. When properly executed, extranets can reduce the cost of sales while enhancing customer relationship management, procurement and LFM and at the same time promote competition and efficiency throughout the value chain.

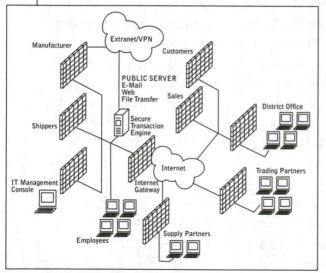

A typical B2B extranet.

Any business adopting a B2B model must have an executive management team with an absolutely clear vision that gives a long view to the future so that the move to a B2B model is one that can be sustained. The executive management team must understand the respective business processes and realize that the future is not only about adoption of all this wondrous new technology but it's also a new business paradigm.

A Morgan Stanley Dean Witter's (www.msdw.com) April 2000 report entitled "The B2B Internet Report — Collaborative Commerce," declared that with the B2B infrastructure up and running, technology can now be viewed as a way of doing business, rather than a cost. It went on to state that B2Bs will use a centralized online trading community to synchronize operations with suppliers and customers and to lower procurement costs. But to reach that point, each B2B must provide an infrastructure that can:

- configure complex products
- generate requests for quotes, proposals or information
- evaluate and respond to bids
- apply for lease or credit lines
- create purchase orders
- secure logistics services
- provide real-time data throughout the order process

AN EFFECTIVE STRATEGY

Many enterprises are still in the first stage of e-business deployment and lack an effective e-business strategy. This assessment is backed up by META Group (www.metagroup.com) (they address the latest technologies, industry trends, and business challenges) through their research report entitled "E-business has Not Yet Become Part of Larger Companies Culture and Strategy." Kirk Reiss, senior VP of META Group Consulting, takes this a bit further. He is of the opinion that, "the low-dollar investment in e-business is indicative of stopgap measures and patch-up thinking — a 'me-too' strategy, where companies are doing e-business because they see other companies in their industry are."

It seems that many business leaders still think that they can ignore a B2B model until it's in a "more mature" phase. They are wrong. By the time e-business is "business as usual" (which will happen in years, rather than decades), it will be too late for the non-adopters. Those enterprises just may have ceased to exist.

What is worrisome is that only about half of the executives that participated in the META Group research think that e-business has had a significant impact on their specific industry. But those who did stated that they see within their enterprise a *probable impetus to a B2B model* due to its ability to shift delivery channels, access a comprehensive knowledge base, and influence commerce. Some are even beginning to understand that interactive relationships within the value chain enable new products and services to be delivered faster and better at a substantially lower cost. The same executives also told META Group that the focus of any B2B investments that their enterprise currently may have in the planning stage is shifting away from customer-facing functions toward business processes such as distribution, logistics and fulfillment management, and supplier management.

To demonstrate what many corporate executives are up against when pursuing a B2B model: When respondents (who expect their e-business revenue contribution to increase from an average of 7% in mid-2000 to 22% by 2002) to the previously mentioned EIU/KPMG study were asked about the potential barriers to e-business implementation, they cited the necessity of re-engineering business processes, the scarcity of e-business skills, and the lack of back- and front-end systems integration.

That same survey pointed out that few enterprises are willing to risk alienating customers (13%), a lower short-term share price (16%), lower short-term revenues (23%), disruptions with established supplier relationships (22%) or cannibalization of existing sources of revenue (22%) in their bid to adopt an e-business model.

According to Harry Tse, director of Internet Computing Strategies at The Yankee Group (www.yankeegroup.com), a recognized leader in technology research and consulting services, "B2B electronic commerce has been treated in the media and Internet marketplace like the ugly stepchild to the more glamorous B2C electronic commerce."

There are some good tidings, Tse went on to state, "B2B e-commerce procurement activity, with its material bottom-line benefits, is spawning rapid adoption by buyers across many industries." That is backed up by a survey conducted at the National Association of Purchasing Management conference on behalf of VisaUSA — more than 50% of the respondents stated that they are using Internet-based software for their procurement. And 60% responded that at least one major supplier had requested an electronic purchasing arrangement from their enterprise.

Have you adopted an B2B model? If so, does it have a robust and scalable infrastructure, do the value chain participants have a 360-degree view? John Katsaros, vice president of Jupiter Research (www.jup.com), advises, "The online trading tidal wave is about to sweep across US business, and the companies that don't invest now will end up struggling to keep their heads above water. We expect unified, online supply chains to become the norm, and companies that don't invest aggressively to build or participate will be unable to compete effectively. Many businesses are already waking up to the efficiency and increased competitiveness they gain through online trading and Net Markets." Katsaros added, "While the rates of Internet trading adoption vary across industries, only one of them, agriculture and farming, is not expected to top $100 billion in online trading by 2005."

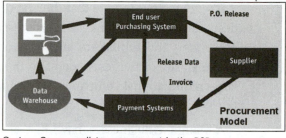

Gartner Group predicts procurement in the B2B market will grow to more than $3 trillion by 2004.

This is supported by a mid-2000 survey conducted by Towers Perrin (www.towers.com), a global management consulting firm, wherein more than 300 executives forecasted a three-fold increase in B2B revenues, and a large-scale shift in each respondent's enterprise's use of strategic alliances and business and management processes. Although most did admit that their enterprise had made very few adjustments in their business processes as a result of e-commerce.

However, according to Peter Bresler, a Towers Perrin consultant and one of the survey's architects, "They accept that large-scale changes are forthcoming and acknowledge the speed required for change in the next two years. It goes well beyond 'business as usual.'" The extent of major operational changes forecast for the next two years in advertising, market and customer research, selling and account management, customer ordering and tracking, and after-sales customer service also range from triple to quadruple of the changes seen over the previous two years, according to the survey.

It's interesting to note that the respondents showed an overwhelming desire to keep customer-centric processes such as customer service, order processing and fulfillment and accounts receivable functions in-house. The majority of the respondents to the Towers Perrin survey were with large multinational companies located in the North America or the UK, but Pan Asian and continental Europe were also represented.

Although e-businesses have just about mastered online commerce, they can't rest. Archaic logistics and fulfillment systems can be a huge barrier to gaining *and keeping* online (and even offline) customers. B2Bs, out of necessity, must put order fulfillment under far greater scrutiny than e-tailers. E-tailers may slip up in delivering a product to their customer; but when it does happen they are only required to deal with one irate customer. Many business executives fear that they will be "betting the firm" on the B2B move. Why? The majority of B2B customers order in the 1000s, not ones and twos. When a B2B misses a shipment, it not only has an angry customer, but a disgruntled supply chain.

ALTERNATIVE SOLUTIONS

Most small to mid-sized B2Bs have been locked out of business opportunities due to the requirement of expensive communication channels and the high cost of back-office integration efforts. Today, these same B2Bs can find many options available to help them get in on the action. The process of linking trading partners together in a neutral environment can be accomplished through behind-the-scenes Web networks that can include application service providers (ASPs) and virtual marketplaces.

E-marketplaces allow the small to mid-sized B2Bs to participate in the electronic sharing of logistics information such as production schedules, parts tracking and financial information and be charged on a per trans-action basis. For example, the readers may have heard about markets such as ChemConnect.com, eSteel.com, TradeXchange.com, Covisint.com, Quoteship.com, Metalspectrum.com, Freemarket.com and Suppliermarket.com.

Jupiter Research a recognized authority on Internet commerce, declares in a study entitled, "US Business-to-Business Trade Projections," that a phenomenal rise in revenues over the next 5 years will emanate from the growth of online supply chains and e-marketplaces. The study finds that 42% of all US business transactions will take place online by 2005, up from its current figure of 3%. In a June 2000 announcement, Jupiter took the step of advising US enterprises to take advantage of this overwhelming growth. But to do so these businesses must act now to incorporate e-business strategies throughout their procurement, sales and fulfillment processes.

Jupiter went on to say that currently the direct channel, a model of one seller to many buyers, dominates 92% of the B2B market. However in 2005, 35% of the B2B trade volume will be conducted via a net market, a model of many buyers and many sellers, or through a coalition market, comprised of a consortium of buyers or sellers.

Due to time-to-market pressures and the volatile nature of B2B applica-tions some e-businesses will look at ASPs for a possible solution. An ASP can provide critical software applications that implement quickly and that can be paid for on a per-use basis, eliminating the need for capital-inten-sive IT hiring, training, development and maintenance costs (discussed in detail later in this section). While the figures vary widely for this new tech-nical offering, International Data Corporation (IDC) (www.idc.com) pro-jects rapid growth over the next several years and estimates that customers will spend over $7.7 billion on ASP services by the year 2004.

ASPs market their services to all ranges of e-businesses and B2Bs can look to an ASP for either the whole back-end solution or a defined por-tion. The critical question for the B2B to pose when considering the ASP route is "Do I really need to run this application inside my enterprise?" If the answer is no, going with an ASP may be the answer. But, for an ASP solution to work, the ASP provider must offer the B2B assurance that it knows how to run a data center in a mission-critical environment.

ASPs deploy, host, implement, manage and support applications from a main data center across a wide-area network, i.e., the Internet, and the end-user (the B2B) accesses these applications remotely and pay for them, for example, on a per-month basis. This allows a B2B to cut its technology budget needs across the board.

The ASP model offers a unique scalability to e-businesses, as applications may be distributed regardless of location to any device running a Web browser with ActiveX plug-ins or Java capabilities.

ASPs have a huge potential as e-businesses seek to outsource applications such as customer relationship management, supply chain management and enterprise resource planning software. In addition, ASPs also provide regular maintenance, upgrade services and ongoing support, in many cases on a 24 x 7 basis.

When it comes to ASPs, Gartner Group's Dataquest (www.dataquest.com) is more bullish than IDC. According to its August 2000 report on the worldwide ASP marketplace, the industry is poised for explosive growth that should reach $3.6 billion by the beginning of 2001 and more than $25 billion by 2004. Despite its promising future, the ASP industry is in a delicate phase of maturation and the period encompassing 2001 will be telling as ASPs scramble for a foothold in the marketspace. Many won't survive. According to Forrester Research (www.forrester.com), 60% of current ASPs will fall victim to bankruptcy, limited venture capital, mergers or market competition by the end of 2001.

E-Marketplaces Might Be the Answer

Another exciting new Internet player is the e-marketplace. E-marketplaces change the way e-businesses buy and sell goods. Most generate revenue by charging fees on transactions and other services.

For many B2Bs, launching a sophisticated Web site with all of its supporting technology and infrastructure may be overkill. These e-businesses may find that they will never establish sufficient "brand" equity or efficien-

DEFINING AN E-MARKETPLACE

The wordsmiths worked overtime and muddied the waters with a variety of words describing functionally similar Web operations. Terms such as, "open market-places," "seller-led buyer cooperatives," "buyer-led selling cooperatives," "seller extranets," and "buyer extranets," "vertical portals," "vortals," "trading net-works," "trading marketplace," "trading hubs," and "trading communities" all describe one thing, the e-marketplace.

Given the confusion in the e-business community surrounding the e-marketplace ter-minology, I wish to take a moment to explain my definition of a B2B e-marketplace — a word you will see frequently in this book.

I use "e-marketplace" to refer to a neutral (as opposed to a marketplace to facili-tate buy-sell interactions between the sponsor e-business and its value chain) Internet-based solution that links businesses interested in buying and selling relat-ed goods or services from one another. The e-marketplace facilitates the exchange by matching buyers and sellers while taking into account the interests of both buy-ers and sellers.

IDC's definition — "an e-marketplace is an Internet-based broker of goods or services in a community of many buyers and many sellers" — also works in this book. Granted there are a variety of other solutions for the B2B community, going by many desig-nations, and while I may refer to these other solutions from time to time, I will use descriptive terminology, and I will not refer to any of them as an "e-marketplace."

cies to make such huge investments pay off. Therefore, some may be better off launching a Web-based storefront and linking it to e-marketplaces that provide advanced functions, and a preset community of qualified buyers.

For example, a B2B can log into an e-marketplace where a variety of suppliers, manufacturers and distributors in its "space" are located. Then B2B "X" describes products *A, B* and *C* and services *D* that it needs. The e-marketplace's system takes this information, including brand prefer-ences, specifications and delivery dates, and notifies (via it's online net-work) the most appropriate member B2Bs that can meet "X's" needs. Of course, this takes sophisticated underlying technology with specialized intelligence to coordinate responses and to make the best choices.

The development of e-marketplaces may also be the solution to the order fulfillment puzzle. Smart entrepreneurs have incorporated into their e-marketplace model the ability to unite a group of businesses (each of which must adopt an e-business model) to buy and sell goods using sophisticated workflow and routing techniques but also supporting pre-production design and collaboration, parts rationalization, order fulfillment and inventory reduction.

Gartner Group, Inc. (www.gartner.com), a research and consulting firm, said at the end of 2000 that there were about 800 functional B2B e-marketplaces and that the number will peak at about 1,100 by 2002. It also defined three unique types of emerging marketplaces.

1. The *commodity e-marketplace*, which supports high-volume trade of products and services of commodity or near-commodity status, as well as financial instruments such as futures contracts.

2. The *business service e-marketplace*, which focuses on supporting specific inter-enterprise processes, such as those related to logistics, financial services, and maintenance, repair and operations procurement.

3. The *integration service e-marketplace*, which focuses on linkages and process definitions, and facilitates process-to-process integration between trading partners.

A Gartner spokesperson states, "Through 2005, the competitive landscape will be significantly transformed to a hub-spoke-Web model of inter-enterprise e-marketplace engagement among the three marketplace models."

If you're thinking about using the e-marketplace option there are some caveats. Forrester Research calculates that the US market will support only about 180 significant e-marketplaces by 2003. And AMR Research (www.amr.com) put the present number of e-marketplaces at about 600 and said that number would shrink to around 100 in 2001. Other industry experts put the number of e-marketplaces in operation today at 1600; but even they state that 90% of neutral e-marketplaces won't be around at the end of 2001. Therefore, do your due diligence before marrying your B2B to an e-marketplace.

One newly formed partnership that thinks e-marketplaces are here to stay is between G-Log (Global Logistics Technologies, Inc.), a logistics software company (www.glogtech.com), and Consolidated Commerce, a software technology company (www.consolidatedcommerce.com). The partnership will market its own brand of e-marketplaces using Consolidated Commerce's eMarketplace software. This software manages online transactions and includes a supply chain optimization module and G-Log's Global Command and Control Center software, better known as GC3, a supply chain and transportation management software. Thus, B2Bs that use an e-marketplace based on these technologies can plan and manage global, multi-carrier shipments (whether by air, land and/or sea) within the same online framework.

According to a G-Log spokesperson, "The joint effort will allow digital marketplace customers to optimize their procurement, order fulfillment, rating, manufacturing planning, and transportation while providing continuous order visibility and managing inventory."

Another e-marketplace champion is Cargill (www.cargill.com). In October 1999 Cargill, through its Corporate Leadership Team, created an e-business platform virtually from scratch. According to Cargill's Vice Chairman Bob Lumpkins, "We went from zero to having a serious team together in no time at all." Once the Cargill team got moving it set the Internet world on fire. On March 1, 2000, less than five months after the propitious October meeting, Rooster.com come online with its two-way e-marketplace for farmers AND Cargill announced its investment in GoCargo.com, the first online exchange for international shippers of container cargo.

Response to the Rooster announcement was immediate and intense. "Our Web site received 28,000 visits in the first two days after the news release rolled out," said Joe Stone, a Cargill Grain Division veteran and now charter member of the Rooster management team. "Our phone never stopped ringing, and the e-mail count was close to 500 on the first day."

Still in March 2000, it announced Novopoint.com, a partnership with software giant Ariba to devise a Rooster.com-like e-marketplace for food and beverage manufacturers and their suppliers. Just as with Rooster, Cargill intends to own a minority interest, with most of the rest of the ownership shared by other players in the industry.

In April 2000 Cargill, along with IBP, Smithfield, Tyson, Gold Kist, and Farmland announced plans for an e-marketplace for the meat and poultry industry that will provide a single, convenient place for buyers and sellers of meat and poultry products to connect with each other. This effort promotes efficiencies by facilitating faster and more direct product comparison and price negotiation, reducing paperwork and other duplication. The marketplace will be open to buyers and sellers of meat and poultry products.

It didn't stop there, for in May global steel trade leaders, Cargill Steel, Duferco, Samsung Corporation and TradeARBED announced that they are creating an independent global exchange for the international trading of steel on the Internet. The exchange is the first to offer online financing, risk management and logistics options as an integral part of the exchange with functionality that eclipses services offered by existing steel Web sites.

Also in May, Cargill's Hohenberg division, along with Allenberg Cotton Co., a division of the Louis Dreyfus Corporation, Dunavant Enterprises, and Plains Cotton Cooperative announced the signing of a letter of intent to pursue a neutral B2B marketplace for cotton and cotton-related products and services. Officials said they hope to create a comprehensive, independent electronic exchange for prospective suppliers of, and customers for, cotton and its products and supplies.

That took care of May. In June 2000 Cargill announced the launch of a new Web site, AGMConnects.com, to better serve grain elevator and farmer customers. AGM is a partnership between AGRI Industries, a federated co-operative, and Cargill. AGMConnects.com will provide local, customized Internet-based services to AGRI Grain Marketing's grain elevator customers.

The summer heat seemed to have put a damper on Cargill's Web initiatives for the last announcement was made in July when Cargill, SYSCO Corporation, Tyson Foods and McDonald's Corporation, through its eMac Digital joint venture with Accel-KKR, announced the formation of electronic Foodservice Network (eFS Network). eFS Network will operate an independent B2B marketplace to facilitate sales and purchases to the foodservice industry and will be open to all segments of the industry —

from foodservice suppliers and distributors to multi-unit operators. eFS Network will help maximize Internet-based efficiencies and savings for its participants across the entire supply chain.

There will probably be more announcements about B2B marketplaces incubated or partially financed by Cargill. The initiatives are as significant for the direction they are taking the Cargill's new e-business model as they are for the speed at which they are coming together — a pace that is practically taken for granted in the fast-forward e-business world of the 21st Century.

E-marketplaces are popping up all over. Marketmile (www.market-mile.com), a joint venture between Ventro (www.ventro.com) and American Express (www.americanexpress.com), is slated to launch about the time this book is published. It will provide supply chain efficiencies and competitive prices — criteria that small to mid-sized e-businesses are looking for in an e-marketplace. "What they really want is one marketplace ... for efficiency and effectiveness in this whole procurement area," said Robin Abrams, chief operating officer for Ventro. Of course, Ventro expects e-businesses that use its other e-marketplaces — Chemdex (www.chemdex.com), Promedix (www.promedix.com), Broadlane (www.broadlane.com), Industria Solutions (www.industria.com), and Amphire Solutions (www.amphire.com) [I hope I got them all!] — to participate in MarketMile.

Instead of building out an entire value chain linked infrastructure, buyers and sellers can just hire Ventro to integrate their systems into an e-

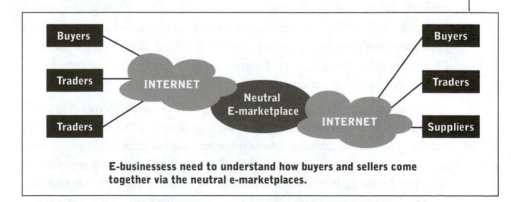

E-businessess need to understand how buyers and sellers come together via the neutral e-marketplaces.

marketplace, offering a variety of features, including automated purchasing and payment, and content aggregation.

Another supporter of e-marketplaces is Mark Hoffman, chairman and CEO of Commerce One (www.commerceone.com). In his keynote address at the EC World 2000 in Orlando, Flordia, he stated, "There's huge demand. So I don't subscribe to this view that we're already overcrowding the marketplace, and that there's going to be an increase in marketplaces and then a decrease, and there's going to be a few running the world."

E-marketplaces are in their infancy. While their marketspace still needs to mature, one thing is certain, they will change the way e-business is transacted over the Internet. Hoffman said, "I don't think today that we even understand the ramifications of what's going on in these marketplaces." I agree wholeheartedly.

The ASP Solution

E-businesses are under pressure to deploy their e-business model in record time and consequently may turn to ASPs as a way to address these demands. As I mentioned earlier in this section, the ASP model can assist an e-business that can't afford the expense and delays of setting up and managing top-tier applications. ASPs typically offer application hosting, consulting and systems integration services for the small to mid-sized e-business market that is commonly underserved by traditional IT solution providers. ASPs also make it possible for e-businesses to use leading software technology without the cost and burden of owning or managing the underlying technology. To run an application, an e-business can simply subscribe to a hosted version, thus reducing its burden of installing, managing and maintaining application software. This allows an e-business's IT staff to take care of the performance and maintenance of other areas in the B2B's infrastructure.

For example, as an e-business addresses the task of implementing applications for their business processes, such as supply chain management, it may be inclined to outsource the entire application deployment and management to an ASP. Using this method the B2B only incurs a monthly fee (and maybe set-up costs) to access its virtual infrastructure instead of a budget crushing expense to install and run its own back-office infrastructure.

Forrester, although a bit skittish when it comes to ASPs, does say that the "concept is compelling," citing the ability for smaller e-businesses to upgrade regularly without great cost. ASPs offer the ability to gain access to software such as PeopleSoft, which is otherwise very expensive and requires extensive customization.

Currently, technology from companies such as Citrix (www.citrix.com), GraphOn (www.graphon.com) and SCO (www.sco.com) allow best-of-breed applications to be leveraged in an ASP environment. Soon an e-business will be able to obtain just about any application it seeks from an outside supplier as a cost-effective solution to the demand of systems ownership. The only difference in the application will be that it's running on a central server managed by the ASP as opposed to the e-business's server, allowing an e-business to avoid up-front capital expenses, implementation challenges, and continuing maintenance, upgrades and customization costs.

The range of services offered by ASPs varies widely — from basic application hosting to full-lifecycle, wholesale installation and management. ASPs can create economies of scale through a centralized infrastructure and a distributed customer base and ASPs have the infrastructure necessary to run applications at high performance and with outstanding reliability, which gives them an edge on all but the largest e-business IT departments.

There are many different types of ASPs, and they vary widely in the applications and services they provide. They encompass the "pure-play" such as TheSupplyChain.com, Applicast (www.applicast.com) and Corio (www.corio.com), to the high-tech giants such as SAP (www.mysap.com), Peoplesoft (peoplesoft.com), Oracle (www.oracle.com), and CommerceOne (www.commerceone.com). There are also ASP options for some small to mid-sized B2B models, such as, Microbond (www.microbond.com), Cayenta, (www.cayenta.com), Usinternetworking (www.usi.com) (who is also a member of the *VARBusiness* E100+25 list of biggest solution providers in North America), and Madisonapps.com. All offer a complete suite of enterprise applications by bolting together best-of-breed applications and hosting them centrally.

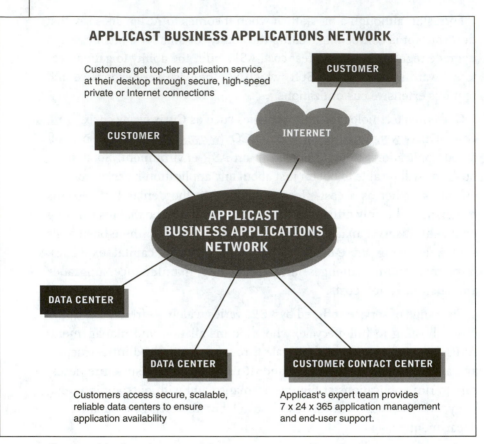

Courtesy of Applicast, Inc.

ASPs seem to be on the verge of being "all the rage" — but they haven't reached that zenith yet. Although the worldwide market for ASPs is forecast to grow from just a little over $3.5 billion in 2000 to more than $25 billion by 2004, according to the Dataquest unit of Gartner Group, Inc. (www.dataquest.com). "The ASP market represents a major computing revolution with the power to dramatically redraw today's IT ecosystem based on the delivery of application services over a network," says Ben Pring, principal analyst for Dataquest's Application Services Worldwide program.

IDC suggests that information regarding ASPs is only slowly penetrating the e-business market. Clare Gillan, group VP of IDC's Applications and Information Access Research, declares, "although buyers are beginning to learn about ASPs, their degree of knowledge is very limited." As of late 2000, knowledge of ASPs was not only low, it varied across IT professionals and corporate executive buyers. Late 2000 surveys conducted by IDC, indicated that only 40% of IT professionals and 50% of corporate executes knew the term ASP as a meaning for application service provider.

Within the next five years, ASP growth will more than triple, with larger enterprises accounting for almost 70% of the growth. At least that is what a study entitled, "Network Hosted Applications: U.S. Market Demand and Segmentation Analysis," from The Phillips Group (www.thephillipsgroup.net), a professional services company specializing in market intelligence for the telecommunications and information technologies industries, proclaims. The mid-2000 study found that "larger businesses recognize the need to adopt a new business model, particularly in the area of e-commerce. This will impact their existing legacy applications, and because they lack the internal skills needed to make this transition, many will turn to ASPs."

Another advocate operating within the same time frame is Scott McNealy, CEO of Sun Microsystems (www.sun.com), he predicts that "five years from now if you're a CIO with a head for business, you won't be buying computers anymore. You won't be buying software either. You will rent all your resources from an Application Service Provider (ASP)."

The ASP model is simply another channel to facilitate an e-business model. What differentiates an ASP from other channels is that its infrastructure delivers services and solutions to e-businesses, and fosters cooperation among many technical providers. Therefore, an ASP can help any enterprise alleviate its capital expenditures when making its move to an e-business model.

To aid an e-business in its ASP decision, on September 14, 2000, *VARBusiness* (www.varbusiness.com) provided a very good Customer Checklist for an e-business thinking about contracting with an ASP:

- Assess your e-business's reasons for opting to go with an ASP solution. Weigh potential trade-offs between in-house and hosted deployments.

Decide which applications make the most sense to host.

- Gather data about potential ASPs — their size, reputation, market experience and existing customer base. Do they serve other customers in your market?

- Assess the flexibility and scalability of the ASP's back-end architecture. Can the ASP facilitate rapid, tight integration? Check to determine the ASP's usage of technologies such as XML and Java.

- Find out whether the ASP has its own data center or if it outsources to a third-party provider. Either way, evaluate the infrastructure on which your chosen applications will run.

- Demand recovery and backup plans. Ask for specifics, including the method of archiving and retrieving data, off-site storage and backup, and alternate power and disaster recovery.

- Closely evaluate the security. Remember that your business systems will reside on the Internet. Make sure the ASP takes security very seriously. Does it offer any added services to help protect your data?

- Service is the key to an ASP. Make sure the ASP provides dedicated management and 24 x 7 help desks. Look into its geographic coverage in your area.

- Pricing in an ASP model can be as confusing as a phone bill. Hidden costs lie in wait for the unsuspecting user. Ask again and again: Do network connections or integration cost extra? If you decide to bring the solution in-house at a later date, what will the transition cost?

- Finally, read the fine print. Remember that a service level agreement (SLA) is a contract and doesn't always work on operant definitions. Nail down SLAs and penalties in writing before proceeding.

Choosing an ASP for the implementation of certain applications can offer tremendous value for some e-businesses. As ASPs fine-tune what amounts to a new service offering, an e-business must weigh the benefits with the trade-offs and assess whether the ASP service is right for it. Just remember to do a thorough due diligence before signing on the dotted line.

THE FULL MONTY (IN-HOUSE SOLUTION)

The true challenge for the enterprise when it has decided to adopt an e-business model is to achieve quick, accurate and successful integration between its back-office business processes and its value chain. Any comprehensive solution requires the blending of software tools, technologies, and expert professional services from consultants, vendors and integrators along with the cooperation of the value chain. Any successful B2B has to integrate its entire value chain so that everyone operates as a winning team.

In this era, a brochureware Web site isn't sufficient for 90% of B2Bs. Most B2Bs have customers, partners, and employees that increasingly require all enterprises in the value chain to provide electronic self-service interaction. Therefore, just about every enterprise must re-think its strategies for doing business within its value chain.

Caught in the middle are the back-office systems and applications (new, old, or packaged) that have enabled B2Bs to automate back-office functions for sales and distribution, order processing, and customer relationship management; allowing e-business enablement tools to satisfy requirements for front-end business activities such as contact management and order entry. The problem is that sometimes in the rush to implement an e-business model the systems and applications that were put in place created "islands of automation." And these "islands" resulted in many business processes requiring some type of manual task for any kind of communication between them. When a B2B chooses to integrate its entire value chain and to host all of its needs in-house it must find a solution to bridge these islands so as to eliminate redundancies, opportunities for error, and other deficiencies inherent with manual processing.

Why Go B2B? Revenue Growth

The businesses that have adopted a B2B model have seen an almost two digit revenue growth in their past fiscal year attributable to the new commerce channels the Internet has provided, far outpacing the e-tailers. Around 20% of the B2Bs state that they derive more than 10% of their total revenue from Internet-related transactions. B2Bs expect their Internet-generated revenue to continue to rise, which means a much higher profit for Internet initiatives.

Take for example, Staples, Inc., its Staples.com (Staples, Inc. owns 88% of Staples.com) is a one-stop shop for office supplies, with sites devoted to selling to the individual and small business and the mid- to large-size enterprises. Staples.com's operations include Staples.com, (of course), an e-tail site devoted to the individual and small businesses; Quill.com, built to service the mid- to large-size companies; and StaplesLink.com, a special service for purchasing managers. "Staples.com is representative of what bricks-and-clicks retailers should be doing online," said Melissa Shore, an analyst with Jupiter Communications Inc.

Of course, Staples.com isn't without competition, Office Depot has its own e-tailer, Officedepot.com and is Staples.com's chief rival. There is other competition in the way of small, mostly regional office supply houses with e-tail sites, although, not one of them seem to have held Staples.com back. Its revenue for the year 2000 soared 513% (No, it's not a typo!) from 1999. Maybe that's why it found itself on the *InternetWeek* 100 list for the year 2000.

Jeanne Lewis, president of Staples.com, says that when all the figures are in she expects her unit to pull down $350 million in revenue for 2000. She went on to state that she has set a goal of one million customers and $1 billion in online sales by 2003. I think she and her team can do it. Forrester thinks Web sales in the office supplies market space will climb to $65 billion by 2003 from $1.3 billion this year.

According to Lewis, one of Staples.com's secrets is getting repeat as well as new Staples shoppers to use its e-tail site. "Existing customers like multiple ways to shop with us," she said. Yet, analysts present a small word of caution for this marketing ploy. "The danger is if you move too quickly in getting on the Net, you risk the reputation of your brand online. This is particularly true if your customer service is poor," said Jim Williamson, analyst with International Data Corp (www.idc.com). E-tailers will have to process orders and customer queries quickly. "Consumer expectations of e-mail response times have moved from days to hours," Shore said.

As you will see throughout this book, the B2B model is quickly becoming an important part of the corporate mix. In addition to boosting sales and revenues, B2Bs are helping enterprises to save on costs in areas such as materials procurement, customer management, and logistics and fulfillment.

According to numerous research studies, global B2B is expected to grow from over $150 billion in 2000 to anywhere between $2 trillion to over $7 trillion in 2004 (it just depends on which research firm you're talking to). Furthermore, these market research figures show that e-marketplaces will facilitate over 700 billion B2B sales transactions in 2004. This volume represents 37% of the overall B2B market, and 2.6% of forecasted global sales transactions.

As a B2B's entire value chain adopts the B2B model, it's possible for their staff to browse, find what is needed and click the buy button and the raw materials, parts or products are automatically delivered (although not via cyberspace — at least not yet) as requested and billed at predetermined prices. This eliminates transaction costs associated with paper-based ordering and, in many cases, it gives the B2B more purchasing leverage.

With the proper integration throughout the value chain and an LFMS in hand, a B2B can optimize its inventory holdings, effortlessly plot the least expensive shipping methods for each instance, and gain reduction in costs through the collaboration of the buying power of its diverse global network.

Manufacturing Challenges

Two major trends are revolutionizing the manufacturing industry, forcing manufacturers to adopt an e-business model to manage their enterprise from the supply chain to the shop floor. Products are becoming more customized while manufacturers are increasingly outsourcing production.

These trends are breaking existing shop floor processes and systems, which are often little more than traditional paper and pencil calculations. Success in the e-business world of manufacturing is being built on a foundation of real-time visibility and collaboration across the value chain, improving speed, flexibility and, ultimately, customer satisfaction.

One of the basic functions of a good B2B model is the management of logistics, distribution and fulfillment. When enterprises link their shipping, warehouse, and logistics functions, they can cut cycle times and raise efficiency. Benefits come through cross-docking, flow-through strategies, and the sharing of delivery and quality information.

For all e-businesses, implementation of a scalable LFMS is a formidable task. For example, a B2B that is a manufacturer, or has a manufacturing division, has distinct requirements, such as:

- Rapid response to changing customer demands, such as making and tracking small runs of customized products.

- Mapping of its customers' orders through the entire value chain.

- Aggregating its shop floor fulfillment process including prioritization and scheduling of the orders, workflow, material, and labor and equipment usage.

- Instituting production reporting and quality management systems.

- Providing individual manufacturing unit management: dispatch and coordinate material and required information for each unit's operation.

- Ability to trace its material stemma and validate same.

- Tracking and reporting the product's progress through production, fulfillment, and shipment throughout the value chain.

One of the primary questions that all e-businesses, but in particular B2Bs need to ask: Does the enterprise's infrastructure mesh with an e-business model and its strategies? That is, can its distribution system handle around-the-clock orders, is its sales organization in tune with the new approach, and can it integrate customer information from ALL channels?

The tools, middleware, messyware, integration issues, and the cost necessary to provide the detailed information is enough to bring tears to the eyes of the most stalwart executive. However, without these details your e-business model cannot succeed.

Supply Management

Some manufacturing B2Bs manage the transformation of raw material into finished goods in the most efficient manner by creating a supply management infrastructure (SMI) that mutually benefits their entire value chain. Within this system are varying sets of demand management relationships that start with the customer and end at the supply base.

Implementation of a SMI allows a B2B to define its procurement and manufacturing strategy on a global basis. It can focus on specific needs and specific suppliers to fill those needs. This enables the B2B to manage a worldwide sourcing strategy, bonded inventory programs and customer-centric just-in-time (JIT) programs. Centralizing this aspect of its business processes affords the B2B a 360-degree view of its suppliers and increases the profit margin of the manufactured product.

Using this scenario, once a sourcing plan is established, the B2B's individual manufacturing units can execute the material flow with its suppliers on a local basis. The requirements of each manufacturing unit stand alone in the planning and execution of needed material and thus are not impacted or delayed by another value chain member's production schedule.

Once everything is in place and operational, a B2B can transmit requests to suppliers, relaying to them the quantities of each item needed via a Web browser or electronically with extensible markup language (XML) messaging instead of electronic data interchange (EDI). With this method you always have an electronic trail of all correspondence, ameliorating the "lost" order or miscommunication syndrome that can occur with "hard" or "white" correspondence and voice communication.

Inventory management that includes allocation processes is important for B2Bs that store their inventory in multiple locations. For without allocation processes many B2Bs won't have capable on-line available-to-promise (ATP) capabilities. Thus, they base promise dates on finished goods stock only, and allocate against a batch download of inventory. But, if and when they adopt the "converged" e-business model and begin to sell to other channels, without an integrated LFMS, inventory could easily become depleted, resulting in backorders, i.e., the 3Rs are not in play.

The response time for delivering ATP must be quick — there are only a few seconds wherein you can capture and maintain your customers' attention. High-end memory-resident technology (large caches) allows systems to determine promise dates in a fraction of a second — this is managed through a complex set of business rules and exceptions.

By improving visibility throughout the value chain B2Bs address three common goals (1) expediting orders, (2) improving customer service (the 3Rs), thus, (3) improving profit margin. Improved visibility allows qualified value chain members to:

- See into cataloged products.
- Access data about committed inventory and scheduled production.
- Check the availability of manufacturing resources and materials.
- Look at engineering change status reports.
- Make sourcing decisions on-line.
- Utilize 360-degree visibility into production data to see what is coming on-line.
- Access transportation options to determine how long it will take to get materials and/or product to a destination.

The same SMI can allow manufacturers that make product to customer specifications to plan based on forecasts and build based on orders, enabling them to strategize in terms of product features that they expect to sell.

CONVINCING THE VALUE CHAIN

At first, when a large B2B tells its trading partners that they must automate and become an integrated member of its value chain, they rebel. It's too scary, the cost is too high, the technology is unstable and the security is problematic, they cry. But with patience they will come around because it's even scarier to refuse to change and deal with those consequences.

Although you have adopted an e-business model, and you have convinced the rest of the value chain that adopting an e-business model is a practical move, they may still want to move cautiously. While, you will, in time, find few that will doubt that the integration of a value chain's systems has merit, how far and how fast it happens will be and remain a bone of contention.

While the value chain presents its share of technical challenges, including the integration of supporting technologies such as electronic resource planning (ERP) and even perhaps electronic data interchange (EDI), the

real problem is the impact automation will have on the business processes of the value chain members. Some B2Bs are just not ready to force
such jarring changes on their suppliers, partners and customers, especially if it's a smaller enterprise.

As J.C. Simbana, an analyst at American Frontier, a Denver-based brokerage firm, told CNET News.com in March 2000, "In my mind there
are a number of issues and concerns that need to be addressed before
this (sector) can move forward." He also voiced concerns about slow
adoption because of standards issues and security problems, as well as
the inevitable compatibility problems between various networks and the
software infrastructure available that could keep many participants on
the sidelines.

In the same article, Mark Ein, chief executive at VentureHouse Group
(www.venturehousegroup.com), a start-up venture fund, stated "the basic
premise behind the excitement over B2B e-commerce — both market
opportunity and size, and the value it will create is incredibly sound. B2B
is going to really revolutionize some industries."

The B2B model brings major changes in the way businesses deal with
each other, from planning to purchasing to paying. It also creates stress
within each enterprise. For example, the sales force may complain that a
B2B model has cut them out of the loop with online ordering systems,
while manufacturing may have to adjust to less than a week's notice on
order changes.

So how do you bring your entire value chain in tow so as to allow accurate and flexible shared planning, true just-in-time production and delivery, and lower inventory costs?

They've no choice — you're the channel master — just tell your partners, suppliers, shippers and customers and whoever that they've no
choice; that is, if they are to continue to participate in the value chain. You
will find plenty of grumbling, especially among your smaller value chain
members, when they are forced to automate and integrate or lose your
business.

If a small business in the value chain is without the resources necessary
to join in the automation movement, and that business is critical to your

profitability, then figure out a way to assist in their transition. Just as Mott's North America has done with some of its smaller trading partners. Perhaps you can let your IT staff handle much of the IT work for that partner for a freeze on the contract price over a set period of time. Any way you go about keeping an essential partner within the value chain, it will pay off in the long run.

Security

When a value chain member joins the integration migration, it may still have concerns whether sharing information might adversely affect its business or its relationships with other partners.

For the most part, familiar security measures, such as encryption, can assure business throughout the value chain that only authenticated individuals see the information that's relevant to them. For example, when you order a personal computer off a Web site — you don't see that Web site's wholesale pricing scheme, its distribution chain or how much inventory it has in stock — you only see what is relevant to you and your order.

Password protection works. But at the same time let it be known that value chain members should behave themselves while traveling the electronic byways. No one wants to deal with a bunch of value chain "hackers." Beyond password security, parameters should be set up that monitors network traffic for transactions or volume that are out of the ordinary.

The question of who gets to see what information goes beyond security to business practice. In reality, the value chain's concern is less about outsiders hackers, and more about how much information and control a member wants to share with other members of the value chain. Some don't want other members of the value chain (who are their competitors) to see their prices or order volumes; there is a fear that sharing too much information will be harmful. It boils down to what information and in what quantity are members of the value chain willing to divulge to each other.

For instance, a value chain manufacturer doesn't want X to know how much capacity it has allocated to Y, or what Z pays for components. Prices fluctuate with volume, it's also difficult if one value chain member feels that another receives better treatment. But for a B2B's LFMS to work, it requires opening up inventory data and the entire value chain must do it and this does decrease the likelihood that any one business gets burned. Yet, e-businesses shouldn't provide full disclosure without a high level of comfort and a long-term relationship.

All B2Bs implementing automated integration will find businesses that absolutely refuse to participate. Some hold out because they are unwilling to share information about the way they do business. Some may make money from investment buys, and experience very thin profit margins and they don't want the other members of the value chain to know what drives their buying patterns.

Stories about security breaches throughout the Internet community make the value chain very nervous. So even the businesses that participate in shared planning — coordinated scheduling of orders, manufacturing, and shipping — don't always trust it completely.

There is one last issue. It centers around a reluctant value chain partner. Some participants, even if they did invest the time and money in integration of their systems into the value chain still don't trust forecasts — they insist on following their own schedule. This reluctance to alter production based on forecast volume brings inconsistency in the forecasting data that dribbles down the value chain and can cause chaos within the chain.

The Trickle-Down Effect

An integrated B2B value chain is an attempt to create a large coordinated organization. However, as difficult as it is to control what it owns, it's a lot harder to control what it doesn't.

The value chain is definitely a coordinated activity, and it's hard to play a team game without teammates. The whole chain suffers if one link is slow to provide information or access or wants to play by itself (but still be a member of the team).

B2Bs, as a whole, implement technology that allows them to anticipate future demand, but this technology is still at the mercy of classic inventory and forecasting problems, such as, the retailer forecasts to customers, distributors forecast to manufacturers, and manufacturers forecast to distributors. However, taking the game analogy, if a defensive tackle is fooled by the fake, the opposition gains yardage and maybe even a touchdown. The trap everyone gets caught in is that everyone is making their best guess (is it a fake?) — but it's still just a guess, if one channel proves to be assessing their needs in a wrong light, then you still end up with turmoil (a touchdown for the opponent).

The only way to eliminate the very real chance of a chaotic inventory forecast is to build front-end and back-end systems that are totally integrated, including the messaging layer, so that definitions and concepts are the same for all systems. Data must not only move throughout the value chain from each partner's front-end to their back-end, it also must only get transmitted once so as to prevent duplication. The right protocol must be established between each system, commit logic must be accurate, and all databases must be in sync.

Be aware that to implement successful communication between front- and back-end systems throughout a value chain often involves a middle layer of sometimes very "messyware" that allows integration of planning and visibility to support Web-based promises of delivery dates. This middle layer can thus notify fulfillment engines of real-time inventory availability, resources, and materials to complete the order and authorized members of the value chain can tap into this data to enable their own forecasting processes.

The middle layer must include an ATP engine, with its own set of business rules, that allows it to offer multidimensional responses. An example of this capability might go something like this: Acme Co. orders 1000 widgets online from Best Widget Corp. The ATP engine confirms production slot based on Acme's request and fulfillment rules. Acme's order information flows automatically through the supply chain. Forecasts and other information pass between Best Widget and its supply chain, allowing the members direct access to both actionable requests and business data to allow them to make the best decision for the customer on behalf of Best Widget.

Return on Investment

Every B2B's goal should be a positive return on investment (ROI). This can be achieved, in part, by the reduction of working capital through increased forecast accuracy, thus allowing lower inventory levels. If a B2B can't accomplish this then it will find itself overcompensating by maintaining a large inventory of its products so it can quickly respond to customer orders. So, set up meetings with the recalcitrant members of your value chain to emphasize the importance of the forecasting process for everyone's balance sheet. This is especially important if the e-business habitually institutes promotional blitzes or regularly launches new product lines.

B2Bs can show a faster and better ROI after implementation of a full-scale LFMS than e-tailers because of the efficiencies permitted throughout the value chain. It can translate its massive investment in this compelling technology into not only satisfied customers and better-managed inventory and forecasting, but also less employee and equipment downtime due to better communications within the value chain. Likewise, with a fully integrated value chain an e-business will know when one of its diverse factories, namely, X has found supplier Y that can provide product Z at a lower cost — no guess work, no remembering to tell fellow divisions about the new found resource.

The Advantages of Integration

With an integrated supply chain B2Bs can access suppliers, distribution channels, and retailers instantly. Managing customer orders means much more than order entry process automation — inquiries, quotes, purchase orders, delivery schedules, acknowledgements, and payments can be processed with the right infrastructure in place. Remember that even B2Bs need an order management process with features such as online product catalogs, fully enabled Web stores, and customer self-service along with an bit of "humanity" thrown in via a call center, which can be a multi-media Web-based center.

Through the proper management, B2Bs can obtain efficient access to information that can have a great impact on the production processes. One scenario might be acquiring the knowledge needed to expand product options or mass-customize to meet customer demands. We all know

UNCOOPERATIVE PARTNERS

A B2B could easily find itself with an uncooperative supply chain member or members when it moves to integrate its value chain. If this happens the B2B's best bet is to classify its individual supply chain members. This will aid the B2B in its strategization of how to handle each situation.

Critical

Supply chain members classified as "critical" have unique capabilities (e.g., raw material availability, product functionality, location, sales channel) that measurably impact or differentiate performance of the a B2B's bottom line and can't be replaced or alternates can't be developed in time without significant cost and resource commitment.

Because critical supply chain members can pose a serious threat to customer responsiveness, and the B2B's profitability, they must be integrated at the same level as in-house business processes.

Important

Supply chain members classified as "important" could measurably impact the B2B's bottom line. While there are alternatives with similar capabilities, it will take some time and effort to court these businesses and integrate them into the value chain. Because of their volume, these members need to be evaluated based on their level of importance in the B2B's operations and how their relationship impacts on your profitability.

Commodity

Supply chain members classified as "commodity" don't measurably impact the B2B's day-to-day operations, have multiple competitors, and it will generally require little effort and time to certify a new business to fill the vacated role in the value chain. It's best to evaluate these members based on their level of importance in the B2B's daily operations.

When considering the impact of each non-cooperative member of the supply chain consider: 1) What is the likelihood that a member will opt to cooperate in time? 2) Should risk minimization strategies, such as inventory build-up, contracts with alternative suppliers or shippers be pursued? Then take the appropriate steps to protect the B2B and its value chain.

of B2Bs that have gained significant competitive advantage when they use e-business solutions such as build or configure-to-order and demand-driven planning.

Herman Miller SQA (a division of Herman Miller) (www.herman-miller.com) has changed the rules of the game in custom-built office furniture and in doing it earned a place on the *InternetWeek* 100 for the year 2000 and was honored by *Industry Week* as one of the world's 100 best managed companies. It has brought the configure-to-order and demand-driven planning concept to reality improving both its Income Statement and Balance Sheet.

Herman Miller's Web site is state-of-the-art (visit it!). The site's great interactivity and dynamic content is pulled from its back-end systems. And although the Web site is a fantastic B2B tool, it carefully avoids industry jargon and instead reinforces the brand presence through clear information hierarchy, intuitive navigation and appropriate technology.

The Customer: Herman Miller SQA
The Challenge: Fast delivery time
The Results:

	Previous	Today
Cycle Times	5 weeks	5 days
On-time delivery	75%	99.7%
Inventory Turns	25	>125
Market Share		Up 20%
Profit		Up 40%

Changing the Rules of the game in office furniture. *Graphic courtesy of SynQuest, Inc.*

And its outside sales staff is still definitely in the loop. Through the use of PC-based configuration software it can quickly and accurately determine a customer's needs. Once that is ascertained, an order is transmitted in real-time to the factory for an immediate delivery commitment. Rush orders can even be promised for completion within two working days and at no extra charge. This information is disseminated as needed throughout the value chain to assure that the order is completed correctly and on time. Herman Miller states that it can go weeks without a single order going out late or delivered incomplete.

Another great benefit of a properly implemented B2B infrastructure is

PC Computing Magazine
E-Commerce Leaders

Top 10 Business-to-Business

Rank	Company	
1	Intel	
2	Cisco Systems	
3	Dell	
4	3Com	
5	IBM	
6	Gateway 2000	
7	Boise Cascade Office Products	E-commerce pioneer and office products supplier to Fortune 500
8	W.W. Grainger	
9	Sabre Group	
10	Office Depot	

PC Computing magazine ranked BCOP No. 7 among all US companies for their leadership in the area of e-commerce. They called BCOP "an e-commerce pioneer" in supplying office products to Fortune 500 companies. Presented at Goldman Sacks Investor Conference on May 2, 2000 in New York City.

that value chain partners can integrate their procurement processes. This allows them to focus their attention on information rather than inventory, and thus enables quick response to fluctuations in supply and demand.

Another shining example of an e-business model is Boise Cascade Office Products (www.bcop.com — "BCOP"), one of the world's premier B2B distributors of products for the office. From its North American, Australian and Europe distribution centers BCOP can provide its global customer-base with virtually any product in its inventory with a strict adherence to the 3Rs (remember — right product, at the right place, at the right time).

Its contract stationer business sells office supplies to a global array of large corporate and government offices. In a speech George J. Harad, chairman and CEO of BCOP, gave at the Goldman Sachs Investor Conference on May 2, 2000, he attributed the growth of BCOP's middle-market initiative in part to "a Web site specifically designed for these customers." He went on to say, "to date, our experience has been very encouraging...."

Harad further told the Goldman Sachs conference attendees, "In another growth initiative, we've made significant progress in developing business opportunities through the Internet and other Web-based technologies. In 1999, office products e-commerce sales reached an annualized rate of $500 million, half of which came over the Internet. In 1998, Internet sales represented only about 2% of BCOP's business. In 1999, it was 12%, and we expect that this year, e-commerce sales will represent 25% to 30% of BCOP's overall sales."

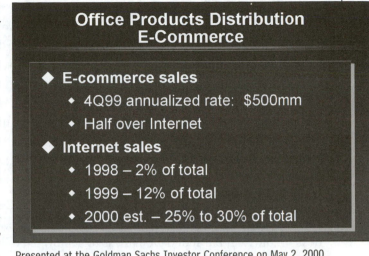

Office Products Distribution E-Commerce

◆ **E-commerce sales**
  ✦ 4Q99 annualized rate: $500mm
  ✦ Half over Internet
◆ **Internet sales**
  ✦ 1998 – 2% of total
  ✦ 1999 – 12% of total
  ✦ 2000 est. – 25% to 30% of total

Presented at the Goldman Sachs Investor Conference on May 2, 2000 in New York City.

Soon you may be quoting a *PC Computing* magazine glowing write-up about your e-business, if you can get a handle on efficiently managing logistics and fulfillment. When a B2B can link its shipping, warehouse, and logistics and other fulfillment functions, it cuts the cycle times and raises efficiency.

Keep in mind that the B2B is likely to be some version of a converged model. This might consist of the traditional enterprise where the day-to-day operations are not dependent upon the mechanizations of an e-business model with a segment of the traditional enterprise (usually a specific division or subsidiary) that has some of its processes online. Added to that may be an e-tail model that allows the e-business to present its products to the individual consumer for purchase and even a pure-play thrown into the mix for tax reasons.

B2Bs have only recently begun to augment their business processes through the use of the Internet so as to speed transactions throughout the value chain. Today, a growing percentage of purchase orders are being presented over the Web to buy materials and goods from strategic suppliers. But still, how many B2Bs have addressed how those goods are going to be processed and shipped?

As a leader in the motion control industry providing solutions for factory automation needs, Compumotor's (www.compumotor.com), a division of manufacturer Parker Hannifin Corp., executives understand customers have and expect access to information they've never had before. Therefore, Compumotor built an extranet to handle orders for not only its 12,500 products, but warranty and non-warranty repair-status issues, along with many other online transactions from its numerous distributors, factory representatives and direct customers, not to mention its internal staff. Now, Compumotor customers, value-added resellers (VARs) and suppliers can use the extranet to enter orders and check order status, product availability or returns and suppliers can access material forecasts and performance statistics.

Take one more look at General Electric. When its CEO, John F. Welch, outlined his sweeping Internet agenda in early 1999, it left no GE business untouched. He added e-business to a short list of broad initiatives — including globalization, customer service and a quality control yardstick called Six Sigma — that each manager would utilize. To paraphrase Welsh: The Internet is no longer just a new medium for buying and selling, it's fundamentally changing how businesses operate.

Since that auspicious beginning GE has moved billions of dollars in sales and spending to the Internet in record time, aided largely by a corporate culture that rewards the "stealing" of ideas within GE's 20 units and 340,000 employees. The result is new buying, selling and manufacturing techniques that spread through the massive company in weeks, not years.

"We've become pretty good at using size to our advantage," Welch says. "Size gives you the ability to experiment, to take risks because you're not going to sink yourself. That is the only advantage of size. The small company is faster, but one wrong swing can wipe them out. They have to be right."

Is the behemoth back? GE makes a pretty good case for the Fortune 500 companies that everyone in the Internet community had discounted since it was felt that they wouldn't try e-business experimentation until absolutely forced.

Not with GE, its private e-auctions are forcing suppliers to fight for its business, squeezing hundreds of millions of dollars out of purchases in 2000 alone. Full-time Internet connections are letting GE remotely monitor heavy equipment — and tell the customers who own the equipment how they could be working more efficiently.

Whole new businesses are sprouting up throughout GE, including, believe it or not, the repackaging of homegrown technology for sale outside the enterprise — the Silicon Valley crowd had better watch out! It's this very e-business ecosystem that has earned GE the No. 1 spot in the *InternetWeek* 100 listing of top e-businesses for the year 2000 and garnered the first position on the *Forbes* 500 in 2000.

"The key revelation is that the Internet is primarily a productivity tool, and secondarily a selling and procurement tool," says Jeanne Terrile, a financial analyst at Merrill Lynch (www.ml.com). "They're using the Internet to eliminate paperwork and run operations a lot more efficiently."

GE expects to slash overhead costs by as much as 50%, which would amount to a staggering $10 billion in as little as two years. Now *that* is a figure executives championing the move to an e-business model can take to their recalcitrant board of directors.

Gary Reiner, GE's corporate CIO, sits at the center of this e-business whirlwind, overseeing e-business and IT activities across all 20 GE businesses. *InternetWeek* senior managing editor David Joachim spoke with Reiner about how the global conglomerate is tuning its business for the Internet Age.

In that interview, Joachim asked Reiner. "Where has the Internet had the largest impact so far?" And Reiner responded that "There are three different areas: the buy side, make side and sell side. On the sell side, it's had a very big impact in GE Plastics. It's had a very big impact on some of the capital businesses, like fleet services. It's having a big impact on the parts side of our heavy equipment businesses. It's having a big impact at NBC, obviously, and CNBC.com and all the Internet investments that we've made there."

Reiner went on to say, "On the buy side, we're doing a ton of e-auctioning across the board. We're putting so much of what we do on the Web in terms of interacting with our suppliers and in terms of negotiations. And that really is changing how we think about sourcing."

Then he addresses the make side where he espouses, "What we're really getting excited about is the shutting down of traditional processes. We're learning that the only way you really take advantage of all of the Web technology is by giving people only one choice in how you do it — the most productive and efficient way. One of the things that we did possibly longer than we should have is allow multiple ways in which transactions could be done and information could be shared internally. We're now at the point where we're saying: This is how you make travel reservations, this is how you get your benefits information, this is how you reserve a conference room. There's only one way to do it. And we're finding that's the real way to drive productivity internally."

Joachim then went to the core by asking, "Do you see those areas of emphasis changing over time, or is it about layering more sophistication on top of those applications?"

Reiner, in response, told Joachim that GE would go "deeper and deeper into those three areas. On the buy side, we separate the world into the negotiation process and the transaction process. We are Web-enabling nearly all of the negotiation process, and we are targeting 100 percent of our transactions on the buy side being done electronically. We're hoping to be mostly there by the end of the year [2000]."

"On the sell side, it's a combination of Web ordering, EDI and fax-to-EDI, depending on what our customers want to do. We're migrating as much as we can electronically on the transaction side. But really there are three areas on the sell side, and we're trying to get more productivity out of all three."

"There's the actual taking of the order. There's providing through the Web all of the information surrounding the order — order status, track and trace information, stock availability, the ability to configure complex orders. All of that stuff we have Web-enabled, and we're migrating more and more of our customers that want to do that, to the Web. And then additional value-added customer services that were traditionally provided either through call centers or not provided at all, are now provided on the Web through something we call *Wizards*."

Joachim asked Reiner how GE has overcome the "large enterprise syndrome" so it could profit from the Internet economy. Reiner's response

— "GE has a history of, when it gets excited about an initiative, moving very fast. When we get focused on an initiative, we hire as many of the right people as we can, focus them, share best practices over and over again, and measure [progress]. It's the way GE operates."

"We can take some examples. E-auctioning on the buy side was something that was launched by our GE Transportation Systems business. It was a software package that was built in two to three weeks by some very talented folks there. We have now taken that and are hosting that for the entire company, and all of the businesses are using that same software tool to do e-auctions. That really started from nothing in December [1999] to where we're targeting $5 billion of volume being e-auctioned by the end of this year [2000]." (Wow!)

Another giant, Cargill (www.cargill.com), isn't just in the e-marketplace arena. It spread its reach into the e-tail sector. Cargill announced on the last day of May 2000 that Cargill Animal Nutrition is offering a select line of animal feed products for purchase over the Internet on its Web site, (www.CargillAnimalNutrition.com).

It's not as if the Internet is virgin territory for the enterprise — Cargill Steel long ago (relatively speaking) set up an extranet site to serve top accounts. It also was one of the first American companies to conduct transactions on the e-STEEL Web site (www.esteel.com). Other Internet-based initiatives have percolated across the corporation — a case in point being February 2000's agreement with J.D. Edwards (www.jdedwards.com) and Ariba (www.ariba.com) to move Cargill's corporate purchasing of items, such as office supplies, chemicals, and airline tickets, to the Internet within three years.

Cargill's e-business initiative has a two-pronged mission: to help the enterprise's existing business units develop e-business tactics to improve their own efficiency and customer service, and to identify and develop e-business opportunities outside the formal Cargill structure through investment, joint ventures and other means. This is why Cargill made it on the *Internet Week* 100 list in 2000.

I believe the stellar examples of Cargill, BCOP, GE, VFC, to name a few, are what the Internet community can expect from the old guard. They may take their time in adopting an e-business model, but when they do finally make the move, they won't do it half way.

THE RIGHT CHOICE

An early 2000 survey by PricewaterhouseCoopers (PWC) (www.e-business.pwcglobal.com), one of the world's largest professional services organization, and The Conference Board, a non-profit educational and research organization, found that 40% of the respondents felt that their companies could handle customer orders electronically, although only 28% could process payments online. When asked about their supply-side connectivity more than 60% stated that they don't have links between their supply chain and more than 10% of the 60% said that they've no future plans for supplier and partnership linkage. The survey entitled, "Electronic Business Outlook for the New Millennium," found that although the respondents acknowledged the importance of e-business, 25% admitted that their enterprise had not moved beyond the brochureware phase.

But we are getting there. "US businesses are universally preparing to buy and sell online, leveraging the Net to build deeper relationships with their business partners," at least according to Steven J. Kafka, eBusiness Trade analyst at Forrester Research.

Cathy Neuman, deputy global e-business leader at PWC, made a good point when she stated, "It's important to remember that, despite how quickly e-business has changed the landscape, it's still a new paradigm, especially for large organizations."

Ultimately, the enterprises that integrate their value chain will be the big winners. "Eventually, companies will have to make sure that they can carry on on-line transactions, manage documents, and make sure that the people on the other end of the line can read their data sheets and have accurate information," says Hadley Reynolds, research director at The Delphi Group (www.delphigroup.com). As discussed previously, today the majority of B2B transactions are handled through traditional processes, e.g., telephone, e-mail, white mail. Yes, currently there are B2B transactions handled through some type of on-line method (EDI, e-marketplaces, supply chain management, VPN, VAN), but most, somewhere along the process chain, revert to traditional processes.

One telling pattern is that many B2Bs don't pay their suppliers electronically because that would mean they'd need to integrate their financials. However, in the end, businesses that don't integrate their systems with all of their value chain lose out on cost savings, the competitive edge. Even more importantly, in the not-too-distant future, systems integration will simply be the cost of doing business.

Building the infrastructure to support a viable B2B e-business model isn't cheap, but in the end everyone from the cantankerous minority stockholder to the forward-looking CEO will praise the benefits of e-business. And, although they may soon come to understand the need for an e-business model, few will grasp the reason for the size of the investment required, even fewer will grasp that a cutting edge, scalable technology infrastructure is a major part of that investment.

The E-Tailers

ALTHOUGH THE FINANCIAL GURUS have lately
been somewhat bearish on e-tailing, consumers remain bullish on online
shopping. Various research groups have touted the number of American
households making their first online purchase during the year 2000 as
being around 11 million, with average online spending increasing more
than 15%. David Pecaut, senior vice president and global co-leader of The
Boston Consulting Group's E-commerce Practice (www.bcg.com) says,
"While financial markets for online stocks are in turmoil, the underlying
growth of the online retailing industry continues unabated. Online retailing
is here to stay and will continue to gain significant share." Not bad for an
industry that is still in its infancy.

Still, there is a problem — too many people adopted a "gold rush" men-
tality in their search for easy money. In doing so, they forgot all the
lessons they learned in Business 101. It takes the same business acumen
to operate an e-tail e-business model as it does to operate a traditional
store on Main Street. The mass marketing of store hosting sites such as
Shopnow.com, Oxygen.com and the venerable Yahoo!Store has given
everyone an easy way to access the bare essentials necessary to put a store
front before the online public, but not to have a viable e-tail business.

Stop and think — would you sign a lease for a storefront on Main Street
without first having a well thought out business plan in hand? You would-
n't even THINK about risking your money and reputation on a traditional retail operation without performing the proper due diligence, and

putting into place the proper planning for customer service, product distribution and order fulfillment — so how does an e-tail operation differ?

I'm not saying that there aren't opportunities available — there are — major ones offering growth and profitability that most e-businesses have yet to exploit, just as there are opportunities in the traditional word. Just do it right — don't jump in blindly. The strongest advice the author can give to any e-preneur is to combine your e-tail efforts with the expertise and resources you would use when building a traditional retail establishment.

Customer Preference to Online or Offline Shopping						
Based on response to following question: "For each of the following categories, if an item is easy to buy both offline and online, I would."						
	Apparel	Electronics	Travel	Books/Video	Groceries	Investing
Always/Mostly Buy Online	5.1%	14.1%	29.8%	28.9%	1.9%	17.9%
Buy Equally On/Offline	21.5%	27.6%	22.8%	34.9%	5.8%	14.1%
Mostly Buy Offline	34.8%	26.3%	17.3%	22.7%	15.2%	13.7%
Always Buy Offline	38.5%	32.0%	30.1%	13.4%	77.2%	54.2%
Source: cPulse						

cPulse found the biggest advantage cited by respondents (primarily online shoppers) was convenience, not price or selection. *Chart courtesy of Internet.com Corp.'s Cyberatlas.*

Currently e-tailers have their work cut out for them — they must increase their revenues through improvement in their checkout procedures so as to capture sales from the more than 50% of online shopping carts that are abandoned before customers complete their transactions.

The great news is that in some categories, such as, books, music and videos, computers and software, e-tailers have begun to pose a real threat to bricks-and-mortars. At the end of 2000 more than 10% of the total sales in these categories occurred online — fantastic!

LESSONS LEARNED

The "good news bad news scenario" is aptly demonstrated by an iGo (www.igo.com) press release in which it stated that iGo "has experienced an *alarming* 2,000% growth rate since its founding in 1993 by Chief Energizing Officer, Ken Hawk. To support, and fuel, the company's growth, on January 1, 1999, iGo went live with its new customer management and fulfillment operating systems." Where else except the Internet would you find a 2000% growth rate deemed "alarming." But

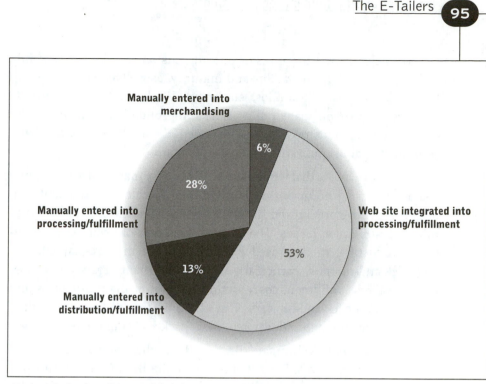

Manually entered into merchandising

6%

28%

Manually entered into processing/fulfillment

Web site integrated into processing/fulfillment

53%

13%

Manually entered into distribution/fulfillment

Most e-tail sites have integrated their front-end with some version of an LFMS

that is exactly how some Web-based businesses look at a spike in growth, mainly due to an insufficient LFMS.

Many e-tailers learned the hard way during the 1999 holiday season that having the ultimate front-end is not enough — customers are much more interested in strong customer service programs, dependable delivery and easy return policies — the 3Rs.

The ones that took those lessons to heart found that their 2000 holiday season was an unbridled e-commerce success. Overall revenues were certainly impressive, of course, that is nothing new in the dot-com world. Industry analysts state that the combination of a strong economy and increasing consumer confidence in the Internet, as a whole, is what drove the numbers to their lofty level. Although the media is still buzzing with horror stories about e-businesses that were not able to fulfill holiday orders in a timely way or touting so-called evidence that e-business is unsafe and unreliable. Some even went so far as to claim that these issues are emblematic of fatal flaws in the overall e-commerce concept!

Nevertheless, what the investor and the customer alike are currently looking for are signs of stability and maturity, as well as the ever elusive black ink on the profit and loss statement. While the financial wizards have put a "pox" on many online stocks, the underlying growth of the online retailing industry continues unabated. E-tail is here to stay and will continue to gain significant share going forward.

The bottom line is that winners in any business market share the same characteristics — no matter what space they operate in — the ability to offer competitive pricing and strong customer service, while experiencing minimal fulfillment issues. The rest will take care of itself. As stated in the Introduction, catalog-based e-tailers outperform pure-play e-tailers and click-and-mortars, particularly in the fulfillment area with catalog-based e-tailers' fulfillment costs around 18% lower than pure-plays and 43% less than click-and-mortars. Why? Because they've been at it longer — they tackled the one and two item pick, pack and ship issues long ago.

A case is point is Intimate Brands, Inc., the parent company of Victoria's Secret, Bath & Body Works and White Barn Candle Company, which stated that the first full year of the company's very successful VictoriasSecret.com business on the Internet was an unbridled success. "At Intimate Brands, we are using VictoriasSecret.com to pioneer a prototype online business," stated Intimate Brands Vice President of Communications and Investor Relations, Debbie Mitchell. "We plan to use this same model of success to bring brand extensions online with the Beauty business of Victoria's Secret and Bath & Body Works."

VictoriasSecret.com uses the technology and infrastructure of Victoria's Secret Catalog, including its real-time inventory tracking, database management and distribution capabilities. This expertise was leveraged not only to deliver high-quality e-commerce service, but to also create a site that has been profitable since inception. Intimate Brands, Inc. is among the *InternetWeek* 100 for the year 2000.

Staples.com uses Staple, Inc.'s mail-order catalog business's operation to give it a ready-made delivery system to fill Web orders. Staples.com keeps no inventory and uses existing Staples distribution centers that also serve its catalog business. Online orders are shipped out in the same way as catalog orders.

"We've been in the delivery business for 11 years. It's not something we have to start from scratch, and with that experience comes ways to efficiently move products from fulfillment centers to our customers," explained Jeanne Lewis, president of Staples.com.

Having an existing delivery system in place also gives companies like Staples a leg up on pure-plays that are new to the game. "It's a lot tougher if you're a retailer that's not already making deliveries," said Barry Parr, an analyst at IDC (www.idc.com).

Ron Hanners, executive vice president of JCPenney.com, (another *InternetWeek* 100 company) told consulting firm, Adventis (www.rens-strategy.com) (formerly Renaissance Strategy), that competitive pressures forced his site to become more user friendly and a stickler for the 3Rs. The overhaul of the site, which launched at the end of 2000, took more than a year and the efforts of over 300 people.

The redesigned site gives customers the option of local pick-up at an Eckards, catalog center or J.C. Penney's store (there is a charge for this service). The site also allows the online customer to place orders using catalog reference numbers. Hanners told Renaissance/Adventis, "When we started the redesign, I thought it'd be easy. Then I moved to thinking of it as extremely impossible. Now I'm somewhere in between. People talk about e-commerce being easy. Well, I'm an old retailer, and I don't recall ever working this hard at retail."

IS THE E-TAILER AN ENDANGERED SPECIES?

New e-tailers are most vulnerable in their LFMS and customer service management. Only 25% of new e-tailers are currently capable of dealing with a sudden surge in traffic on their Web site, especially in the areas of Web response rates, levels of customer service and fulfillment. The survival of many e-tailers is threatened unless drastic measures are taken immediately.

The picture isn't as bleak for the more established e-tailers; but they also have weak spots in the same areas. The year 2000 gave the entire online community a roller-coaster ride; however, the e-tailers with a strong consumer focus and an eye toward maximizing profits came through relatively unscathed — just a few bumps and bruises here and there.

Although online shopping is exploding, less than one-half of e-tailers make a profit on a one-item product order, except for the e-tailers offering high-ticket products. For others the profit comes only when the customer purchases more than one item, but even then profit is dependent upon efficiencies in the e-tailer's LFMS.

Many e-tailers feel that fulfillment is a black hole that they are being sucked into and don't know if and when they will ever escape. And all e-tailers have to find a way to overcome the cost of continually shipping out small packages where the shipping cost sometimes is at least one-half of the overall value of the product purchased. This high distribution cost is one reason why the Web has not progressed past the "rapidly emerging sales channel" stage, except in a few specific areas — books (most e-tailers offer a 20-50% discount on books), music and videos, high ticket items, and virtual products (software).

Unless the customer is shopping for a specific hard-to-find product or finds the convenience of shopping online outweighs additional costs — the e-tailer has an uphill battle. For many products, it's much less expensive to go to the local retail store, even when the cost of gas and the time to drive and shop is factored into the equation. Of course, the e-tailer also has to overcome the fact that shopping at a local retail store brings immediate gratification — the product is in-hand and the customer is not forced to wait for its arrival. However, the demand on the individual consumer's time is growing and one compromise is to find quicker ways to handle everyday tasks. The Web is part of the solution, if e-businesses can get it right.

Taking an online order is the easy part. Getting the product to the customer is a logistical nightmare. That last yard — completing the sale to the satisfaction of the customers so they return and order again — takes planning and organization. The key word is "completing" and the sale is not complete until the product is in the customer's hands and the customer is satisfied. It's the least glamorous part of operating an e-tail site and it's the hardest to get right. Getting a product from the e-tailer's virtual checkout counter to its customer's doorstep is what order fulfillment is all about and it's remarkably complex.

Post-Transaction Anxiety Disorder

Believe it or not there is now a medical term for the frustrations online customers experience from the aftermath of buying an item online — Post-Transaction Anxiety Disorder (PTAD). What will they think of next? Shelley Taylor & Associates (www.shelly-taylor.com), a management consulting and research publishing firm, highlighted this new definition in a mid-2000 study entitled "Return to Sender," an international study of the success factors in online order fulfillment and post-transaction communication. To gather information for the study, Taylor's staff purchased items from 100 retail sites in the US and UK. They then tracked the checkout process, order fulfillment and returns to identify 200 user experience metrics that normally ensure repeat business and customer loyalty, such as factors in online order fulfillment and post-transaction communication.

The Taylor study pointed out that shipping charges, sticker shock and anxiety over whether items ordered online would ever truly arrive bring on this new malady. But it also prescribed a cure; it found that a faultless checkout process, good post-transaction communication, quick receipt and return of goods would stop PTAD in its tracks. This same prescription is also destined to develop into the defining standard of any successful e-business.

According to Taylor, the e-businesses that ranked highest in order fulfillment in the US include Amazon, Sports Authority, Outpost and Drugstore. In the UK Blackstar, HMV and Jungle.com were among the highest, although the US e-businesses did run laps around their UK counterparts.

Taylor told a May 3, 2000 Silicon Valley Breakfast Briefing, "I was astonished to find that some of the hottest online retailers have yet to adopt the rudimentary customer services practices of their bricks-and-mortar counterparts. The success of online stores will depend upon bridging the gap between the purchase and delivery of goods and effectively managing customer expectations through post-transaction communication."

A Forrester Report titled "Mastering Commerce Logistics" seems to confirm PTAD. The research shows that online customers check the status of their orders an average of seven times to determine when their order will arrive — is that stressing or what?

As such, e-tailers must make delivery promises based on "the total order cycle," not just "in-transit times" as buyers are demanding package rerouting and precise delivery times.

Taylor goes on to give the seemingly cryptic and confusing advice of "tell them what you're going to tell them, tell them, and then tell them what you told them." Read it a couple of times and you will find that it's actually very good advice. According to Taylor, "There are several points in the post-transaction process where companies have an opportunity to communicate with the customer. These include the sending of online receipts, e-mail confirmations, shipping confirmations and packing slips." However, Taylor says that:

- Less than half of online receipts inform the customer of the total charges that will be debited against the credit card.

- 36% indicate whether the products are actually in stock before the customer submits a credit card number.

- 16% spell out their return policy during the checkout process.

- 57% provide live online order tracking.

- 7% provide a link to order status on their home page.

- 48% of items ordered by Shelley Taylor & Associates during the study arrived when expected.

- 30% provide free shipping.

- The e-businesses that charge for shipping — the average shipping charge was 37% of the total cost of the order in the US and 20% in the UK (with a 2-3 day shipping option on products that averaged $25 in the US and £20 in the UK).

- 64% of stores included return instructions in the box with the items (75% in US but only 37% in the UK).

Educate the Customer — The Reality

As Stacey McCullough, a senior analyst at Forrester Research told the *New York Times* (www.nytimes.com), "I can order a book on my lunch break, but if I have to wait a week to get something, it becomes less valuable." In the June 7, 2000 article the *Times* made an effort to plainly set out the frustration that currently sends many potential online shoppers to the mall.

The article goes on to explain that delivery delays are often attributed to the parcel carrier, but mishaps frequently occur before an order leaves the warehouse. Not that this matters to the customer, who knows only that the order did not arrive on time.

The article pointed to a Boston Consulting Group (www.bcg.com) study, wherein 19% of online customers said the delivery of their orders either took longer than they expected or they never arrived. As a result, many stopped shopping online, while others simply refused to do more business with the offending e-tailer. While the orders that were never delivered are definitely a problem, the ones that took longer than expected, may, in reality, be "business as usual." Customers don't expect 24 to 48 hour delivery from telephone-based catalog orders, so they need to be educated that e-businesses deal with the same shipping factors that bricks-and-mortar catalog companies deal with.

Especially during a holiday and its shopping madness, online customers, sucked in by the media hype, don't leave enough time for normal ground shipping to get their orders (gifts) delivered in time. Educate your customer that giving the e-business a reasonable amount of time to get the product to them can lower shipping costs and that an order that necessitates priority shipment adds to the overall shipping charges and therefore can significantly raise the cost of a product.

Theresia Gouw Ranzetta, a partner at Accel Partners (www.accel.com), a venture capital firm, says, "We haven't figured out how to beam things, but that's sort of what people expect. The Internet has trained consumers that they should be able to access information anytime, anywhere." While the author agrees with Ranzetta's comments about the expectations of the customer, she does feel that the Internet should provide the customer with access to information anytime, anywhere.

You notice I said "Internet" not "Web site." If an e-business wants to provide optimal service it should provide access to information including a living, breathing, talking, customer service agent on a 24 x 7 basis.

E-businesses should strive to make clear to their customers that, *as of now*, beaming a product to the customer isn't an option. The package must go through channels, some of which are outside the e-business's control, although the e-business will make every effort to keep the customer informed. E-businesses *can* provide instant gratification IF they offer software, music, video and/or written material (such as the industry reports referred to in this book) — through downloads, which is somewhat akin to the "beam me up Scotty" technology. If you do take the time and effort to educate your customer then they won't be as disappointed when something goes awry or their expectations are not met.

If you offer next day delivery, you must deliver it; BUT at the same time you must educate your customer about the cost to *them* for the convenience of next day delivery. What is most shocking to customers is the expectation of having the product in their hands within 48 hours (at the most) and then receiving the billing statement and finding out how much of the cost was attributable to shipping.

Is there hope that when the remaining 50% of the population become online customers, that they will realize that the Web isn't full of freebies — that maybe they'll expect to pay a higher price in exchange for convenience? Expecting the higher price may be asking a bit much; but e-businesses do need to retrain online customers not to expect free gifts and free shipping, loss-leader products and that sort of thing. It won't be easy, the current crop of online customers are spoiled, though some will stick around. Many online consumers will realize that "it couldn't last forever," and appreciate that they were in on the "grand opening sales." At least that is what numerous focus groups have told the surveyors.

CLICK-AND-MORTARS

Getting to the Internet is proving difficult for some bricks-and-mortars. Take for example, Lord & Taylor, Ann Taylor, and Wal-Mart with its on-again-off-again e-tail site. Even the much-heralded Harrods.com's Web site for the US market was inoperative at the time this book was written. Many bricks-and-mortars find that the implementation issues, including order fulfillment and customer service are roadblocks in their drive to an online presence.

A study conducted by Deloitte & Touche (www.deloitte.com) in the first quarter of 2000 looked at how bricks-and-mortars handled the formidable task of building and operating an online store. Deloitte & Touche surveyed 156 bricks-and mortar executives. Out of those 156 stores, 76% have an online presence but only 29% of that 76% have e-commerce capabilities. All of the 29% stated that their online sales and profits were marginal at best. For example, 48% of the e-commerce-enabled sites generated only 1% or less of the combined "bricks" and "clicks" overall sales. Even sadder (and maybe one of the reasons for such a poor performance) is that a full 50% of the bricks-and-mortars use profitability as a measure of success of their "click," and only 15% generated a profit.

What about implementation issues such as order fulfillment? Many executives in the study admitted that they were currently fulfilling online orders through a process of picking items for shipment from either their stores or current distribution centers. The study goes on to document that only about 20% of the e-commerce-enabled sites offered even close to the full product line and 33% offered fewer than 60 items. And many offer product that is only available online. A little good news was that 60% of the operational Web stores could track an order and provide a purchasing history per customer.

Almost 40% of click-and-mortars have counterparts that consider them to be a strategic necessity but not a full partner in their overall sales strategy. The same bricks-and-mortars that have not had the foresight to lead their e-tail counterpart into a fully integrated, value-added service also

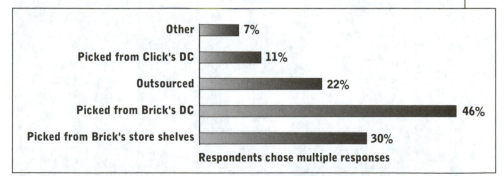

How e-tail orders are currently filled. Statistics courtesy of Deloitte & Touche Survey of 156 bricks-and-mortar executives.

have failed to seek out the full-time e-tail leadership and staff necessary for the realization of a successful e-business model. In fact, it's clear that the vast majority in this group doesn't even have an e-business leader in the bricks-and-mortar's executive suite. It seems that a majority of the bricks-and-mortar retailers have opted to institute an e-business operation without a clearly articulated strategy. Many have taken the tack of just "dipping their toes in the water" to gauge online demand.

The brave souls who have taken a realistic proactive approach to e-business opportunities have surged ahead of their competitors. These click-and-mortars have instituted an e-business strategy that enables them to fully integrate their e-business efforts with their entire value chain, allowing them to win market share and customer loyalty with their resourceful forethought. They've a viable e-tail presence that is advanced enough to automatically integrate Web purchases with their fulfillment and distribution systems.

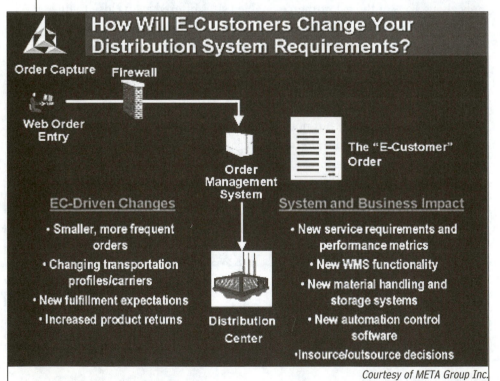

How Will E-Customers Change Your Distribution System Requirements?

Order Capture   Firewall

Web Order Entry

Order Management System

The "E-Customer" Order

EC-Driven Changes

- Smaller, more frequent orders
- Changing transportation profiles/carriers
- New fulfillment expectations
- Increased product returns

Distribution Center

System and Business Impact

- New service requirements and performance metrics
- New WMS functionality
- New material handling and storage systems
- New automation control software
- Insource/outsource decisions

Courtesy of META Group Inc.

The e-tailers that have been handicapped by their traditional counter-parts will have a tough row to hoe once the decision-markers finally wake up. The realization that *the Internet is here to stay,* will come too late for many retail businesses — by then the customers will have developed low expectations for these neglected Web sites and will have already established relationships with other e-tailers.

Congratulations to the respected high-end retailer, Saks Inc (www.saks-fifthavenue.com). It has just recently jumped on the e-tail bandwagon and expanded its e-tail operations so as to have a viable e-business operation on all fronts.

CHALLENGES

The daily challenges that e-tailers face continue to grow by leaps and bounds. No longer are customers enthralled with the ability to buy a product over their PC — it's old hat now. E-tailers have become complacent — buying online used to be such a cool novelty that early-adopter users would forgive some inconvenience and hassles — those days are over, so get moving.

I am constantly hearing, "We're still in the early stage," or "The Internet is an evolutionary process — it was years before the telephone and television provided consistently reliable service." Sorry — the customers expect more from an e-tail model as they become more "online savvy." Unfortunately, some e-tailers don't seem to understand that.

E-tailers, out of necessity, are compelled to continually re-evaluate their offerings, their front-end, back-end and entire infrastructure to ensure they are (hopefully) one step ahead of their customers' ever-expanding expectations.

To prove your business is a viable e-tail model, you must:

- Cost-efficiently attract customers.
- Efficiently capture customer orders.
- Initiate a viable, full-scale fulfillment system.
- Provide excellent customer service through all channels.
- Reduce overall costs so as to present a positive cash flow.

Many e-tailers have already proven their prowess in attracting customers — but at what cost? They've built a system that efficiently captures the customer's orders but that is where many customers have found themselves left high and dry. To avoid the necessity of continually competing on price alone, e-tailers need to distinguish themselves in the fulfillment area through speed, accuracy, and completeness of each order. Customer loyalty doesn't come by way of low price — flawless order fulfillment (and excellent customer service) is what ensures customer retention and loyalty. E-tailers must prove that they can provide the 3Rs and respond to customer inquiries in a timely manner or they will find it difficult to build a loyal customer base.

An August 2000 survey conducted by Gartner-owned cPulse (www.cpulse.com), an Internet satisfaction monitor, concluded that of the more than 137,000 online shoppers surveyed almost a quarter were extremely dissatisfied with their online experience. What caused most concern were security, shipping costs and timely delivery.

Bluefly.com, a pure-play discount apparel e-tailer, told the *New York Times* in April 2000 that it had found a way to add to its profit margin through order fulfillment. Rather than rely on a single delivery service, Bluefly.com has a system whereby it can determine the most cost-effective and efficient carrier to send a package to various regions of the country. As Jonathan Morris, executive vice president of Bluefly.com told the *Times*, "that can play a huge role in lowering costs," adding that fulfillment managers — whether inside the company or outside contractors — "are getting smarter about this, because they're being forced to."

Fulfillment

An e-tail site cannot just lay back and take orders without knowing what that next step will be. According to Optum's (www.optum.com) vice president of corporate marketing, Henry Bruce, "Delivery is still a physical act, even if you order everything over the Web. You can always get what you want in the timeframe you want it from a company like Amazon, even next-day delivery, if you pay for it, and it's expensive. But the product still has to be physically delivered to your doorstep. This is where most companies are failing — they have not really thought out their fulfillment strategies. Thanks to the Web, we are moving from pallets to pieces with lot sizes shrinking, resulting in changes in packing and shipping requirements and processes."

Bruce goes on, "A lot of [bricks-and-mortar] companies weren't ready to enter the world of 'e'. They were still traditional 'one-size-fits-all' operations relying on a traditional back-end. In e-fulfillment, customers are often different and sometimes completely unknown, and there is a shift to small, fragmented buying habits with returns more likely to occur." Optum is a leading provider of configurable end-to-end fulfillment solutions for e-businesses.

The e-tail leaders have clearly come to grips with the fundamentals of exceptional customer service, especially the issues revolving around order fulfillment and Web-based call centers. They know that the more customers they get, the higher the number of customer inquiries that need to be addressed — therefore they worked diligently to get customer relationship management systems in place. These savvy e-tailers also took note that without an efficient LFMS to handle the high volume of order requests, customer service would become an even bigger challenge. The smart ones addressed these two issues as one.

Here is an on-target (pardon the pun) example — Target Corp. (www.target.com), a national US retailer, reported in July 2000 that it was in the midst of integrating the business processes of its various sales channels to streamline fulfillment, boost sales, and improve the customer experience. In adopting this e-business strategy Target will be able to integrate order processing for its e-business, 12 catalog companies and five retail chains including call centers. Then order entry and management, warehouse management, fulfillment, shipping, and customer service will be integrated and linked with enterprise resource planning, warehouse management, and merchandising systems for Target's multi-channel retail operations.

Improved customer service is another benefit of Target's new system. For example, if a customer places an order through a catalog, he or she can go to the Web site and check the status or if the order is placed through the Web site, a quick call to Target's customer service representative will give the customer the status.

With its new system Target can view its customer activity across the different channels, providing it with a 360-degree view of the customer — this is what all e-tailers should aim towards.

Fulfillment is a logistical wilderness for the entire e-business community. Take note of the following debacle. In a July 2000 ruling by the U.S. Federal Trade Commission (FTC), seven e-tail sites, including well-known click-and-mortars and pure-plays, were fined a total of $1.5 million. The settlement put an end to the FTC's lawsuit arising out of bungled deliveries during the 1999 Christmas season. In the lawsuit, the FTC charged the seven e-tailers with violating its mail-and-telephone order rule by promising delivery dates they could not meet and failing to notify their customers that shipments would be late. FTC took the position that its mail and telephone order rule is not a requirement for only the bricks-and-mortar and catalog companies, but that it also applies to e-tailers. The strict penalties were designed to put the Internet community on notice that the

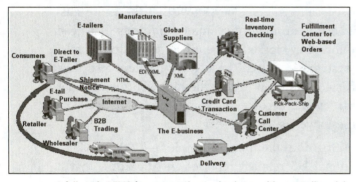

A full-scale LFMS for a stage three e-business with an e-tail model.

FTC will continue to monitor its actions. This means all e-businesses must get their logistical and fulfillment system in well-oiled running order or face the consequences — loss of the customer base (eToys), governmental agency action (Macys), lawsuits (Toys 'R Us) and even bankruptcy (Value America).

In response to the FTC's actions, CDNow.com Inc. made changes in the policies that governs its shipping and back-order processes so it can give more specific shipping dates. Instead of giving the customers a generic response that their orders will be shipped in one to four weeks.

After being caught once, Patriot Computer Corp. (www.patriot.com) built an automated customer-response system that automatically sends a customer notice if delivery will be delayed in hopes of staying out of the FTC's line of sight. The company is also installing a new accounting system, and once the 1999 holiday season was over, it began installation of a factory-floor application to manage production, warehousing, and inventory. Patriot also negotiated new contracts with logistics companies to ensure on-time delivery.

Let the Customer Do the Walking

Some click-and-mortars have tried to come to grips with their fulfillment issue by taking an entirely different route. They hope their path to fulfillment heaven is via their customers doing the walking, i.e., letting them use the Web to access inventory data segregated by store location, then picking up their heart's desire from their local store. This solves some online shoppers' complaint of long waits for ordered items and it also provides an answer to many e-tailers' "how do we provide fulfillment" question. However, this fulfillment model requires tightly integrated back-office systems in order to provide the customer, the e-tailer, and the bricks-and-mortar with accurate data.

On September 24, 2000, Found, Inc. (www.found.com), a technology solution provider, announced a partnership with Apropos Retail Management Systems (www.apropos.com), a provider of retail technologies for chain specialty retailers. This partnership allows Apropos' point-of-sale (POS) solution to integrate directly with Found's Integrated Clicks and Mortar (ICaM) technology, thus enabling retailers to integrate their "bricks" and "clicks" allowing for true multi-channel retailing.

This solution enables the seamless integration of commerce operations and in-store inventory systems, providing real-time remote access to inventory information across the store network and the ability to complete in-store transactions online. As a result, the "brick's" and "click's" customers can utilize the Internet to easily find and purchase what they want, when and where they want it, from their local store, i.e., let the customer do the walking.

Finish Line (www.finishline.com), a specialty retailer of athletic and lifestyle apparel and accessories, is implementing the ICaM technology into its infrastructure. The same holds true for bebe Stores, Inc.

(www.bebe.com), a leading designer and retailer of contemporary women's apparel and accessories. To provide its customers with a more complete, multi-channel shopping experience, bebe will begin testing the Found technology in selected markets throughout the US. So will ICON, a leading manufacturer of home fitness equipment, who is beta testing the ICaM Solution to connect NordicTrack retail stores to online activities.

Malibu.com hosts Web sites for the RiverTown Crossings Mall retailers in Grandville, Michigan, and one of the services it offers is an option for its "mall customers" to buy merchandise online through a centralized ordering system, then have it delivered or held at the mall for pickup.

The executives in both the click and the bricks sides of click-and-mortars feel that they've come up with a win-win solution. By letting their customers do the walking, they can wrest more value from their bricks-and-mortars that already carry the costs of receiving, storing, and merchandising goods. Then getting the online customer into a local storefront also can add to that stores bottom line through the well-known and easily exploited "impulse purchase syndrome." Does the author see click and brick executives licking their chops? I believe so, if it works...

Some other Web sites jumping on the "let the customer do the walking" bandwagon is Payless Shoes (www.payless.com), Circuit City Stores Inc. (circuitcity.com), Office Depot (www.officedepot.com), and Toys 'R Us (www.toysrus.com).

Customer Confidence

In a traditional store the customers know they can buy a product off the shelf and walk out the door with it. E-tailers need to provide their customers with that same level of confidence when they're buying online. How? The e-tailer must provide its customers with the ability on its Web site for its customers to check if the product is in stock and, if ordered, how or when it will be delivered. That is one part of LFM — the integration of systems from the browse mode to the click of the buy button all the way through to the customer signing for the package, including managing the complex task of delivering thousands of mostly small packages daily to their unique destinations.

According to a META Group (www.metagroup.com) analysis, most e-tailers have simply shrugged off the demands of the back-end, leaving their customers frustrated — they can't obtain the information necessary to make an intelligent decision about the e-tailer's product availability much less delivery. An e-tail site must instill confidence in its ability to provide the right product at the right time in the right place or suffer from high shopping cart abandonment rate.

Saks Inc. (mentioned previously) was late in entering the e-business arena with a viable, fully automated e-business operation. Although late, Saks did take the time to do it right. SaksFifthAvenue.com initially went live in 1999 as a static storefront and took a bit of media drubbing for its timidness — customers could only request catalogs and get store locations. The corporation knew the Saks brand was an asset and well worth protecting. It took the time and made the effort to procure an experienced in-house Web team and astutely divided it into four distinct units: technology operations, applications, site development, and data architecture, and it enlisted a third-party integrator for implementation help. Saks' staff spent its time wisely after its inauspicious beginning in 1999 by carefully planning and mapping out its e-business strategy so the totally revamped site could have the appropriate technical base to not only build customer confidence, but to draw in new customers.

E-tailers should bear in mind that to inform customers accurately about product availability requires real-time capabilities and the translation of these real-time communications to the customer — either by removing out-of-stock items from the site or by clearly indicating that the item is not available. Although informing customers about stock outages (without the ability to offer cross-selling and up-selling) might result in lost sales with the customers taking their business elsewhere, the door has been left open for the customer to return later. If customers are given a false promise and are disappointed, they slam the door as they leave, never to return.

Another great example of an e-business with a good LFMS is Neiman Marcus — another esteemed brand. Neiman Marcus has taken the lead in state-of-the-art fashion retailing. "Our challenge has been to translate the distinctive Neiman Marcus experience to the Web. We've met that challenge by creating an entirely fresh approach to online shopping," at least so says Burton M. Tansky, president and COO, The Neiman Marcus Group. Forbes.com placed Neimanmarcus.com in their top 100 Best of the Web, Best of the Best.

FOUR LITTLE STEPS

For the majority of the e-tailers, I have this bit of advice — institute the following four steps into your e-tailing strategy to give you the necessary tools to gain customer confidence in your brand.

1. Establish a well-designed, properly maintained customer service strategy that allows you to provide good customer service on the Web, i.e., new lines of communication. E-mail is universal but must be well managed. FAQ pages and a dynamic knowledge base are easy to set up and when managed properly and kept current (through help provided by the proper software) can consistently be an asset for a Web site. Web Chat can be especially effective for quick real-time queries, since it can be faster than a phone call and call centers can deal quickly and efficiently with queries that cannot be dealt with via any other method.

2. Implement logistical business processes and solutions throughout the value chain. With the proper LFMS any e-tailer can provide the *right* product at the *right* place at the *right* time (the 3Rs). This includes ensuring that delivery and storage facilities are adequate to meet customer demand. You can provide your LFMS through an in-house operation or through a fulfillment partner (use your Logistics Plan to show you what would be the best fit your e-business's specific needs). The specifics of drawing up a Logistics Plan are set out in Chapter 8.

3. Post-sales infrastructure is as important as pre-sales. An e-tailer must provide its customers with a foolproof mechanism for easy returns, quick response to warranty questions, and technical support.

4. A top running front-end is a must. The Web's key appeal to the buying public is its perceived ability to provide immediate gratification. When customers come to an e-tailer's site they expect to immediately find information and/or products, then to solve the problem or purchase the product — fast!

With these four steps in place, the e-tail model has a system wherein the customer's complete experience, from the moment a customer enters the Web site through fulfillment, delivery and return, is easy and fast — at least from the customer's viewpoint (whether handled in-house or outsourced).

THE E-TAILERS THAT DON'T GET IT

Although a bit late, Macy's (www.macys.com) did launch a Web site for a select offering of products to its online customers. And it follows JCPenney.com's example and allows its customers to place orders online using the printed Macy's By Mail catalog. But it has many problems, including a disgruntled FTC, a fractured inventory and general confusion. For example, on its Web site it states for all to see on its "shipping policy" page, "In stock merchandise usually is processed and shipped (in other words, leaves our fulfillment center) within _7 business days_ [emphasis added]. macys.com will let you know at checkout or by a follow-up message if the merchandise you have selected is not currently in stock or if we need to confirm availability. For that merchandise, we will give you an expected shipping time at checkout." What this typifies is a woeful LFMS.

Look at Sears' online e-tail site, www.sears.com, it has a pitiful number of product offerings compared to its bricks-and-mortar, but does have a well-trafficked site, since it features the well-known Kenmore and Craftsman brands. It also has a pretty good B2B global exchange set up. Sears does seem to have confidence in its LFMS. It provides product availability on the "product summary page," which states "two business days" for the majority of the products; this means the product is in the hands of the shipper within two business days after the order is placed versus Macy's seven business days.

In a June 2000 report by the consulting firm, Creative Good (www.creativegood.com), it was pointed out that e-tailers, in general, could make a good deal of headway in their uphill climb to profitability by focusing on the customers' basic needs, i.e., the 3Rs. According to the report, e-tailers could realize over $20 billion more in sales by implementing strategic improvements in their LFMS.

For example, the report criticized MarthaStewart.com for letting customers unknowingly add out-of-stock items to the shopping cart, they were told about the backorder status only when they reached the final checkout page — I bet she has a high shopping cart abandonment rate. When Creative Good brought the issue up with Martha Stewart, the chief executive of Martha Stewart Living Omnimedia, it was told, "We're working on that. But the coordination between the catalog and the Internet operations has to be perfect before we can do it."

Stewart went on to tell Creative Good that her fulfillment service provider (FSP), Time Customer Service (a unit of Time Warner), has an older computer system that can't handle the "Internet speed" database searches to provide real-time in stock reports to the Web site. Due to this inadequacy of its FSP, MarthaStewart.com was forced to hold off on inventory notification until checkout so the site wouldn't drag due to the performance of a real-time inventory check of each item as a shopper selects it. However, Stewart did state that she was looking for a FSP that could provide speedy real-time inventory data. She also added, "It's a minute-to-minute task, to keep up with technology and customer demands. It's a constant thing."

LESSONS LEARNED

Since its inception, the Internet community has faced a barrage of obstacles that it has consistently managed to overcome. The e-tailer is no exception. Any retailer, bricks-and-mortar, click-and-mortar or pure-play, will tell you that upwards to 50% of its annual sales occur during the Thanksgiving to New Years holiday season. For example in July 2000, Gary Gerdermann, eToys' senior director of communications told *The Standard* (www.thestandard.com), "Ideally, everything from inventory forecasting to Web technology that will withstand a tsunami of traffic will have been mapped out ahead of time. We started Dec. 26, 1999."

One thing that is crucial for a happy holiday season is procuring the inventory so it's available when needed. However, it doesn't stop there, moving product out the back door to the customer's front door also requires special planning.

Another step that should not be overlooked if you want to prevent problems like outages, missed ship dates or unacceptably slow fulfillment, is to troubleshoot the entire operative structure of your Web-based business long before the holiday buying rush so you don't get burned. It seems that many e-tail executives are "quick learners." According to the aforementioned *The Standard* article, today's e-tail executives know that "last-minute plans, such as revamping sites and cutting corners on distribution and fulfillment, are out."

The opportunity still exists for bricks-and-mortars to transform and dominate the e-tailing segment of the Internet, but the window of opportunity is becoming smaller. For a successful e-tail operation you must shift purchasing, logistics, and overall supply management to the Internet. In doing so, you can shorten your supply chain, obtain better information about schedules and inventory throughout the supply chain. This allows the e-tailer and the supply chain to inject cost-efficiencies through fine-tuning of manufacturing levels, allowing postponement of final configuration decisions and cuts in the distribution network. This, in turn, eliminates unnecessary transportation and warehousing costs. By itself, technology doesn't accomplish much. But, in the hands of the right executives who aren't averse to intelligent risk-taking, technology can be a dynamic force that can change any business's future for the good.

The Partners: Outsourcing the Tech

THE EFFECTIVE EXECUTION OF e-business strategies requires a complex mix of elements, which include substantial resources, strategic vision, speed, and *skills that are hard to find and keep*. In considering their options, many e-businesses look at outsourcing as a means to achieving their business's transformation while minimizing risk. Tech partners are the key to an e-business's future. The smart e-business will choose its partners wisely.

The IT market is a complex ecosystem, with revolutionary changes occurring at warp speed. It's a market where tech solution providers such as consultants, integrators and product vendors struggle on a daily basis to survive and, if lucky, thrive. Any e-business looking for a tech solution provider should interview a lot of companies, but before you interview, know exactly what you want and what your initiatives and objectives are. Talk to other companies in your industry (if possible) that have completed similar projects. Also ensure that in the interview process you actually get to meet and talk with the people who would be working on your specific project.

The current tech solution provider market is suffering an "identity crisis." It's hard to differentiate between a software company as opposed to a services company or a network company, much less, who is a consultant, an integrator, or a vendor. Carefully separate your potential partners from the throng, a tough job in such a crowded market.

What was a relatively stable Internet solutions provider landscape seems to have become a giant free-for-all of clashing and competing business models, fueled by technical breakthroughs and entrepreneurial zeal. This is exacerbated by the fact that traditional tech solution providers are increasingly challenged by other e-business service companies that are quickly expanding their rich consulting, design and development skills from being exclusively project-based to encompassing ongoing comprehensive e-business advisory and management services.

E-businesses looking for single-source solutions for their IT-enabled e-business requirements should go with those tech solution providers that offer the strongest comprehensive solutions and understands the intricacies of LFM, real-time inventory availability, value chain integration and legacy systems. In the near future, however, I perceive that comprehensive solutions will increasingly be delivered via partnerships or a consortium approach.

According to Gartner Group, through the year 2002 more than 65% of e-businesses will engage in selective or comprehensive outsourcing to meet their e-business requirements. And Gartner states that 75% of all e-business service companies (your potential tech partners) will offer some form of e-business management service, such as hosting. Thus, differentiation will increasingly stem from relationship management, business process expertise, and vertical market capabilities — this is what Cisco is doing now.

Strategies and approaches differ widely, influenced by geography, history, expertise, gut instinct and, of course, customer need. Fierce competitors partner with each other to win enterprise accounts. Some touch the hardware; others wouldn't be caught dead doing so. Some embrace the Web; others stick to more tried-and-true solutions. Most differ in strategic approach, but all swear they are motivated by one overriding influence: the customer — you, the e-business.

Take a look at the VARBusiness 500. Its 2000 qualification form took the 1999's "Web integrators" business model option and expanded "Web integrators" to "Internet professional services organizations." At the same time *VARBusiness* (www.varbusiness.com) sliced and diced the "Internet professional services organizations" model to encompass five distinct business models: ASPs, ISPs, interactive agencies, strategic Web consultants, and Web integrators and developers.

In e-business, continual change is an opportunity rather than a threat; therefore flourishing partnerships are almost always a must if an e-business is to attain the heights of success. Hence, this chapter is written on the premise that e-businesses will form strategic partnerships with tech solution providers to ease the integration of multiple technologies into a total solution that can better meet the logistic and fulfillment needs of their specific e-business model.

TECH PARTNERSHIPS ARE A TWO-WAY-STREET

Don't forget that a partnership is a two-way street. Tom Rodenhauser, an industry analyst and head of ConsultingInfo.com, goes even further, saying that during the next few years, e-business consultants' chance for success will hinge on the strength of their clients (the e-businesses).

Your potential tech partner is looking (just as you are) for a partnership that can give the most bang for the buck. Here are how some tech solution providers look at e-business partnering opportunities.

If your e-business is a cutting-edge start-up you may have problems finding the right tech partners. ConsultingInfo.com's Rodenhauser says working with start-ups is a gamble. "A lot of the start-ups are flaming out now," he notes. "From a consulting point of view, it's not a good thing to be associated with a start-up unless it's an Amazon-type true start-up."

Instead, successful tech providers are embracing the traditional old guard companies with deep pockets, established track records and a strong desire to adopt an e-business model. Experts say tech solution providers want a good mix today — this means about 30% to 40% start-up work, with the rest being established companies, such as, Fortune 500 and blue chip companies.

"A Fortune 500-type company with good name recognition and a broad business sense is something a consultant can really dig into," Rodenhauser says. The tech solution providers "want to be linked with the Dow Chemicals and other big Blue Chip clients that are moving to the Web because, for the most part, these projects are not going to fail."

The tech provider is also performing their due diligence on potential e-business clients. No matter how interesting or challenging a particular e-business's needs are, if it can't commit to a concrete reimbursement plan from the start, chances are it's a risky idea and the tech solution provider will pass. "You have to look at the economics of a job, the profitability for your company," says Kevin Rowe, president of Agency.com's North American business practice. "Customers who are constantly trying to beat us down over a nickel or a dime are the ones we'll try to shy away from." Agency.com is a global Internet solutions provider offering integrated strategic, creative, technology and media services to businesses adopting an e-business model.

Today's tech providers will also embrace alternative payment schedules that usually include, as part of the compensation package, an equity stake in an e-business rather than straight payment. This type of alternative compensation arrangement, however, is dependent upon the specific e-business, according to experts.

Michael Fagan, president, CEO and founder of Web builder MokoNet Inc. (www.mokonet.com), says tech providers look closely at a prospective client's financial resources and business plan to figure out an appropriate course of action. "In high-flying Internet work, people loosen up a bit and try to take more risks," says Fagan. "I think the right approach is to take a balance. If you're too conservative, you will miss opportunities, and if you're too wild, you will get burned."

Ask any successful tech provider about its work and, chances are, one of the first things the company will offer up is a list of Fortune 500 clients or other big-name companies it has worked with. "Today, customers are not only the calling cards, but they will define who is really successful in this space in the next couple of years," Rodenhauser says. "So little is known about what these firms [the tech providers] do that the client is much more than a calling card. It's a reason to exist."

Integrators like Fagan agree, saying high-profile e-business customers can increase a tech solution provider's image and lead to even bigger clients signing on. "Having high-profile customers is critical," he says. "There is an attraction from many levels, future customers who pay more attention to you, then there are the venture capital folks and prospective employees who are more knowledgeable about the industry these days."

Luminant Worldwide Corp.'s (www.luminant.com) president/CEO, Richard Scruggs, says his company tries to align itself with e-businesses that will promote the work Luminant performs for them. It can be in the role of a reference for future e-business clients or perhaps participating in case studies or publicity announcements. It must have worked for *VARBusiness* placed them on its E100+25 list for the year 2000.

Many tech providers have established very efficient methods of weeding out potential e-business clients that will present a "windfall" from the ones that will end up being a headache. MokoNet evaluates smaller-sized e-businesses through the use of a quiz of about 50 questions ranging from an e-business's goals to its financial resources and Web expectations.

"We give that to potential clients to get a feel for how serious they are," says Mike Fagan, president of the four-year-old MokoNet, which has companies such as Barnes & Noble and Canon U.S.A. Inc. on its client roster. "One of the first measuring devices is if they even fill out the questionnaire. If they won't even do that, then it means they are not really serious." Another common problem for many tech providers is that they are burdened with clients that have unrealistic expectations of what "e-business solutions" actually require.

Agency.com's Kevin Rowe, says that his company (one of *VARBusiness* E100+25 companies) seeks out e-business clients who understand the implications of e-business and who are prepared to put in the time and money to create a successful initiative. "We look for those who are committed to using the Web." He goes on to say that to really work, e-business must understand and want integration, "as opposed to just a freak show designed on the side to say you have a Web presence."

Agency.com boasts clients such as 3M, Coca-Cola, British Airways, Colgate-Palmolive and Deutsche Bank. According to Kyle Shannon, co-founder and chief people officer, Agency.com's clients consist of primarily Fortune 1000, Global 1000 kind of e-businesses. "We don't have a lot of dot-com risks, meaning we do some dot-com start-ups, but not a tremendous amount."

Agency.com builds business Web portals for global e-businesses. It proclaims that it doesn't create "brochureware." As Chan Suh, Agency.com's co-founder/CEO/chairman put it, "We build businesses. A lot of what we do is not visible to the consumer."

Tyler Niess, director of business development for Organic Inc. (www.organic.com), gauges the likelihood of a potential e-business partner's success on any given project based on the level of executives who get initially involved. "Who are the people we are talking to? If we don't have visibility and conversations with the CEO or another high-level executive, then we try to establish if he or she is involved in the initiative in any way, shape or form," he says. "If they are not, then [the e-business] is probably going at it at half-speed. Work with them, and you're not doing yourself any favors." *VARBusiness* liked Organic's philosophy since they placed the company on their E100+25 list for the year 2000.

Kevin Greenan, vice president of Emerald Solutions' (www.emeraldsolutions) customer interaction practice, says his company works to establish long-term relationships with its e-business clients, rather than just basing business on single-sell engagements. *VARBusiness* thought enough of Emerald to place it among its E100+25 list of the biggest solution providers in North America. Emerald actively seeks out e-businesses that will work as a partner to build comprehensive Web initiatives, rather than those seeking small fixes.

But the other side, says MokoNet's Fagan, is that it's sometimes worth doing a relatively small job for an e-business if the work will put the tech provider in touch with the enterprise's executive suite decision-makers. "If you are talking to the right set of people to make a good impression, then maybe it's worth doing."

Agency.com also tries to establish e-business partnerships that provide new challenges and that also can keep its staff interested in their day-to-day responsibilities. "We are in a tough market in terms of keeping talented employees," says Rowe. "So it's important to keep them working on jobs that interest and challenge them. If you do that, then they'll work like dogs for the client, but on the other hand, if they are struggling to stay motivated, then it's not good for anyone involved."

Rowe says Agency.com also has no qualms dumping an e-business that makes working conditions unbearable for its employees, whether it's by treating them with a lack of respect, putting undue pressure on them or nitpicking over every decision they make. "That's something we want to avoid," Rowe says. "It's so hard holding on to talented people right now that we don't need our clients chasing them away."

E-BUSINESS START-UP CHALLENGES

The pure-play e-business model presents unique challenges for many tech solution providers. Some will come to the table with nothing more than a sketchy, albeit grandiose, idea for their e-business and expect the solution provider to bring it to life in a matter of weeks. Many may have an ill-conceived notion of what an e-business solution actually requires, neglecting to factor in value chain integration, real-time inventory solutions and a viable LFMS.

When approaching a potential tech partner the imaginative entrepreneur usually has on its agenda one or more of the following:

Hot Technology: Kevin Greenan, vice president of Emerald Solutions Inc.'s customer interaction practice, says many e-businesses get caught up in trendy technology. "They are seeing everywhere this great new technology that's allowing companies to throw out an e-business of some sort," he says. "They are very focused on what the slickest spit-new technology is that they need to buy and deploy to get their presence out there." If you fit within this group then be aware that your potential tech partner *must* stress the notion that e-business is a complicated marriage of new and existing technology coupled with proven business processes. Therefore, they are not "talking down to you" but are trying to help your fledgling e-business to grow.

Breaking All the Rules: Michael Fagan, CEO of MokoNet Inc., says most e-businesses want solutions so fast that they are willing to bend or break every rule of business engagement, from RFPs to contract negotiations to work schedules. Oftentimes, it's up to the tech solution provider to draw a line in the sand and enforce it. "It's OK to break some rules," he says. "But you can't break every rule." So if this rings a bell, you should take notes and heed what the "expert" says.

Too Much, Too Fast: When working with well-funded pure-play start-ups, Greenan says energetic e-businesses can sometimes convince their tech partners to spread themselves too thin, designing a Web site, building a data warehouse and fulfillment infrastructure, implementing an ERP package and then trying to integrate it all. "You try to do too much, too quickly, and you choke the horse a little bit," says Greenan. "Yes, we need to go fast in a lot of these initiatives, but we need to do it in a fashion that the client can digest without totally derailing the company." When a tech provider hollers "uncle," listen. You're paying big bucks for the expert advice and skills so tread carefully if you decide to circumvent the advice given.

Validate Me: E-business start-ups often look to their tech solution providers to validate their still-unproven business models to attract investors. One of the best ways to do that is to provide the e-business with a "prototype." "It's a semi-functional, scaled-down version that can show potential output," says Tyler Niess, director of business development for Organic Inc. "But the downside to that is that it may not be possible to validate a complex site with a half-baked version of it." Again, an entrepreneur should heed the counsel of its tech partner.

The Global 1000 want-a-bes are quick learners. Tech providers also find realistic approaches to building a viable e-business on the agendas of their pure-play suitors, such as:

Going Behind the Curtain: In the wake of last year's breakdown of several high-profile e-tailing sites, most new e-businesses realize the need for reliable back-end fulfillment solutions to go hand-in-hand with their new e-business model. As a result, Greenan says it's becoming much easier for integrators to get clients to build fully integrated product fulfillment infrastructures for their e-commerce sites.

E-Business Intelligence: Start-ups are increasingly realizing that it's no longer enough to simply adopt an e-business model and hope it will generate revenue. With pressure increasing from investors, they need tech solution providers to give them more reliable ways to predict profitability, pinpoint strengths and weaknesses and leverage existing information to target specific customers.

SPECIALIZATION VS. GENERALIZATION

The great divide in the tech provider field, according to many industry players, is specialization versus generalization. When an e-business approaches a tech provider it needs to bring to the table a clear differentiation. Does it want a tech partner that's a general contractor with myriad interests and the ability to integrate various technologies for its clients (the e-business)? Or does the e-business need a tech partner that favors the specialist role, focusing on technology excellence in a narrow field or discipline? These two categories seem to be the emerging dividing line, especially for those heavily involved in Web integration and services.

Focus on Technology

Nelson Carbonell, president and CEO of Cysive Inc. (www.cysive.com), believes hiring a tech solution provider that has a more limited, focused approach is central to the success of an e-business. "We provide one critical service," Carbonell explains. "We allow [our customers — the e-business] to build the technology platform they need to run their businesses. And we don't do anything else." In Carbonell's view, the best technology determines the winning business model, especially with more businesses gravitating to an e-business model. (You can find Cysive on *VARBusiness's* year 2000 E100+25 list.)

Carbonell states that the fact that some tech solution providers prefer to offer one-stop shopping is evidence of a still-maturing market. According to Carbonell, at Cysive "we focus on really executing on the technology. And I think largely immature markets tend to breed one-stop shopping. As marketplaces mature, people hire people because they are good at something. You certainly aren't going to walk out the door and go to the French restaurant/dry cleaners/bowling alley because you don't really think anybody can be in all those businesses and be good in all of them." In the end, the jack-of-all-trades truly is master of none.

He adds, "What ends up happening is that none of those services is the best it can be. Our stake in the ground is this: As this marketplace matures — and it's continuing to grow very rapidly — you are going to get hired for two reasons: It's important to the customer, and they can't do it for themselves. We believe that with technology being probably where 80% of the dollars are going to get spent, that's the place to be."

Many other solution providers don't see it that way. In their view, the winning tech provider offers a broad array of services to its e-business customers.

Martin Wright, CEO of Emerald Solutions Inc., defines his company as "an end-to-end e-business solution provider" that takes clients through three phases: business strategy, digital strategy (where creative work is done and applications developed) and integration. Wright proudly states, "we're better positioned focused on business modeling and Web and legacy systems integration." This may very well be the type of solution provider an enterprise adopting an e-business model wants on its team, especially when digging into the vagaries of LFMS. Emerald will even partner with ISPs and ASPs to manage or host applications, if need be.

"I think [our approach] is accountability, ease of a single vendor," Wright says. "The problem with a strictly management vs. general contractor kind of [approach] is, do you have the capabilities in-house to manage three different delivery organizations? It's much easier to have one person on the hook for that, and that's the role we step up to."

Although many in the tech solution provider industry would disagree, in Wright's view, a very focused, specific approach is based on an underlying and imperfect assumption: "You can be best-of-breed in one area, and that means, by definition, you are not going to be best-of-breed in the other two. That's not something we believe." Wright explains that Emerald has three distinct divisions that work together seamlessly for the client to deliver strategy, interactive and then technical solutions.

"We've set those up such that even the physical environments for those groups can be slightly different to make sure that we still attract the very best strategy people," he says. "We want to be recognized as doing business strategy at the same level as a McKinsey or a Bain, and digital strategy at the same level as a DiamondCluster International Inc. [formerly Diamond Technology Partners]. We want to be recognized for our creative capabilities to be superior in the industry. And the Emerald Solutions brand is probably best known already for the ability to deliver the best technical Web solutions. So we don't buy into the concept that focusing on one area means you have to be bad in the others."

Wright sees traditional systems integrators rapidly reengineering themselves to become Internet professional services companies. "[The Internet] is just another technology now," he says. "And we believe you do need creative capabilities to be a really good Internet services company."

Through "e-business engineering," Emerald claims to balance Internet innovation and business strategy while leveraging IT assets to deliver an integrated solution.

Still, some tech solution providers believe such a broad approach can set up unrealistic expectations by the e-business customer and create problems for the integrators. One popular view is to just make sure the technology works and the implementation is sound, and success will flow from there.

For example, Joseph Beninati, CEO of Greenwich Technology Partners, Inc. (www.greenwich.com), says, "We actually are very focused, and the focus is on engineering around the network infrastructure. That has been our charter now for 36 consecutive months. We are typically providing the security engineering services, performance engineering or Internetworking engineering services as it all relates to the network." Greenwich is another *VARBusiness* year 2000 E100+25 alumnus. Greenwich's business model is simple — it specializes in providing network consulting and engineering services that deliver complex network infrastructure solutions to enterprise clients.

"[The] underlying theme is that, in the technology industry, there are 25 ways to build substantial wealth, and the surefire way to fail is to focus on more than one or two at any one given time," Beninati explains. "Things change very quickly, and focus is important. You have to pick a market that's big, that's growing fast and in which you can make a difference. There are almost too many options...you have to pick one or two to be successful, to be meaningful in a given market."

Ask Beninati what do his customers want most and he'll tell you, "besides delivering the project on time and with the functionality desired, they want engineering excellence and attention to detail, attention to their satisfaction."

Cysive's Carbonell believes the growth of e-businesses makes almost every application mission-critical, placing greater importance on the success of the technology. "What fundamentally shifted in this industry is that 10 years ago, if the system you built didn't work, it didn't matter," he says. "If the accounts payable system you hired a Big Five firm to build was 18 months late, nobody got hurt. But if the e-business system you build [now] doesn't get delivered, the customer has no business."

Carbonell adds, "You are going to find focused, best-of-breed players that really hone a skill to do something," he says. "There's a specialization that takes place in order to be good." Customers are becoming more technology-dependent, and Carbonell believes that favors the specialist.

Cysive is working with Cisco Systems' Global Services Unit to create an e-business platform that will enable Cisco to rapidly build applications to respond to customer needs, to reduce maintenance costs and to flexibly modify its e-business strategy.

PARTNER FOR SUCCESS

For an e-business, the successful build out and management of its entire e-business (including an infrastructure with faultless logistics and fulfillment and real-time inventory solutions), depends on choosing the right technology and business partners.

Just as the 21st Century is the era of technology it's also the era of tech specialists and, as such, hiring a full-time specialist can be not only expensive, but also almost impossible due to the lack of good, experienced technical personnel.

In the August 28, 2000's issue of *InternetWeek*, Robert Preston, its editor, discusses how partnership-oriented relationships are central to an e-business's success. He goes on by holding Cisco up as an example of how to manage an e-business and its partnerships. He states that Cisco is a phenomenal e-business not only because it's good at selling networking gear on its Web site, but because it coordinates its myriad outsourced manufacturing and logistics operations over the Internet in lockstep with internal R&D, sales, customer service and other competencies. He further states that Amazon.com is an online market leader because it recognizes what it's good at (customer service, order fulfillment) and taps specialized partners like Toys 'R Us for what it's not so good at (toy purchasing, inventory management).

Preston then poses some very good questions to ponder before an e-business begins its search for the right tech partner:

- Is the e-business or department built for such partnerships?

- On an IT infrastructure level, does the e-business have the networking, security, directory and other tools in place to give key "outsiders" access to the internal data they need to serve its interests?

- Up front, is the e-business prepared to select a partner, negotiate a flexible multi-year contract and oversee that relationship?

Most e-businesses aren't prepared; and they have no idea how to oversee alliances with integrators, consultants, fulfillment houses, transportation companies and other strategic partners. The result is that benefits accrue mostly to the other partner, or the relationship deteriorates because of mismanagement or neglect.

But also an e-business has to foster a culture in which employees give partners the same priority (and respect) that they accord co-workers. If a tech partner isn't considered part of the team, it's just another vendor/consultant/integrator.

Some of the Issues

There are many issues that an e-business needs to consider when contracting with a tech solutions provider, be it an integrator, consultant, vendor or one of the many other names these tech specialists use today. They are the best friends any e-business can have, but they can also be their worst enemy if not chosen intelligently.

Although you may have sufficient project management experience in-house to enable you to create e-business architectures, project teams, implementation timelines and milestones, you will find that eventually you still need the services of a tech specialist.

E-businesses of all shapes and sizes are evaluating their move to an e-business model (whether ongoing, projected or under consideration), and they're turning to tech solution providers to craft e-business strategies so as to increase sales through effective e-business initiatives. In doing so, they are working through numerous issues: cost, capability, competitive pressure. Some businesses are in emerging markets; others are in traditional old-line industries. One common trait they share, however, is the desire to expand by adopting an e-business model whether enterprise-wide or within a specific division, to reach a wider, sometimes global, market. Typically, an e-business will seek out a "Web integrator" that can provide its specifically outlined skillsets coupled with a willingness to think creatively and respond quickly to its changing needs.

The scenario is probably familiar. Your project must be up and running as quickly as possible, but you realize you don't have all the skills in-house to accomplish your goals — you need help. But finding the right tech partner isn't an easy task. Choosing the right tech partner is a lot like choosing a marriage partner. You can pick the right partner and live happily ever after (or at least harmoniously until the project is complete), or it can end in a messy divorce where the innocent (in this case, your e-business) suffer.

There are the patently obvious things to keep in mind, such as the due diligence for any company you hire to work with you; but there's more to it than that. Compatibility is the first and foremost concern. "[Disagreements] happen when you're dealing with a company where one is profit-oriented and one is revenue- and market share-oriented; it happens with an East Coast and West Coast company, where the attitudes are different," says Jennifer Pigg, executive vice president of the Yankee Group (www.yankeegroup.com).

Look at a potential partner the same way you'd look at a merger partner. Lorin Coles, senior vice president of worldwide alliances for iXL Inc. (www.ixl.com), an e-business services firm, says, "When you think about an acquisition, you're almost doing the same thing [as choosing a partner], only here you're dealing with two [separate] organizations. That's why cultural fit is so important."

An e-business can use its internal people to build contacts. Many times, people move on from a large company like Arthur Andersen or Electronic Data Systems (EDS) to join a startup or an e-business and they may know people back at their old companies who can help out in a particular situation.

Remember that at the end of the day, all e-businesses are competing for a highly skilled group of people and there aren't enough of them to go around. You have three choices: develop them yourself, hire them from someone, or find a tech partner who has the necessary skills in-house.

Let potential partners do some of the homework for you. Ask them who their competitors are. In this roundabout way, you could easily get several companies to show you who the real leader is. "Eventually, you find out who the market leader is because if the same company is being mentioned by all the competitors, then you know who's leading the market," says Tim Nelson, CTO of ITConsult.com, which offers e-business consulting services.

Another key point: Don't play the part of the matchmaker and try to force an "arranged marriage" on your tech partners. This happens more often than you think. An e-business will choose two tech partners for a deployment or development effort, and the two tech partners don't work well together. Remember that you entered into a "partnership" with your tech solution providers and you have to treat them as partners, not as hired hands. Most tech partners won't agree to work with another tech provider just because you, as their client, want them to, unless *they* think the match is a good one. Permit your tech partners to get involved, allow them to do the usual due diligence on the "new kid on the block." Let them tell you if they don't think it will work. Of course, they must offer specific reasons that make good business sense.

Before any new player is brought into an established partner mix, make sure it's clear who's the quarterback in the technology arena. "The key thing is to try and mitigate any chance of finger-pointing," says Theo Forbath, senior strategist with NerveWire (www.nervewire.com), a consulting firm. "So, up front, you have to define areas of responsibility and who owns different portions of it, where the interfaces are and how you handle escalations of issues."

The contracts should clearly state what each party has to gain or lose. You don't want a partner with nothing to lose, because you might be left holding the bag. "Contracts should be written so there's skin in the game on all parties' parts, so there's both revenue- and risk-sharing involved," Jennifer Pigg with Yankee Group advises. A privately held tech company might have more to lose, since public companies tend to be bigger and have greater cash flow, she adds. Also, when working with a privately held company, there's the opportunity for the e-business to have its work done in "stealth mode," when it wants to keep what it's doing under wraps.

Conversely, don't shaft your partner. You'd think most people would know this, but not so, says ITConsult.com's Nelson. "People will try to negotiate away as much of the power and revenue as they can, as opposed to leaving money on the table for their partner to be profitable," he says. E-business should be looking for follow-up business and should rather have its partner gain a point or two on the project than miss out on that partner's expertise in a future upgrade.

If you're a large enterprise, keep an eye on your divisions and subsidiaries. Many tech partnerships are entered into on the local level and fly under the radar of the main office. You may discover that your enterprise has partnered with a tech firm successfully on several occasions through your far-flung divisions and you didn't even know it. "Having a relationship 'bubble up' is a great model," iXL's Coles says. Some of the best relationships happen that way.

Take the example of Red Sky (www.redsky.com), an Internet professional services organization and among *VARBusiness's* list of E100+25. Howard Belk, president of Red Sky says it has a two-year $2 million contract with Texaco to consult on innovative approaches to the company's e-business plans. He asserts that Red Sky will likely become involved in up to 20 different e-business projects for Texaco, "We also expect to be doing some things with their service-station network." And he expects Red Sky to work with Texaco's Fuel and Marine Marketing unit to develop a wireless- and Web-based order and procurement system that tracks fuel shipments and deliveries around the world.

The Texaco contract underscores another important consideration for bricks-and-mortar companies: flexibility. Red Sky is essentially offering cutting-edge technology solutions to a variety of entrepreneurial business units that are widely spread divisions of a global Fortune 1000 giant. It's also leveraging its vertical market expertise with its knowledge of technology.

"We've earmarked different resources to build a Texaco team of about 50 different people in our New York and Houston offices," Belk says. "We have established a very high level of comfort with them through the Houston office, and we have a lot of vertical expertise in the oil industry. There was clearly a need for this at Texaco."

Invite that Sales Person In

Cold calls can be an effortless way for an e-business to obtain introduction to a potential tech partner — don't shut the door on them. If they've shown the initiative to contact you, at least add them to your list of potential tech partners. Keep a running list of tech people who contact you.

Stan Hock, director of communications for Trinchero Family Estates in California's Napa wine region, used two integrators to supplement internal IT efforts to launch and operate the Sutter Home winery and four other related Web sites. He remembers when executives with local integrator Free Run Technologies began talking to Sutter and to competing California wineries about the Web's value as a marketing tool back in 1993. Initially, Free Run was rebuffed. "They came knocking on the door in 1993 and said, 'Here's the Internet! Here's what it's about, and here's how we can make it happen,'" Hock recalls. "I was resistant." But his resistance wore down as he saw competitors start Web sites and realized that major consumer brands similar to Sutter were establishing Web presences.

"They were evangelists. They were persistent," Hock says of the local integrators. "They were largely responsible for getting most of the wine industry online." (The tech company lists 30 clients, including vineyards, resorts and a limousine service in California's wine country.) Hock used Free Run to launch Sutter's first Web site — which he describes as an online brochure — in 1996. Eventually, with Free Run's help in creating a shopping-cart model, the site was upgraded and used more strategically for marketing ventures and then as a marketing platform for limited e-commerce activities. Now, the site is being used "to create synergy between our online and offline marketing programs, like the ones we have with grocery stores," Hock says. He uses his own Web designer to make Web site changes, but hosts the site on Free Run's high-capacity servers (which are co-located at Exodus). Why? Because, according to Hock, "they are really not the area [of expertise] of our own MIS department, and I can't afford to have the Web site out of commission. Free Run is very reliable," he says. Hock notes that his IT department (like in many e-businesses) "really isn't involved with the Web sites," but focused more on internal networking issues.

Look for Partners in all the Right Places

But don't wait for potential tech partners to come to you. Go to the major conferences and seminars. "It's important to be in the places where other people are looking for partners as well," Todd Knight, head of strategic vendor partnerships for Luminant Worldwide says. And, just as important, send your people for training. If you're looking to beef up your area of expertise, training your key staffers is a good way for them to meet and establish relationships with other people learning the same technology.

Stay Alert and Be Cautious

Once you've located a potential partner, do your due diligence. Don't rely just on the CIO or their end users as references. Talk to the implementers at the company. "It's great to have a successful implementation, but did it kill everyone to get there?" asks Nuforia's Sherwood (Nuforia, incorporating Net Explorer and Belk Mignogna Associates, is now Red Sky). You want to make sure the customer is happy, but also talk to whomever implemented the project so you understand what it took to get there. "You may find buried bodies along the way," he warns.

Get bad references, too. The usual assumption when asking for references is to get happy customers, but no one bats a thousand. There will be misses, problems and failures in any business, and a company can be more telling in failure than success. "Quite often, the way you deal with adversity will say more about how well you work than [what you do when things] are going well," Knight says.

Make sure the people who are courting the e-business as a partner are the same people that will be on the project. "Sometimes a consultancy will send in their A-team players to get the contract, then send in whomever is available for the job [later on]," Nelson says. Make sure you request that at least some of the people who will be assigned to the job will be in the initial interview.

Avoid narrow-minded tech solution providers. "[E-business doesn't present] a repetitive set of problems that every customer has, like delivering an ERP system might," says NerveWire's Forbath. "In most cases, people are trying to innovate on what they deliver, so it's important to have an original, out-of-the-box thinker."

Sometimes it's better to start with a small working relationship before going into a full-fledged, legally binding alliance. It's not until you do a full job that you'll know if the partner is compatible. Until then, it's guesswork — 75% an e-business can get when it sits down in a meeting, but the last 25% comes from going through one cycle, and that last 25% is vital.

ONE SIZE DOESN'T FIT ALL

An e-business needs to have an intimate and detailed knowledge of the potential partner from the very beginning. Ask them to lay out for you their core competencies, but listen to Keith Lauver, president and CEO of Gearworks.com, a Web integrator, whose advice is to have them boil it down to what they really do best. For example Lauver says, "I define our core competency as [being] business problem-solvers." Gearworks.com focuses its expertise on transportation, logistics, and supply chain solutions. Among its clients are Ford Motor Company, 3M, Carlson Companies, and Tires Plus.

Determine if there's a fit by assessing what your e-business is trying to accomplish, then find out what your potential tech solution provider's sweet spot is, this will allow you to determine if there's truly a match. "We're not the right company for everybody," says Joe Neely, senior vice president of sales and marketing Nuforia (now part of Red Sky). So, if the match isn't there, let it go.

Ask the potential tech solution provider for previous customer examples of similar work they've successfully completed. Howard Belk, Nuforia's president (Nuforia merged with Red Sky in mid-2000), clarifies, "We're not a low-cost provider, so there's some legitimate skepticism on the part of [our prospective clients]." Nuforia normally offers a taste of original thinking about the project under consideration at no charge to the courting e-business. If, after a bit of discussion, there is a hint that a "marriage" is in the making, he follows with real-life, successful implementation stories that fits with the e-business's wants and needs.

Can the potential tech solution provider anticipate the e-business's needs? Since many tech solution providers specialize in necessary, but disruptive solutions, such as creating new processes, like real-time inventory solutions, for e-businesses, Gearworks.com's Lauver says it's critical to anticipate needs rather than react to them. "Technology doesn't mean anything if it can't be integrated into an organization," he continued.

Is the potential tech solution provider a One-Stop Shop? Sometimes it's easier to work with a small group of outsourcers than a disruptive crowd. "Nobody prefers to work with multiple vendors on a single effort," Belk says. For example, Nuforia (Red Sky) strategizes, consults on builds, and provides the creative element as well. Few companies have bona fide credentials in all three areas. According to Belk, if a potential tech solution provider can wear more than one hat, it will let you know. The caveat is to be sure the tech provider truly has the skill sets to do all it states it can accomplish.

Set clear and honest expectations; but to do this you need to make sure you're honest with yourself and your potential partners about the resources and time lines you have to accomplish your e-business's goals. Determine, through due diligence, if the potential partner is consistent in its methodology and can implement and even re-implement solutions that work.

Does the potential tech solution provider work "outside the box"? In other words does the potential partner have an environment that is creative and invites innovative thinking? If so, the potential provider will let you know. At the same time you want to find a partner that has a road map, for while they may think out of the box, an e-business also needs a partner that keeps on track, and keeps their e-business clients informed throughout the process (that's a partnership).

Finally, it's imperative that whichever tech solution providers you partner with, you must promote a strong working relationship with each and every one of them. The kinds of projects you're entrusting to them are business makers or breakers for you, so you not only have to believe your partners can do the job and help your e-business achieve its goals, but you need to like working with them and their team.

THE INTEGRATOR OR SOLUTION PROVIDER

Almost all enterprises adopting an e-business model will enter into a partnership with an integrator (a/k/a Web integrator or an Internet solution provider — of course these days it could be almost any title). Bear in mind that integrators who offer a combination of business strategy, consulting and basic IT skills are very much in demand. Roy Wetterstrom, CEO and founder of e-business integrator, Plural, Inc. (www.plural.com), feels that in addition to technology and general business expertise, it's becoming increasingly important for integrators to have a deep knowledge of the specific industries they serve. "That is different than having just a great client list," he says. "It's truly understanding the business so clients are hiring you just as much for your industry knowledge as [for] your technical expertise." *VARBusiness* thinks Plural Inc. follows its own advice, *VARBusiness* placed them in its year 2000 E100+25 list.

One of Plural, Inc.'s clients is ValueVision International, a leading national shopping network. ValueVision and Plural collaborated on the successful launch of the ValueVision Web site (www.vvtv.com) in time for the 1999 holiday season. The site offers an extensive product line in an easy-to-use and searchable format, with integrated cross-selling and real-time inventory updates. "We are very pleased with our decision to use Plural to build, integrate and complete our Web development, which was on an accelerated timeline. We now have a completely integrated technology solution combining a contemporary storefront look and functionality, a highly popular auction element, and true TV-Internet convergence," espoused Kevin Hanson, senior vice president and chief technology officer of ValueVision.

Make sure that the integrator doesn't stint on back-end integration — even if the marketing and sales people (who seem to head up many Web initiative teams) don't list it on the top of their agenda. Unhappily, thousands of online customers have experienced online shopping nightmares. Each of these, in all likelihood, resulted from sloppy or nonexistent e-business fulfillment systems when the integrator that built their site neglected proper back-end integration. All the flash and interactivity designed to attract customers to a Web site is for naught if the customer doesn't get their ordered products when promised.

To get an e-business up and running quickly (whether an e-tail site, a B2B solution or a hybrid) requires a integrator/tech solution partner that is one-part drill sergeant, one-part guidance counselor, one-part workflow expert and one-part technologist.

The drill sergeant makes sure his team lives by the project plan and calendar. Fast-implementation specialists break a massive project down into pieces. They adhere to clear time lines and have written goals for each phase of a project. "From the minute an integrator enters a fixed-price contract situation, the clock is ticking," says Glen Mella, senior vice president of marketing and alliances for TenFold Corp. (www.10fold.com), an e-applications provider. "There's no room for inefficiency if you plan on making any money."

TenFold states in writing what is going to be delivered in each phase of a project and when written approval of each phase is needed. "You have to remove ambiguity and uncertainty from these projects to be successful," says Mella.

The guidance counselor comes in to help the e-business chart its Web site's path and prepare everyone for staying the course. No e-business can thrive on a foundation of broken business processes. Yet, people within the e-business have probably been denying or trying to hide the cracks in the foundation for some time. That's why many tech solution providers have a discovery, or "profiling," phase where they listen to what the e-business's staff says as well as what they *don't* say.

Many integrators get inside knowledge about an e-business's processes by putting some of the e-business's own staff on the project team. Besides providing training that helps the e-business self-administer and use the solution later, this involvement keeps lines of communication open between the e-business and the integrator partner.

Once discovery is completed, integrators do more than suggest which products to buy. An e-business wants a tech partner that will work with it to develop the right strategy, implement the right cultural environment and organization, define the right knowledge management processes, and provide the right technology platform and infrastructure.

"Super-fast implementation only occurs after you identify and correctly engineer all the business processes involved in the application," says

Jeff Frederick, project executive for Crowe Chizek Systems Consulting Group (www.crowechizek), an e-solutions provider. "A large part of our methodology for fast implementation involves getting existing business processes ready."

The technologist is always at work on the project, from discovery to completion. In discovery, for instance, the technologist uncovers infrastructure flaws, which if left uncorrected can mean death to even successful Web sites.

Many integrators speed implementation by putting the e-business staff to work on version one of an actual solution, rather than developing a prototype. "Customers often don't know what they like or hate until they get hands-on experience," says Mella.

Also an integrator's job is to come in and get the job done and get out as quickly as possible. While an e-business may have an integrator's staff in-house for long periods of time, they don't spend too much time on one project. Integrators say the most important written agreement is a definition of the goals and sign-off procedures that enable both parties to leave well enough alone.

Plural, Inc. is an 11-year-old company that got its start building high-end technology solutions for the financial industry. By 1996, the company had begun to focus heavily on e-commerce and Internet applications. Its two-tiered expertise in the financial industry and its technology proved invaluable for Restor Johnson, president of small cap market portal RedChip.com Inc., which recently launched a new Web strategy under Plural's Propeller incubation program.

"I'm a stock guy, so I can't talk technology," Johnson says. "They can, but they also understand stocks, and more importantly, research. That 'been there, done that' experience is worth paying for." Johnson continued, "Those guys moved mountains for us."

Sometimes the water gets a bit muddy and you don't know where your potential tech solutions partner fits into the integrator-vendor-consultant channel. For example, Joe Bellini, CEO of C-bridge Internet Solutions (www.cbridge.com), sees his company as a hybrid of old and new worlds: a services-driven company leveraging a product-oriented sales model. *VARBusiness* put C-Bridge among the biggest and best when it included it among its E100+25 in 2000. C-bridge began in early 1997, and quickly found a niche building compartmentalized Internet solutions that could be easily implemented and upgraded. However, when Bellini entered the scene in 1998, he began to focus exclusively on services rather than products. In 1998 Bellini built a new center for interface design and created learning centers to support research programs, workshops and seminars on e-business.

C-bridge is one of the tech solution partners working with Fosters Brewing Group to develop its B2B portal for the hospitality industry. C-bridge, working with Oracle, is providing the technical, project management, and organizational framework to empower Fosters and its vendors to order, track goods and services, and to take advantage of such things as promotions and delivery options, once the portal is completed.

When Central Carolina Bank Inc. in Durham, NC made the decision to expand its Internet strategy and build a full-service financial portal, the bank tapped C-bridge because of the integrator's expertise as well as its willingness to work in a true partnership. "They came in with a value proposition where they would transfer knowledge and methodologies to us so we could keep it going," says Howard Brooks, Central Carolina Bank's senior vice president of Internet banking. "That was the biggest point of sale."

But C-bridge isn't standing still; it has entered into partnerships with USinternetworking Inc. and Qwest Communications Corp. to provide virtual ASP services in a move that is a logical extension of C-bridge's strength in building compartmental solutions. "As we assemble these Legos, the client sees it's a homogeneous environment and asks if we could come in on a monthly fee basis and support the systems for them," Bellini says.

Sometimes when trying to figure out where a solutions provider fits in, you can take a look at the businesses it competes with, at least that is what Bob Clarkson, COO of marchFirst, Inc. (www.marchfirst.com), a professional services company, advises.

The author could have just as easily placed marchFirst (www.marchfirst.com) in the consultant section of this chapter but decided its main strength lay in the integrator arena. It was formed in early 2000 through a merger of Whittman-Hart Inc. and USWeb/CKS and placed eighth on ZDNet's year 2000 Smart 100 companies and was among *VARBusiness's* E100+25 list of the best solution providers in North America. According to Clarkson, it competes with Web pure-plays such as Scient Corp. (www.scient.com) and Viant Corp. (www.viant.com), traditional IT giants such as EDS (www.eds.com) and IBM Global Services, strategy business-es such as Bain & Co. (www.bain.com) and McKinsey & Co. (www.mckinsey.com), and even digital advertising companies such as McCann Erickson Worldwide (www.mccann.com).

Although marchFirst may be a new name to you, Clarkson says the combined resources of the two companies that make up marchFirst include more than $1.1 billion in 2000 revenue and approximately 9,000 employees working in 72 offices in 15 countries. It also has, thanks to the merger, an expansive client list of e-businesses that includes pure-plays, midsize corporations and global Fortune 1000 companies. But marchFirst's main selling point, according to Clarkson, is it can provide creative solutions to rival any Web design boutique.

That's probably why Pottery Barn (www.potterybarn.com) and its parent company , Williams-Sonoma (www.williams-sonoma.com), decided to use marchFirst when the decision was made to go online. Finding an integrator that could maintain the business discipline the successful retailer already practiced was of utmost concern. Shelley Nandkeolyar, vice president of Pottery Barn's e-commerce division, says they found the right integrator in marchFirst, which built an online presence that achieved all of their goals, and ahead of schedule to boot.

While marchFirst's work on the site was critical to its success, Pottery Barn also has a full integration team and built the site in tandem with the integrator, according to Nandkeolyar. marchFirst created the GUI and the business architecture, but the majority of the operation infrastructure and integration to the back-end legacy systems was done internally. The author notes that both the Pottery Barn and Williams-Sonoma sites were built on the Allaire ColdFusion platform.

"Most technology integrators are coming from the systems and solutions perspectives. Not many people would believe that a company like

IBM Global Services (www.ibm.com) can bring world-class creative skills to a site," Clarkson says. "On the other hand, I don't think anybody would look at a McKinsey, OgilvyInteractive (www.ogilvy.com), or Bain and say they have the technology chops to put in a system that feeds into a back-end infrastructure. In fact, we can take those three things and leverage them with best-of-breed capabilities." As part of its ongoing strategy, marchFirst looks for customers with high-profile brands and deep supply chain processes, which might include a need for a first-class LFMS and real-time inventory management. What's more, the company wants clients who are willing to fundamentally restructure the base of their businesses to better compete in the new digital economy — not necessarily those who simply want to add a Web site to an existing business.

Keith Lauver, CEO and founder of Gearworks.com Inc., doesn't consider his company a consulting or technology company. Instead, he calls it "an engine all about innovation" — a new one on the author — but ... as a result, Gearworks.com has managed to differentiate itself by focusing on back-end and supply chain processes. "People don't come to us if they want a Web site," Lauver says. "They come if they are into the supply chain and are part of a logistics or transportation company that needs to leverage the data collection and data-delivery capabilities that come from the latest mobile data technology."

Despite its modest size, Lauver says his $2 million company's greatest strength is the level of talent it attracts through its professional staffers. "If I do the job successfully, we will be able to attract and retain world-class people," Lauver says. Gearworks.com encourages its people to spend about a quarter of their time in what he calls the technology "sandbox," playing with the newest technologies and then regrouping with peers to brainstorm on ways to solve customers' problems.

Way back in 1997 Web integrator AppNet and its founder, IT veteran Ken Bajaj, knew where the e-business industry would end up — even then they were focusing on enterprise and B2B projects, courting established bricks-and-mortar clients instead of flashier start-ups. "A year ago, B2C was all the rage, so in some ways, Wall Street was knocking us a bit because we didn't have a strong B2C focus," says John Berry, AppNet's vice president of marketing. "But with Ken's background, he understood from the beginning that the better focus for long-term growth would be in working with large corporations in developing their e-business solutions. Now, as we see, the market has directly moved to that area."

According to Berry, AppNet managed to carve out its own B2B niche early on by focusing on three key areas: business strategy consulting and support, effective user interface applications and killer e-business technology. Over the years, it has won client contracts with companies such as Citibank, Daimler-Chrysler and Ford. He goes on to state that "eighty percent of our work now is with Fortune 1000-type clients."

Berry feels that AppNet is better-suited for B2B work due to its deeper understanding of the business processes and strategies that are imperative to the integration of Internet technology with back-office systems and legacy applications that make up a faultless LFMS and real-time inventory solutions. "There is a lot of heavy lifting on the back-end," Berry espouses. "Reports say that 50% or more of all e-business activity in the next few years will be heavy application development work and systems integration. You'll have a lot of problems going to a company that is trying to morph from a pure-play Web design shop to a full systems integrator."

One of its satisfied clients is Burton Snowboards. Burton partnered with AppNet to implement an Internet solution for managing its business infrastructure including the integration and streamlining of all business processes. This was achieved by building a secure extranet that enabled suppliers and dealers to update, check and place orders in real-time and in five different languages — English, French, German, Italian and Kanjii.

VARBusiness thinks AppNet has its act together since it placed the company among its E100+25 list in 2000, which sets out the top solution providers in North America focused on e-business. CommerceOne is also smitten with AppNet; in September 2000 they acquired the company.

Incorporated as a systems integrator in 1997, AnswerThink Consulting Group Inc. (www.answerthink.com) believes it knows the answer to the e-business outsourcing quandary. So does *VARBusiness*, it placed AnswerThink in its E100+25. According to Lee Fields, executive vice president of sales for AnswerThink, "We do a good job of bringing in the

Green Berets, not necessarily the entire infantry. We believe in co-managed projects with our clients, so we will bring in folks who are self-sufficient right from the start."

Among AnswerThink's client list are high-profilers such as Bostonian Footware, Isuzu Motors Ltd. and Time Warner Corp. The company has striven to position itself as a full-service provider for e-business, leveraging many of the skills it developed as a traditional systems integrator.

"Let's assume you want to do interactive development with Web skills and an e-business strategy," Fields says. "Then you may want to add a supply chain behind the scenes, CRM and back-office integration to a legacy fulfillment system and tie it all into a pure-play infrastructure. We play in all those areas, and have for the last several years. We can bring together a cross-functional team very quickly without having different silos that have to be brought together."

AnswerThink recognized early on the importance of industry research when it came to supporting its methodologies and with that idea in mind, it acquired Hackett Benchmarking Group in 1997. Field stated, "From a benchmarking standpoint, they basically had in their database 80% of the Dow Jones industrials and 80% of the Fortune 500. We felt we could bake that information into our methodologies and practices, so when we go out on client engagements we can use best practices."

Fields says the company practices what it preaches. "You can sell as much as you want, but if you are actually using the tools you tell clients you can build, then that is more important than anything else."

Another key acquisition for AnswerThink was a merger last year with e-solutions provider Think New Ideas Inc., which brought the company to a new level of interactive development. "We created the first marriage of a front-end creative piece with middleware and back-end solutions integration pieces," Fields says. "You will be seeing more of that over time, but we have a head start."

Fifth on ZDNet's Smart 100 Companies list, integrator powerhouse Scient may be only three years old, but ZDNet thinks "it already has the look of an industry veteran." *VARBusiness* agrees, it placed Scient on its year 2000 E100+25 list. Unlike other tech solution providers, Scient demands that it be allowed to build the entire e-business, refusing to unbundle its services. "We don't do systems; we do e-businesses, from business strategy, to architecture and implementation, to marketing," says Stephen Mucchetti, Scient's president. "We provide complete e-businesses from front to back." This "my way or nothing" approach doesn't seem to have hurt its business; it has launched some 20 pure-play start-ups and bricks-and-mortar spin-offs with more in the pipeline, including a few B2B exchanges.

One of Scient's clients, out of many that you may recognize, is PlanetRx (www.planetrx.com). The online drugstore partnered with Scient to accelerate its time to market while at the same time defining its business processes. Scient determined the functional requirements and technical specifications needed to support the e-business and based on that assessment, it rapidly designed, architected, and implemented an e-business system for PlanetRx in only six months.

EASING THE MOVE FOR THE ESTABLISHED ENTERPRISE

Bricks-and-mortar players realize (just as B2Bs do) that the launch of a Web site will have a tremendous impact on their existing enterprise in everything from the sales channel to customer fulfillment to call centers and they choose their tech partners accordingly.

"Corporations that are just starting their e-business initiatives don't want to have to deal with the huge complexities of all the new Internet technologies," said MimEcom's (www.mimecom.com) CEO Darl Davidson. "They don't have the internal staffing or knowledge to manage these sites. And they don't want to." MimEcom claims the middle ground between web-hosting/data centers such as Exodus Communications (www.exodus.com), and web design shops like Scient. It boosts Kmart's BlueLight.com and the now defunct Gardens.com among its client list. How? By giving them what is essentially an offsite IT department. MimEcom coordinates and oversees all the operations of an online initiative from getting an array of software and hardware tools to meshing everything together in a seamless fashion so as to assure secure transactions and prompt customer responses to fixing glitches without bothering the client.

"It's just too costly to maintain the staff and talent and competency in-house that MimEcom can provide on an outsourced basis," said the chief Web officer at BlueLight.com.

Bricks-and-mortars and B2Bs, in general, have shown that they're more interested in traditional, financial metrics than the pure-play start-ups, which includes return on investment, net profits and customer-acquisition costs. This more mature approach, though lauded, doesn't mean that these enterprises aren't using the Web to boost company sales. Most bricks-and-mortars and B2Bs just took their time; but at the same time nearly killed themselves while trying to figure out a viable strategy. Many, to their credit, sought expert advice and partnered with the best when it came to adopting an e-business model.

Office supply giant Staples, for example, launched its Staples.com online site in early 1999, largely as an extension to its existing retail and catalog business. To expedite its online ventures, Staples.com partnered with professional services firms to complement its existing staff, resources and skills in the design and development of its Web sites. One company provided Web-based server tools and integrated the technology components; another provided advice on improving site usability; and an Internet marketing firm managed affiliate sales and marketing.

One risk to established bricks-and-mortars as they make the move to the Web is disaffected stockholders. The expense associated with the Staples' Web effort pummeled its stock price while generating just an estimated $94 million in online revenue — about 1% of Staples' total 1999 revenue of $8.9 billion. Staples completely revamped the site in May 2000, adding new search tools, small-business services and a streamlined checkout procedure with a reasonable LFMS. It has also promoted the site heavily in its existing stores and through newspaper advertisements sporting rebates to online customers, and since then the e-tail sites have seen heavy traffic and expansive sales.

Staples partnered with Manhattan Associates, Inc. for the implementation of a suite of supply chain solutions — PkMS for advanced warehouse management, Productivity Manager for productivity tracking and labor management, and SLOT-IT for pickline optimization. These applications were implemented at multiple Staples Contract and Commercial fulfillment centers to help in the establishment of cost efficiencies.

J.C. Penney is another old-line company grappling with a Web strategy. J.C. Penney has had an online presence since August 1996, when it initiated secure ordering on the Web but has struggled ever since. In November 1999, JCP Internet Commerce Solutions, Inc., a wholly owned subsidiary of J.C. Penney, brought the full catalog merchandise assortment online. The JCPenney.com e-tail operation pulled in an estimated $102 million in 1999, less than one-half of 1% of J.C. Penney's $32.5 billion in 1999 total revenue.

Despite the miniscule percentages of the enterprises' total sales as noted above, JCPenney.com and Staples are deemed successful, when judged against Internet-only competitors. Web retailer Bluefly, for example, racked up just $5 million in annual sales resulting in a hugh net loss. Another online retailer, Boo.com, went out of business in spring 2000 after posting heavy losses (although it had a rebirth as a portal). JCPenney.com received a complete make-over in March 2000, adding a browser tool for female shoppers that allows them to model clothes on a replica of their body dimensions before an actual purchase (a concept executives of Lands' End, a direct merchant of casual clothing, said they pioneered in 1999). In November 2000, JCPenney.com yet again received an overhaul in preparation for the crucial 2000 holiday season.

Waiting in the wings are giant discounters Wal-Mart and Kmart's BlueLight.com. Both undertook huge site revamps and expansions for the 2000 holiday shopping season, but kept close-mouthed about their specific tech solution providers for the redos (though Wal-Mart has already sued Amazon.com for allegedly hiring away some of its employees). Both bricks-and-mortar companies have opened offices in Silicon Valley, a sign the competitive fray is indeed getting serious.

New alliances and new Web strategies in the e-tail sector are being formed at a time when many traditional enterprises have just begun to struggle with development of an e-business model. A report released in early 2000 by consulting firm Deloitte Consulting (www.dc.com) found that while two-thirds of 400 surveyed retailers had Web sites, only one-fourth of those surveyed were actually selling online. Of those that had Web sites, nearly one-third believed they served no strategic purpose.

(Ouch!) Among the retailers that had viable e-commerce sites, nearly half reported they were filling orders from the same distribution centers used by their bricks-and-mortar operations. Another 30% said they were fulfilling the orders directly from their store shelves. Deloitte's concluded that to be successful the bricks-and-mortars would need to evolve their business models, develop multi-channel sales and invest heavily in technology including a viable LFMS.

Understanding the beneficial impact technology can have throughout an enterprise organization — and the way it can change the entire customer equation — stands in stark contrast to the e-business community's early emphasis on building name recognition instead of infrastructure.

"There is a whole class of systems integrator who, two to three years ago, were doing client-server or ERP implementations," says Stephen Lane, research director of the Professional Services Practice at Aberdeen Group. The Web is extending further into the existing infrastructure of e-businesses, affecting supply chain management, LFM and inventory management. Lane remarks, "The front-end piece is less important. Companies need strategy realization and lack the resources to do it themselves."

Has the integrator market soured on e-tail? Somewhat. It's definitely difficult to get one of the top-tier integrators to work with a pure-play e-tail startup. Mainly because with alarming frequency, pure-play e-tailers are announcing they've run out of cash and Wall Street seems to be abandoning them. Further, the design-oriented services required by pure-play e-tailers have become commodities.

However, the story is a bit different for bricks-and-mortars adopting an e-business model, they often have the same back-end integration needs as the B2Bs and everyone is cognizant of that fact. Thus they are treated as an equal to the B2Bs in the tech solution provider community.

Conversely, the skills required by B2Bs are complex. Integrating the inventory, general ledger and information systems, and LFMS of a well-established enterprise making its move to a B2B model (with multitudes of suppliers) is a huge technical hurdle. Back-end systems integrators need to be knowledgeable about mainframe and client-server systems as well as databases, data warehousing and packaged applications. Tech firms that provide those skills can charge premium rates.

Founded in 1993, Inventa (www.inventa.com) began in the client-server arena. Within two years, it moved to B2B e-commerce Web integration. Inventa never pursued the B2C market despite requests from clients because of the difference in transaction complexity, value and effect.

"B2B requires a higher order of intellectual capital," Toby Younis, vice president of marketing and i-strategies at Inventa, comments. "We take on the tough stuff is how Inventa positions itself." Younis says he believes that the B2B model requires more intellectual effort than the e-tail model, is more challenging, and over the long-term, will have more value and impact.

"B2B is an easier case to make than B2C because it's not creating a whole new sales channel," states Aberdeen Group's Lane. "The suppliers are already there. Also, companies are more willing to invest in things that help them reduce costs." While the Web is just another sales channel for e-tail, it fundamentally changes business practices in the B2Bs and they know it. Therefore they are willing to invest the capital to do it right; such as integration of their value chain and legacy systems, implementation of a fail-safe LFMS and real-time inventory solutions, and so forth.

Contrary to what most experts advise, Inventa's Youngis says, "Financial performance as the primary measure of business performance has been replaced by temporal performance. The faster you do things, the better. If you can do things faster, you will derive other benefits, such as increases in revenue, decreases in costs or increases in customer satisfaction."

American Consolidation Services (ACS) (www.acslogistics.com), a subsidiary of American President Lines, books, consolidates, and tracks shipments from Asian vendor manufacturing facilities to delivery locations at large retail customers in the US. "Inventa really helped us further our strategic goals through their technology expertise," boasted Peter Weis, CIO, American Consolidation Services.

Inventa designed the architecture for ACS's global network, electronically linking all their customers and vendors (i.e., manufacturers) to a central database and to the ACS's legacy mainframe systems. The electronic booking system automated the time-consuming cargo booking and validation process, allowing manufacturers to make cargo bookings online. In addition, Inventa designed and built a customer information system that allowed ACS customers to obtain shipment status online and to analyze the information for improved decision-making.

Jim Ruggiero, vice president of technology at Novo Corp. (www.novo-corp.com), a Web integrator that has a well-rounded e-business client roster and is a member of *VARBusiness* E100+25 group, says his company has no intention of abandoning e-tail, which comprises half of Novo's revenue. But Novo takes a different approach to each market. "B2B is more focused on functionality and usability, while marketing is downplayed. And you don't have to look at market segmentation; in B2B the set of users is well-defined. B2B is business-process-oriented and more granular than B2C. There's a strong focus on architectural planning."

"Companies are taking a much more holistic approach to the Web," says Phillip Say, e-business strategist for Novo. "Established businesses are now looking to apply Web technology to their core business." This means bricks-to-click undertakings will assess the entire impact of the Web throughout a corporate business, i.e., integration of the back-end systems including the messyware necessary to deal with legacy systems, not to mention customer management and fulfillment solutions.

Novo, for example, has developed bricks-to-click strategies for large national retailers such as Proctor & Gamble (www.pg.com) and Krause's Furniture (www.krausesfurniture.com). The integrator is working to design and engineer new Web portals for United, Delta, Continental and Northwest Airlines. Say believes such large clients are interested in adopting new technology, but want to know its impact on their internal processes and procedures before they proceed.

Krause Furniture's chairman and CEO, Philip M. Hawley, on choosing Novo as its e-business professional services provider, stated, "Our goal is not only to better serve our existing retail customers but also to provide a business-to-business solution for other furniture e-tailers, independent bricks-and-mortar retailers and the hospitality industry. Leveraging Novo's e-business strategy and planning expertise during the first phase of the relationship will help us quickly determine the risks, strategies and opportunities in developing our e-business framework."

Larry Tanning, president of Denver-based IT services provider Tanning Technology (www.tanning.com), believes that enterprises making the e-business move should take a methodological approach to make the turn from "bricks" to "click." Many old guard enterprises have been slow to respond to the promise of the Web, he concedes, but that is because they are forced to deal with significant value chain and infrastructure issues, such as legacy systems and logistics and fulfillment, before moving forward. "I believe the bricks-and-mortar guys are going to be the real drivers in the next wave of the Internet," Tanning predicted.

In Tanning's view, the successful approach stresses integration of Web technology with existing business processes and procedures. "It's all about exposing your business processes to the Web in a way that allows you to be responsive [to customers] and bring new things to market." That also means taking a deliberate, collaborative, "engineered approach" to Web technology. Tanning goes on, "The challenge is to develop an architecture and a road map [for enterprise clients] that stands the test of time."

Not only did Tanning gain a spot on the *VARBusiness* E100+25 list; it also was awarded Forrester Research's top score in the Technology Category (which includes Systems Architecture and Systems Development) in Forrester's report, entitled "eCommerce Integrators Exposed." Forrester's report stated, "Tanning's services are best suited for Fortune 1000 companies and established Dot Coms that must build out global e-business platforms in Unix environments."

DiamondCluster International Inc. (formerly Diamond Technology Partners Inc.) (www.diamtech.com) is a solution provider that has customers on both sides of the market. But it does admit the B2B model has some compelling advantages. "The size of the deal is much bigger. B2B is more attractive when you go out to get capital," says Anthony Abbattista, a Diamond partner. "With B2B, the economics of the value chain are more precise and there's a better correlation between expenditures and investment."

Abbattista also believes a full-service approach such as Diamond's is important because execution cannot be accomplished without strategy. *Forbes* magazine has ranked Diamond 56th on its Forbes 200 Best Small Companies for 2000. Quoting *Forbes*, "The Forbes 200 Best

Small Companies list is more than just a numbers game. We comb candidates' financial documents for bad debt, lawsuits and slow receivables — all of which are grounds for dismissal. Those that make the final cut are truly survivors."

EXCHANGE OF KNOWLEDGE

Since the dawn of e-business (just a few short years ago), one of the most notable changes is the increased sophistication of the tech solution provider's e-business customers. Today these e-businesses know what's possible and know that they need partners who can "carry them across the threshold," says Michael Boyd, who heads Eddie Bauer's online efforts (www.eddiebauer.com). At the same time, integrators and solution providers are no longer relying on just their hard-earned reputations to bring in big-name e-business customers. "We saw a stream of start-up entities knocking on the doors of established companies," Boyd says. "We saw them as less interested in bringing value than they were in getting a chance to leverage our brand name for their own businesses' benefit."

However, before dismissing these new tech providers out-of-hand, consider what they have to offer. Many times these young upstarts have the necessary tools to lead a business into the e-business world at a reasonable cost. Just perform the appropriate due diligence before signing on the dotted line.

Giant Step (www.giantstep.com), an Internet solution provider, developed an online commerce strategy for a leading grower of agricultural products that leveraged the client's proprietary inventory management system and drove incremental revenues. The client initially assumed that its best online opportunity was to gain additional margin by selling directly to its business customers. After performing a business process and market analysis, Giant Step recommended a new approach.

The agricultural industry follows the just-in-time/build-to-order model, with capacity for early-stage growers committed up to 16-weeks in advance of delivery. Most early stage growers must allocate 30% of capacity as insurance to guarantee coverage of its orders; however, Giant Step's client had an inventory management system that allowed it to maintain insurance levels of only 10%. As orders approach shipping date and their insurance inventory is deemed unnecessary, this overage is taken online and integrated into a Giant Step-modeled catalog of available inventory. This allows the Giant Step client to provide real-time, on-demand availability, online ordering of on-demand inventory for brokers and real-time fulfillment and shipping status of all orders (build-to-order and on-demand).

The argicultural firm (and other e-businesses) partnered with Giant Step with the knowledge that the Internet was the key to their future. The Hub Group Inc.'s (www.hubgroup.com) story points out another benefet of adopting the e-business model. When it approached Cysive Inc. (www.cysive.com), one of the premier builders of e-business architectures, the Hub Group (moves cargo in trailers over railroads and behind trucks) knew it had a degree of redundancy in its operations to cope with inconsistencies in the railroads. As David Yeager, vice chairman and CEO of Hub Group explained, "Every time there'd be a merger between rail lines, we'd have a brief disruption. We had to have the resources to deal with these situations."

But when it came time to introduce a Web-based system for managing the trucking side of Hub Group's business, the process of organizing the data revealed Hub had been so focused on heading off customer outages that efficiency had slipped. According to Yeager, "I hate to admit it, but this process showed we had a lot more redundancy than we had envisioned. Just going through the preliminary steps of Webifying our trucking operations helped us function much more economically."

Cysive and Hub Group worked together to install a new system that provides Hub Group customers with the option to access their accounts via the Internet to track shipments, thus positioning Hub Group as one of the industry leader in online tracking.

The phenomenon of unexpected returns isn't unique to the Hub Group, says Cysive CEO Nelson Carbonell. "It doesn't matter how smooth you are. You're always going to learn something new when you roll out a solution. We think that the technology, in most cases, differentiates the winners from the losers. In the end, when you can't get the system to work, it doesn't really matter if the rest of the stuff [provided] was great."

LEGACY SYSTEMS

All tech solution providers struggle to match new-age technologies with legacy systems. The e-business space is migrating from a community of pure-play Web-based businesses to one quickly becoming dominated by the old guard enterprises. However, as they begin muscling their way into the e-business domain the established old guard must deal with their substantial investments in legacy systems that they loathe to abandon.

Integrators definitely earn their substantial fee when searching for the solution to the perplexity of linking a Web site with an e-business's legacy systems. To do this, many integrators form their own partnerships with established vendors, or relationships with other tech experts, or perhaps may rely on consultants to provide specific expertise for the e-business. An e-business needs to know prior to entering into any contract with an integrator who their partners will be, or might be. Because, even if the integrator is a good fit for the e-business, the partners may not be.

Vignette Corp. (www.vignette.com), for instance, relies on large consulting firms such as Andersen Consulting (www.ac.com) and PriceWaterhouseCoopers (www.pwcglobal.com) to provide an overall solution for its e-business clients; for a SME adopting an e-business model this may be overkill. Therefore, Vignette may agree to another partner in the place of Andersen or PWC although the suggested partner may be essentially an unknown quantity that doesn't fit comfortably in a working relationship. However, Vignette also is in bed with IBM Corp., Microsoft Corp., Oracle Corp. and Sun Microsystems Inc. and one of these firms may have an overall solution provider that will solve everyone's dilemma.

One example of how Vignette and other tech solution providers work with a host of tech experts to get a project out the door is when PlanetOutdoors.com recently launched WomenOutdoors.com in record time. Steve Styczynsky, PlanetOutdoors.com's director of future technology simply stated, "We chose Vignette because they've established themselves as the leader in content management and personalization, and they offer a broad suite of complementary enterprise applications."

PlanetOutdoors.com then selected Saillant Consulting Group (www.saillant.com, a Vignette Solution Provider, to provide in-depth Vignette product expertise and accelerated deployment strategies. Saillant's challenge was to meet aggressive goals for site availability without compromising production quality. To do this, Saillant's consultants engaged in a collaborative team approach to prioritize key business objectives for the site. The team then streamlined technical design and execution to best leverage Vignette software for the immediate goals and to create an underlying platform to efficiently update the site over the long term.

But you also can look at the Vignette Corp. and Asista.com (www.asista.com) partnership to see an example of legacy integration. In September 2000, Asista, a digital marketplace for the sale and purchase of indirect goods and services in Latin America, and Vignette successfully completed the first B2B integration ever between an electronic marketplace and a company's back-end system in Latin America.

"The real value of B2B e-commerce comes through integration: the in-house automation of one company's operating processes are merely necessary, while the integration of companies within a virtual marketplace, is revolutionary," said Carlos A. Guajardo, founder and CEO of Asista.com

Here's a look at some projects. These tech solution providers have all had involvement with the necessary integration of an enterprise's legacy systems when adopting an e-business model.

Fort Point Partners Inc. (www.ftpoint.com), an ATG (www.atg.com) partner and a resident of the *VARBusiness* year 2000 E100+25 list, recently completed a project that involved extensive legacy integration consisting of a Web site re-launch of Kaplan Inc., a New York-based provider of educational and career services who wanted to redesign its internally developed kaptest.com site. The site, one of several operated by Kaplan, offers comprehensive test preparation and admissions services. Kaplan wanted a more seamless registration system combined with the ability to sell books and software. In addition to ATG application servers, the project involved an Apache Web server, Sun servers and an existing Oracle database. James Roche, CEO of Fort Point, says his company's experience in working with legacy systems in real time helped to cinch the deal.

Although it doesn't address directly the subject of this book — LFM — the tech experts did meet the bogeyman a few times. They had to integrate kaptest.com with six legacy systems. Another major challenge was the company's desire to implement a high level of personalization so the new site could assess test results and recommend personalized product offerings based on those results without human intervention. The process took five months. "Scalability was an important issue," Roche says.

E-businesses that have developed their Web sites in-house often rely on well-established vendors and solutions. For instance, when West Marine (www.westmarine.com), an international reseller of boats and boating supplies, wanted to overhaul its Web site, it turned to Web Emporium LLC (www.webemporium.com), a premier IBM software partner. As such, Web Emporium builds customized platforms using IBM WebSphere Commerce Suite and is a member of IBM's Web Initiatives program.

"Our site wasn't robust [or] scalable, the user interface was embarrassing and our customers hated it," admits Michelle Farabaugh, West Marine's vice president of e-commerce. West Marine is standardized on IBM, using AS/400 hardware and DB2 database software, and had no interest in changing its core technology. IBM suggested Web Emporium when West Marine asked for a recommendation. "We gave [Web Emporium] four days to put together a proposal. They really understood the hardware and software, and they had great references," Farabaugh says. "They came through and exceeded our expectations."

One of West Marine's requirements was a 90-day turnaround on the project, which was daunting considering that the project called for full back-end integration and catalog integration of 50,000 SKUs. The project was particularly complex because West Marine had mostly mainframe data and more than one database, adds Marshall Freiman, co-founder and CTO of Web Emporium. Those factors worked against any major technology overhauls. Therefore, the best solution was for Web Emporium to act as an ASP serving West Marine. There is back-end integration with West Marine's JDA system, which runs on an AS/400 platform. Web Emporium upgraded West Marine from JDA Version 1 to Version 4. IBM's WebSphere application server is also part of the package. "There is a lot of IBM hardware involved, including Netfinity servers and an RS/6000," Freiman says. "IBM provides good support, and we like their products." Web Emporium has received recognition as a leading integrator with ranking in *Sm@rtReseller's* (www.smartreseller.com) Smart 50 List.

Many of the Fortune 1000 companies can probably find their e-business tech partner already in-house. The traditional integrators like EDS and Computer Sciences Corp. (www.csc.com) have a history of working with legacy systems and therefore have the skills in abundance. Then factor in that the traditional integrators have long-term outsourcing work within Fortune 1000 companies, new e-business projects at those customers are "theirs to lose," says Greg Jacobsen, chief executive officer of e-business integrator and managed services provider XOR Inc. (www.xor.com). The challenge for the longtime players, he says, "is staffing to a different skill set," i.e., the e-business model's needs.

Even start-ups with no legacy system baggage find they may want to rely on traditional vendors for solutions. With time-to-market a crucial element there's less risk involved with a known solution. Frans Johansson, co-founder of Inka.net, an e-business that creates and extends trading platforms for services marketplaces, turned to integrator Primix Solutions Inc. (www.primix.com) for assistance. Good choice, *VARBusiness* likes them too, they put them in the E100+25 list for 2000. In this instance, Primix offered office space as well as a quick implementation to Johansson.

Serendipitously, Primix had just formulated its e-Catalyst incubator program for start-ups, and Inka.net became the test case. In addition to office space and equipment, e-Catalyst also provided access to business development, IT and human-resource professionals. Inka.net found that access invaluable.

Thanks to smart partnering, Inka's new product, InkaStructure, launched in mid-2000, just slightly behind schedule. It's 100 percent Java-based, and runs on Windows NT and Sun Solaris platforms. Inka.net uses Sun hardware, a Sun-Netscape Web server, an IBM WebSphere application server and an Oracle database.

Integrators partnering with traditional vendors can be an advantage for an e-business looking to launch, upgrade or re-launch a Web site. Traditional vendors train their integrator partners on their products and provide technical support as long as the integrators recommend their products. But again I remind the reader looking to hire an integrator — find out who the integrator's partners are and be sure those partners are a good fit for your e-business.

Rare Medium Inc. (www.raremedium.com), for example, is an integrator that has forged solid alliances with Microsoft, IBM and Sun Microsystems, thus ensuring that best-of-breed solutions can be quickly deployed to meet the specific needs of each of its clients. "It's imperative that we align with best-of-breed products, technologies and companies," says Brian Francis, Rare Medium's senior vice president of global alliances.

When Epson (www.epson.com) partnered with Rare Medium (listed in *VARBusiness* E100+25 in 2000) to give it a viable online presence, Rare Medium had to solve a few prickly challenges. Such as how to sell directly to users a complete complement of Genuine Epson Supplies and Media for all Epson discontinued and current products (regardless of geography) without damaging existing channel relationships. At the same time, Rare Medium had to integrate everything with Epson's legacy systems. Rare Medium came up with a modular product catalog, customer product search interface and checkout system and integrated it all with Epson's legacy back-end systems including direct mail inventory and fulfillment systems.

"With traditional companies, we take a different approach," says Anish Dhanda, president of NetNumina Solutions (www.netnumina.com), a Web integrator that provides e-business solutions to Fortune 1000 companies. "Our approach focuses on more of an architectural level. We'll come in and look at the existing technology, evaluate their existing skillsets and then ask how they want to move forward." When dealing with bricks-and-mortars, Dhanda believes, it's critical to address their specific technology needs, provide the right tools and build the solution around existing legacy systems.

"You can't have a solution that is pre-determined before you come in," he says. "You have to study their specific needs and be prepared to work with them as a team. You have to take more of an architected approach and provide the right tools." It's also important to accept existing legacy systems and build the new solution to leverage off them. "You can't be afraid of it," Dhanda says. "Just because they have a legacy hole, it doesn't mean it doesn't work."

Martin Adams, executive vice president of Petrossian Paris (www.petrossianparis.com), had, in his view, only one obstacle — retaining a tech partner skilled enough to make his vision a reality. "We interviewed three or four different companies, but decided that Vizy Interactive ((www.vizy-interactive.com) was the best around," he says. "We liked the staff we met and the references that came out of Vizy's camp. They're young and dynamic," he adds.

When he envisioned Petrossian's new online strategy, Adams was not concerned with becoming the best, but with staying the best. "Petrossian is a very well-known brand name, and we had to recreate the feel and ambience that Petrossian evokes," says Tracy Richards, account manager at Vizy. "We were integrating with Petrossian's internal systems, so the site could connect with all the existing ways that Petroissian does business."

Integration at this scale was not that simple, however, and that's where Scott Kilroy, director of technology at Vizy Interactive came in. "Our biggest challenge has been integrating the SQL database with Petrossian's order fulfillment system, which is based on FoxPro," he says. "FoxPro isn't a very Internet-savvy database, so we've built almost everything we needed from the ground up in MS SQL 7.0. That way, we could concentrate on sharing the data between the two systems, instead of trying to adapt our tools to FoxPro," Kilroy explains. With a tool belt equipped with MS SQL 7.0, ColdFusion, Perl, C++ and FoxPro, Vizy's architects had Petrossian's site up and running in time for the 2000 holiday season.

E-business should keep in mind what Stan Lepeak, an analyst at META Group Inc. (www.metagroup.com), has to say about the current cadre of integrators who are using a mix of new breed and traditional solutions. He believes that traditional vendors have one distinct advantage — they are consistent, something some of the new breed of integrators can't always accomplish. "And sometimes it's up to the e-business to decide whether they want something safe or cutting-edge," he says.

EVERYONE WANTS IN ON THE E-BUSINESS ACTION

Tech providers — who are they and what *exactly* do they provide and what is their core expertise? Finding the answers to those three little questions when looking for a tech solution provider can instill uncertainty and confusion in the smartest e-business executive. Are they a Web-, Internet-, e-integrator, an e-business consultant, and Internet advisor, a digital architect, a VAR, a vendor, a Web producer. The so-called "descriptive" nomenclatures go on and on.

Instead of helping to clarify roles, the industry's love affair with all things "e" has forever blurred traditional dividing lines. "Everybody related to IT today is e-business this or e-commerce that," says John Berry, vice president of marketing for Web integrator AppNet Inc. "It's hard to differentiate. You can't even tell who is a software company as opposed to a services company or network company."

"It's becoming an increasingly crowded market, so the ability to differentiate yourself [the tech or solutions provider] is an important ingredient for long-term success," says Roy Wetterstrom, CEO and founder of e-business integrator Plural Inc., which changed its name from Micro Modeling Associates to better express its Internet services focus.

The large technology enterprises want in on the action too. In March 2000, Sun Microsystems Inc. announced an ambitious $300 million program to help start-ups quickly initiate e-business models in an effort to better marry itself to the integrator market. IBM is offering the Startup Essentials program, which can help start-ups become eligible for deeply discounted hardware, software, consulting, Web design and business plan development services from participating Sun "e-integrators."

IBM also has a program with the stated goal of training and supporting integrators so they can recommend IBM products. In addition, IBM offers mentoring and provides co-marketing funds. The company now has more than 1,200 participatory integrators and has trained more than 2,500 technical integrator employees on its e-commerce software.

"IBM needs these firms to build on technology so it can be recognized as a market leader in e-business," Mark Hanny, vice president of integrator initiatives at IBM, says. He characterizes IBM's approach to the program as "give to get" business. The level of IBM's investment in an integrator depends on the integrator's level of commitment in building on IBM platforms and training its people on IBM technology.

Compaq and Hewlett-Packard Co. have each designed programs for

Web developers and integrators that provide leads, equipment discount programs, co-marketing and sales support. For all of these technology giants the objective is to have the integrators deploy Internet solutions on their respective systems.

THE VENDOR PARTNERSHIP

The development of an independent partnership with a tech vendor should not be undertaken without the input of your tech solution partner. That's because, in part, it's imperative that an e-business ensures the product (application, tool, middleware, software) is a well-thought-out solution that will bring not only synergy to the e-business, but scalability.

A vendor is relatively unfamiliar with the specific needs of the e-business. Providing a tech solution for an e-business is very different from the traditional software application sale. Most e-business models have their own uniqueness. For instance, you find very few businesses that adopt an e-business model for its entire enterprise in one fell-swoop. Therefore, more users are added to the implementation base over a period of time as the e-business brings its assorted divisions into the e-business model with their diverse infrastructures. There is also a tremendous need for speed and reliability, e-businesses demand that they be up and running quickly. Normally, they want the solution yesterday and a vendor operating "out in the cold" may not have the necessary skillsets in-house to provide the total solution.

In general, vendors themselves look to integrators who have hardware integration and software development skills to help them get their products into e-businesses. A good example is ERP, which may be too complex for most integrators to provide; nonetheless, some ERP middleware vendors are looking for integrators to sell their products to the e-business client. Most vendors are smart enough to realize that they need Web-savvy integrators to tie their products into Web sites and business processes.

Vendors are also searching for integrators who have the internal resources necessary to host software applications as ASPs and/or CSPs. For a vendor, these are just other venues in which it can get its product to the e-business.

In the point-of-sale (POS) market, tying the Web store with the bricks-and-mortar store is a priority with larger retailers as they begin to make their move to an e-business model. Now, this need is trickling down — companies such as Cougar Mountain Software (www.cougarmtn.com) are unveiling software packages that marry data from physical POS stations to Web storefronts and they need integrators who are prepared to handle these intricacies.

The same is true with Savvion (www.savvion.com), an innovative global provider of Internet-deployed business management solutions. It actively seeks out system integrators and consultants to help get its product to the end user (the e-business). A scant couple of years ago Savvion was known as TDI Inc. — one of the top integrators in Silicon Valley. Today, Savvion's products give e-businesses the tools to quickly transform business processes into flexible, distributed Web applications. "The Internet has created an opportunity to fundamentally change the way business process management is delivered, by integrating customers, suppliers, and employees into a seamless e-business process," said Dr. Ketabchi, Savvion founder and CEO.

When looking at your potential tech vendor partners, recognize the synergies that are in play within the vendor/integrator/consultant community so you can address them.

Another area that requires close scrutiny involves payment — vendors generally expect to be paid up-front, while many e-business will want to pay on a tiered basis.

Training is an area that many e-businesses overlook. Its staff must be trained in the daily and technical operation to use and support the application(s) and platforms. The customer wants training that's thorough but also fast, convenient and ongoing. The slam-bam-I'm-out-of-here seven-day training course doesn't work in the e-business world.

Vendors are slowing realizing that e-business has a two layer training need. One is focused training for the tech support of the application in the appropriate department (payroll, fulfillment, customer service, etc.) and the other is cursory training for the employees using the applications. All of this must be ongoing training as each division is gradually integrated into the e-business model. Another training issue comes out with pure-play start-ups — mainly due to staffing constraints pure-plays see in-house training as the only option.

I have set out some selection criteria that an e-business should consider when choosing a vendor partner:

- solid product line

- speed of solutions deployment

- speed in authorizing other partners

- emphasis on teamwork

- emphasis on implementing the e-business's stepped adoption rate

- minimal internal barriers

- comprehensive training

- full access to professional services and specialized training

- support for the product's sales cycle

- flexibility and adaptability to changing landscape of players and their needs

- increased use of the Internet, intranets and extranets for communication, training, etc.

THE CONSULTING FIRM

A good consulting firm should begin with an e-business strategy plan. Take an inventory of the relevant technology in place in your enterprise and within the value chain, and then lay out a set of scenarios on different ways you could proceed to accomplish your e-business goals. Each scenario should be laid out in detail to enable you and your staff to reach optimal implementation strategy. This is much the same framework process that a movie producer works when making a movie.

Then you, your staff and the consultants should begin checking out possible tech solutions and providers. Generally, no one tech solution or provider will fit all of an e-business's needs. An e-business will need to contract and form several tech partnerships before its systems are fully operational. These partners will include integrators to deal with the "messyware" of integrating legacy systems, the value chain's systems, LFM and inventory systems. How much an e-business should outsource depends on its core competency in the IT area.

A Tour of the Consultancy Arena

Most enterprises need the services of a consulting firm not only to take them into the e-business arena but also to define its LFM strategy within the e-business strategy including a blueprint that lays out its design, architecture, development and implementation. The following is a balanced sampling (in no particular order of reference) of consultants currently providing services that can help an e-business tackle its LFM issues.

One consultancy that many of the large e-businesses tap to help them manage their logistics and fulfillment strategy is Sapient (www.sapient.com). The author notes that this is the second consecutive year that Sapient has landed at the top of ZDNet's Smart 100 Companies list; and it also found its way onto *VARBusiness* E100+25 list. According to ZDNet, "like the New York Yankees, Sapient Corp. is beginning to resemble a dynasty." Sapient is the only e-services company to be included in the S&P 500! Sapient avers to be the leading provider of Internet strategy consulting, providing sophisticated end-to-end solutions, and launch support to Global 1000 and startup companies. You won't get an argument from me. Sapient can help an e-business (with deep pockets) to define its strategy and design, then architect, develop and implement solutions to execute that strategy.

Sapient has developed practices in several key industries including retail and manufacturing and distribution (primarily the automobile and high-tech industries) with only 15% of its business coming from start-ups. The bulk (85%) of the company's business is from established, bricks-and-mortars that are trying to make the e-business move, sometimes through the spin off of an independent Web-based division.

Before approaching Sapient to be a consultant partner, an e-business should be aware that Sapient has adopted the "one team" approach. This means Sapient brings its consultants and the e-business's staff together to work as a cohesive unit. This team-building technique requires that Sapient's staff and the e-business's staff occupy the same physical space, whether at one of Sapient's offices or on the e-business's premises.

With roots as a computer systems integrator, Sapient has an impressive list of Fortune 1000 clients, including United Airlines (redesigned Web site) Nordstrom Shoes (built a Web site that offers more than 20 million pairs of shoes) and Hallmark (built Hallmark.com).

As I hinted at previously, Sapient's services aren't for the average guys, you have to pay to play in Sapient's ball park. The average Sapient engagement will cost an e-business more than $5 million, and $10 to $15 million projects are not uncommon.

For a young company, Viant (www.viant.com), has an impressive pedigree. It placed second on the ZDNet's Smart 100 Company's list; is a member of the *VARBusiness* year 2000 E100+25 list; and was named one of the Top 100 Information Technology companies in the world by *Business Week's* 2000 "Info Tech 100" report. Added to those kudos is a year 2000 *Forbes* ASAP survey wherein Viant was named one of the Top 20 Best-Managed, fastest growing tech companies in the world. And perhaps, most important, in 2000, an independent client satisfaction survey showed 100% of Viant's clients that participated in the survey said that Viant made a significant contribution in helping them take their product to the Web. Some clients are old-line businesses like Schering-Plough and Sears, others are pure-play startups like WIT Capital and CMGI and still others are Global 2000 companies. All opted for Viant due to its expertise in designing, building, and launching the next generation of e-businesses. From eCast.com and Della.com (now part of WeddingChannel.com) to Sears, Polaroid and Fortuneoff, Viant has helped a number of companies realize value in the e-business arena.

But there are many more high rated consultancies out there. In 2000, Proxicom Inc. (www.proxicom.com) ranked fourth on ZDNet's Smart 100 Companies list and also is among the *VARBusiness's* E100+25. Proxicom is no shrinking violet, it states that it has set the standard as the original Internet consulting firm. With such blue-chip customers as BMW and General Motors Corp., it may be right. It focuses on a handful of vertical markets that include retail and manufacturing; but Proxicom has worked with hundreds of Global 1000 companies in helping them develop their global e-business strategy, many of which included management of a diverse value chain.

For example, Harman Consumer Systems Group (www.harman.com), a leader in designing, manufacturing and marketing audio products such as JBL and Infinity Systems, engaged Proxicom to define its e-business strategy and to build an integrated online supply chain solution for its dealer network and consumers. In doing so, Harman increased sales, improved customer service and created a new communications channel, along with improved purchasing, forecasting and inventory management. In the long run, this brought lowered cost and improved performance of customer service. But Proxicom and Harman didn't stop there, they built a back-end system that could provide real-time pricing and complete access to account information and history. And let's not forget the processing of returns along with leveraging investments and saving money through full integration with Harman's SAP ERP system.

DiamondCluster International Inc. (formerly Diamond Technology Partners Inc.) managed a sixth place on the ZDNet Smart 100 Companies list in 2000 for its pure "digital strategy consultancy" and also can be found among *VARBusiness's* elite E100+25 (in addition to its *Forbes* honors). Diamond's mission is to get enterprises to understand how the Internet can transform their business and then to help them devise their e-business strategy. And since founders (a group from Andersen Consulting) started Diamond in 1994, it got at least a 12- to 18-month head start on its Big Five competitors.

Its customers are drawn from the Fortune 500, not Nasdaq — pure-plays account for roughly 5% of revenues. "Diamond is emerging as the McKinsey [the guru of management gurus] of the Net," says Mark D'Annolfo, an analyst with Deutsche Bank Alex. Brown.

The readers may be interested in *Context*, DiamondCluster International Inc.'s well-regarded business strategies magazine. It regularly features articles from the movers and shakers in the leading high tech industries giving it a cutting edge editorial bent with material on topics of interest to both its existing and potential e-business clientele.

Diamond even had a hand in Covisint, the planned automotive e-business trading exchange, supported by General Motors, Ford and DaimlerChrysler (Renault/Nissan has also joined the group). Covisint's goal is to allow OEMs and suppliers to reduce cost in their respective supply chains and bring efficiencies to their business operations.

Of course, Diamond's services don't come cheap, so before jumping on their bandwagon decide whether your e-business *really* needs their kind of expertise. Many e-businesses can do very well with a less "lofty" consulting partner.

One e-business that benefited from Diamond's services is Praxair, Inc. (www.praxair.com), the largest industrial gas company in the Americas, which produces, sells and distributes atmospheric, process, medical and specialty gases, as well as high-performance surface coatings. One of the major markets Praxair serves is the metal fabrication industry. Metal fabricators use the company's gases for metal cutting, welding, processing and finishing. Praxair's customers include manufacturers of automobiles, farm equipment, prefab housing and many others.

Instead of merely using the Web to focus on welding gases for Praxair customers, Diamond proposed helping the company build a unique, broader-based Internet marketplace and resource community, designed both to help its customers acquire new business and to run their operations better. The new business is MetFabCitySM Inc., a B2B Web-based marketplace (www.metfabcity.com) initially funded by Praxair.

Praxair CEO, John Clerico, says, "Diamond helped us to create a unique offering to the major industry segments, including automotive, aircraft, industrial machinery and durable goods. MetFabCity is a resource of truly unique scope and scale and one that we believe will revolutionize the metal fabrication industry's supply chains."

iXL (www.ixl.com) is the tenth company on the ZDNet Smart 100 Companies list and also is on the *VARBusiness's* E100+25 list for 2000. Although ZDNet classifies iXL as an "e-integrator" I believe it fits better under consultants since it *modes operande* is more "consultant-like" than "integrator-like." iXL knows it can't tackle everything by itself and as ZDNet writes, "CEO Bill Nussey and his lieutenants have polished iXL's alliance strategy into one of the gems of the e-biz channel." Gartner Group credits iXL with having the second-best alliance strategy in the business, trailing only that of Andersen Consulting (see, even they compare iXL to a consulting firm). For iXL, this has translated into tight relationships with major e-commerce vendors like BroadVision and computing giants such as Sun Microsystems.

NerveWire (www.nervewire.com), who merged with Northeast Consulting Resources in late 1999, provides Internet consulting and services including strategic counsel, system integration, business planning, and design and implementation for Web-based businesses. NerveWire might be just the firm for start-ups, its NerveWire Ventures will take an equity stake in selected e-business start-ups that the consultancy advises. As Jim Schoonmaker, head of NerveWire Ventures puts it, "It's not simply migrating existing business processes onto the Internet. Rather, given the existence of the Internet, how do you revise your business and processes to keep up? It's the sort of fundamental decision that we approach as a partner, not as an outsider."

One start-up that sought NerveWire assistance was Mesania (www.mesania.com), a new online gift exchange that hopes to rope in Europe's fragmented gift and housewares industry. Mesania partnered with NerveWire to help it deal with the complex business and technical issues along with e-business strategy and implementation of the exchange technology. "We're using this period as a learning experience," Gajen Kandiah, senior vice president of operations at NerveWire, says of the testing phase. "We're talking to buyers and suppliers and asking them what they need and we'll add that functionality."

It's internal partnerships include Asera (www.asera.com), Net Market Partners (www.netmarketpartners.com), Sun Microsystems, and Idapta (www.idapta.com). It has an impressive customer list with such industry giants as Cisco Systems, Nokia, ABN AMRO, BDirect Capital, Tivoli, Mesania, and Sun Microsystems.

The Big Five

When it comes to e-business consulting services, the days of the traditional Big Five auditing/consulting firms are clearly numbered. With the pressure of SEC regulations forcing the separation of consulting work from traditional audit and tax services, and the emergence of Internet services undermining the need for end-to-end consulting giants, traditional auditing firms KPMG, Ernst & Young and Arthur Andersen have been cutting ties with their IT consulting sides. In some cases, the result has been the creation of smaller, sleeker independent companies that look a lot more like pure-play Internet service companies than they do the staunch old-economy giants that gave them life.

Ernst & Young was among the first to formally shed its consulting business, selling Ernst & Young Consulting to European IT giant Cap Gemini (www.capgemini.com) in early 2000. And in August 2000, the company spun out its Ernst & Young Technologies IT arm into an independent ASP called EYT (www.eyt.com). And although the author felt it may be a bit too soon to recommend them as a lead tech partner, *VARBusiness* did place them among its year 2000 E100+25 list.

KPMG LLP chose a similar route, spinning off KPMG Consulting as an independent, IPO-bound company. Andersen Consulting, on the other hand, fought long and hard for its independence from Arthur Andersen in a recently settled arbitration case.

The move to independence will likely help companies such as Andersen Consulting, EYT and KPMG Consulting establish themselves as viable Internet players, however, these companies are in flux at the moment and as such, I have hesitated to include them in any depth in this chapter. Nonetheless, I felt due to their prominence in the tech solution providers arena, they deserved some mention.

The same holds true for Deloitte & Touche and PricewaterhouseCoopers, both of which have also voiced intent to either sell off or spin out their respective consulting divisions. Currently the Big Five's e-business services brings in between $1.5 and $2 billion in revenue, which is far greater than even marchFirst's or Razorfish's (www.razorfish.com) annual take.

"The irony is that all those guys are making money hand over fist in the consulting business, but they are being forced by both the marketplace and the regulatory environment to distance themselves from what has been the golden goose," says Tom Rodenhauser, industry analyst with

Consulting Information Services (www.consultinginfo.com). "None of them are going to be able to hold onto consulting in the future, so they have to get as much money out of it as they can right now." Keep in mind that many industry experts warn against judging a company's e-savviness based solely on revenue. For example, who's to say an IT service company can't build a legacy ERP system, throw a Web site on top of it and mark it off as a $10 million e-business project, according to Cathy Benko, global leader of Deloitte Consulting's e-business practice.

Here's a look at what each company is doing in the Internet service space.

KPMG: Formed in 1997 as a distinct business unit of KPMG International LLC, the consultancy officially incorporated in 2000. It serves some 2,000 clients, ranging from Fortune 1000 companies to small and midsize businesses, e-tailers, B2Bs, e-marketplaces and government agencies. KPMG made its formal push into the Web service space almost two years ago, when it acquired a number of smaller shops specializing in projects such as Web design and Java development. According to Paul Ciandrini, executive vice president of the high-tech practice for KPMG Consulting, "Now all business is e-business. The playing field is kind of changing, but we feel pretty good about where we are right now."

KPMG merged the new acquisitions into a separate company called Metrius (www.metrius.com). "There are still a number of organizations out there trying to integrate the pure Internet services with what were the more traditional services, but we feel pretty comfortable knowing that we got there about a good year-and-a-half ago," touted Ciandrini. "I'd like to say it's because we had a big crystal ball, but it probably wasn't. You know how business kind of anticipates and reacts," he added.

Aside from metrius.com's backing from its parent company, infrastructure heavyweight Cisco has a $1 billion stake in KPMG/metrius.com. It also has an e-business alliance with Microsoft to build a co-branded Collaborative Development Lab for creating e-businesses. The consultancy has been making a few strategic investments of its own. It's getting behind e-business solution companies such as WebMethods and diving headfirst into the emerging ASP space with Qwest Cyber.Solutions (QCS), a joint venture with Qwest Communications to provide clients with end-to-end Web hosting and application management services. KPMG, which owns 49% of the new entity, lends its Internet methodologies and professionals to QCS and in return has a solid partner for its hosting needs.

KPMG attacks the Internet service space via six industry units: high-tech, health care, public sector, financial services, communications, and consumer and industrial markets. Then it further breaks each down into subsegments. "Those businesses are not big businesses," Ciandrini says. "They are the size of the little guys who say they are really nimble." Like other large companies, KPMG Consulting is now throwing its weight behind B2B marketplaces with clients that include Chevron's Petrocosm exchange for the gas and oil community and TRADE.com. It's also moving into the e-marketing space, managing and automating clients' Internet content for multiple media. "We have made enough investments in different areas and have gotten enough traction to remain and grow," Ciandrini says. "The reality is, I would put my Internet guys against anyone and beat them, and I do."

Deloitte Consulting: Len Prokopets considers the market for e-services a two-year sprint. "Everything kicked off with a lot of hype," the senior manager for the B2B practice of Deloitte Consulting says. "Now it's time to bring that hype to reality." The strategy is simple: Make e-business the company's entire business. Deloitte is striving to do just that by transforming existing consultants, establishing distinct units and pursuing new alliances. Deloitte says it can offer clients a full menu of Internet-related services covering technology, strategy and processes, and targeting specific e-business requirements, including things such as e-learning and strategy. For the most part, it directs the bulk of its energy on B2B work, taking on clients in need of major transformations and aligning itself with major platform providers and vendors.

In late 1999, Deloitte Consulting made a move to dramatically transform its delivery model, creating what it calls a "mothership/pod" model, in which the larger consultancy spins out separate business units. The company's flagship "pod" is RoundArch.com, the joint solutions venture it created with partners BroadVision and advertising giant WPP. "This is a pod that lives outside the mothership," Deloitte Consulting's Benko says. "It's a solutions-based start-up that provides a front-end solution — from e-strategy to the technology platform, systems and process integration, and the creative and advertising and interactive marketing elements."

Deloitte Consulting also created an internal unit called DC.com to accelerate Internet initiatives and target clients' e-business services and solutions in North America. "It's essentially an e-consultancy — one of those pure-plays everybody's talking about," Benko says. The company also created a ventures practice in late 1999 for Web-focused spin-offs. Its first project was a joint venture with Chase Manhattan that focused on e-procurement services. In looking to the future, the company's key touch-point for client engagements will be the supply chain, which it sees as the critical element when deriving value for its clients. "The key, moving forward, is heavy-lifting," Benko says. "It's an area for which we are very well-known and have been for a long time. It's in our DNA."

PricewaterhouseCoopers Management Consulting (PWC): Its first formal push into the Internet service space came in 1996 when it saw a new breed of Web integrators emerge with the skills to design and build Web sites quickly. According to Stewart Morick, e-business leader for the Americas division, what those competitors couldn't do was integrate those sites with a client's overall business strategy. PWC created its first formal Internet strategy entity, called the Global E-Business Group, with separate divisions for the Americas; Europe, Africa and the Middle East; and Asia-Pacific. Concerned with end-to-end solutions, the group created a methodology surrounding four solution sets: e-markets, business-to-enterprise solutions, dot coms and "e-transformation" services. On top of those, the company built specific service offerings, including call centers, e-procurement and e-logistics services. It has vendor alliances with more than 140 leading e-business companies.

PWC claims it builds internal competencies and vendor profiles to fit each area so it can automatically locate the right kind of employees, vendors and teams to meet specific needs. That way it can build customized solutions for clients under tight deadlines, while still providing them with an overall vision for their company's future. "We know all the touch points, and we know how to unplug [products], what overlaps and where they fit," Morick says.

Its "e-transformation" services — bring Fortune 1000 and other larger companies to the Internet. "We are just touching the tip of the iceberg," Morick says about B2B and exchanges. "Design and develop and exchange is all relatively easy. It's getting the suppliers, vendors and members, and putting them into the system, maintaining the system, marketing [it] and making it run, that is going to be much larger."

Andersen Consulting: Its road to independence was certainly bumpy, but at the moment Andersen Consulting may be in the best position to provide full-service consulting to an e-business, analysts say. The New York-based consultancy recently won independence after a bitter two-year arbitration case with parent Arthur Andersen. "The predictable outcome is that [the split] allows Andersen Consulting to expand what it was already doing," Consulting Information Services' Rodenhauser says. "It's not going to recast itself as some big behemoth with thousands of people. It's really going to become a collection of smaller groups and become much more aggressive." However, Arthur Andersen, may be in for tough times ahead, according to Rodenhauser. He called the company "damaged goods" in the consulting world.

Joe Forehand, Andersen Consulting's CEO, in a report to shareholders, stated that the consultancy's new mission statement is "helping clients create their future." Anderson Consulting works with roughly 4,500 clients globally, including Fortune 500 and Global 1000 leaders in areas such as telecommunications, utilities and banking. The company's strategy has included a renewed focus on its core business, as well as the launch of AC Ventures, a venture capitalist unit to invest in new economy companies. The unit has plans to invest up to $1 billion globally during the next five years.

Andersen Consulting has also created Dot-Com Launch Centres, which it describes as "post-incubation" sites to help funded e-commerce start-ups and spin-offs expand their operations. "The importance of the Launch Centres was to catalyze our activity in the dot-com launch space," says Larry Leisure, managing partner of the firm's Global Business Launch Centres. "Before we had really just had a Global 1000 focus, and Joe [Forehand] believed it was critically important that we play a much larger role in serving these future Global 1000 companies and accelerate activity in that space." The company has also been expanding its strategic alliance with e-business players, including a partnership with Microsoft and the joint formation of Internet services company Avanade, as well as partnerships with some 175 vendors, including Asera, Blue Martini and Commerce One.

MITIGATING OUTSOURCING RISKS

As stated throughout this chapter, partnerships are essential in expanding and creating a successful e-business — no one company can handle all facets of an e-business without compromising efficiency and its core competency. But outsourcing is a complicated matter rather than a simple one-dimensional "make or buy" decision. There are risks in outsourcing, and understanding those risks is the first step to mitigating them. It is the opinion of IT metrics expert Michael Mah that setting realistic goals for any outsourcing partnership will provide the most promising results.

At the Cutter Consortium Summit 2000, Mah told the audience that "outsourcing relationships are high risk because each side has a completely different set of goals. The client [e-business] wants to save money. It also wants to find a high productivity partner to decrease its IT backlogs, get rid of its biggest IT headaches, and slim its operation down to its core competency. The supplier [tech solution provider] wants to make money by growing its business, making high-profit deals, and leveraging its position in the market."

Mah pointed out that an e-business should take a number of important steps in choosing the right outsourcing relationship:

- Create a strong internal sourcing group, then a governance group.
- Assemble an internal metrics SWAT team.
- Benchmark your IT capability to establish a productivity baseline.
- Ask your potential tech solution provider to show you their productivity benchmarks. If they are reluctant, carefully weigh the risks involved with selecting a provider with no metrics.
- Get an outside advocate to help you through the contract and initial management stages.
- Determine your priorities with regard to schedule, effort and defects.
- Update your baseline periodically to assess whether contract goals are being met for each dimension of your balanced scorecard.

Just keep in mind that once you've made your potential partner list, you should perform your due diligence so you know up front who is dependable and who isn't. Sign up with Hoovers Online (www.hoovers.com) for its proprietary company and industry information. It has an unblemished reputation for the quality, accuracy, and reliability of the information it provides and will make your due diligence task much easier.

THE SEARCH BEGINS

I am indebted to *VARBusiness* (www.varbusiness.com), the magazine for the architects of the new economy, for many of the quotes in this chapter. Even though the magazine and Web site is "created as a personal connection for today's solution providers," it's a wonderful source for any e-business looking for a tech partner. Use their "E100+25 Listing" of the biggest solution providers in North America focused on e-business as a jumping off point in your search for the best-fit tech partner for your e-business.

Although not as focused, ZDNet's Smart 100 Companies listing (www.zdnet.com) compiled by the *Sm@rt Reseller's* staff is another good source for finding the right tech partner. This is their third year of selecting and profiling the most successful and dynamic businesses, which include those in the solution providers arena.

Lastly, be careful, for it's not uncommon for a company today to pursue several related, but different, approaches concurrently. Even some of the smaller companies consider themselves immersed in several divergent businesses. In some instances, they seem to be operating effectively (or perhaps ineffectively) as ASPs, CSPs, e-integrators, consultants and more in answer to the growing number of e-businesses that demand one-stop shopping.

Shipping

ALTHOUGH THE MAJORITY OF the pure-plays, small e-tailers and B2Bs will not have a fleet of trucks and containers, they still must deal with and understand the ins and outs of the shipping industry to truly provide first-class logistics and fulfillment.

E-businesses are continually grappling with shipping costs and many consider shipping the bane of their existence. Some 8 billion packages are shipped by businesses each year at an average cost of $16 apiece, for a total of $128 billion. "And almost no one in the company has any idea what the real cost of any one shipment is," opines Stamps.com senior vice president and general manager David Duckwitz.

Meanwhile, the e-business phenomenon is also having a profound effect on the shipping industry. As e-businesses mature they

Modes of Transportation

- ◆ Rail
  - ◆ mass movement of goods
  - ◆ large capabilities
  - ◆ low unit cost
- ◆ Water
  - ◆ lowest costs
  - ◆ large capabilities
  - ◆ mass movement of bulk commodities
- ◆ Air
  - ◆ fastest for long distances
  - ◆ broad service range
- ◆ Truck
  - ◆ point-to-point service
  - ◆ flexible
  - ◆ fast

become more proactive in demanding better information on the whereabouts of their intransit packages, but also, technology is making that process more thorough — and less expensive.

"With residential deliveries expected to exceed 2.1 billion by 2003, a strategic battle over the consumer doorstep is under way," Stacie McCullough, business applications research analyst at Forrester said. "Shippers have figured out that whichever vendor establishes an ongoing relationship with the consumer becomes the online retail gateway."

Recognizing how the customer uses a Web site is the first step in knowing which business processes need immediate integration. Some e-businesses will find that real-time information from the shipping department is what customers want access to most.

There is also the fact that although an online product's cost is generally lower, and out of state delivery often excludes sales tax, the shipping can end up making the product more expensive to the customer than a bricks-and-mortar purchase. Shipping schemes vary, but the customer generally picks up the actual freight charge and then the e-business spends about 12-18% of the purchase price of any given item on handling.

Most online customers are wary of shipping charges. They see them as a hidden cost that e-businesses pad to increase their profit margin.

As Chan Suh, co-founder/CEO/chairman of Agency.com states, "I believe the [Web] evolution has just started. The first couple of steps were taken by early adopters and gold-rushers, and the real business will be by those companies that use the medium in a smart fashion." Getting a handle on shipping is an important part of effectively using the Web as a business tool.

For instance, December 11th is the approximate peak order-taking day of the season for e-tailers, and yet the shipping companies that the e-tail community uses to deliver their products to the customers don't see a spike in their shipping requests until about December 22. Why? Lack of first-class LFM. The result is chaos in the back-offices and distribution centers. This unconscionable delay serves to put the shipper's neck in the proverbial noose; but it also spells disaster for the e-tailers — late deliveries cause dissatisfied customers, which translates into no repeat business.

The e-business model is also radically altering the rules of the shipping game for the international market — just ask Jean-Peter Jansen, chairman of the executive board of Lufthansa Cargo (www.lufthansa-cargo.com). "Traditional linear relations between customers and suppliers have been replaced by 'multi-dimensional' link-ups between market participants," Jansen told the Eurocargo 2000 international trade fair in Dusseldorf. He goes on to explain that the global expansion of e-business is having a twofold impact on logistics services. On the one hand, it's responsible for the actual fulfillment or provision of commercial services, such as the shipment of goods purchased via the Internet. On the other hand, e-business also provides a basis for logistics companies to optimize their own business processes.

"Air cargo and e-commerce are interdependent. The trend is from coop-eration to integration," Jansen said. However, he did add that the logistics sector is lagging and needs to make a concerted effort to close the gap. He also reaffirmed Lufthansa Cargo's determination to play a leading role in the development of e-business. "The transition from the old to the new economy in the air cargo business has already begun."

The Internet has raised the online customer's expectations by allowing goods and services to be offered in real time on a global basis. One of the key benefits offered by the Internet is the downfall of geographical advan-tages. When a customer places an online order, it's done in real time, so the customer expects that once the buying cycle is complete, everything else that follows should also happen in real time.

Customer expectations are such that the delivery process must emulate a real-time model. Hence, express transportation companies are poised to play even bigger roles in facilitating the movement of goods in global, regional and national trade.

YOUR SHIPPING PARTNER?

For the e-business, selecting the right carrier can be a difficult chore. So many options are offered that the best choice is not always clear. When looking for a shipping partner-type relationship ask:

- Do they offer a full range of shipping services, i.e., same day, next day, ground, air, etc.?

- How late can a package get into their hands and still be delivered the next day?

- Do they have online real-time tracking and tracing that can integrate into a Web site's back-end and its warehousing systems?

- Do they offer complete transportation management services, including palletized inbound shipments as well as small package services?

- Can they offer the same connectivity and tracking services if shipments move outside the shipper's network (a commercial airline or rail or ocean container)?

- Can they handle orders 24 x 7? If not, what is the latest they will eccept a package and what is the latest they will pickup a package?

- Do they provide import/export compliance checks (if the e-business is shipping internationally)?

- Do they provide documentation for global transactions?

- Do they have automated, easy return service that is customer friendly?

Shipping is one of the most costly factors of order fulfillment. Keep in mind that shipping rates are determined by three major factors: travel mileage, package weight and delivery times. Let's say you're shipping a package from San Francisco to New York City and the weight of the package is five pounds or less. Using FedEx Standard Overnight or UPS Next Day Air Saver would cost approximately $30 (FedEx being a few pennies more), Airborne Next Afternoon Service runs approximately $21, and the U.S. Postal Service Express Mail runs $24 dollars. Second day service is more reasonable, although still expensive — FedEx and UPS both running around $16 (again FedEx is a few pennies more), Airborne runs a little over $10 and the U.S. Postal Service charges $6.50 for its Priority Mail service.

Now lets look at what the shipper does to earn the $6.50 to $30:

- Transports the package whether it's 5 miles or 5000 miles.

- Provides tracking information so you and your customer can know exactly where in the shipping cycle the package is located.

- Delivers the package to the customer's front door.

- Records when the package is actually delivered.

B2B'S SHIPPING NEEDS

To get an ordered product to the customer on time requires precise information from real-time data. This typically requires integrated systems and processes that cross over departmental borders. The information should enable a shipping department and shipping company to start shipment planning as soon as possible. This includes selecton of the best carrier, based on speed, weighted share allocation, and costs. At the same time, the appropriate documentation should be automatically generated. Delivery status information and the ability to track promised versus actual delivery dates must also be provided to ensure quality control, and of course, there should be seamless communication between the carrier and the e-business.

Essentially, the B2Bs are content with their current shipping infrastructure; but many do say that they would like to streamline a bit by leveraging the power and ubiquitousness of the Internet to reduce delay and shipping errors.

DHL Worldwide Express (www.dhl.com), one of the leaders in international air express shipping, has heard the B2B community loud and clear. DHL is moving quickly to ensure it continues to meet the B2B's shipping needs. In September 2000 DHL partnered with BEA Systems, Inc. (www.beasys.com) to build its next-generation system on the BEA E-Commerce Transaction Platform. Stephen McGuckin, DHL International's IT development director proudly states, "All of our customers require the utmost in dependability. But for our large customers with high-volume B2B shipping requirements, we believe BEA can provide the 'industrial-strength' performance that's needed."

DHL's new systems will provide a dependable environment to speed online customer services such as pickup requests, shipment tracking, and import/export compliance checks. Sometime during the first quarter of 2001, B2B customers can look for the first DHL product suites built on BEA — the next generation DHL Connect service, which will allow B2B customers to ship and track express packages from their desktops.

Freight forwarders move industrial products from plant to plant or from plant to distribution center on airliners or ocean liners. Such industrial freight is 10 to 20 times heavier than a typical small package delivered by the likes of FedEx and UPS, explained Brian Clancy, principal at logistics consultancy MergeGlobal Inc (www.mergeglobal.com).

B2Bs have flocked to U-Freight (www.ufreight.com), the international logistics and freight services group, because it was one of the early freight forwarder pioneers on the Internet. In 1996 it gave its customers access to its AFSA (Air Freight Systems Architecture) Communications System and has continued to stay apace with cutting edge technology through regular upgrades and the introduction of new systems. Gene Boyer, head of U-Freight's North American operations, explains, "We always try to offer our customers more than our competitors. Unlike many other forwarders, our Web site is not just a home page, it interacts with our AFSA system so that customers can use it for a whole range of real-time options such as tracking and tracing shipments, and checking documents and records."

Today, U-Freight customers can take advantage of a number of distinct benefits:

- A system that provides, for example, real-time tracking and state-of-the-art pre-alerts, allowing customers to be more aware of the consignment progress and status.
- An ocean freight module that covers both import and export shipments.
- A shipment manifest application.
- Pickup and delivery details in terms of timings and progress information.
- Templates to save time in accessing data and reduce errors.

The ocean freight module shares the air freight customer database and can perform a number of financial functions such as accounts and costing. The U-Freight system offers its customers a flexible reporting tool with a range of templated formats or customization to meet a B2B's specific needs.

Freight forwarder Danzas AEI Inc. (www.aeilogistics.com) mixes the Web and legacy applications to deliver what customers want. Danzas AEI decisively won the *InternetWeek* 100 transportation category, besting two companies for which IT supremacy is all but a birthright: UPS and FedEx Corp. It also topped industry giants such as the US Postal Service and CSX Corp. How? According to *InternetWeek*, by giving its customers what they wanted: the latest and most detailed information on material being transported or inventory being managed.

Danzas AEI's Web and legacy applications offer customers everything from simple access to the status of a shipment to end-to-end supply chain management. The heart of Danzas AEI's infrastructure is a cluster of legacy and Web apps, some of them homegrown and some off-the-shelf, called the AEI Interactive Suite. Thus customers can order transportation over EDI links (VAN and Web-based), track and trace shipments, gain real-time visibility into the location of their goods and even check status of inventory in facilities managed by Danzas AEI.

The AEI suite includes:

- Ship AEI for shipment booking and tracking online, which includes pre-shipment alerts to customers through their messaging systems;

- Logistics Information System (LOGIS) Cargo Management System, which lets customers track and query shipment data by purchase order number, item number, transportation container number and so on;

- LOGIS Warehouse Management System, which gives customers real-time visibility into inventory levels and lets them release inventory from any of Danzas AEI's 21 warehouses worldwide; and

- LOGIS Exception Management, which alerts customers of unplanned events — such as a disrupted delivery — and identifies corrective measures.

One of Danzas AEI's clients is 3M Co. in Germany. 3M's Omer Denturck, transportation manager Europe, stated, "You have easy interconnection and an easy transfer of data from one side of the world to another. Some companies have different systems." 3M uses Danzas AEI in Europe for, among other things, "floor-to-door" transport of goods from electronics manufacturing facilities all the way to customers.

Danzas AEI is also constantly questioning and surveying its customers. According to Danzas AEI, many customers select it solely on the strength of its IT and e-business capabilities. That is backed up by Eric Vargas, Danzas AEI vice president of logistics applications, who states that some 35% to 40% of customer requests for quotation focus on those capabilities. He also adds that price is no longer the big driver.

High tech is one of Danzas AEI's strongest assets. According to Mike Powers, transportation procurement manager at Caterpillar, "Such rich integration of systems was the main reason Caterpillar Inc. chose Danzas AEI to manage air freight forwarding for its heavy construction equipment. It's the information technology that really brought it to the forefront."

"There are some Band-Aids going on," says MergeGlobal's Brian Clancy regarding the existing legacy applications that have been made accessible through a browser. "The technology may not be super elegant, but it's practical."

There are other transportation companies doing close to the same thing and many are very aggressive IT innovators. "IT integration is the biggest challenge we face," says Jay Walsh, CIO of the UPS Logistics Group (www.upslogistics.com), citing demand planning and supply chain management as functions critical to customers. "We need systems to keep track of that information as we deal with customers' legacy or ERP systems."

Sometimes a strong relationship is created from emergency situations. Such was the case when Gerber Technologies was ready to ship a textile machine to a customer. Due to the large size of its machine, Gerber can ship only one at a time. Also, once a machine is ready for the customer, it's imperative that it be shipped immediately, so Gerber can continue its production line. A delay in shipment can mess up Gerber's whole production schedule.

Once upon a time, Gerber had one of its immense Textuke machines ready for shipment and the poor Textuke had been stood up — dressed up with no place to go! When the afternoon of the fourth day arrived and the Textuke machine was still out on the dock forlornly awaiting shipment, Gerber dumped its existing transport partner and contracted with Bulk Connection, Inc. (www.bulkconnection.com), a full-service transportation brokerage carrier for the US and its neighbors. The next morning at 5:30 a.m., Bulk Connection had a truck at Gerber's facility to give the Textuke the attention it deserved. Bulk Connection's rapid response was the beginning of a close relationship with Gerber. It has recommended Bulk Connection to Gerber customers with shipping challenges.

Bulk Connection has a history of dealing with the unusual and even the occasional emergency. It utilized its vast network of carrier partners to transport fuel oil during the winter freezes of 1994 and 1996, and provided food grade pneumatic units to assist General Mills when they had tons of flour to be moved due to rail problems. And after coming to Potomac Electric's aid, a grateful Susann Felton, vice present materials at Potomac Electric Power Company, states, "It's indeed reassuring to know that Bulk Connection shares our commitment to the health and welfare of the community at all times, and particularly in crisis." Bulk Connection also came through when E.C.C. International could not supply product to their customers because railcars were not in position and their regular carriers did not have equipment. And it showed up for Rhone Poulenc during Thanksgiving when no one else would, to ensure their delivery schedules were met.

When an interruption occurs it's up to the e-business to keep production running smoothly; however, looking for the correct transportation facilities, making sure it meets the e-business's requirements while still being cost effective, can be very time consuming. E-business should look for carriers, such as Bulk Connection that have the network necessary to handle not only the daily shipping necessities, but also the unusual or emergency situation.

E-TAIL'S SIZE & WEIGHT ISSUES

Shipping becomes more of a difficult issue as the range of products offered online continues to expand. While books, CDs and apparel are relatively light and easy to pack and ship, furniture, consumer electronics, and groceries present much more difficult shipping dilemmas. E-tailers also need to ease the frustration of many online customers, who wade through the maze of Web pages in hopes of finding a clear, concise explanation of the e-business's shipping policy and what is charged to ship the customer's selected product(s). Often it's not until the payment process is almost complete that information of the actual shipping charges are displayed and long before that happens the customer has abandoned the shopping cart.

As reported in a June 2000 issue of *Fortune* magazine, Alex Rivera, executive vice president of online electronics retailer etronics.com, was pleased with the volume of sales his Web-based business produced. The problem was the delivery: his shipping department was a revolving door since many of his big-ticket items, like big-screen televisions, were being returned as quickly as he sold them.

Big screen televisions exceed the size and weight limitations of courier services such as FedEx and UPS, so Rivera relied on regional carriers and that was the crux of the problem. The regional carriers weren't set up to handle home deliveries; therefore, the products were often damaged or left unattended on the customers' doorstep, if they arrived at all.

Rivera's problems came to an end when NationStreet rode into town offering to arrange for the home delivery of etronics.com's large items, including the lucrative but problematic big-screen TVs. NationStreet (www.nationstreet.com) not only delivers, but also performs any necessary unpacking, assembly, and installation. As an added benefit to the customer, it removes excess packaging from the premises. Rivera wondered if he was dreaming — NationStreet offered to do all this good stuff for about the same price Rivera was already paying for delivery. "It seemed too good to be true," Rivera said, "Competitive rates with so many value-added services."

The *Fortune* article stated that "NationStreet wants to be the place e-tailers, catalog merchants, and bricks-and-mortar retailers go for delivery of furniture, appliances, and other large consumer products." The shocker is that NationStreet doesn't own a fleet of trucks; it doesn't own any trucks. Instead, NationStreet uses a sophisticated logistics system to manage a network of almost 1500 trucking companies (located throughout the US) that it has personally selected for their quality of service.

NationStreet knows that there is room for growth. It cites Jupiter Communications' report that projects that the online sale of appliances, furniture, and housewares will reach $3 billion by 2003. That's without factoring in sales of large electronic items like etronics.com's big-screen TVs. According to John Fontanella, a supply chain execution specialist at AMR Research, "If you are an Internet retailer with products that are bigger than a breadbox or require setup or configuration, you will be hard-pressed to find a way to get your products to the customer." At the moment there's no infrastructure in place to support the predicted growth in the online sale of "large items."

"The expense of owning and maintaining a fleet of delivery vehicles is well beyond most enterprises' capabilities," Fontanella says. "There is no question the market needs the services NationStreet is offering." Along with etronics.com, NationStreet includes in its customer list Mercata, Amazon.com, upscale catalog house Garnet Hill and mattress giant Simmons.

NationStreet doesn't have the "oversize home delivery package" playground all to itself. The Bekins Co., for example, launched HomeDirect USA (www.homedirectusa.com) to provide white-glove delivery of high-end internet purchases. This service includes unpacking, setting up the product, removing packing materials and, in some cases, being eco-friendly by taking away old products that are being replaced.

As Jean V. Murphy reported in her article for supplychainbrain.com entitled, "Home Delivery: Conquering the Long, Last Mile," HomeDirect USA was spawned from a Bekins service that initially focused on moving B2B electronics products. This expanded into delivering high-end home products for catalog companies like Williams-Sonoma, American Express and Nieman Marcus. Larry Marzullo, chairman and CEO of Bekins, said, "Suddenly we found we were getting very good at this service." Marzullo attributes HomeDirect's success not only to the quality of its in-home service, but to its technology — EXE fulfillment software (www.exe.com) is installed in all of its distribution centers, and thus the company is able to provide visibility of all shipments to the customer. Tracking is available via the Web, which also is used to provide exception reports if the schedule becomes muddled.

Marzullo declared that the biggest challenge with home deliveries is trying to schedule them with a customer who has limited hours at home. "We work evenings to try and increase the window, but that is one of the reasons we are investing a lot in information systems. In addition to EXE, we are about to put in a supply chain management piece from i2 Technologies (www.i2.com) to help us with things like merge-in-transit. If you buy a headline product from a furniture e-tailer, you will likely be prompted to buy other pieces for the room. If you purchase 15 items there will be 15 deliveries, some as small as an ashtray or lamp and some much larger, unless there is some consolidation. What we are moving toward is being able to merge those shipments from different manufacturers into a single delivery at the DC closest to the customer. This way the consumer can take a single day off work and have everything delivered at once." To help minimize returns, HomeDirect also provides a deluxe service, which involves touching up small nicks or scratches on furniture before delivery to the customer.

Exel (www.exel.com), until recently known as Exel Logistics, also is licking its chops at the opportunity that it sees in the big-ticket home delivery market. In 1999 it sidled up a little closer to its sister company, Merchants Home Delivery. Merchants has around 1,500 delivery teams that make on average close to 15,000 home deliveries per day in the US and Canada, although at the moment most of these deliveries are for traditional retailers. Excel and Merchants realigned, in part, to help Merchants tap the e-business market through the use of Exel's information technology and supply chain management resources. "All the researchers out there say that by 2005 one third of all furniture purchases will take place over the internet," says Jim Allyn, president of Merchants. "That's an awful lot of product."

And, there is even more good news for e-businesses, Hub Group (discussed in the previous chapter) is eyeing the same marketspace with its Hub Group Distribution Services (HGDS) (www.hdgs.com). Hub Group president Dave Yeager told Jean V. Murphy (for supplychainbrain.com) that HGDS is leveraging its expertise to create a home delivery service for Web purchases that are too large or heavy for services like UPS to handle.

"With large shipments consumers run into situations where delivery is made by an LTL carrier, and the item is taken no farther than the truck gate, or they have to go to a truck terminal and pick it up themselves," says Yeager. "There is a need for this kind of home delivery service and we think we will have a ready market among many of our existing customers that are moving into the e-commerce environment." Yeager admits the challenges are considerable. "You have to deal with going up flights of stairs, with parking limitations in major metropolitan areas and with a multitude of other variables that make this type of service exceedingly complex. B2B is a heck of a lot easier."

The regional carriers are in the same predicament as the bricks-and-mortars — they aren't set up to handle small-boxed products in ones and twos, and residential delivery is not their forte. Not that the well-known carriers such as Bekins, North American Van Lines, and CNF don't try — just like the bricks-and-mortars they've adopted some version of an e-business model, some better than others. But home delivery of e-tail products is a sideline for most (although not all); they are set up to ship large containers of merchandise from one loading dock to another and not deliver single-item retail orders to people's homes. It's not possible for many of them to offer NationStreet's level of service and reliability, says Len Smolinski, director of logistics for Simmons. "I looked at all the alternatives and made my decision based on the quality of NationStreet's information system."

E-TAIL SHIPPING CONUNDRUM

One problem all e-tail establishments are grappling with is that their customers (at least some of them) don't want to pay for shipping (the last couple of years have spoiled them) and they certainly don't want delivery costs to outweigh the cost of the item purchased. A number of e-tailers have gone belly-up or are just hanging on by their teeth because they didn't fully account for shipping costs.

Smart e-tailers use ground shipping for the normal product shipment, and allow their customers to upgrade to next-day air only at serious cost. However, even these e-tailers need to work on their shipping options — especially how they delineate them for their customers.

Shipping

UPS STANDARD DELIVERY. Your package will arrive within 5-7 business days after you place your order. Please refer to the following chart when calculating charges for shipping.

Merchandise Total	Standard Delivery
Up to $25.00	$5.00
$25.01 to $50.00	$7.50
$50.01 to $100.00	$10.00
$100.01 to $200.00	$12.50
$200.01 to $300.00	$15.00
$300.01 to $500.00	$16.50
$500.01 to $700.00	$18.00
Over $700.01	$19.50

UPS 3-DAY RUSH DELIVERY. Your package will arrive 3 business days after you place your order. Add $7.50 to the Standard Delivery Charge.
UPS OVERNIGHT DELIVERY. Your order must be placed before 1 p.m. Eastern Standard Time and will arrive the next business day. Add $15 to the Standard Delivery Charge.
UPS OVERNIGHT SATURDAY DELIVERY. Your order must be placed before 1 p.m. Eastern Standard Time on Friday. Add $30 to the Standard Delivery Charge. Currently, this service is not available to all zip codes, so if you are unsure as to whether or not UPS delivers to your area on Saturday, please call Customer Service at [telephone number] and we will gladly assist you.
USPS STANDARD DELIVERY - P.O. BOX & APO ADDRESSES. If your address is a P.O. Box or APO, you must select the United States Postal Service option. Your package will arrive within 5-7 business days after you place your order. Please refer to the Standard Delivery Charges when calculating charges for shipping.

Within the U.S.

When making a purchase from us online, shipping and handling rates are approximate until you select a shipping option (standard delivery, two-day delivery, or overnight delivery). The following standard shipping costs are for shipments within the continental U.S. only and are calculated according to the total cost of merchandise in your order. For two-day shipping, please add $6.00 to the cost below. For overnight shipping, please add $12.00 to the cost below. You are required to sign for your deliveries.

All prices on this Web site are expressed in U.S. currency. For more information concerning pricing, see our pricing policy.

Merchandise Total	Add to Total
25.00 and under	5.00
25.01 - 50.00	7.50
50.01 - 100.00	10.00
100.01 - 200.00	12.50
200.01 - 300.00	15.00
300.01 - 500.00	17.50
500.01 and over	20.00

Outside the U.S.

At this time, we are unable to fulfill international orders online. We regret that this is beyond our control and will strive to serve our international customers through our web site as soon as we can put the timeliest, most responsive shipping process into place.

Shipping to Multiple Addresses

During the checkout process, you will be asked to select the shipping address for your order. At this time, you can ship your online order to only one location. We realize that your order may include gifts that require shipping to several different locations. We can solve this dilemma in one of two ways: You can break your items into separate online orders. Or, you can contact one of our customer service representatives at [telephone number] and we will gladly handle your order request any time of day, any day of the year.

Questions?

Should you have any questions concerning the shipment of an order, please contact us. To verify the shipping status of your order, please see your order history.

These are unedited copies of the shipping options displayed on two top-tier click-and-mortar Web sites. Note the differences and consider how each might be made more concise.

Shipping Vagaries Affect Sales

While the cost of a product isn't always the determining factor for making an on-line purchase, it still is a consideration. A late 2000 study by NFO Interactive (www.nfoi.com), a market research firm, indicated that more than one-third of the surveyees stated that shipping fees affected their buying decision. These fees are often "a huge consideration" for the online customer, said Ann Green, vice president of e-commerce and retail at NFO. Often, two sites will offer the same product at the same price, and "the decision factor will really be the shipping fee itself," Green stated. That holds true for the author.

Whether the purchase is offline or online, customers do look at the "total" price when deciding to pull out the credit card. For instance, when the author found a product online that she wanted and that was priced competitively, she clicked the "buy" button and entered her shipping and billing information. But, although she noted that there was no sales tax, there was a shipping entry that had more than $30 displayed, so guess what, she abandoned that shopping cart as if it were on fire.

In an article that Julie Bort wrote for microtimes.com entitled, "Even With E-com's Gains, Caveat Emptor," she stated in a discussion about her online gift buying experience: "I found very few items that cost less than $35 plus shipping charges. Normally, I spend about $20 per gift. (Fine, call me cheap.) In most cases, I couldn't even determine what the total cost of my purchase would be, because the vendor wouldn't tally shipping costs until after I had entered my credit card information. Having to play this guessing game was an immediate turnoff, and I surfed away."

A report published by Shelley Taylor & Associates (www.infofarm.com), and titled "Return to Sender," concluded that the lack of personal contact with the online e-tailer means that the customer is very likely to start worrying about what might go wrong with their purchase (one of the symptoms of Post-Transaction Anxiety Disorder). The survey on which the report was based found that close to 40% of sites fail to provide shipping options (e.g., next day, 2nd day, standard, etc.).

The report also indicated that there were several points in the post-transaction process where an e-business has the opportunity to communicate with the customer. These include the sending of online receipts, e-mail confirmations, shipping confirmations and packing slips. Nonetheless, not even 50% informed the customer of the total charges that will be debited against their credit card and only 57% of the surveyed sites provide live online order tracking. Perhaps worse, the study noted that only 48% of items ordered by Shelley Taylor & Associates during the survey actually arrived when expected.

Numerous research reports published in 2000 pointed out that online shoppers aren't as unobservant as some e-tailers think. A Forrester Research study showed that more than 80% of the respondents stated that the cost of shipping was a factor in their decision to type in their credit card number. An Ernst & Young study of 3,900 online shoppers, revealed that more than half of the shoppers said high cost of shipping was a main concern when considering online purchases. Finally, a Bizrate report found that the most important drivers for repeat online sales were quality of customer service (65%), on-time delivery (58%), and shipping (49%), with price dragging in last at 19%.

Shipping Options

Many e-businesses try to approximate the offline shopping experience by offering same-day, next-day or nearly immediate shipping. It's obvious that online shoppers want immediate shipping — or as close to instant gratification as an e-business can get. Yet, at this point in time, you can't "beam" most products to the customer at time of payment — most customers have to wait. I say "most" because you can "beam" software, music, and text-based products.

E-tailers will not be able to sell the common everyday variety of merchandise if they can't get a handle on their shipping. Today, many online shoppers are penalized with higher shipping and handling costs for spending more money at the online store. It should actually be the reverse. Online shoppers should be rewarded for stuffing shopping carts to overflowing.

Shipping represents a serious issue. Even the research firms have begun tracking e-tail shipping practices. As stated previously, the research firm, Shelly Taylor & Associates released a report in mid-2000 that highlighted the shipping game that some e-tailers play with their customers. The Taylor report pointed out that many e-tail sites use "grab bag" shipping, i.e., you never know from one order to the next what the shipping charges will entail. Although the Taylor study didn't go so far as to address why many e-tail sites had unfathomable pricing methods for delivery of their products, it may be that some use shipping to supplement their gross profits.

The study did point out that lesser-priced items are hardest hit by high shipping charges. For example, a $12 item Taylor researchers ordered from the MarthaStewart.com cost $18.90 to ship, leaving the hapless customer's final credit card charge of $31.89. Or take the author's recent online experience. I bought three items from the struggling eToys.com, totaling $25.38 and my shipping (ground USPS) was $9.40. None of the items were large (a book, a video and a toy bank). It was Christmas so I swallowed hard and typed in my credit card number. Just as appalling are the figures, which indicated that of online stores who charge for shipping, the average charge added up to a whopping 37% of the total cost of the order in the US and 20% in the UK.

As Mark Hawkins, vice president of marketing for SmartShip.com, stated: "E-tailers have a pretty big job. They go through the pain of finding and buying merchandise to sell. In some cases, they spend hundreds of thousands of dollars developing their Web sites using the latest technology. Yet, while they are busy investing in the finest technologies, many of them forget to employ the basics of sound retailing." He hit the nail right on the head — what really counts is the total figure that will show up on the customer's next credit card statement.

Matrix-type Option

Based on market research carried out in late 1999, many e-tailers decided to adopt a matrix-type shipping option where the scale of shipping charges is tied to the value of an order, said Lee Pritchard, vice president, operations, Harrods Online. "That's something that customers understand," he adds. For good examples of the matrix option see the graphic on page 189.

It can also be based on the volume of orders — you order 10 CDs and you get next-day shipping for the cost of ground shipment. Or perhaps if you order two of the daily special and your total shopping cart value is over $100, you get free ground shipping or discounted next-day shipping. You can even offer free next-day shipping in certain situations — just be sure the shipping charge that you decide to "eat" doesn't bring you a loss on that sale.

With this option, you can play in the "who ships the fastest" game but still protect your profit margin. For although the delivery schedule may not be as tight as for the online grocer, many online customers expect quick deliveries. Consequently, e-tailers are using next-day or even same-day services as a way to differentiate themselves in what has become a crowded market. For example, BarnesandNoble.com offers same-day delivery in specific markets, such as New York City, but only when a product has displayed beneath the title "In Stock: 24 hours (Same Day)."

Tier Option

With tiered delivery fees customers can choose between low-cost, and relatively slow service, or higher-cost and fast delivery. This is nothing new; a charging structure based on speed of delivery is old hat in the B2B community. And as Scott Rosenberger, managing director for transportation, KPMG Consulting points out, customers may not want nor need to receive the goods they order online within a very narrow time frame.

An e-business can offer its customers a tier shipment option and also play the "more you spend the less the shipping costs" game. However, if you build the cost of shipping into the shopping cart total price equation, it can reflect negatively when price comparison is facilitated online.

Shipping Prices
We've changed the way we calculate shipping rates to save you money. Since carriers charge us for the total weight of your order, we've created a tiered, per pound system to share the savings with you.

Shipping Method	Per Shipment	Per Pound	
Standard	$2.99	0-9.99 pounds	= $.65 per pound
		10-19.99 pounds	= $.60 per pound
		20-34.99 pounds	= $.55 per pound
		35-49.99 pounds	= $.50 per pound
		50 pounds and up	= $.45 per pound
Premium*	$6.99	0-9.99 pounds	= $1.99 per pound
		10-19.99 pounds	= $1.89 per pound
		20 pounds and up	= $1.79 per pound
Express*	$8.99	0-19.99 pounds	= $2.79 per pound
		20 pounds and up	= $2.59 per pound

*Not available for P.O. Boxes, APO/FPO, HI, AK, USVI, PR, and Guam

- We calculate our rates per shipment, based on total weight.
- The more your shipment weighs, the less you pay per pound.
- If you're shipping to more than one address, we'll charge you the base and per pound rate for each separate shipment.
- We calculate shipping cost this way: Base Price + (Total Weight x Price Per Pound) = Total
- We add a shipping surcharge to a few items because of their large size. You'll find surcharge information included in the product description.

This is an exact replica of KBkids.com's "Shipping Prices" as it was displayed at the end of 2000. It's a good example of the tier shopping option.

Free Shipping Option

Most e-tailers know they have a problem when it comes to implementing the correct shipping option for their products. Many, rather than dealing with the issue head-on, decided to offer free shipping as an incentive to purchase products. Forrester surveys indicate that e-tailers who offer free shipping to bring in the crowds could face problems, if and when they change their policy (and they will, for they must) because online shoppers take shipping very seriously — cost-wise and time-wise.

Staples.com and its other e-business subsidiaries seem to be using the free delivery option effectively (a 500+% growth rate). One of its online customers gives a sampling of why many e-tailers opt for the free shipping option. Chris Gwynn is president of FridgeDoor.com, a small firm in Quincy, Mass. that sells refrigerator magnets. It processes orders daily and can't afford to run out of supplies such as printer toner or copy paper. "It takes an hour to drive to the nearest Staples outlet. But if I use the Web site, Staples delivers the next morning <u>for free</u>," Gwynn said.

Cyberian Outpost (<u>www.outpost.com</u>), which specializes in computer and electronic goods, offers free overnight shipping. Cyberian Outpost's CEO, Darryl Peck, explains that although his e-business cuts shipping costs it also has its warehouse next to Airborne Express which ameliorates the effect that free shipping might have on its profit margin. Peck understands that many online customers are often put off when they click the buy button only to discover near the end of the purchase that they have to pay for shipping. He remarked, "We really felt it was important to help the customer cut through the clutter."

Scott Rosenberger, KPMG Consulting, says, "On top there are marketing costs for customer acquisition which can be real high." In such a climate, offering free delivery is risky. "All in the name of building density to justify expansion," as Rosenberger puts it, describing the free-delivery model as "ground zero" in the evolution of this market. He goes on to state, "It's questionable as to whether this is a good model."

In the end, free shipping is a lose-lose situation in most cases. It raises the product cost or the e-tailer is shipping 60% of its orders at a loss. I didn't pull that figure out of my hat — Forrester Research (they are everywhere) did a study of online merchants, which indicated that 60% lose money on each shipment and 75% can't calculate the total delivery cost of a given shipment until after they get the bill (Wow!).

The exception may be to use free shipping as an incentive for customers to place an order above a certain dollar level. Catalog firms have been doing this for years — find some of the many Victoria Secret catalogs that are littering most households — one or more will have "free shipping" or "free next day shipping" for orders over $100 or $150 dollars. It's one way in which retailers can breed customer loyalty.

<u>Customer Pick-Up Option</u>: Another type of "free" shipping is to let the customer do the work. Some e-tailers, such as Payless Shoes, Toys 'R Us and fxsalon.com (to name a few) are offering this option with their "bricks" counterparts. For example, as soon as the online transaction is complete, a click-and-mortar's customer can avoid shipping charges and pick up the product at the counterpart's local retail store. This model is discussed also in Chapter 4, in the section entitled "Let the Customer Do the Walking" and in Chapter 7, in the section entitled "Local Fulfillment."

Amazon used the free shipping incentive during the 2000 holiday season. *Graphic courtesy of Amazon.com*

A Practical E-tail Shipping Option

Offering accurate shipping information to the customer at the time of check-out isn't that difficult. Just ask SmartShip.com's vice president of online marketing, Mark Hawkins. He says that there are three information elements to the process:

1. Fulfillment center zip code
2. Deliver zip code
3. Properties (weight, dim weight) of the SKU

Once an e-business has these three elements in hand, it can link them with a multi-carrier service like SmartShip.com, thus allowing the e-business to give its customer full disclosure at the point of purchase. This includes shipping options, the actual shipping rates between the two zip codes, one-on-one communication as to when the customer will receive the purchase, and how much the shipping will cost — all displayed during the shopping and the checkout process.

Another service an e-business could go to for shipping help is iship.com. It offers a template that allows an e-business to find the best options for shipping a package based on delivery times, weight and destination, with a comparison of UPS, FedEx, Airborne, and the US Postal Service. Just fill out the online form with the appropriate information — shipment dimensions, postal codes and loss-protection options. It even has a place for an e-business to add handling charges (if any). It also offers an integration tool that will allow a Web-based business to provide the service directly on its Web pages as a convenience for its customers.

A more sophisticated alternative is InterShipper.net. This site also provides comparison of rates among multiple carriers (domestic and international). But it goes further with tracking, drop-off locations, pickup scheduling, zip code lookups, along with an integration tool so an e-business can provide the service to its customers

According to Hawkins, if you adopt the shipping model he outlines and use the technology already in place in most e-tail back-ends, you could cut the shipping cost charged per customer by almost 50%. As a result of the freedom offered by a practical shipping model, customer expectations are met while profits are preserved. And isn't that what the wonderful World Wide Web is all about?

Shipping Dilemmas

Drop shipping: With drop-shipping, multiple manufacturers and distributors own and hold the inventory for the e-business. Once an order is received that involves multiple fulfillers, a shared shipping carrier (like USPS) can be used to ship the order. If a single fulfiller is involved, then the site queries the fulfiller in real-time for up-to-date delivery options and provides the same to the customer. When there are multiple fulfillers, managing trouble-free shipping with this option is very complicated. One issue that must be dealt with is multiple ship-to addresses for the same order. For example, say I order a HoKu CD for my adopted niece, a computer game for my boyfriend, the "Star Wars Trilogy" for the son of a friend, "Spellbound" in DVD format for my best friend, and I want the latest science fiction book for myself — how does the e-business ensure that each order goes to the right address and that I am notified when each is delivered?

Or perhaps I place three distinctly different products in one shopping cart requiring three different fulfillers, and I still want to get a single package within a few days — not an installment of packages and the inconvenience that involves. Unconsolidated shipping weakens the customer experience, providing a good reason for them to go elsewhere.

Turning again to the author's previously-mentioned order she placed with eToys.com — the order was split into what was to eventually be two orders although I guess I'm lucky it wasn't three orders since I ordered three separate items. I must admit eToys.com did initially keep me informed all along the way. After the initial acknowledgement e-mail, I received an e-mail stating in part: "As promised, here's an update on the shipping status of your order. You'll see that we've split your order into more than one shipment. We've done this to ensure that you receive your items as quickly as possible. Read below for more details. Of course, if you have any questions, please let us know by replying to this message. — eToys Customer Service Order Team." One last note: I only received two of the three items ordered prior to Christmas Day — but not before coming down with a case of PTAD.

Shipping from Multiple Fulfillment Sites: Macys.com is shipping product out of five sites, including two stores. Kent Anderson, president of Macys.com, stated that the store-based fulfillment is staffed through a dedicated macys.com team, not store employees. According to Anderson, the store-based approach is the best way to source fast-moving fashion merchandise, including apparel and accessories. Basic merchandise with more predictable sales patterns is being shipped from traditional warehouses. "We think using stores for fashion fulfillment gives us the ability to provide the freshest fashionable merchandise, which is a competitive advantage," he said.

Macys.com pays the price for using multiple fulfillment sites. Online orders average three items and, if those products are found in two or three different fulfillment sites, Macy.com pays the extra shipping, not the customer — at least that's what Anderson vows. The macy.com shipping policy Web page is also explicit on this point: "Since the merchandise you order may be filled from several locations, items may arrive separately. You will not incur additional shipping charges under these circumstances."

Anderson did point to research, which shows that many customers prefer to shop online, even when the added cost of shipping and the lack of promotional pricing is factored in. "The tradeoff on the Internet is the additional cost of shipping and not being able to physically see the merchandise, but you have the convenience of being able to shop in your bathrobe at 2 o'clock in the morning," remarks Anderson.

How did macys.com, toysrus.com, and cdnow.com — three of the companies fined by the FTC for failing to deliver last year — respond to their shipping dilemma? Rather than making radical changes in their procedures, these three e-businesses decided to exercise caution about what they promise. None are offering a shipping schedule that even comes close to the instant gratification of making a purchase at a bricks-and-mortar store, and all three are charging fees that would choke a horse.

Macy's states that customers should generally expect standard delivery to take 7-10 days after the customer's order leaves the macys.com fulfillment center (which, if you remember, macys.com advises may happen up to 7 business days after placement of the order). At the end of 2000, macys.com's shipping charge for ground shipment started at $8.00, second-day air costs were at least $14, and shipment by next-day air ran a minimum of $18.00.

As of December 2000, CDNow.com's "Shipping Charges and Information" Web page (located when you click the "Help" tab on the home page) provided uninformative and confusing information although it goes on for five pages. However, unlike macys.com, CDNow.com is not willing to "eat" shipping charges due to its fractured shipping methods. It clearly states in its shipping information that "CDNOW fills orders from many different locations. Therefore, various items, even items from the same product line, may not ship from the same shipping center.

Please, be aware that when you combine orders that include items shipping from different centers, you will incur some additional shipping charges. However, your total shipping charge will be less than if you placed your orders separately."

CDNow goes on to tell its US customers that "shipping and handling charges to destinations within the U.S. are determined by the quantity and type of merchandise ordered and the shipping method(s) you choose." Its shipping costs are so complex that I won't even go into them — the reader can check out the page.

As further indication that CDNow's LFMS isn't state of the art: "Due to occasional backorders at our distribution centers, product shown as 'in-stock' at CDNow may become backordered. If this occurs, your order will ship when the product is re-stocked at our distribution centers." No mention of when, how or even if the e-tailer notifies its disappointed customer that an item has been backordered.

I've discussed the shipping policies of macys.com and CDNow.com to show the reader how difficult it is to institute a fair, reasonable and accurate shipping system. Macy's is one of the largest department retailers in the US and CDNow.com is one of the most popular pure-play e-tailers today, and they're wrestling with their LFMS just as many of the readers are in their e-business. Learn from their mistakes.

The number one e-tailer, according to many analysts, is Amazon. The company has made a Herculean effort to clarify its shipping policy. I'll let the reader be the judge of whether its method works.

Custom Shipping Structure

Dr. Steve Banker, director of supply chain solutions at consultants ARC Advisory Group (www.arcweb.com), expects a new service structure to emerge that takes into account the physical constraints associated with delivering goods in urban areas. "Not just same-day, but one that depends on the time of day," he said. For example, consumers could pay a premium for deliveries made during rush-hour periods.

Also important is that e-tailers need to be realistic when it comes to incorporating delivery costs into the overall cost of the products they sell

Refer to the chart below to get it there on time!

December	Shipping Rates	Visit Gifts to find items with 24-hour availability
	All ordering deadlines are 11:59 p.m. Pacific standard time, for delivery by December 23.	

December	For continental U.S. orders only: (Click here for international shipments)
14	Last day to order items that say "Usually ships in 24 hours" using Standard Shipping.
15	Last day to order items that say "Usually ships in 5 business days" using 2nd Day Air. Last day to order a paper gift certificate.
16	Last day to order: • items that say "Usually ships in 2-3 days" using 2nd Day Air. • items that say "Usually ships in 5 business days" using Next Day Air.
17	Last day to order items that say "Usually ships in 2-3 days" using Next Day Air.
19	Last day to order items that say "Usually ships in 24 hours" using 2nd Day Air.
20	Last day to order items that say "Usually ships in 24 hours" using Next Day Air.
21	First night of Hanukkah Last day to order items that say "Usually ships in 24 hours" using Holiday Saturday Delivery.
22	There's still time to send an e-mail gift certificate with an e-card.
23	Last day to order items that say "Usually ships in 24 hours" using Holiday Christmas Delivery. To see if your order qualifies, please enter the recipient's ZIP code here: [ ] Submit
24	Christmas Eve Orders placed today will arrive after Christmas, but there's still time to send an e-mail gift certificate with an e-card.
25	Merry Christmas! Best holiday wishes from all of us at Amazon.com! You can still send an e-mail gift certificate with an e-card.

For gifts sent to international addresses:
The last day to order products is Monday, December 11.
(Last day to order products for shipment to Canada is Saturday, December 16.)
• Item's detail page must say "Usually ships in 24 hours."
• Items must be shipped via international priority shipping.

You can also order directly from our international sites: amazon.co.uk, amazon.de, amazon.fr, or amazon.co.jp.

Amazon.com 2000 holiday shipping policy.

online, he said. "If they want to differentiate themselves by offering same-day service, they need to charge a premium for that. Otherwise they will not survive," he said.

"We advocate establishing profitability benchmarks up front so they are not throwing money away," said KPMG's Rosenberger. But calculating the tradeoff between pandering to the customers' taste for convenience and the incremental costs involved is more complicated at a time when there is a tight labor market and high fuel costs.

Ravi Kalakota, CEO and chairman of the online hospitality supply industry marketplace h.supply.com, thinks an even more specialized subset of the logistics market is emerging. According to Kalakota it's, "What you might call local 3PLs — people who take a geographic market like a city, interface it with a web and deliver within a 50-mile radius." This is a growth market, he said, that requires special skills such as an intimate knowledge of the traffic patterns in localized areas. "There is a huge opportunity for players to step in who are what I call localized 3PLs," speculates Kalakota.

Who these players are has yet to be determined. Rosenberger points out that there are thousands of local delivery firms, but relatively few with the technological capacity to be part of a sophisticated, Web-based supply chain. "This is the most significant impediment to their growth," he said. However, the majority of established 3PLs haven't decided whether investing in local delivery infrastructure is cost effective. "Where are the niches profitable enough for these people to play in?" asked Rosenberger.

"LAST MILE" SOLUTIONS

Shipping may become easier to answer as e-marketplaces offering transportation services come online. Once it becomes easier to sell local delivery services over the Internet, the market may attract more big-name players. This also will open more options for e-businesses, allowing them an easy way to make shipping choices outside the norm, i.e., UPS, FedEx, Airborne and the US Postal Service, when trying to get the products to their customers, in a quick, efficient, cost-effective manner.

Another sign that the shipping market is beginning to adopt an e-business model itself is the growth of support services. For example, Traffic.com provides real-time traffic and logistics information on highways, airports and ports. It offers proprietary features such as the actual travel times between two points in a city and comparisons to historical conditions to quantify delays for routing.

By the time this book hits the store shelves, Traffic.com should have its service deployed in at least 15 markets according to spokesman Jim Smith. He goes on to state that Traffic.com's data center is updated at intervals of less than one minute. "We will cover fleet optimization and 'last mile' solutions," Smith said. He would not divulge the names of the carriers involved, "but the plan is to cover the economics and systems of a regional carrier and a large, technically sophisticated carrier," he said.

Such developments will help to create "last mile" delivery solutions that are more attuned to the e-business market, ARC Advisory Group's Banker believes. He explains that the traditional approach to routing is to put together schedules a few days or a week in advance. "That doesn't work too well with e-fulfillment where you want next-day delivery," he said. Dynamic routing is needed, so those operators can recreate routes as conditions change. "The market potential is there," advised Rosenberger. The e-business community just needs to seek out the carriers with the knowledge and wherewithal to determine the value of incentives, such as a high-speed delivery service in relation to the profitability of the customers that the same would attract. If it's determined dynamic delivery has merit, then carriers need to follow through with the implementation of the technology necessary to make the service happen. Of course, the carrier offering next-day services at reduced prices because of dynamic routing technology must ensure that having made the promise, it can deliver the service.

COST OF SHIPPING

E-businesses are presented with so many shipping options that the best choice is not always clear. For the e-tailer, selecting the right shipping option has always been like navigating a maze. Yet large e-tail sites with high volume can almost always negotiate a flat-rate fee for each item shipped, giving them an edge over the smaller e-tail sites. The click-and-mortars might be able to ride on the shirttail of their counterpart and negotiate an overall discounted fee schedule for the multi-channel shipping needs of the entire enterprise. Once shipping volume is taken out of the equation, the bottom line is that rates are determined by three major factors: delivery distance, package weight and delivery times.

If an online customer in Portland, Oregon buys a couple of books from XYZBooks.com, and another customer in Portland, Maine buys the same two books from XYZBooks.com and each book is actually shipped from a New York-based publisher, should the shipping costs be the same for each customer? That is the quandary that most e-businesses are grappling with in their search for shipping equality for all. Add to that the reality that e-businesses, in general, are subject to the complex, shifting rates determined by the various carriers in the e-business-shipment marketplace, and an e-business quickly learns that it mustn't fall into the trap of trying to model its shipping costs to the penny. Most e-commerce systems, except perhaps some custom-built solutions, simply aren't equipped to calculate the exact cost of picking, packing and shipping. And few e-businesses would benefit from modeling shipments to that level of detail. Keep it simple, and focus on making shipping costs reasonable and predictable.

As part of the purchasing process, online customers should be able to select a shipping method and see exactly what they'll pay before the order is processed. To do this, an e-business should integrate with application programming interfaces (APIs) from the shipping companies, which compute approximate shipping costs. If you have multiple shipping methods, make sure your system can compute and show the costs of each at the time the method is chosen. This gives the online customer more choices and creates a sense of comfort level that is conducive to repeat visits.

Always have a Web page that sets out clear, reasonable, and fair shipping choices and policies. If your e-business offers overnight service, clarify the time by which orders must be received for same-day shipping, and whether orders received on weekends and holidays are shipped immediately or on the next business day.

Many e-businesses who are still operating in the red place part of the blame on their pricing strategy for shipping — either charging standard fees for packages regardless of size or weight or not charging for shipping at all. Forrester's report entitled "Mastering Commerce Logistics," based on interviews with 40 logistics officials at manufacturing, retail and Internet companies, included some telling quotes:

"We lose money on most of our orders. We charge a flat rate per order that is less than

Shipping Options Gap Online ships to all fifty United States and the following U.S. territories; American Samoa, Guam, Marianas Islands, Puerto Rico, and the U.S. Virgin Islands. Normal standard shipping costs apply to orders to U.S. territories. Overnight delivery is not available to U.S. territories.

We do not ship or bill orders internationally. If you are outside of the United States or its territories, please use our Store Locator to find the store nearest you.

Gap Online ships via the United States Postal Service or Federal Express (either standard or overnight delivery) as you specify. Deliveries are made only Monday through Friday (holidays excluded).

Standard Delivery

Standard shipments via USPS or FedEx economy service should arrive within 7 business days. Shipments to U.S. territories are delivered via USPS only.

The cost depends on the total amount of the order:

purchase total	shipping & handling fee
$0 - $50	$5.00
$50.01 - $100	$7.00
$100.01 - $175	$9.00
$175.01 and over	$11.00

Overnight Delivery

Federal Express handles all Gap Online overnight deliveries. Overnight orders ship the same business day, pending order verification, if received by 12 noon EST. Overnight deliveries cost the same as standard delivery plus an additional $9.00. Overnight delivery is not available for shipping to U.S. territories.

Gap.com has a clear, concise shipping policy.

the average cost to fulfill the order. We want to make a little money or at least break even by 2001. We will do this by getting rid of our flat rate — what we will move to is yet to be determined" (click-and-mortar e-tailer).

"We absorb 100% of the costs of our shipments. As the manufacturer, we don't mind paying the $4 shipping fee to make a $45 sale. We make sure customers can shop at our online store at the same price as our retail stores. So if they can walk into a department store and buy an item for $50, that is how much we'll charge them online — delivered. We have to deal with the fact that online sales may not be quite as profitable as store sales" (catalog e-tailer).

"We lose money on a per-order basis because we charge the consumer less for the shipping than we pay. It's amplified even more if a customer orders three products from three different suppliers because we ship in three different boxes — one from each supplier — and lose money three times over. In the future, we'll try to reduce charges, but for now we're just trying to build momentum" (pure-play e-tailer).

The Entrepreneur to the Rescue

Enter GoShip.com, a new startup that has developed a tailor-made software system that it says can provide shipping rates and services from different carriers and be integrated into an e-business's back-end within 24 hours. GoShip.com touts that it's the first application service provider to offer e-businesses and their customers flexible, real-time choice in shipping solutions.

GoShip.com lets the customer complete a purchase and then choose (from a pop-up window) a matrix of carrier services — including delivery times and costs for selection. After the selection is made, the shipping cost is added to the merchandise total for customer acceptance. GoShip.com then gets a percentage of the transaction.

GoShip.com has entered into agreements with e-commerce service providers such as InterShop. A spokesperson

GoShip Store - Whole Order Demo - Microsoft Internet Explorer

Step 4. Choose Carrier and Services

(a) If you wish to change the destination of this order, please input the new ZIP code *first*.
   -Once entered, please click the "Update" button.
   -This will display a new set of Carrier/Services based on the new destination selection.
(b) Select a Carrier/Service by clicking on the "Select" button.
   -The Service Levels are displayed and show approximate delivery time.
   -The Rates are also displayed to show the differences in shipping cost.
(c) When complete, click the "Select" button at the bottom of the page.

Destination for this shipment from: 92612
US: 10028   Update

Choose shipping carrier/service

Select	Group	Carrier/Service Name	Service Level	Rate
	Least Cost	UPS Ground Residential	6th day by 6 PM	$39.03
	3 Day Del.	UPS 3 Day Select Commercial	3rd day by 6 PM	$89.10
		Fedex Express Saver	3rd day by 4:30 PM	$110.98
	2 Day Del.	UPS 2nd Day Air	2nd day by 6 PM	$127.56
		ABX Second Day	2nd day by 6 PM	$84.00
	Next Day	Fedex Priority Overnight	Next day by 10:30 AM	$177.42
		DHL Express	Next day by 10:30 AM	$150.17

Select

advises that GoShip.com serves more than 100,000 e-businesses, including Compaq and Sony. The company is also working with e-businesses who ship from multiple locations to set up "real/virtual" warehouses so, says Neal Anstadt, GoShip.com's CEO, "The customer gets the local shipping prices based on regional costs no matter where the product is coming from." The reader should visit GoShip.com and, while there, download their white papers — every e-business will find them useful.

Also take a look at the sophisticated iLink Global (www.ilinkglobal.com) that can as easily serve the B2B as the e-tail sector. It's a carrier-neutral, global e-business shipping and logistics service provider. iLink Global has a broad network of carrier alliances and a state-of-the-art back-end sporting systems that allow it to provide 100% door-to-door eLogistics services and technology to the growing e-business community. iLink Global plainly states it can "enable the seamless delivery of any product to any customer, anywhere in the world. According to iLink Global "by integrating our state-of-the-art rate engine, logistics software, and Web-centric tracking system" into an e-business's Web site, "we can help [e-businesses] turn their shipping challenge into a competitive advantage."

The reader MUST check out their CanTRACK "commercial" not only for the entertainment value but also for the solution the product offers to the e-business community.

Look also into the services of AnythingOvernight.com (AO). It bills itself as the "Shipping Information Technology Company" and is a Web-based service provider (read ASP) that consolidates all parcel and freight activity and data onto

To give the reader a taste of what iLink Global and CanTRACK offer.

one platform. AO provides shipping information solutions including innovative data importing, management reporting of all product fulfillment activity and costs, online pricing, shipment initiation, package tracking and other value-added support to e-businesses. This technology may be accessed via the Web site at www.anythingovernight.com, or through an application programming interface (API).

With AO in their corner, e-businesses can simplify, economize and fulfill their needs for shipping and receiving anything, both domestically and internationally. AO has entered into a partnership with TNT, one of the world's top four providers of global express distribution services. This allows e-business customers to use TNT for international express shipping through AO. "It's a natural fit," said Mark Gunton, President of TNT International Express, North America. "This is a major step in our continuing effort to provide the most efficient, accessible and advanced international shipping functionality to our clientele, online and off. Our partnership with AO promotes the alliance between unmatched technology and our global reach."

Mark Edwards, AnythingOvernight.com President and COO, added, "TNT's first class international service is a crucial piece of the total business and e-commerce solution that AnythingOvernight.com offers." Take the example of a TNT customer who clicks on the TNT logo and accesses TNT's comprehensive range of express services for international shipping. After specifying the packages dimension, time constraints, and destination, the TNT customer can view pre-negotiated rates, print shipping labels, schedule a pick-up, track packages, and notify the recipients. In addition, customers can generate real-time reports on historical TNT shipping activity and costs.

Dana Commercial Credit (DCC), operates some 320 major facilities in 33 countries and employs more than 82,000 people. After evaluating AO's suite of services, it chose AO's ASP technology to unify and streamline the shipping and information technology components within the DCC network.

"We feel that AnythingOvernight.com's ASP technology is easy to use, provides us with vast reporting functionality, and helps us control costs," said Calvin Axtell, senior vice president of DCC. "The benefits of uniting our DCC offices via AnythingOvernight.com's shipping services and information technology are endless."

TECHNOLOGY

Two constantly recurring little questions, "Where is my order now?" and "When can I have it?," have transformed supply chain management (SCM). If an order is placed, customers want to be 100% sure that the e-business can guarantee delivery. The problem in answering such questions arises when the front-end system is not properly integrated with the back-end system, creating an information disconnect between the online customer and the e-business. Enter companies like Optum (www.optum.com) that can track products across the Internet, in real-time including knowing where the products should be shipped from for the best delivery time and lowest cost.

A company that has put technology in the forefront to enable e-business shipment is the Internet logistics company, ShipChem.com, formed by Eastman Chemicals and Global Logistics Technologies (a.k.a. G-Log) in February 2000. ShipChem was born out of the need to handle logistics and distribution for the chemicals and plastics industries, according to P.J. White, vice president of sales and marketing for the company.

And, who was its first customer? Eastman Chemicals, naturally. White further states that around the spring of 2001, ShipChem will make its offering to all businesses through an all-Internet-based product "with no fancy IT integration." White also makes it clear that ShipChem is not building an e-markeplace. "We are strictly logistics," she says. However, ShipChem will provide rating and routing, tracking, tracing and documentation for global transactions.

ShipChem isn't doing all of this alone; it has formed and is forming multiple partnerships while implementing a variety of software solutions. For instance, G-Log (www.glog.com) is the engine behind ShipChem. Then there is NextLinx Corp. (www.nextlinx.com), an international trade logistics company that will provide global documentation to get product in and out of different countries. Worldwide Testing will handle testing documents. ShipChem has also brought on board EDS (www.eds.com) to provide technical support and BDP (www.bdpinternational.com) to provide logistics, such as freight forwarding, customs house brokerage, warehousing and distribution.

Of course, such behind-the-scenes action fits perfectly into G-Log's strategy — using their technology to power Internet logistics companies and marketplaces. Mitch Weseley, founder and CEO of G-Log, told *Traffic World Magazine* (www.trafficworld.com) in late 2000 that he plans to make G-Log the answer across all modes of transportation around the globe. "Initially, our clients are American, Canadian and European. But they are shipping freight all over the world," he said. Routing, tracking and tracing, tendering payment, estimating arrival times, paying bills, handling claims — all of this will be handled by G-Log. "It's soup to nuts," he said.

How does G-Log plan to accomplish such a grandiose plan? G-Log will work behind the scenes allowing e-businesses to utilize G-Log as a seamless part of their Web site, according to Jane Biddle, a spokesperson for G-Log. "Very few people use our front-end," added Weseley.

Companies using G-Log technology include Logistics Gateway, an Internet-based freight forwarder fulfillment service for small and midsize companies (www.loggate.com); SupplyLinks (www.supplylinks.com), an Internet-based supply chain network for the high-tech, aerospace, heavy equipment, pharmaceutical and health care fields; and the previously mentioned Consolidated Commerce (www.consolidatedcommerce.com), a software technology company.

Not only do these companies use G-Log technology; they are a key part of G-Log's strategy, Weseley told *Traffic World Magazine*. Many B2Bs have trouble understanding transportation. "We go after the B2B market with a partner like SupplyLinks. SupplyLinks negotiates the rates (with carriers) and gives [the e-business] a fully loaded system they can use," Weseley said. "Around 80 percent of the B2Bs we call on, we bring a partner [SupplyLink is a good example]. They [the e-businesses] are not sophisticated enough — they need one of those intermediaries," to help in the transportation area.

Freight Tools LLC (www.ltlrates.com) has announced software that enables e-businesses to compare rates, transit times and delivery points for up to six less-than-truckload carriers over the Internet. "The software is a specialized Web browser that retrieves specific information on carrier Web sites. In most cases all six answers are returned in less than 60 seconds and often faster," said the spokesperson. The software can be downloaded at www.ltlrates.com.

Kewill.Net, a B2B site for small and midsize companies, announced its "suite of applications, Kewill.Trade, Kewill.Ship, Kewill.Trace, and Kewill. Receive, which enables e-businesses to view, transact, trace and control goods as they move through the supply chain." Readers can investigate further at the Web site, www.kewill.net.

Also take a look at the National Transportation Exchange's (www.nte.net) new version of its Internet trading exchange, NTEx 2.0, which has "full browser capabilities and trading functionality for both shippers and carriers. Shippers can communicate online and monitor freight movement through the Web. Carriers can define and change routes, capacities and price specifications at any time, according to a spokesperson.

And finally, check out UPS Logistics Group (www.upslogistics.com). It's advanced technology solutions utilizing Roadnet MobileCast systems provide routing and scheduling, dispatch, driver and delivery tracking, and driver support mobile computing. Online grocers such as Albertsons.com and GroceryWorks.com are Roadnet MobileCast users.

Handling the Exceptions

"Commerce sites must now focus on...preparing crisis plans for addressing issues that their company might face during an outage or product delivery problem," said David Schatsky, an analyst with Jupiter Communications (www.jup.com). Jupiter warns that many e-businesses will be unprepared for demand that is expected to increase 11-fold in the next four years.

Chris Guzik of TanData (www.tandata.com) agrees and says that TanData addresses the problem of shipping commitments, their irregularities and exceptions. TanData's business focus is on the e-business. Once an e-business has committed to getting an order to a customer by a certain time, it's the carrier's responsibility to see that it happens (at least once the carrier picks up the package).

Although Guzik recommends tight integration of the supply chain, warehouse, and fulfillment processes, he stresses that an e-business's shipping operations can really make a difference in satisfying the customer. TanData's ChainLink shipping software is designed to enable an e-business to meet its shipping commitment to the customer via customizable shipping options.

Service	Commitment	Arrival Date	Total Charge*	Messages
FedEx First Overnight	Next Day 8:00 AM	12/13/00	$66.56	Success
UPS Next Day Air Early A.M.	Next Day 8:30 AM	12/13/00	$62.27	Success
UPS Next Day Air	Next Day 10:30 AM	12/13/00	$36.96	Success
FedEx Priority Overnight	Next Day 10:30 AM	12/13/00	$40.56	Success
DHL USA Overnight	Next Day 12:00 Noon	12/13/00	$42.90	Success
UPS Next Day Air Saver	Next Day 3:00 PM	12/13/00	$32.40	Success
FedEx Standard Overnight	Next Day 4:30 PM	12/13/00	$34.06	Success
UPS 2nd Day Air A.M.	2nd Day 12:00 Noon	12/14/00	$18.12	Success
FedEx 2Day	2nd Day 5:00 PM	12/14/00	$17.58	Success
UPS 2nd Day Air	2nd Day	12/14/00	$16.30	Success
FedEx Express Saver	3 Days 4:30 PM	12/15/00	$16.07	Success
UPS 3 Day Select	3 Days	12/15/00	$10.23	Success

A sample of what a user might see using TanData's ChainLink shipping software.

For example, an e-business using just-in-time inventory management usually has its LFMS ironed out only to the point that products come into its warehouse from its suppliers when it expects them, allowing the e-business to get the product to its customers by the date it promised. However, many systems can't handle the exceptions and those failures are what can really damage an e-business's reputation.

Suppose the e-business told its customer that the product requested would get to the customer's premises within five days of its order. Now the e-business had made that promise based on the assumption that the ordered product would arrive in its warehouse from its supplier within two days after the customer ordered the product. The e-business would then turn around and immediately ship the product to the customer, but that's not the end of the story. The e-business chose the time frame and the shipping option based on what it would take to meet the five-day delivery commitment. So when the product comes from the supplier two days late (as sometimes happens with those pesky suppliers), there isn't a system in place to customize the shipping options; the e-business's LFMS isn't equipped to stray from that original three-day ground shipping decision.

Solutions such as TanData's ChainLink can give an e-business options at that critical point. It's specifically designed to let an e-business make late decisions/alterations by allowing it to override the original shipping choice (by selecting, say, an overnight courier service) to meet its original five-day delivery commitment to the customer.

ChainLink lets an e-business keep track of carrier rates so it can know what the options might be if and when the supply chain drops a stitch and runs behind schedule. In Guzik's estimation, few e-businesses have adopted such technology.

Here is a company that has big plans for the future. Although initially formed to sell postage over the Internet, Stamps.com currently provides one-click services to e-business users that will instantly allow them to compare shipping costs for online orders, while taking into account the weight, distance and priority of a shipment. It's managed to make quite a reputation for itself in a very short time. For example, Stamps.com was named one of the 200 most important B2B Web sites in 2000 by Forbes.com and was listed in *PC Magazine's* e-tailing category for one of the most helpful Web sites on the Internet in 2000.

Stamps.com acquired technology that allows it to merge carrier and rate information on a single screen and also enables instant orders using the selected carrier, including Airborne Express, FedEx, UPS, and the US Postal Service, as well as most small package and freight carriers. It's the one-stop service e-businesses are looking for, said one observer.

The iShip feature that Stamps.com offers allows users to centrally manage and control costs from mailing and shipping activities across multiple carriers and can be distributed to an unlimited number of corporate desktops using only a Web browser. Management can overlay the system with corporate shipping rules (like the limitations that an enterprise places on corporate travel). With Stamps.com's embedded services for corporate desktops, an e-business can limit access, build in special negotiated rates, add or drop carriers and make other changes. This allows an e-business shipping a package to look at all the options available, or limits its employees to only the options the e-business wants shown. The service can work on either the buy or sell side of a transaction.

Stamps.com is moving decisively into international trading environments. The company recently formed Stamps.com International Inc., a wholly owned subsidiary focused on markets in Europe and Asia.

Another one-click service is E-Stamp Corporation (www.estamp.com), a leading provider of secure Internet-based transactions, which provides Web-based shipping and logistics solutions. E-Stamp has phased out its Internet postage operation and "phased-in" e-Warehouse, a client/server software designed to run on Windows operating systems. According to Robert (Bo) Ewald, president and CEO of E-Stamp Corporation, its comprehensive multi-carrier shipping solution, DigitalShipper Enterprise, is fully compliant with virtually all of the major small package and freight carriers, making E-Stamp a driving force in the e-business shipping process. DigitalShipper Enterprise's variety of integration modes enables two-way communication and data exchange with an e-business's order management system, allowing the e-business to eliminate errors and repetitive data entry, and provide immediate shipping information enterprise-wide.

"Someone shipping a package within a company can look at all the options available, or only the ones the company wants you to see," remarked Rod Witmond, E-Stamp's vice president and general manager of shipping. The services can work on either the buy or sell side of a transaction. Customers of iPrint.com, an online print shop, can use E-Stamp's DigitalShipper.com to select transport options, commented Royal Farros, chairman and chief executive of iPrint.com. DigitalShipper is embedded into the iPrint.com Web site.

Neopost Inc. (www.neopost.com), a worldwide provider of logistics systems, also offers one click service through its iLS.X suite of products. iLS.X offers enterprise-wide shipping management, outbound logistics, tracking, and departmental budgeting solutions, thus allowing e-businesses of any size to combine various functionalities to create their own customized virtual shipping room internally and at a customer's place of business. "The Internet's ability to provide online access to daily transactions is rapidly changing today's business landscape," asserted Jean Weber, vice president of Neopost's Logistics Systems Division. To back up that statement, Neopost has entered into a strategic partnership with From2.com, an international logistics company, that allows Neopost to embed a link to From2.com's international rating module, the Global Delivered Cost Calculator, in its Neopost Logistics Systems software.

With the Global Delivered Cost Calculator in residence, Neopost Logistics Systems users can determine the best rate and methodology for international shipping based on variables such as destination, contents and required delivery time, and then choose from a variety of air, ground and ocean transportation options. By clicking on an icon, Neopost Logistics Systems users can establish in real-time the cost for international door-to-door transportation. An international shipper can also upload product information, which automatically assigns the international product codes necessary to determine duties, weights, and customs limitations. The Neopost customer then downloads the documentation necessary to meet trade compliances at international borders.

"We are delighted to provide added value to our logistics customers through this agreement with From2.com," said Jean Weber of Neopost. "As e-commerce portals and traditional businesses continue to offer their products across international borders, Neopost Logistic Systems, through this agreement, provides the best domestic and international shipping solutions to meet their needs."

E-BUSINESS'S CARRIER CHOICES

While the "last mile" of delivery is often quoted as being the hardest challenge, in residential delivery the last few feet to the door can actually be the most challenging piece of the puzzle. According to numerous surveys, today's online customers are an affluent and professional group. Many shop online because their lives are too busy to shop in retail stores, and thus are also unlikely to be willing to sit at home waiting for the delivery truck to arrive. The resulting narrow time interval for possible delivery serves to put the e-tail establishment in a vise.

United Parcel Service and the US Postal Service (USPS), with their unequaled infrastructure, currently dominate the package segment of the fragmented "last mile" market (delivery of individual orders into the hands of the customer). But they had better watch their backs — competitors are working hard to bring new value propositions to what Jean V. Murphy, writing for supplychainbrain.com, calls "the longest mile." Murphy further states that other providers are focusing on non-package home delivery, a segment being fueled by rising online purchases of furniture, large electronics and appliances.

Roadway Express Inc. is a transportation company that carries primarily less-than-truckload shipments, or shipments of less than 500 pounds for its more than 10,000 customers. My.roadway.com, Roadway Express' extranet, has allowed it to expand its customer list because it has been able to reach the smaller customers. This is an important consideration for the small business community, since traditional technologies such as electronic data interchange are too costly for the smaller busineses to implement, says Dave Pavlich, director of e-commerce technologies at Roadway Express. Customers can use My.roadway.com to check invoices and payment history, access shipping rates, and obtain proof of delivery and other shipping documents.

Courting the USPS

Airborne (www.airborne.com) made a radical move — it partnered with the US Postal Service (www.usps.com). Airborne uses the USPS's trucks and personnel to serve the final leg of its residential deliveries. Although Airborne wanted to stay active in the residential delivery arena, it no longer wanted to manage the residential business itself because it's not cost effective for its business model. Airborne's plan is to make its profits at the regional level and discount residential fares through USPS stamp subsidization.

Another USPS "partner" is SmartMail Services (www.smartmail.com), an emerging leader of expedited flat-sized mail and light parcel shipping services. It's using most of the $45 million received in a third round of fundraising to complete a national build out of its technology-driven distribution network and expand its light parcel shipping services to customers. A SmartMail spokesperson states that the e-business sector is significantly dependent on logistics as increasing numbers of people shop online and thus can benefit from the SmartMail delivery solution.

SmartMail provides an alternative to traditional mail and parcel delivery and offers significant discounts off USPS First Class and Priority rates for the large volume e-business. Through its innovative business model and workshare partnership with the USPS, the company retrieves, sorts and aggregates small parcels, expediting delivery and minimizing infrastructure costs for its customers. The company offers state-of-the-art tracking technology and serves the financial, manufacturing, retail and public sectors. The company has more than 400 customers including BarnesandNoble.com, CVS Pharmacy, Nissan, Gateway, CD Universe, Talbot's, Snapfish.com, Tower Records, TD Waterhouse, CitiStreet and Sony Electronics.

SmartMail and Airborne provide delivery and service savings through their efficient, national network of distribution centers and leveraging of the USPS's existing infrastructure for that final mile delivery.

And there are more carriers introducing business models that leverage the existing infrastructure of the USPS — GATX Logistics launched its Paxis unit (www.paxis.net) that collects and aggregates parcels for delivery to the USPS, which makes the final residential delivery. Although delivery time is about a day slower than UPS, according to Tom Scanlin of GATX Logistics, the cost is less. Paxis currently has a number of facilities around the US where an e-business can truck their packages. They are then broken down and sorted for drop-off at various postal facilities in the region.

"I think people ordering products on the Web are initially going to expect a pretty quick service time, perhaps two to three days," says Scanlin. "On the other hand, once dotcom companies are forced to actually make money, they will look for ways to save on delivery and I think that is where a service like Paxis comes in, because it can provide dependable delivery at a much lower cost."

Emery Worldwide Global Logistics (www.emeryworld.com) also wants on the USPS bandwagon. It's studiously searching for ways to leverage its existing relationship with the postal service. "If you look at the postal service in North America, who else goes to every residential and every business address?" Don Cox, Emery's managing director asked. According to Cox, Emery is also exploring the possibility of picking up packages from manufacturers or other businesses and using a hub to sort and consolidate them before handing off to the postal service.

Forrester had a comment on this little bit of partnering (doesn't it always) and states that it thinks this will work for a few carriers, but overloading the USPS's existing network could dampen the Internet experience and threaten further online opportunities.

However, the USPS isn't counting on partnerships being the "only game in town" for it in the e-business delivery stratosphere. It's spending millions of dollars to advertise its Priority Mail two- and three-day delivery service, betting that few people are willing to pay more simply to get an item overnight.

The USPS is also testing tiny radio transmitter tags — RFIDs — inserted on test envelopes that are then sent through the regular mail system. In the future, it hopes to be able to track Priority, Express and other high-value packages throughout its mail-flow system through the use of this technology. Sensors in 250 post offices and processing centers listen for identifying signals from the tagged envelopes and distribute data about the tags' whereabouts; then information on service bottlenecks is fed into the USPS' intranet system. "This technology allows us to see flow problems that have been invisible up until now," said project manager Glenn McDonald.

UPS and FedEx

Of course, any conversation about shipping requires the inclusion of the venerable UPS (www.ups.com) and FedEx (www.fedex.com) — the giants in the residential delivery sector. "Electronic commerce is empowering buyers like never before. UPS OnLine Tools support this trend by giving businesses and consumers product and shipping information where, when and how they need it, ultimately turning customer support and internal purchasing costs from dollars to dimes," said Dale Hayes, vice president of electronic commerce marketing for UPS.

UPS OnLine Tools Package:

- Enables the e-business and its customers to track packages using their own internally generated reference number (e.g., a P.O. number).

- Enables users to view Published Rate & Service Selection

- Enables an e-business's customers to compare UPS published rates for different levels of UPS service.

- Enables e-businesses to customize their rate tables to include a handling charge, to allow the buyer to compare total shipping and handling charges.

- Catches discrepancies in city-state-zip code combinations and thus helps e-businesses to improve customer service and reduce costs by ensuring that shipping addresses are correct at the point of order entry, before the order has left the shipping dock.

- Provides the time-in-transit in business days for UPS ground shipments between any two postal codes within the continental U.S.

- Generates a color-coded map displaying UPS ground transit time for any origin zip code within the continental U.S. Service. This feature is intended to be especially useful for just-in-time inventory planning.

- Enables e-businesses that use a non-UPS OnLine compatible shipping system to upload shipment manifest information to the UPS mainframe, which is required for reference number package tracking. This enables UPS e-businesses to designate their own tracking number, such as a purchase order or invoice number, to shipments.

Federal Express, which was a step or two behind its archrival UPS in the home delivery market, is gaining ground. In March 2000, FedEx began using its RPS network, renamed FedEx Ground, to provide a new residential service, FedEx Home Delivery, in its major US markets. This delivery-only service is dedicated to the needs of e-tailers. The company says the new service provides customized delivery options, including delivery by appointment day or evening, with a money-back guarantee.

FedEx Home Delivery takes advantage of the FedEx Ground operational network for pickup and package sorting to maintain a low cost structure. FedEx says the new business's focus is on meeting the distinct requirements of residential customers while giving e-tailers an option that combines reliability with lower cost ground transportation.

FedEx also offers Web-based shipping application forms that allow shippers to print out a bar-coded label on plain paper using a laser printer instead of filling out waybill forms by hand. The service, called FedEx interNetShip, lets the customer review a 45-day shipping history and offers e-mail notification of the shipment to the sender, recipient or third parties. The e-mail includes a brief greeting or a list of the package contents.

New Shipping Models

The newest shipping models in the residential delivery sector are carriers like Peapod.com, Streamline.com and Webvan.com. Peapod sees its in-house local delivery services as a key advantage in Internet commerce. These pure-plays have drivers making grocery deliveries but who can also drop off other items — prescription drugs, dry cleaning, restaurant meals, even books and CDs — with the fresh meat and veggies. "Groceries as the core enables you to put trucks on the street," said Peapod chief executive Andrew Parkinson. "Then you can add other products to deliver, and you can do it cheaper than to drop-ship them."

For example, Streamline.com states that its shipping model is to facilitate unattended deliveries by providing installed garage boxes or returnable insulated tote bins to hold perishable products until the customer comes home. After it sold its Chicago and Washington D.C. operations to Peapod, Streamline.com began focusing on delivering groceries and providing other services, e.g., dry cleaning, shoe repair, film processing and bottled water delivery in Massachusetts and northern New Jersey. Those markets are its stronghold and Streamline.com predicts that a positive profit margin is in its near future. Keep an eye on Streamline.com; it may produce some inventive delivery options for the e-business community.

Webvan is building an infrastructure of local, almost totally automated distribution centers using Optum software. There is no doubt that Webvan has more than groceries in mind with such an ambitious build out. Look for announcements any day as to what the company has planned. According to a Webvan spokesperson, customers can schedule a half-hour delivery slot up to seven days in advance when ordering online. In its report, "Mastering Commerce Logistics," Forrester predicts that as the "fight for the consumer doorstep" shakes out in 2001, "players like Webvan will manage consumer relationships." Put Webvan in your address book.

Some e-businesses are going it alone. Sears, taking a page from Peapod's and Webvan's play books, delivers appliances sold on its Web site by using the delivery services in place at its local Sears or dealer store locations.

Shipping Lines (the Big Boats)

Many e-businesses have interaction with shipping lines. As shipping lines become more sophisticated in their use of the Internet, they are moving beyond the basic Web site to provide much needed value-added services. At the moment, however the quality of services being offered by these first adopters remain a little uneven. "Most lines think it means putting a picture of a vessel on the Web site," said Ted Prince, senior vice president of sales and marketing at Kleinschmidt Inc., one of the largest worldwide providers of B2B Electronic Commerce (EC) services, such as Electronic Data Interchange (EDI) Value-Added Network (VAN). "If it's really good, it's java-enhanced and the boat will move," he said.

Shipping executives agree with Prince. "E-commerce is just starting to revolutionize the way business is conducted in the transportation industry," said Robert Beilin, senior vice president-North America at Australia-New Zealand Direct Line. "Quite honestly, not every carrier is able to offer the same level of traditional customer service, and this holds true for online services as well," he said.

E-businesses that use shipping lines should look for ocean carriers that design their online presence around the needs of the customer, rather than using it only as a marketing tool, said Cindy Yamamoto, director of customer products at Orient Overseas Container Line. They have to bring the customer into their process, by providing detailed rate and schedule information as well as access to cargo tracking and electronic bills of lading.

Customers who ship regularly with an ocean carrier want a personalized site that includes all of the pertinent information involving their recent transactions. Carriers must therefore design "customer-centric" e-commerce products, Yamamoto added.

Providing convenient, personalized information will help carriers by freeing their personnel to perform true customer-service work. Yamamoto advised, the carrier "employees will be more exception handlers than re-keyers of data." E-businesses state that carriers who offer valuable electronic products save all participants in the supply chain time and money. "They take time-consuming administrative work out of the supply chain," said Tom Craig, president of LTD Shippers Association.

Ocean carrier Web-based technology is in its infancy. J.C. Penney Co., which ships with multiple carriers, uses carrier e-commerce products sparingly, according to Mark Maleski, international distribution manager. Currently, if he and his staff wanted to use carrier Web sites, they would be forced to jump from one site to another, so his department relies mostly upon established relationships with consolidators. Although Maleski did feel that "ideally, there should be an industry e-commerce effort that puts all of the information into one source for tracking and tracing."

If you visit ANZDL (www.anzdl.com), you'll find that it has separated its Web page into two sites, one for marketing its services and the other dedicated solely to conducting freight transactions. "If we really want shippers [e-business], freight forwarders and NVOCCs to use the site regularly, we needed to make it fast and user-friendly, without slowing them down with large graphics or flashing marketing messages," Beilin said.

E-business should look for an ocean carrier that has a back-end that allows the e-business to coordinate and integrate the work of the line's different departments, and follow transactions from beginning to end. The Web site should integrate the front-end system, the Web application and at least some version of EDI with the back-end system.

One e-business in this field that gets it is Greybox Logistics Services (GLS), a wholly owned subsidiary of Transamerica Leasing. Its eGreybox.com is a groundbreaking online service that offers a one-click solution for transport information exchange. In addition to delivering a single source solution, eGreybox.com can be tailored to meet an individual e-business's requirements.

The egreybox.com systems were designed to harness the fast-evolving and cost-effective Internet technologies developed by GLS to meet the demands for easily accessible data transfer in real-time across international time zones.

eGreybox.com supplies shippers, steamship lines, leasing companies and other transport operators with access to online systems.

This comprehensive, neutral system can be effective regardless of which enterprise owns the assets or which line/operator is transporting the freight. eGreybox.com states that other specialist, equipment-related data services will become available in the near future.

Don't overlook the online transportation auction sites (although most are still in the formative stage) since these let e-businesses shop for rates and book freight over the Internet; they have many implications for both the e-business and the carrier that should be investigated. "There's a lot of hype, but it's too early to make the call," Craig said. E-businesses who are as concerned about service as with price will still prefer to deal direct-ly with carrier representatives and sign service contracts, he said. However, for spot bookings, the online auctions could be valuable. "If I'm a rate shopper, I just go to one or two sites and take care of my shipping needs," he said.

You might also find e-marketplace LevelSeas (www.levelseas.com) of interest. It was founded in April 2000 with the backing of BP Amoco, Cargill, shipbroker Clarksons and the Royal Dutch/Shell Group to deliv-er the benefits of new technology to bulk ocean transportation through the provision of voyage management services and a life-of-voyage char-tering system. LevelSeas states that its main goal is to provide greater market access, reduce costs, increase efficiencies and deliver significant value to a broad community of large and small industry players, includ-ing intermediaries, that are in today's shipping environment.

LevelSeas provides comprehensive freight management services encompassing market intelligence, online chartering, pre- and post-fix-ture activities and risk management tools, including freight derivatives. Gary Weston, Chairman of Clarksons commented, "The advent of LevelSeas.com provides a real opportunity to create an electronic market place for the shipping industry. We believe LevelSeas.com will provide liquidity as well as a level playing field for all participants to trade on. This is an environment in which Clarksons can assist our clients in making the move to on-line trading." Tom Intrator, vice president, Ocean Transportation Division of Cargill, went on record as saying, "LevelSeas.com will combine the latest internet technology together with deep shipping expertise to provide the central point for what is today a complex and dispersed global industry. We see this as a tremendous opportunity to fundamentally change the way we and the industry man-age our freight business."

THEY NEED IT YESTERDAY

Here are a few courier services that specialize in helping the e-business ser-vice the "I needed it yesterday" customer. Put them in your address book, for every e-business will have a need for these services at some time or the other. Just bear in mind that revved-up delivery isn't for the bean counters.

UPS's Sonic Air (www.sonicair.com) will express-ship packages any-where in the world within about 12 hours. Although a service like Sonic's is costly, at some time or another most e-businesses, no matter what size, will require emergency delivery service, no matter what the cost.

Velocity Express (www.velocityexp.com), a long-time player in the same-day game, believes there is demand for same-day delivery through-out the e-business community. Velocity Express, formerly known as Corporate Express Delivery and a subsidiary of United Shipping and Technology (US&T), is a network of couriers working from 200 offices and using 10,000 delivery vehicles allowing Velocity to cover 83 of the top 100 US markets on any given day.

NextJet (www.nextjet.com), which claims to be the "fastest package delivery system in the world," uses a network of couriers and space on commercial airlines to move packages as fast as humanly possible. NextJet states that it has the technology to allow e-businesses to integrate its transportation system into their Web site, then NextJet can determine the routing, schedule the flight and quote a price for them and their cus-tomers in less than five seconds.

Technology and the ability to integrate its same-day solution into an e-business site is what sets NextJet apart from its myriad competitors, at least according to Joseph P. Lane, NextJet's co-founder and co-CEO. Lane states that most same-day solutions rely heavily on the phone, and NextJet has automated everything, shaving time from an already speedy process.

NextJet isn't targeting the e-tail market but is focusing its sights on the blossoming B2B e-marketplaces where businesses, for example, buy and sell parts for oil rigs, elevators, aviation and the automotive industry. In this atmosphere, NextJet could provide constant tracking information while the shipment was en route.

NextJet's average shipment cost for a lightweight object is about $150, com-petitive with the integrated carriers in the zero-to-50-pound range, said Lane. Lane started the company in 1999 and brought in top executives from FedEx and UPS's Sonic Air for shipping expertise. "There is just a huge market opportunity," said Lane. "We like to call what we are doing 'disruptive tech-nology.' We are shaking up the way people view their shipping solutions."

"This is a challenging business," said David S. Quin, vice president and managing director of Emery Expedite. Emery Worldwide's successful same-day business, which has grown from nothing to $100 million in five years, works because of the air freight experience behind the company. "It's complex because so much depends on just knowing how airlines work, which flights to avoid, allowing for enough time at certain hubs and knowing where the freight is at all times," said Quin. "We are delivering production line material or payroll, things with disastrous ramifications if it doesn't arrive."

The bulk of e-tail products aren't urgently needed. "Same-day transportation has been around for years and they've always catered to law firms where the costs can be billed to clients," said Satish Jindel, principal of SJ Consulting (www.jindel.com). He warned that the shakeup e-tailers are experiencing can hit the e-tail shippers too if they operate on the main principal that all customers want their orders immediately. "People always want something for free. For it to work, customers have to be willing to pay for it," he said.

THINKING IN THE BOX

As the time-pressed population increasingly embraces the convenience of Web shopping, the demand for home deliveries will continue to grow.

Your online customer has ordered a new MP3 player from your e-tail site because the overall cost was a good deal and the customer decided that the anxiety of awaiting its delivery was worth the savings. However, if a week later that customer arrives at his or her doorstep and finds a telltale long retangle slip on the door, he or she is no longer sure the decision was a correct one. Now the customer has several (unappealing) options:

- Sign the slip and risk the delivery service leaving the package unprotected at the door step the next day. This is not only exposing the customer to post-transaction anxiety disorder, but it's also costly for the delivery service (extra visits cut into their profit margin) and the e-tailer runs the risk that the package won't be there when the customer gets home.

- If the customer lives in a managed apartment building or complex, he or she may find that the delivery service has left the package with the

management office which most likely is only open when the customer is at work.

- The customer might also have the option of going to a local distribution center to retrieve the package, but it also probably has limited operating hours.

All of a sudden the "convenience" of ordering online, starts to appear to be a little less convenient.

How does an e-tailer get the goods to the customer and still provide convenience?

- Consolidate the residential delivery of a neighborhood at one location that offers after-business-hours pick-up, eliminating the need for some-one to be home for delivery. This would reduce the costs for delivery companies by limiting the number of spread out stops and unsuccessful attempts, but would provide customer with after-business-hours access to packages. Thus, the customer is happy, the delivery service is happy and the e-tail establishment is satisfied that it has provided the 3Rs. Another benefit of this solution is that an e-tailer could, in all probabili-ty, negotiate lower delivery rates based on this type of set up.

- Partner with an existing multi-neighborhood bricks-and-mortar, such as video rental, convenience store, dry cleaner, fast-food establishment, etc., that offers long hours, easy parking, and quick pick-up of packages. Drive through options would be an additional bonus. Offer a discount on your Web site for customers that select this delivery method. Once you have your "pick-up" partnerships in place you could start negotiating discounts from the various shippers for you're also saving them money.

TIPS

It's essential for an e-business to integrate tracking information into its systems and make that data available to customers. For example, Federal Express has a customized shipping system that allows qualified e-busi-nesses to track deliveries once every hour. This allows an e-business to not only check when a package was delivered and who signed for it, but also the orders that were returned because of a problem with delivery

itself. Then this information can be sent to the e-business's customers via e-mail. UPS, Airborne and DHL offer similar services.

If you choose to offer your customers shipping options, post clear, concise and fair shipping choices and policies on your Web site. If overnight service is offered, clarify what time orders must be received for same day shipping, and whether orders placed on weekends and holidays are shipped the next business day. It's better to be honest about delivery times than give the impression that an express service is guaranteed when that isn't the case. If you don't have the infrastructure for a two-day turnaround, or even if there is a possibility you can't hold to that schedule, you need to be honest with your customers.

Prior to a predictable surge in purchases on its Web site due to a new product, special promotion, marketing campaign, beginning of the school year, holidays, etc., an e-business should assemble its management staff, and go over the following:

- Inventory, staffing, equipment, shipping partners and team issues.
- Determine if you have made your shipping partners aware of your forecast volume.
- Find out if you need to add extra pickups.
- Certify that your current shipping and receiving layout is adequate for your planned volume surge.

It's imperative that an e-business addresses these issues as far in advance of the predicted upswing as possible.

Speed is an expensive commodity — however the Internet is all about speed and so many Web-based businesses are in a catch 22 situation — a speedy delivery of products but *inexpensively* — eek!

Logistics and/or Fulfillment Models

TIME AND A LITTLE MONEY is all it takes to post a Web site to sell a product, but actually filling the orders that come in is an entirely different matter, and a much more challenging one. Many e-businesses — manufacturers, trading partners, suppliers, distributors, pure-plays, and click-and-mortars — face that dilemma. In response, e-businesses have conceived innovative ways to approach the adaptation of their traditional business model to an e-business model so as to have a viable LFMS and that is where the logistics and/or fulfillment models come into play.

Logistics is all of the activities that are involved in the management of product movement from the moment the product is finalized on the drawing board until the time it's in the end-user's possession. Its partner, fulfillment, is the back-office systems that provide the link between the customer experience and the actual physical delivery of goods to the customer. This includes inventory management as well as order capture and management and reconciliation, and sometimes even customer service is brought under the fulfillment umbrella.

Logistics and fulfillment management is the nuts and bolts of the 3Rs — *the right product at the right place at the right time.* If an e-business doesn't put the right nut or bolt in the right hole and tighten it sufficiently, all the design awards in the world won't help. That's why the best e-businesses have invested so heavily in LFM. Witness Amazon.com's installation of its own state of the art system. It has paid off. In a mid-2000 survey conducted by Leo J. Shapiro & Associates on behalf of National Retail

Federation *STORES* Magazine (www.stores.org), and sponsored by VeriFone (www.verifone.com) and Russell Reynolds Associates (www.russreyn.com), Amazon was ranked number two (eBay came in first) in online sales to US customers and tied with Sears.com for the 11th position in the repeat purchase potential index.

Many traditional catalog companies already had an LFM system in place so when they adopted an e-business model, they were able to use these same systems as the cornerstone of their Web-based division, albeit with some tweaking, upgrades and so forth. In that same mid-2000 *STORES* survey, seven of the top twenty had a "catalog competency" in-house prior to adopting an e-business model. Then also, the same survey confirmed that the top-ranked apparel sites remain concentrated in the hands of the catalog-to-e-business models. Landsend.com received a 15 ranking, with the Spiegel Group (spiegel.com, eddiebauer.com, newport-news.com) right behind at 16. They were followed closely by JCPenney.com and LLBean.com. Even these e-businesses are constantly finding ways to upgrade their online services. Each have undergone as

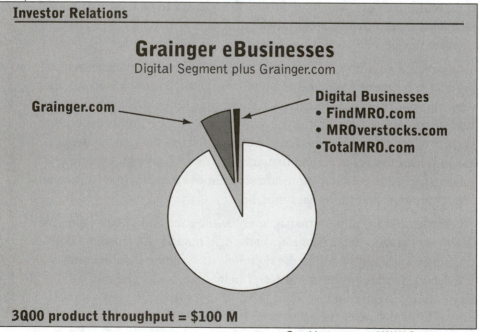

Investor Relations

Grainger eBusinesses
Digital Segment plus Grainger.com

Grainger.com

Digital Businesses
• FindMRO.com
• MROverstocks.com
• TotalMRO.com

3Q00 product throughput = $100 M

Graphic courtesy of W.W.Grainger, Inc

many as five site revisions, each time seeking improved navigation, order management and customer service initiatives. But although The Limited's Victoriassecret.com and Lanebryant.com were in the running at 37, along with jcrew.com at 39, there was nary a pure-play apparel e-business in sight.

The catalogers' telephone-based fulfillment systems, originally designed to accommodate individual consumers, were ideally suited to e-commerce. As a result, catalog retailers have the lowest backorder rate among e-tailers (6%), compared with 9% for pure-plays and as much as 11% for click-and-mortars. Again, this is due in main part to the catalogers' sophisticated back-ends, which include established inventory and fulfillment systems.

Jim Ryan, president of Grainger.com, understands the place that logistics and fulfillment has in a successful e-business model. He is on record as stating, "Grainger's digital businesses are expanding rapidly, but one of the challenges of e-commerce is integrating smoothly with the back-end fulfillment system. Getting the product out the back door to a customer at the right place and right time is critical, no matter what business you are in."

But not all fulfillment is equal. E-tail does generally fit into most of the models discussed herein and many of the models are converging, causing a blurring of the demarcation lines that once were very clear. When you start digging into the B2B models, there is much obscurity because of the multi-channels in the B2B space.

Yet, it gets murkier than that. In Chapter 2 of this book I introduced the reader to three basic e-business models: B2B, e-tail and converged. But you can't stop there, to get to the meat of the matter you must break these three basic models into fulfillment and logistics models and those models into sub-models and subsets. You can't just say you're handling your fulfillment in-house or outsourcing it. It goes deeper than that. For instance, in-house fulfillment models such as the "pure-play in-house," the "click-and-mortar" (which is 90% of the time in-house) and the "catalog" (basically 100% in-house) all have different fulfillment challenges. Factor in B2B in-house fulfillment challenges and the reader can see how the models were born, how they're now merging into what will eventually become one model for all but the small e-business — the multi-channel model.

For instance, Compaq and Hewlett-Packard depend on retailers, distributors and other middlemen to sell most of their computer systems and peripherals, but each e-business has taken a different route when it comes to catering to the customer who prefers a one-to-one relationship.

Then we have a pure-play that partnered with a click-and-mortar. Amazon.com may be an icon of the dotcom movement, but its new alliance with Toys 'R Us acknowledges the fact that Amazon won't develop its own toy purchasing and inventory management skills but will rely on its click-and-mortar partner instead. Likewise, Toys 'R Us now concedes that Amazon's customer service, order fulfillment and other Web retailing capabilities are light years ahead of its own.

The lines are blurring everywhere. General Motors is inserting itself into its traditional sales channel and more. Already aggressive in helping its dealers peddle GM vehicles online, the company is plotting a Web site to sell cars made by other manufacturers as well.

What all e-businesses are realizing is that e-business isn't a one-size-fits-all medium. Customers (and suppliers) demand multiple buying (and selling) sources, so it's not a sign of weakness or indecision for an e-business to spread its bets around. Some companies, like Staples, are building out their own multi-channel strategies and infrastructures, but most have or will tap partners.

Internet time accelerates the pace of change, making yesterday's strategic masterstroke today's bumbling miscalculation. Be prepared to adapt quickly or fall way behind your nimbler competitors. Look at CompUSA, *Internetweek* reported in mid-2000 that it's installing a Gigabit Ethernet backbone mainly to support core bricks-and-mortar retail applications. CIO Cathy Witt was frank when she told *Internetweek* that the company is still feeling its way around e-business, so CompUSA is covering its bases with an IT infrastructure that can accommodate future online growth and changes in direction. In other words, CompUSA can't always predict what's coming around the corner, but it's ready to mobilize for the next strategic project.

There is yet another model to consider when looking at how e-businesses manage their logistics and fulfillment needs: online marketplaces. Online marketplaces are just coming into their own, especially for the small to mid-size e-business operating a B2B model. Over the last couple of years online marketplaces have proliferated throughout the e-business community. A full discussion of this model and the ramifications and technology employed is beyond the scope of this book. Suffice it to say that some online marketplaces, out of necessity, have among their repertoire logistics and fulfillment solutions.

As stated earlier in this book, online marketplaces can be known as e-marketplaces, procurement marketplaces, digital marketplaces, open marketplaces, seller-led buyer cooperatives, buyer-led selling cooperatives, seller extranets, and buyer extranets, vertical portals, vortals, trading networks, trading marketplace, trading hubs, trading communities, and so forth. Whatever name they use, the main goal of each and every one of them is to facilitate the buy-sell interaction in the e-business community due to the changes in business processes brought about by the adoption of the e-business model.

B2B BUY-SELL MODEL

One way some e-businesses are handling the fundamental change an Internet-based system represents to their value chain is by formation of an online marketplace, which has resulted in a variety of new B2B models, technologies and application designs. Consequently, an e-business that adopts one of the "marketplace" models makes it possible for its value chain to work and communicate in real-time with an automated flow of information and transactions, while still supporting individual business and contractual relationships between the value chain members.

An online marketplace is a Web site that some B2Bs implement to optimize their buy-sell activities. However, to do this the B2B must understand how its value chain will come together with the Internet as the enabler. It also greatly accelerates the speed of every value chain interaction, thus increasing the rate at which members of the value chain companies must disseminate information and process transactions, which puts a tremendous strain on an LFMS.

Of course, this means that the B2B implementing the online market (whether as a buyer or seller) must dictate the solutions and/or standards with which all members of the value chain must comply if the market-place is to meet the needs of the value chain.

Sell-side Online Marketplace

For example, a supplier might create a sell-side online marketplace to lower its cost of sales through automation of the order entry and ful-fillment processes. This is in reality a B2B e-commerce Web site or "storefront" which operates 24 x 7, offering its latest inventory, and enabling self-service ordering and tracking. In short, suppliers are cap-italizing on the Internet's potential by bringing their existing value chain and processes online. A good example of this model is Staples.com's three entities:

- Staples.com — devoted to the small businesses;

- Quill.com — servicing the midsize companies; and

- StaplesLink.com — a special service for purchasing managers.

Buy-side Online Market

There are also e-businesses that want more control over their procure-ment processes. These e-businesses have implemented their own version of the online marketplace where they can have control over pricing or the handling of pre-negotiated contracts. Many times these online markets are referred to as simply a corporate intranet or portal. The best known example is Wal-Mart which uses its current online marketplace — Retail Link — to cut its costs through e-procurement applications operated as a browser-based front-end for back-office ERP and legacy purchasing sys-tems. Wal-Mart's procurement departments have access to a multitude of "approved" supplier catalogs, which have been morphed into Wal-Mart's own one-stop shopping catalog of approved supplier products and ser-vices. This allows the deployment of self-service requisitioning and order processing to the internal user's desktop, while aggregating enterprise-wide expenditures across a consistent supplier and product portfolio. Suppliers can also track how their products are selling in Wal-Mart stores.

At the time this book was written, Wal-Mart and Atlas Commerce (www.atlascommerce.com) (a startup that got the nod to update Retail

Link) were testing a new private internet marketplace that will allow Wal-Mart to automate its global sourcing processes. For example, the upgraded Retail Link will give Wal-Mart the ability to collect and aggregate inventory forecasts across Wal-Mart stores worldwide, and then buy the supplies through a reverse auction.

Both of these sub-models of the B2B buy-sell fulfillment model offer cost savings throughout the value chain and allow for stable logistics and fulfillment solutions to be implemented. The result is further savings with the added bonus of improved customer satisfaction.

E-Marketplaces

The above two buy-sell sub-models are not for every B2B. Only the large enterprise can afford to aggregate catalog content, link the value chain and develop a comprehensive LFMS. Accordingly, the remaining e-businesses have turned to third-party online marketplaces (which for clarity's sake I refer to as "e-marketplaces") to streamline the order process and expedite fulfillment.

The development of e-marketplaces may be tomorrow's answer to enhancing order fulfillment, as they unite a group of e-businesses to enable the buy and sell process using sophisticated workflow and routing techniques. The process of linking trading partners together in a neutral environment can either be done behind-the-scenes without the user's knowledge or the user may contact the network. i2 Technologies' (www.i2.com) Burghli says, "A user may describe the products they are looking for on a general Web site that a variety of suppliers, manufacturers, and distributors support. The system takes the user's needs, including brand preferences and delivery dates, and notifies the most appropriate supplier via the online network that can meet the user's needs." The system and underlying network needs intelligence to coordinate responses and be able to make the best choices.

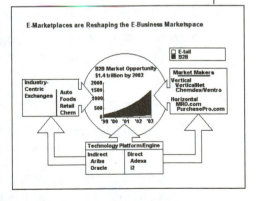

Logility (www.logility.com) vice president, Andrew White, takes an opposing view. He opines that to bring together multiple buyers and sellers is a risky model for e-business commerce because to do so eliminates healthy competition. White goes on to say, "Buyers shouldn't have all information about suppliers. Trading exchanges actually compete with the collaboration process. If price were the only reason a user wanted to buy a product, which may be the case in business-to-consumer markets, then trading exchanges would make sense. But, if you are looking for service too, exchanges are not the answer."

White does admit that the issue of optimizing order fulfillment may be the mitigating factor in the eventual success or downfall of many new e-businesses. "Many of the new dot-com firms are fairly naïve about what supply chain really means. They are just grabbing at old practices and trying to deal with big demand on the front-end and insufficiencies [in the] back-end. They are rushing to build warehouses and overcompensating with inventory. All it takes is a drop in demand or a specific promotion, and they will be phased out because they can't swallow their costs."

E-marketplaces are in a state of flux — as stated earlier in the book, this sector is due for a major shakeout in the next two or three years — a B2B needs to be very careful when ponying-up to a third-party e-market solution. E-marketplaces are meant to provide multi-buyer/multi-seller interaction and collaboration through a common trading hub. Typical e-marketplaces might be implemented by:

- A trade organization to aggregate its members' orders from approved suppliers by providing online procurement services.

- A new market maker that is trying to replace existing distribution channels by offering online information and services to a specific industry.

- A large distributor who seeks to automate processes among several buyers, suppliers or manufacturers.

- A third-party service provider who wants to create a common marketplace by providing hosted procurement services to a specific set of suppliers and their customers.

Many feel that e-marketplaces will change the way the entire business community thinks about e-business and its commerce. The Gartner Group is an online marketplace champion, as it has predicted that within a year 70% of distributors who operate online will attribute more than 80% of their sales through e-marketplaces.

E-Marketplaces impact every element of the E-Business Supply Chain

Although there is doubt about the viability of the vast majority of e-marketplaces flooding the Internet's byways, it's clear that the formation of these shared marketplaces is necessary if e-business and its commerce are to reach full potential. It's like the US's food supply at the beginning of the 20th Century — if the great majority of the populace wanted fresh vegetables, it grew its own in either a small backyard garden or a truck garden on a farm. But as time went on and the populace became more urbanized and time pressures took their toll, there came a growth of vegetable wholesalers operating through a cooperative or a shared network and delivery model to get the fresh produce to the end-users, the housewives and cooks.

Equally important, these e-marketplaces can bring with them innovative new methods of dynamic exchange. Look at the Web sites of many of the first B2B adopters. They were (and some still are) little more than an Internet-based front-end for the traditional business applications. Many e-businesses have done little to advance commerce to the new Internet standard. On the other hand, e-marketplaces create entirely new methods of commerce, such as online sourcing, auctions and negotiations. They also enable trading communities to share common information and knowledge more easily, and they can bring calm to what has been logistics and fulfillment chaos for many e-businesses.

While the specific benefits of an e-marketplace, including logistics and fulfillment, will differ across the online market models, a general set of core benefits can be recognized.

Rooster.com is quickly becoming a comprehensive online e-marketplace for the agriculture community to service the wants and needs of both agribusiness and agricultural producers. Rooster.com is where pro-

Benefits of a Digital Marketplace		
To Seller	**To Market Host**	**To Buyer**
• Provides new marketing and distribution channel to customers • Provides better customer service through online interaction • Provides more complete product information to buyer • Automates order & fulfillment processes • Lowers overall operational costs	• Protects current role or creates new role within the commerce chain • Establishes high "value-add" in digital economy • Increases service levels to existing customers • Leverages current information and customers • Provides access to more information and suppliers	• Lowers up-front costs and risks • Provides access to more information and suppliers • Provides access to secondary and excess supply auctions • Provides a more comprehensive solution • Eliminates on-going software upgrades & Maintenance costs • Utilizes outsourced expertise

Table courtesy of NetMarket Makers (www.netmarketmakers.com).

ducers can utilize the Internet to market their crops and buy their seed, fertilizer, crop protection products, equipment and other supplies. It provides a 24 x 7 one-stop shop connecting producers, dealers and manufacturers with new marketing opportunities. Gary Carlson, president and chief executive officer of Rooster.com, states, "Combined, all facets of agriculture will help make Rooster.com the premiere purchasing and marketing transactional Internet site for the agriculture community."

Rooster.com tapped tech solution provider, NerveWire, Inc. (www.nervewire.com), as its network architectural provider to implement a software platform for all of its on-line commerce transactions. Instigating the NerveWire relationship was among the first steps Rooster.com's executives took to design, build, test and deploy its e-marketplace. NerveWire defined the detailed functional and technical blueprint for Rooster.com. Rooster.com and NerveWire then aligned with Ariba, Inc. (www.ariba.com) to deploy the Ariba Trading Dynamics. Thus allowing the e-marketplace to "enable buyers and sellers to transact back and forth on product specifications, delivery dates, payment methods and other terms," says Tim Moulton, Rooster.com's chief technology officer. He added, "This technology not only provides comprehensive functionality and total interaction for all players, but it also has the potential to go global."

One of the main benefits of the e-marketplace model is that a B2B can expand its online revenues by selling through the numerous online marketplaces that are currently proliferating throughout the Web. A B2B can also reduce its per customer service costs by taking advantage of the online marketplaces' efforts in the area of customer service, fulfillment and shipment. Finally, this sub-model of the buy-sell fulfillment model lets a B2B have a credible presence thereby allowing it to maintain a competitive edge.

B2B SPONSORED MODEL

With this model, an e-business has a brochureware Web site sporting a full product catalog, online customer service attributes such as frequently asked questions, a knowledge base, technical manuals, and maybe even a newsletter. However, it channels all potential customers to its distributors' Web sites, and the actual "commerce" takes place on the distributor's site.

Thus a B2B sponsored model has the distributor closing the actual sale with the individual customer and acting as merchant of record. Shipment and fulfillment can occur either from the distributor or from the channel sponsor, depending on the sub-model; but the "B2B sponsor" does sell to the distributor at wholesale prices and the distributor does mark up the products. In the year 2000, sponsor e-businesses using distributor Web sites expected 50% of the purchases initiated on these sites to be transacted and closed online, up from 28% in 1999 according to Reality Research (www.realityresearch.com).

The major benefit of this model is that it lets everyone take advantage of e-commerce revenues in a method that supports existing distribution channels. It allows a B2B to utilize traffic coming to its Web site by disbursing it to distribution channel partners, hence allowing the B2B to strengthen its relationships with its distribution channel and also drive up the volume of sales. An example of this model is Girard Equipment, Inc. (www.girardequip.com), one of North America's leading builders of safety equipment for the tank trailer industry. Another is Lincoln Electric Company (www.lincolnelectric.com), who states it's "the world leader in welding and cutting products."

You can take this model a bit further to give the e-business and its partners/distributors the ability to extend across corporate boundaries to link and integrate business processes. For example, a customer who places a product order can directly provision it via the sponsoring e-business's ordering system. Of course, to have viable logistics and fulfillment within this model a solid Web-based security system is critical, especially when operating a distributor/wholesaler's online order entry program.

Square D Company, a leading manufacturer and supplier of electrical distribution, automation and industrial control products, has its systems and services linked via its Web site (www.squared.com). Therefore by "linking our site with distributors [we] offer a whole range of new opportunities for our customers," said Scott Harris, vice president, channel marketing. "Once they've downloaded the product data and specifications they need from our site, they can jump over to a distributor's to learn more about local service availability, support and training. They can even place orders on many distributor sites; as well as track the current status and ship date of previous orders. All of these things save time and help our customers and distributors get the information they need, when they need it."

Another variation is where a B2B sponsor has established a "personalized" distributor "Web site product" that their distributors can use. In other words, each distributor's Web site can be a "replica" of the B2B sponsor's site, but with the inclusion of e-commerce capabilities. A distributor's Web site might display product availability, price changes, unique price configurations, upgrade information and shipping processes.

A good example of this model is Compaq's new online initiative, CompaqPlus, an e-tail program Compaq developed to sell its high-value product range to the end-user over the Internet with fulfillment through an authorized channel partner. CompaqPlus consists of an e-commerce enabled Web site (for example, www.compaqplus.co.za), toll free CRM Call Center, printed catalogs targeted at small and medium businesses, and an on-line order management system for CompaqPlus channel partners. Customers, ordering via the Web site or the call center, simply select the products they require as well as their preferred channel partner. Once the order is placed, the channel partner the customer chose is notified automatically. The partner can then process the order and initiate the delivery using the integrated order management system.

Another example of the B2B sponsor model is AGMConnects.com, a partnership between AGRI Industries (a federated co-operative) and Cargill, which provides local, customized Internet-based services to AGRI Grain Marketing's grain elevator customers. The local elevators customize the sites for grain producers. "As new technologies emerge, we will continue to offer products and services that help our members provide increased value to farmers," said Jerry Van Der Kamp, CEO of AGRI Industries.

Any of the aforementioned variations of this fulfillment model allows an e-business to strengthen its relationship with its distribution channel and increase sales volume by sponsoring their e-commerce presence.

One final variation on this model is that in which an e-business might support its VIP customers with customized Web sites tied to the e-business's systems that can provide information and services a VIP customer expects. For example, pre-negotiated contract pricing, order status, problem resolution status, product warranties, billing, and customized reports.

With personalized or customized Web sites, business policies, procedures, and practices can be implemented by creating and managing numerous customized applications for major accounts and partners through the Web.

For example, Staples Contract (www.staplescontract.com) creates and operates stores for its corporate customers to purchase Staples products via the Web. Each of these online stores is tailored to the unique requirements of the corporate customer who uses the store. Pre-negotiated product prices, product availability, shipping addresses, billing addresses, and more are all automatically set up for the customer before they ever browse through the store.

So the B2B sponsored Web site model (and its many variations) allows a large e-business to optimize its sales but also provides savings in time and cost. All the while it provides the crucial 3Rs of LFM, so that its ultimate end-user, the customers, receive exemplary service throughout the ordering and fulfillment process.

MANUFACTURER MODEL

As manufacturers adopt the e-business model, they must grapple, not only with the cooperation of their value chain members and their ensuing integration, but also just how to offer real-time visibility into their planning processes. To do this causes paranoia tendencies in some executives; many within such enterprises are hesitant to share vital information to those outside the enterprise.

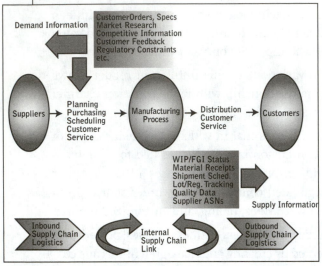

Common order fulfillment and manufacturing challenges.

The forward thinking manufacturing e-business will jump this hurdle and move forward to a full e-business integration as SMTC Manufacturing (www.smtc.com) did through its innovative supply chain management that "accentuates forward thinking business processes and value added supply management. Focusing on electronic links that provide customers and suppliers secure Web sites for real time and interactive relationships," per SMTC documentation. This manufacturer's adoption of an e-business model allows it to provide a virtual environment for demand management, flexible manufacturing and complete logistical services that are all customer specific solutions. According to SMTC, "be it finished goods management of PCBAs, build to order system configuration, end product packaging, warranty and repair or world wide product distribution," it has the systems in place to handle the process.

SMTC is a Toronto-based contract manufacturer for the electronics industry and has built what I call an LFMS on steroids. It established a global SMTC e-business commerce trading community, where manufacturing plants, customers and suppliers can collaborate and transact business in real-time, over the Web. Through the adoption of a manufacturing fulfillment model, it not only provides its suppliers and customers access to its production scheduling, manufacturing planning, and forecasting data, but can provide enhanced supply planning and order promising as well.

"What used to take days now takes hours," says Phil Woodard, a senior vice president for SMTC. "We send e-mails with a list of changes in demand, and manufacturing plans to our suppliers, who in turn, update their reports. When a change occurs in our master production schedule, our suppliers are notified. When we realized how the system increased efficiency on the supply side, we were eager to try it for our customers," continued Woodard. The system offers customers different options depending on the data they need. One option is viewing SMTC's entire master production schedule, which can be published on customers' Web sites. "This allows customers to see hard orders, forecasts, constraints, and production schedules for each finished product," says Woodard.

SMCT has also built in the ability to give its value chain ATP or ship dates. If the system detects that an item will fall outside the committed ship date, it sends out an alert of the potential problem. "It gives them time to go back and fix problems to prevent late deliveries," Woodard explains. Then there is its capable-to-promise, which performs "what-if?" scenarios for order changes. "The system identifies the trading partners involved for each customer and scans the entire supply chain to come back with an accurate date," says Woodard. "Customers can have an order promising Web page in their sales order cycle that checks our system simultaneously when orders are taken."

SMTC isn't the only e-business manufacturer optimizing its value chain through its e-business model. Mott's North America (B2B Web site unavailabile to outsiders) upgraded its SAP (www.sap.com) software to let third-party brokers of its products make inquiries electronically. However, Motts knew some of its smaller business partners had limited IT resources, so the company handled much of the IT work for them.

Once everything was in place, Mott's began using techniques including ATP, capable-to-promise, and collaborative planning. Mott's manufactures more than 300 products, although it's probably best known for its applesauce and juices. Mott's reduced working capital through increased forecast accuracy and lower inventory. Jeff Morgan, a Mott's vice president explained, "We overcompensated with a large inventory of many items to be able to respond to customers. We wanted to emphasize supply chain rather than sales in our forecasting process, and still respond to customer requirements. We needed a stronger forecasting method due to our heavy promotional activity and new product launches."

As Bill Green, a vice president for Adexa (formerly Paragon Management Systems) (www.adexa.com), explains: Although having real-time ATP data is a crucial piece in the value chain planning puzzle, a number of other functions initially must take place. A good starting point is collaborative demand planning, where the entire value chain develops a forecast of what they believe they will sell. Once there is a general idea of demand, the members of the chain need to plan distribution, manufacturing, and resources, accessing information from the enterprise system to consider material and capacity constraints.

Once the members of the chain get numbers back from their suppliers, they can use a value chain planner component to determine which items can be sold to which customers, and whether they need to raise prices or look for alternative suppliers. When implemented correctly, and if all functional constraints are considered simultaneously, the value chain can support synchronized concurrent planning.

In the past, enterprises had a centralized department for high-level planning processes, but with the adoption of the e-business model, many are seeing the practicality of giving each division or subsidiary responsibility for developing plans for its own operations. "Companies used to be forced to do planning sequentially, where one plant developed a plan and sent it to the next site, and so on," says Green. "More of today's businesses distribute corporate plans down to the plant level and merge them with local constraints."

But, Stacie McCullough, a senior analyst for Forrester, says de-centralized planning might not be the solution for all e-businesses, particularly in make-to-order, discrete environments. "Some functions still need to be coordinated centrally, such as when working with virtual inventory, or where components are sourced from multiple channels," she ventured.

However, some inventory allocation processes, such as ATP, are important for enterprises that store inventory in multiple locations. "Many companies don't have capable on-line available-to-promise," says McCullough. "They base promise dates on finished goods stock only, and allocate against a batch download of inventory. But, if they sell to other channels, inventory easily can be depleted, and back-orders occur."

The response time for delivering ATP must be fast because systems only have a few seconds to capture and maintain users' attention. Memory-resident technology allows systems to determine promise dates in a fraction of a second as it manages by exception. "This *allows* a company to replan on every order, but only *requires* them to replan when changes occur," says McCullough.

Through the adoption of systems and processes that allow visibility throughout a value chain and thus avoid classic inventory problems, e-businesses can address expediting orders and improving customer service.

ATP requires communication between value chain members about committed inventory, scheduled production, and the availability of manufacturing resources and materials. Michael Lipton, director of supply chain consulting for SAP gives the example of, "a computer manufacturer needs visibility into the stage production components are in and where they are located in the supply chain. They must plan based on forecasts and build based on orders, thinking in terms of features they expect to sell."

Many e-businesses are making great progress in anticipating demand, but their systems and processes still are at the mercy of classic inventory and fore-

---

BULLWHIP EFFECT

Legend has it that the Pampers manufacturer Procter & Gamble (P&G) coined the phrase "bullwhip effect." In studying its diaper sales to retailers P&G found that despite the steady rate of demand among babies for diapers there was a puzzling, dramatic fluctuation in the retailers' orders to wholesalers. The fluctuations were even greater in orders that P&G received from the wholesalers. P&G began to wonder — the variability in demand by babies for dry diapers was small — why was there such a marked variability in demand from the retailers to the wholesalers? Next, why was the variability even more extreme when the wholesalers placed their orders with the manufacturers?

Thus the bullwhip effect is what happens in manufacturing when information about consumer demand — for diapers or for any other product — becomes increasingly distorted as it moves upstream in the manufacturing process. This distortion leads to excessive inventory throughout the system, poor product forecasts, insufficient or excessive capacities, product unavailability, and higher costs generally.

Therefore, the term "bullwhip effect" refers to the magnification of demand fluctuations as orders move up the supply chain. Improved forecasting techniques at just one level in the supply chain cannot eliminate the bullwhip effect and can even worsen it. *Information flow and coordination of orders across the supply chain offer the only hope of taming the bullwhip effect.*

casting problems. Here Lipton gave the example of an e-tailer that "may forecast to customers, distributors forecast to manufacturers, and manufacturers forecast to distributors. This creates the bullwhip effect, where the variability of downstream demand is light, but high upstream. Everyone is making their best guesses and the right demand signal gets lost in all the chaos."

One way to counteract the bullwhip effect is to ensure that front-end and back-end systems are fully integrated, including the messaging layer — whether using EDI or XML — as well as in semantics, so that definitions and concepts are the same for both systems.

VENDOR MANAGED INVENTORY MODEL

A streamlined approach to inventory and order fulfillment is the vendor managed inventory (VMI) model. With it, the supplier, not its e-business customer, is responsible for managing and replenishing inventory. VMI lets companies reduce overhead by shifting responsibility for managing and replenishing inventory to vendors.

VMI can cut costs and keep inventory levels low throughout the value chain. Look at some of the world-class enterprises that have adopted this model — Kraft Inc., Mott's North America, Cisco and Wal-Mart. Often you will find it as a subset of the extended enterprise model.

"If you're smart enough to transfer the ownership of inventory to your vendors, your raw materials and work-in-process inventory comes off your balance sheets. Your assets go down, and you need less working capital to run your business," says Ron Barris, global leader of supply chain management for the high-tech industry at Ernst & Young LLP (www.ey.com).

Using the VMI model, the e-business's vendors track the number of products shipped to distributors and retail outlets and thus stay informed as to whether or not more supplies are needed. Once an "alarm goes off" products are automatically replenished, but merchandise isn't shipped until its needed, consequently lowering inventory for the vendor's customers. Suppliers and buyers use written contracts to determine payment terms, frequency of replenishment and other terms of the agreement.

At the moment the most prevalent technology in VMI is electronic data interchange (EDI), an ordering system traditionally conducted over private

WEB-BASED TRANSACTION SERVICES

The notion of using the Internet as an inexpensive conduit for EDI-formatted transaction traffic isn't a new innovation. General Electric's Global Exchange and the auto, retail and financial services industries have been working on Internet EDI standards for some time.

However, St. Paul Software Inc. (a provider of translation software for EDI) seems to have taken the lead. It has repositioned itself from an EDI software supplier to a provider of Web-based transaction services. At the same time it received a new name and logo — SPS Commerce Inc. Some of the "biggies" availing themselves of SPS's services are Dayton Hudson Corp. (Target), Fingerhut, Kmart, Cisco Systems, Rite Aid and Sears.

The SPS Commerce Service Center (www.spscommerce.com) lets suppliers use a Web browser to exchange transactions and documents with the EDI systems of buyers. SPS converts HTML data from a supplier's browser into EDI transaction sets of XML or other format used by the buyer company. SPS charges the supplier company $1.50 per transaction, with volume discounts available.

"The Web isn't just for the small vendor anymore. Retailers and manufacturers of all sizes can automate any type of B2B transactions using a Web browser through our trading community." says SPS Commerce president and CEO Steve Waldron.

The Small Vendors Benefit

Getting the small vendors to participate cuts costs — electronic transactions can cost just 5% of what it costs to process a transaction on paper, according to Forrester. Also, it's much easier for small vendors to go the hosted route because of the complexity of administration typical of EDI.

Services such as SPS is also a benefit for the small vendor. "Target requires every vendor to be EDI-compliant, and although we work very hard to help small companies do that, sometimes it's very difficult," said Jerry Storch, president of financial services and new business at Target.

"If we can get smaller vendors to participate [in a Web-based transaction service], we can reduce our overhead and the amount of paper we need to push," said Fingerhut's EDI operations manager Scott Bolduc.

value-added networks (VANs) but due to the high costs of the VANs e-businesses have "EDI replacement technology" high on their "to do" list. Typically, the vendor/manufacturer gets a daily review of inventory by downloading EDI files from its customers. The vendor/manufacturer then uses the inventory data to put together an anticipated order for the customers and after receipt of an electronic acknowledgment, it ships the order. After the shipment is received and approved by the customer, payment is made with an electronic funds transfer from the customer's financial institution.

According to Scott Stratman, president of the consulting company, The Distribution Team (www.dteam.com), distributors of hard goods such as auto parts and electrical supplies began experiencing the benefits of EDI-based VMI several years ago. Stratman estimates the VMI model allowed the distributors to lower inventory levels and eliminate paperwork resulting in a substantial reduction in overall inventory overhead and it cut the time for order fulfillment from a range of 22 to 29 days to one of 14 to 17 days.

Not all VMI implementations use EDI, especially the ones implemented within the last 2 or 3 years. Customizable software from providers like E3 Corp. (www.e3.com), Manugistics (www.manugistics.com), and Supply Chain Solutions have started infiltrating this arena. You can also find VMI integration in larger supply chain implementations that combine the inventory management, order fulfillment and product replenishment of VMI with collaborative sales planning and forecasting such as the SAP Advanced Planner and Optimizer (APO) solution which provides a range of collaborative planning tools and components that can store common information in the SAP APO server or in a standalone collaboration server.

For the most part, manufacturers haven't integrated VMI with their internal ERP systems because software vendors haven't built interfaces. "The two systems use different data models," explained Ron Girard, an analyst at AMR Research (www.amrresearch.com). For the most part, ERP components haven't scaled to the item location volume demanded in a manufacturer direct to customer environment. So unless an enterprise fully adopts an e-business model and takes on the burden of full systems integration, it's faced with what Girard calls "a sneaker net" — a live person (usually wearing sneakers) eyeballing the items in stock on the shelves.

One of the early adopters of VMI was Wal-Mart, which moved to automate

VMI in the late 1980s. But also VF Corp., maker of brands like Healthtex, Lee and Jantzen, has implemented a sophisticated system that integrates retail inventory data from VMI into floor-space management at the store level.

EXTENDED ENTERPRISE MODEL

Carl Redfield, Cisco Systems senior VP of manufacturing and worldwide logistics, cuts to the chase, "Networked [Internet] manufacturing processes have enabled Cisco to manufacture new world products with new world processes, resulting in a competitive advantage for Cisco and enhanced satisfaction for Cisco customers." Cisco's value chain management solution helped it to build an extended enterprise to accommodate higher order volume while minimizing administrative overhead. The Cisco solution fuses the entire value chain — partners, suppliers, manufacturers, distributors, retailers, customers and Cisco's internal operations — into an Internet-based network extension of a single enterprise to serve the customer.

The benefits of Cisco's integrated systems include:

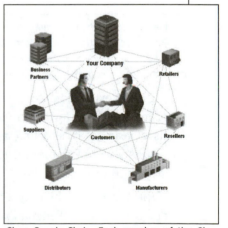

- Faster inventory turns throughout the supply chain, reducing both inventory carrying costs and a product's overall cost base.

- Improved customer satisfaction through a sophisticated LFMS that enables online order entry and configuration and speedy delivery of the product to the customer through rapid sharing of customer demand information across the supply chain.

- Shorter engineering-to-production cycle times thus allowing Cisco and its supply chain partners to increase market share.

- Flexibility to design, ramp, and retire products rapidly in response to market

Cisco Supply Chain. Each member of the Cisco value chain benefits through secure access to key business information giving it the power to make its own decisions, thus amplifying the speed, responsiveness, and efficiency of each member of the value chain. *Graphic courtesy of Cisco Systems.*

demand, allowing Cisco and its supply chain partners to improve inventory carrying costs.

- Ability to sustain product quality while outsourcing major portions of the fulfillment process.

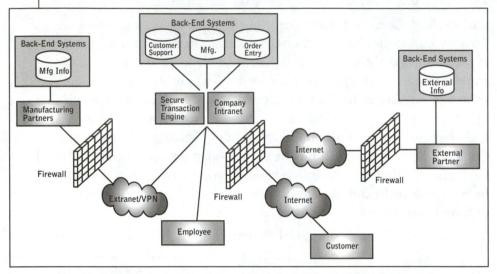

The extended enterprise is built upon a scalable and reliable network infrastructure and uses end-to-end connectivity strategies to support business requirements. Over these secure connections travel critical business transactions, product information, test scripts and results, and customer demand signals. *Graphic courtesy of Cisco Systems.*

Cisco's extended enterprise e-business model has been a critical enabler of its net sales growth from $2 billion in 1995 to almost $19 billion for its fiscal year 2000, showing a 55.7% net sales growth. Its fiscal year 2000 results also reflect the networking equipment vendor's best year-on-year growth in three years.

But Cisco isn't the only e-business reaping the benefits of an extended enterprise model. Federal Express saves $20 million annually by providing package tracking information and shipping management via the Web. And Wal-Mart, as discussed earlier in this book, has created direct Internet links between its inventory control system and its suppliers, such as Proctor & Gamble. Each time Wal-Mart sells an item, the sale automatically triggers a replenishment request at P&G. The result is a dramatic improvement in customer satisfaction as inventory is always fully stocked.

E-businesses implementing the extended enterprise model can quickly communicate customer demand and changes throughout the value chain. This allows suppliers to meet order demand more quickly and also ship the product directly to the customer. Thereby enabling the customer to receive the ordered product on time with higher consistency and enjoy greater control by self-serve processes — ordering, configuring, checking order status — all online.

Order fulfillment process activities occur across multiple value chain members and range from order entry and confirmation to scheduling and production. These include packaging, delivery, and payment that are optimized with an extended enterprise model. With increased coordination, standardization, systemization and connectivity between supply partners comes a reduction in operating costs for all members of the supply chain.

The extended e-business enterprise model allows the entire value chain to share actions that were once isolated within each individual enterprise. A single business action triggers cross-enterprise transactions and changes in market demand can be communicated directly to the supply chain allowing suppliers to respond appropriately to minimize inventory buildup, sustain quality levels, and operate profitably. Thus, automated processes within the value chain remove redundant steps and add efficiencies, which contribute to a positive profit margin for all.

Going back to Cisco's model for a moment, as of the time this book was written, Cisco's supply chain members had achieved a 45% reduction in inventory because they were armed with real-time demand and inventory signals to manage replenishment of subassemblies and components. The result has been a doubling of inventory turns with no impact to on-time shipment.

Direct Fulfillment Model

Within the extended enterprise model is a subset, which I call the direct fulfillment model (a kissing cousin of the e-tail drop-ship model). For example, Cisco has implemented a direct fulfillment model and a merge-in-transit program for materials flowing from various contract manufacturers into a single destination. Subcontract manufacturers were brought into the network so that a product would have the same look and feel, regardless of origin. Third-party logistics providers were plugged into Cisco's database via the Web, giving customers complete information on shipment status. Direct fulfillment means reduced inventories, labor costs and shipping expense. Cisco pegs savings at $10 per unit.

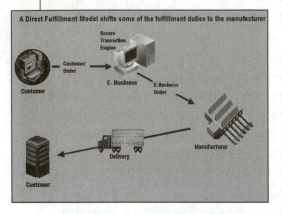

A Direct Fulfillment Model shifts some of the fulfillment duties to the manufacturer

Hold on to your hat — Cisco saves more than $75 million annually as a direct result of the combination of its Internet-linked or networked value chain and the implementation of a direct fulfillment model. Over 75% of Cisco's products are ordered over the Internet, which can be broken down to a figure of more than $22 million in business each day. Cisco outsources 55% of its product fulfillment to its supply chain partners who build and ship product directly to the customer. Cisco personnel never touch the product from order through the fulfillment process. "Cisco does the design and the partners do the rest," says Lance Travis of AMR Research, Inc.

Also, Cisco states that 97% of its products ship on the date promised to the customer. Cisco customers place more than 75% of their orders online, which automatically flow to Cisco and its manufacturing partners to fulfill. Cisco's value chain management system, which incorporates a robust LFMS, allows Cisco to be more responsive to customer requirements and reduces the cycle time from 6-8 weeks to 1-3 weeks.

"The idea of drop-shipping packages directly to the end user is also appealing to companies looking to streamline the delivery process," said Bob Moncrieff, a director of management consulting firm Pittiglio Rabin Todd & McGrath (www.prtm.com). As the e-business model becomes the norm, more enterprises will begin to make available inventory, shipment tracking, and product availability information to their value chain through their online site. In doing so, they are furthering the adoption of direct fulfillment (drop shipping) since the necessary data is easy to find and access.

To show how hybrid the fulfillment models have become, you can place

Bccomponents (passive-component manufacturer), National Semiconductor, V3 Semiconductor, Dell, Lands End, Eddie Bauer, and a host of other e-businesses within the direct fulfillment model (at least with some products). In the case of Dell, shipping cost is typically only about one or two percent of the cost of the average order, so the direct fulfillment model works well. And even when you dig around to come up with an average order at e-tailers such as Eddie Bauer and Lands End, this model still seems to be cost effective.

Build-to-Order/Just-In-Time Model

The build-to-order/just-in-time manufacturing or supply model has been around for quite some time and is closely related to and many times used along with the JIT shipping model (273). Dell is a perfect example of the build-to-order end of this model. Although it doesn't strictly have to be a subset of the extended enterprise model, most of the time that is where it's found.

Dell sells custom-configured PCs to consumers and businesses. It started as a mail-order company that sold its computers over the phone. Dell's e-business model is so widely publicized because Dell was one of the first e-business to sell a large volume of merchandise over the Web. Although Dell has no stores, it registers $14 million in revenues per day through its Web site.

Its customers have been conditioned to expect custom-built computer systems in a couple of days. Those same customers are part of a shift towards "customer pull" where goods are supplied to meet individual consumers' specifications. Dell has set the standard — and captured the lead in the PC market — by assembling computers to individual specifications and shipping them on the same day.

In today's customer pull climate, if an e-business's current manufacturing operations are set up around guessing demand, it will find itself forever in a loop of producing and holding the wrong items and not having enough of what the customer actually wants. David Rucker, director of business development at TBM Institute, a manufacturing consulting firm tries to clarify, "with pull production [in response to customer pull], you have to set up your order management system to be able to respond daily to changing demand." He went on to add, "The most effective manufacturing is to make it when the customer wants it. The trick is to figure out how to set up a system that runs on demand."

For example, when a Dell customer orders a computer system, Dell then transmits the order to its suppliers throughout its supply chain and those suppliers, in turn, transmit orders to their suppliers, and so forth. (In all probability, some of the supply chain members have also adopted a just-in-time manufacturing, supply and/or shipping model.) The customers track the status of their order easily since shippers like Federal Express and UPS provide the systems to track the exact location of an order. Then, there are similar systems that provide Dell manufacturers with exact and timely information about the location of each component and the status of each order in the supply chain. Finally, the Internet enables the fast and safe transfer of money between the different agents.

While the built-to-order/just-in-time model isn't new, its beginning to mushroom. Dell set the standard, Cisco pursued it with a vengeance and others, such as Intel, are quickly following their lead. The Internet has become a catalyst that will make e-businesses re-examine their sourcing strategies and cause them to invest in the IT systems necessary to increase responsiveness of their back-office systems and processes. The capabilities and infrastructure an e-business puts in place now should be built so that they can evolve over time to a less asset-intense, more IT-intense system. In the future, there will be less emphasis on inventory and more emphasis on the build-to-order or just-in-time approach, particularly for high-specification items.

E-TAIL MODEL

"The 'e' in e-commerce is misplaced," said Kevin Silverman, an analyst with securities firm ABN Amro (www.abnamro.com). "It's 'd-commerce' or 'f-commerce' — distribution or fulfillment. You can't e-mail a sweater to somebody."

E-tail has its own specific logistics and fulfillment puzzle to solve. As stated *ad nauseam* throughout this book, to have a truly effective e-tail business necessitates more than just a well-designed, easy to use catalog and shopping cart that enables the customers to browser for products, choose products and click a buy button. E-tailers also must have the ability to seamlessly integrate with an inventory or warehouse system to perform fulfillment functions (in-house or outsourced) along with automated shipping that allows real-time tracking of the package until it's in the customer's hands.

According to Access Media International USA (www.accessmedia-int.com), a technology consulting company that tracks technology-adoption trends in small and medium size e-businesses, an order fulfillment or distribution system is the key to leveraging technology for the small e-tailer. Access Media says that one of the key factors in building online customer loyalty is to meet four basic customer needs: order fulfillment, price, customer service, and Web-site functionality.

In both apparel and groceries, Access Media's analysis shows that improvements in order fulfillment and dependability can have a large impact on customer loyalty. Furthermore, improving customer satisfaction scores in order fulfillment can have an impact on increase implied customer retention rates. A surprising number of customers told Access Media that they had experienced fulfillment frustration and disappoint from e-tail sites because:

- The product received was not exactly what they thought they had ordered.

- The e-tailer had not made them aware of the total price when they placed their order.

- Product delivery was late or lacking in one respect or the other.

- The e-tailer's return policy and service commitments were not met.

Bricks-and-mortar retailers expend huge resources developing world-class capabilities in these areas. Online customers are the same as bricks-and-mortar customers. One of the main reasons Amazon.com is among the top five of almost any "best of ..." list is because it has concentrated on providing its customers with the very best in order fulfillment and dependability (and even Amazon has room for improvement). Of course, Amazon.com was fortunate. It was an early adopter and its first product offerings were relatively easy to handle since few people return books. Hence, Amazon was able to slowly build a distribution arm and, with it, the goodwill of its customers

The value of best-in-class fulfillment cannot be overstated, as many e-businesses found out again this past Christmas season. The e-business that over-invested in marketing or advertising at the expense of fulfillment and basic site functionality may have succeeded in drawing customers to its site, only to lose them forever through poor logistics and fulfillment management.

As reported by Julie Vallone in the May 2000 issue of *Business Start-Ups* magazine, when triathlete Laura Stanford decided to start an e-business selling exercise apparel, she thought that it would be simple. All she needed to do was to attend a few trade shows, set up an attractive site, take the orders and ship them out. "I had no idea what I was getting into," Stanford told Vallone, speaking about her sports apparel boutique, Pro Se Sports (www.pro-se-sports.com). "If I could do it again, I probably wouldn't go into a business that involves inventory or fulfillment."

Stanford told Vallone that her main difficulties were coping with long lead times from manufacturers and managing the logistics and fulfillment in such a way that her customers would be happy. Currently, all of Pro Se's fulfillment operations are handled in-house, although, as sales increased, Stanford did investigate the possibility of outsourcing her fulfillment operations. However, she found it was not the cure-all that she thought it would be. Since women's exercise apparel is a fairly new industry, there were few choices for partnering with fulfillment houses. The ones she found that might have been suitable wanted to charge her around $8 per package — too high for Pro Se Sports to make a profit. "It's prohibitively expensive," says Stanford, "and it doesn't appear that the groups [FSPs] have the kind of customer care we're interested in providing."

All e-tailers must realize that integration between the Web site and the technical infrastructure that supports all commerce transactions is critical. With successful integration, when a Web-based transaction occurs, the order can be processed, the products allocated, each individual order picked and packed, and the package can then be sent on its merry way to the customer's eager hands. Without the integration of the Web site with all the systems that support these processes, customer service, fulfillment, and data integrity are all at risk.

Walk into an e-tailer's executive suite and ask what software packages are used to integrate their Web site with their legacy systems and a full two thirds will not know. The pitiful truth of the matter is that many so-called e-businesses are in reality manually entering order information into their legacy systems or outsourcing their logistics and fulfillment. Of course, the other one third that responded with "custom code," "secure

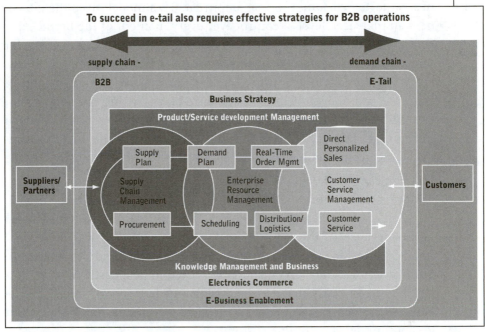

The e-tailer (pure-play or click-and-mortar) that will survive is the e-business that not only provides its customers with a seamless and consistent shopping experience, but also adopts an e-business model that allows for improved efficiencies throughout the supply chain.

transfer," or named a packaged solution, does give hope that this dismal under utilization of the e-business model can be turned around.

Pure-Play In-house Model

Logistics and fulfillment operations, including stock inventory and shipping, are the biggest issues e-tailers must grapple with. The only logical way to do this is to ensure that the whole supply chain process is under control. Outsourcing these critical functions won't work in the long term. Frequent out-of-stock notices, late deliveries and sub-standard or defective products will bring on the dreaded negative "word of mouse" and with it a declining customer base.

The pure-play in-house model is exemplified by the scenario whereby a product is ordered off the Web site and shipped from an in-house fulfillment center (a basement or garage for a home-based e-business, a warehouse or distribution center (possibly automated) for larger e-businesses) to the customer in one shipment. This model gives the e-business an increased level of control over every moment of the brand experience, which is what the mail order catalog business has been doing for years. However, it does require know-how, labor, facilities and often, special equipment and software, all of which may be outside the area of expertise and budget of the average pure-play. The big disadvantage of this model is that there is usually only the one shipping location, which means that same-day delivery is impossible (except in the direct proximity of the distribution center) and next-day delivery is costly for the majority of shipments.

More and more e-businesses are adopting this model. SmarterKids.com has opened its own 140,000 square foot fulfillment facility because its executive board felt that its success was dependent upon SmarterKids.com handling its own shipments and not relying on outsourcing. Reliance on outsourcing proved to be a costly mistake during the 1999 holiday season — a mistake made by nearly every other e-tailer — that resulted in missed or botched shipments, and a significant loss of confidence by online customers.

The oft quoted Forrester has, across its many different research reports, fallen squarely into the camp of those who believe that e-businesses who rely on third party fulfillment providers have a tough row to hoe and in all probability will not survive. Forrester attributes the near demise of Peapod to its unprofitable grocer-fulfilled operations. The markets in which it did its own fulfillment, from its own warehouses, were its profitable markets, but not enough to overcome the disadvantages of relying on others for a large percentage of its fulfillment needs.

And, while some analysts saw Amazon's move to in-house fulfillment as a bad move, Forrester saw it differently. According to Forrester, as long as an in-house fulfillment facility, staffing, capacity and technology allows an e-business to handle its own fulfillment, it has a good thing going. The overwhelming success of catalog-based e-businesses such as LandsEnd.com, EddieBauer.com and JCrew.com (ranked, respectively, 15, 16 and 39 in the Russell Reynolds Associates/VeriFone Top 100 Internet Retailers survey), which have their own fulfillment centers, supports Forrester's counter-intuitive position.

It's not only the "big guys" that should consider in-house fulfillment. Tony Rayder, the founder of RedWagons.com, an e-tailer that sells Radio Flyer children's wagons quickly achieved success in its niche market space. However, this very prosperity necessitated the decision to make a quick move toward handling its own fulfillment instead of using its distributor, Radio Flyers' resources. RedWagons.com initially acquired a 1,000-square foot warehouse to ship its own product, but when projections showed that it would soon outgrow the space, it added an additional 1,000 feet prior to the 1999 holiday season. "This was really a mission-critical decision," Rayder says, one which he has not regretted making.

Outsourced Model

Full-service fulfillment companies offer up an end-to-end solution: They take your products from warehouse shelves, pack them, hand them to shippers and then send an automated e-mail response to your customers to let them know their packages are in transit. They can also handle your credit-card processing, supply current inventory levels to your Web site, reorder products, offer call-center services, send notices of shipment, and handle returns. There are literally thousands of these companies to choose from, but experts say the best way to find one that suits your needs is by word-of-mouth.

If you're using your Web hosting company for shopping cart and credit-card functions or doing this in-house, you can just use some of the fulfillment companies' options — such as pick-and-pack, returns processing and customer service support.

So, should you outsource? Art Avery, principal consultant of Avery & Associates (www.elogistics101.com), an e-commerce distribution and logistics consulting firm, advises that outsourcing your fulfillment only makes good financial sense if the e-business has more money than time. "When you need every penny, you should do it yourself," he explains. "When you can earn more doing other things with your time, look outside." In addition, he says you should outsource only when your present method has to be expanded and the incremental cost of expansion would be expensive.

Before you choose a fulfillment company, however, make sure that it wants your business (many might not) and is reliable. "If your fulfillment company screws up in your peak season, you can lose your entire business," Avery says. And, no matter what type of fulfillment operation you set up, it shouldn't cost more than 10% of sales, plus the actual shipping costs.

Your Web site gets tons of orders, but how do you fill them? If you're asking this question, then don't go it alone — outsourcing makes fulfillment and distribution simpler and more efficient. If you're a small e-business owner, you probably won't need to worry about setting up an efficient nation-wide distribution facility — yet. The companies offering these services are called fulfillment service providers, fulfillment partners or fulfillment houses (they will be referred to as fulfillment service provider or FSP in this book).

The outsourcing model gives the e-business a good deal of control over all aspects of product quality, distribution and messaging. This model could utilize one or multiple distribution centers strategically located nationwide or worldwide, each center carrying inventory levels relative to their regional market.

The FSP receives merchandise from the e-business and numerous other businesses and it stores the merchandise in its warehouse(s). It picks, packs and ships the orders received by its clients. Since the FSP provides this service to numerous businesses, it can spread the costs of the operation across a large base. However, e-businesses may find that maintaining the optimum service levels will require adjustments — give everyone at least 4 or 5 months to work out all of the bugs. In particular, many of these providers make it difficult for an e-business to obtain real-time information about inventory status and order status. So don't sign a contract with a new FSP just a month or so before the Christmas buying rush.

Many large e-tailers are currently using this model. There are e-businesses that feel (and rightly so) it's good business practice to concentrate on their core strengths and contract with experts, such as a FSP. The FSP will, for an up-front agreed price, provide whatever services are needed. The FSP will receive a Web site's products, warehouse them, and when customers orders are received, it will pick and fill the customers orders, and pack and ship each order to the customers by the method that the Web site and/or its customers choose. The FSP works for the e-business and therefore the labels and packing lists carry the e-business's name and logo.

Although Wal-Mart has an "up and down" relationship with its e-tail site, Jeanne Jackson, chief executive of Walmart.com states that Wal-Mart will eventually handle its own fulfillment of Internet orders. Until it does, it will continue to use Fingerhut Inc., a Federated Department Stores Inc. subsidiary, and Airborne Express Co.'s Airborne Logistics division to take orders and deliver products. Walmart.com is building a warehouse in Carrollton, GA that Jackson says will begin to fulfill Internet orders in August 2001. "We've made the decision to start with one facility and make the thing work," Jackson explains.

Why did Wal-Mart with its notable logistics and fulfillment talent choose to outsouce its online fulfillment needs? I believe one reason is to test the waters so it can fully understand the online demand for its products — what does the online customer expect, order, return? When Walmart.com does open its distribution center in the summer of 2001, it will have been down the road once, albeit as an observer, but it will have an experience curve, which will allow it to build in-house, scale-based capabilities.

Drop-Ship Model

Many entrepreneurs initially adopted the drop-ship model because they bought into the hype of easy sales worldwide. The drop-ship manufacturers or distributors would ship the product directly to the entrepreneur's customers with the e-tailer's name on the merchandise, without the entrepreneur having to pay a cent upfront, but it would hear the "kerching" of its cash register with every purchase.

It's not quite that simple. I'm not saying it can't be done, but it takes a lot of work — i.e., it can be done. And this model is popular with many small e-tailers, particularly because it reduces initial capital expenditures. There are large e-tailers also utilizing drop shippers, i.e, CDNow.com.

When using this model, a customer clicks the buy button on the Web site, the e-tailer then forward's the order to its drop shipper(s) (a wholesaler or distributor that owns a variety of products). The drop shipper then fills that order by shipping product directly to the Web site's customers. The e-tailer owns the customer database, while the drop shipper owns the products. The drop shipper pays the e-tailer a sales commission. The drawbacks of this arrangement are that there is little or no control over how the products are packed and shipped. Unless negotiated in advance, your products can be shipped with the drop shipper's name on the packaging instead of the e-tailer's brand causing difficulties in retaining a loyal customer base. The drop-ship model generally functions best if an e-tail site offers a wide range or generalized base of products but doesn't want to worry about managing the entire chain of the order fulfillment process.

The drop-ship model requires that the e-tailer give up much of its control over the fulfillment process. Although an e-tailer may determinedly establish rigid guidelines for its drop-ship suppliers, it's still putting its brand in the hands of strangers. This includes everything from quality of product, delivery to the customers, communication with customers concerning tracking, shipping, delivery dates, returns, and so forth.

When it comes to integrating the front-end customer experience with the drop-ship fulfillment process the disadvantages of this model become apparent.

- An e-tailer probably won't have any control over when the order will be shipped to the customer or in how many packages. It might not even know if the product the customer ordered is in stock.

- An e-tail site may not have a way to provide customers with tracking or shipping status information.

- The products ordered from the e-tailer may be shipped with the drop shipper's own name on the labels and packing lists, negating the Web site's branding efforts and causing customer confusion on receipt of the package.

This model isn't hopeless. If an e-tailer does decide to use the drop-ship model for some or all of its products it needs to iron out the peccadilloes prior to entering into any written contract. An e-tailer determined to make the drop-ship model work should consider utilizing a service for its order management, such as OrderTrust (www.ordertrust.net),

---

General shipping information

Shipping charges are affected by a variety of factors, especially when shipping to a non-U.S. destination. CDNOW is always working to improve the quality and cost of shipping for both our U.S. and non-U.S. customers. For this reason, shipping rates and policies are subject to change without notice.

- **All available shipping options and your exact shipping and handling charges (and any applicable taxes) will be shown in your Shopping Cart after you login to your account (or create an account).** Because CDNOW ships worldwide, it is not possible to calculate your shipping and handling charges before you login.

- **Orders combining different shipping centers** CDNOW fills orders from many different locations. Therefore, various items, even items from the same product line, may not ship from the same shipping center. Please, be aware that when you combine orders that include items shipping from different centers, you will incur some additional shipping charges. However, your total shipping charge will be less than if you placed your orders separately.

- **Please verify your shipping address before placing your order.** An additional shipping charge will be applied if we have to re-ship an item because of an address error.

- Shipping upgrades may not apply to items that are backordered at the time your order is placed.

As this graphic indicates a drop-ship model provides challenges for the e-tailer and can cause inconvenience for the online customer.

Netship (www.netship.com) or Dotcom Distribution (www.dotcomdist.com) to help it maintain control over the fulfillment process. Or some of this can be accomplished by establishing internal monitoring processes, assigning employees to drop-ship monitoring, and leveraging technologies that will help to integrate the Web site with the drop-shipper's systems to aid it in keeping the customer informed.

Click-and-Mortar

Click-and-mortars are beginning to figure out how to use their distinct advantage over pure-plays — capitalizing on the years of experience their "bricks" have in the traditional world getting logistics and fulfillment down to a science. Heed some sage advice given by Randall S. Hancock, senior vice president of eStrategy at Mainspring (www.mainspring.com): "While e-commerce is indeed taking off across many sectors, the growth of the online market will be limited unless Internet retailers can overcome fundamental obstacles such as channel management, fulfillment, and customer service." The study's findings indicate that bricks-and-mortar assets are crucial to meeting the challenges of building a profitable online business, adds Chris Zook, head of Bain's Global Strategy Practice (www.bain.com).

Making the transition to a click-and-mortar involves building and stocking warehouses, investing in warehouse staff, packing the boxes and handling customer queries, complaints and returns. RISNews.com figures show that 46% of click-and-mortars use the same distribution center that serve their traditional counterpart, which can be efficient if warehouse management systems and at least part of the distribution center layout are designed for small household orders. E-tailers are beginning to learn the ropes, although some will still make a few expensive mistakes along the way.

There are numerous examples of this model, Nordstrom.com, Saksfifthavenue.com, Borders.com, and Sears.com, to name a few.

Local Fulfillment Model

Many bricks-and-mortar retailers are encouraging their online counterpart's customers to pickup online purchases at their local stores. Not only do in-store pickups provide another level of customer service for the online customer, but they also help to optimize the cost structure of the bricks-and-mortar retailers. The pure click-and-mortar (no catalog) doesn't have the experience nor facilities for shipping directly to the customers. The regional warehouses load trucks bound for stores with merchandise in bulk that is later unpacked and put on display in a store for sale to the customer. In essence, bricks-and-mortar retailers are optimized to deliver products to customers on a local basis at the store level. Therefore, some of them decided to make use of this competence — have the online customer come into the local store to pick up the product (that they had ordered or reserved online).

In a keynote speech delivered by analyst Patricia Seybold, she noted that the best-positioned retailers are those with so-called "click-and-mortar capabilities," that let customers do things like order online and pickup goods at local stores. According to Seybold, e-tailers will continue to increase their distribution networks via local delivery services in 2001.

Using stores for returns and in-store pickups is a good example of local fulfillment, but this is just a base hit compared to the home run delivered through the option of near immediate delivery of online orders from local stores or warehouses (both e-tail and B2B). This convergence edge may be devastating to the prospects of most pure-plays because customers may see it as representing the ultimate in online customer service. I feel strongly that pure-plays need to look closely at a local fulfillment model and determine how they can adopt it as a subset to their logistics and fulfillment model.

Once the various entities have merged into a single e-business enterprise, they can offer local fulfillment allowing the click-and-mortar to change the customer's buying process from one based solely on breadth of selection and price, to include immediacy of service. An added benefit is the very real chance of an additional impulse purchase while the customer is in the store to pickup their order.

This model also means that click-and mortars have the chance to out perform their pure-play competitors. They can beat them on speed of service and do so in a way that will leverage, at little incremental cost, every bit of their bricks-and-mortar infrastructure. The pure-plays have no option but to build, buy or enter into a partnership to obtain what the click-and-mortars already control. But this puts the pure-plays at risk since they will be subjected to the full cost impact of positioning themselves to compete on the new service dimension of immediate fulfillment unless they take the partnership route (Amazon/Toys 'R Us).

One local delivery option, which many pure-plays may opt for, is for an e-business to align with a local convenience store (a Seven Eleven, dry cleaning or gasoline franchise, for instance). This way their customers can shop online but pickup the order (and maybe even pay) at the local establishment. The examples cited above are very convenient (chains are numerous and generally keep long hours). They make a great alternative for local delivery convenience if the e-business wishes to take this route.

One pure-play, Kozmo.com, is making a move toward the local fulfillment model by entering into an agreement with Starbucks Coffee stores. The agreement allows for Kozmo.com to use local Starbucks Coffee storefronts in several major cities as drop-off depots for Kozmo.com customers who use its Internet-based service to rent videocassettes, DVDs and other items.

Toy retailer KB Toys and its "click," KBkids.com, recently formed a committee from both organizations to explore ideas such as allowing customers to order products online and then pick them up at stores. "Those are things we're looking at," said Mike Wagner, vice president and chief operating officer at KBkids.com. "But we're not there yet."

Don't try to convince luxury retailer Neiman Marcus to support pick-up at or delivery from local stores. Its online counterpart doesn't believe it needs to replicate its bricks-and-mortar stores. Jo Marie Lilly, senior VP states, "We're not trying to put each individual store online. It would actually be quite cumbersome to keep the sites up to date with all their inventory. Linking those systems doesn't seem cost-effective or desired by our customers."

In-Store Fulfillment Model

This is another local fulfillment model for the click-and-mortars. When an online order is received by a click-and-mortar it's fulfilled by employees who pick stock from its counterpart's traditional retail store shelves. Then the product delivery process is basically the same as with any other model. This model does incur less startup costs, and some bricks-and-mortars use this model when testing the waters in the e-tail arena. In the end though, this model can be very expensive due to overhead and the complexity in tracking and pricing and billing the same inventory for both store and Web sales.

While many e-businesses can achieve fulfillment speed with this model, most have probably not achieved efficiency. According to RISNews.com, 30% of e-tailers are picking at least part of their online orders from their counterpart's store shelves — an expensive effort.

Don't talk to Williams-Sonoma about redirecting its catalog and online customer orders to a local store. Their spokesperson doesn't think it's cost-effective, citing that retailers ship merchandise to local stores in bulk packaging. Store employees then unpack the merchandise and put it on display. If customers order merchandise to be shipped to them from a local outlet rather than the main warehouse, the store has to repackage the goods for delivery. "Those costs are then passed on to the customer. It's not an efficient model or it would have come together years ago," the Williams-Sonoma spokesperson added.

However, the in-store fulfillment model can give speed to market, although it must be a short-term solution. The UK grocer, Tesco's, approach of crowding the store aisles and check-out stands with its self-styled "pick-pack-and-ship" personnel did allow it to have an almost immediate online presence once its executive officers decided to take the plunge. But as scale builds, Tesco will need to adopt a more efficient approach, this model is awkward, inefficient and cost-intensive.

A US grocer providing in-store personal shoppers is Haggen. Haggen operates two Web-based businesses www.topfoods.com, a value-oriented site and www.haggen.com, a high-service site. ShopEaze (www.shopeaze.com) provides a turnkey online approach for the Haggen chain. Haggen and Tops don't offer delivery, instead the online customer's shopping list is downloaded as pick lists for in-store personal shoppers to fulfill the order and the customer picks up the order at designated drive-through lanes at all Haggen chain storefronts.

An innovative Internet start-up, myButler.com, provides click-and-mortars with a fully supported, turnkey Internet service that gets grocery businesses online, fast. The myButler.com services include a customized easy-to-use shopping interface, in-store fulfillment procedures and an innovative e-commerce enabled, multi-partner Web site. IGA stores served by Sobeys', a major supermarket retailer in Canada, will use myButler.com's technology and Symbol's CS2000 (www.symbol.com) for selling products over the Web.

Another start-up, deliverEnow.com, provides an end-to-end solution for click-and-mortars wanting to give their online customers access to local store inventories as well as same-day delivery. Stock Clerk 1.0 is its proprietary in-store fulfillment, managing, and monitoring system that allows Web-based orders to be paid for, picked, packed and shipped from a local store. deliverEnow.com has also introduced an easy, nationwide delivery system, plugging into Stock Clerk 1.0, it enables click-and-mortars to provide immediate, same-day delivery from every store in their network.

Kiosk Order Model

This model is often a subset of local fulfillment. More and more click-and-mortars are beginning to use this model, and in the future you will find pure-plays in this space as well. For example, 80% of retailers plan to roll out kiosks and Web-linked point-of-sale systems in physical stores by 2002 according to a Forrester survey of 30 bricks-and-mortar executives. Forrester analyst, Seema Williams, is bullish on in-store Web access since it gives shoppers another route to find detailed information on goods, compare prices, and order goods not stocked in stores.

According to Matt Hyde, REI's vice president for online sales, that's why outdoor goods retailer REI (www.rei.com) installed online kiosks in 58 of its stores. Hyde says, "Now we're finding customers are using (kiosks) for transactions, and we're finding transactions are happening at an increasing frequency. If you look at the aggregate sales across all our kiosks, it's about the same as sales for one of our physical stores." Not bad!

The basic concept is simple; a customer orders products, using a Kiosk with a computer and high-speed connection, located at a store or mall. With this model the customer doesn't need a home computer and most of the time can even pay in person for the products ordered. In this model it's possible to order products offered online and pay in cash. Customers then choose to pickup the order on their next trip to the kiosk or have it shipped to a specified location.

One advantage of this model is a possible increase in customer loyalty by introducing human interaction (the store clerk that takes the payment and hands over the products). Also, an almost unlimited range of products can be made available for pickup at a neighborhood store — provided the customer can wait a couple of days. Soon Internet Kiosks may be as prevalent as ATMs, and ordering your favorite books, wine, clothing and gourmet food at your corner coffee shop or dry cleaners for later pickup may be a common occurance.

The big retailers that have adopted an e-business model, such as Office Depot, Home Depot, and Nordstrom's, are struggling with the challenge of how to entice traditional customers to shop through the their e-tail site. Many are coming up with the same solution — install kiosks in their stores. In doing so, they hope to condition customers to shop at their virtual store using an in-house Web connection installed in a kiosk-like environment. Kmart in cooperation with its counterpart, Bluelight.com, rolled out Web kiosks in 1,600 of its 2,000+ stores just before the big holiday shopping rush in 2000.

Borders Books and Music stores, one of the nation's top booksellers, currently offers its customers the ease of its in-store Title Sleuth kiosk that utilizes the latest in Web-based technologies to put millions of titles at the fingertips of their in-store customers.

The kiosk lets Borders customers perform self-directed searches of more than 400 subject areas including top-selling books, music and videos/DVDs. This allows customers to check availability of a desired title within the retail store (for immediately purchase or in the company-wide stock supply for quick delivery).

"Title Sleuth is a significant milestone in our retail convergence strategy," said Mary Jean Raab, senior vice president, retail direct and convergence for Borders. "We are taking our fundamental strength in customer service to a new level by bringing the range and convenience of the Internet to the store and marrying it with the insight and knowledge of our staff to create a powerful customer experience."

Borders believes that retail convergence — the integration of bricks-and-mortar and emerging retail channels (such as e-tail) and technology to provide customers with a compelling and enhanced shopping experience is the future for all e-businesses. Early results of the rollout of Title Sleuth kiosks — based on customer reaction and increased special order sales — are very encouraging.

This is something all click-and-mortars should do. Borders started the trend in 1999. It's the best customer service process a click-and-mortar can do and one that will generate more sales. Why should you lose a sale, when a customer is in your store?

Suppose you were to find the book you want online, and Barnesand Noble.com with its network of storefronts had a way where you wouldn't have to wait three to seven days to receive the book. If you wanted to, you could determine, online, the nearest Barnes & Noble retail store carrying that particular book in current inventory, reserve it there, and pick it up that evening. If you wanted to, you could return something to the store that the e-tailer had delivered to you last week. While you're in the store, you could grab a latte, sit down at a kiosk, and see the same collaborative-filtering generated recommendations you normally only get from online.

These kiosks could even tell you in which aisle to pick up a copy. Add to that BarnesandNoble.com's ability to send you personalized e-mails saying: "We know you like Cat in the Hat books, and your local Barnes & Noble store will be hosting a Cat in the Hat costume party next month. We'll reserve a ticket for you." Or, because it knows you're a mystery reader, "We're having a 'Who Done It' festival on Monday evening at the Midtown store, and Saturday afternoon at the 96th Street store."

Click-to-Bricks

A variation of the local fulfillment model, which has aspects of the in-store model is click-to-bricks. The idea is quite simple. Go online to find a nearby bricks-and-mortar retailer that has what you're looking for in stock. Then go to that store with the confidence that you can pick up what you're looking for. "It's increasingly important to let consumers choose how they want to get their product," says James Vogtle, Boston Consulting Group's (www.bcg.com) e-commerce research director. As reported in an April 24, 2000 issue of BusinessWeekOnline, in theory, there's a payoff for retailers, too. By letting buyers place orders and make pickups themselves, they wring more value from locations that already carry the costs of receiving, storing, and merchandising goods.

But so far, only a handful of traditional retailers have opted to tryout this fulfillment model — various egrocers, food.com, circuitcity.com, and webhealthcenter.com, to name a few. But, the malls are getting into the act. Check out malibu.com, the online division of Rivertown Crossings Mall in Grandville, Michigan. Also, browse www.futureshop/photos, this site allows customers to upload, download, enhance, print, share and distribute high-quality photo images across Canada or around the world in digital form. Then after viewing the photos the customer can order any number of prints in standard photographic sizes. The finished photos can either be made available for pickup at a Future Shop location or mailed to the customer.

Internet pure-plays are turning the tables and Gateway Computer is an obvious example, with its recent opening of physical stores — Gateway Country. Gateway, as usual, is doing it a bit differently. Their "bricks" don't hold inventory. The stores allow customers to "test drive" the hardware, learn how to use software, and ask questions (especially good for the technically challenged). Then, once a decision is made, the customer can order customized Gateway systems via the Internet — all from within the physical store (a hybrid click-to-bricks and kiosk model).

Retailer Circuit City built a robust Web presence (www.circuitcity.com) that replicated its customer's bricks-and-mortar experience offering comparison capabilities, large inventory and immediate inventory information. Its e-business strategy was for the enterprise to be tightly interlinked and interdependent while providing quality online service.

Circuit City offers its "Express Delivery," which allows online shoppers to search the real-time inventory database of three stores. Dennis Bowman, Circuit City's CIO says that 50% of their Web site visits end up at one of their bricks-and-mortar stores to buy the product. Against pureplays "the major source of leverage we have is our stores," he adds. Plus, this fulfillment model is perfect for electronics since shoppers do most of their research online prior to purchasing a product, but like to have a hands-on experience before the actual purchase takes place. Bowman also feels that the click-to-bricks model helps to reduce any conflict that might occur between the "brick," staff and the "click" staff.

As far back as October 1999 Cnet.com reported that businesses are betting that physical stores will help capture shoppers who are not yet online — and give customers a convenient way to return goods and try out products — a benefit that analysts say is missing from Web-based stores. "The retail business of the future has a bricks-and-mortar and Internet side," said Jupiter Communications analyst Ken Cassar.

This thinking follows industry analyst predictions that successful retailers in the future will operate online and offline. "This is absolutely where bricks-and-mortar merchants need to be in the future," says Forrester Research Inc. analyst Lisa Allen.

Of course, as with any new idea there are the naysayers. One is Don Paschal, manager of global store marketing for ICL Retail Systems Inc. (www.iclretail.com), designer of retail computers who asks, "If you've found an item online, how can you be sure it isn't sold in the store before you get there?"

There are downsides to this model. The "brick" has to find a way to integrate its complex and many times legacy systems — inventory systems, cash-register data (point-of-sale), with its Web-based catalog (which describes the items). And don't forget there also needs to be a system in place to retrieve the items within the actual store. Most have come up with only one solution to that puzzle — a clerk who can search up and down and aisles and in the backrooms for the requested item.

As Fulton R. Macdonald, with retail consultancy International Business Development (www.idbcorporation.com), another naysayer states: "All kinds of errors occur in physical stores that can mess up inventory status," and you still might end up with an unhappy customer. Only this time the customer made an extra effort by physically visiting a store with a "promise" that the item would be available. How will the e-business handle this problem?

SAME-DAY DELIVERY MODEL

This e-business model is utilized by both B2Bs and e-tailers. Although e-tails use of this model can be "normal operating procedure," B2Bs use of this model is more on the "exception basis." Numerous e-businesses have discovered the hard way that there's a lot more to building a successful e-business than enticing the customer to click the "buy" button. The most challenging corner of e-business can be where the customer wants the product delivered not in a week or a few days, but within hours. Setting up a Web site that displays products and takes orders is just the beginning; the remainder is delivering the 3Rs and still make a profit.

As I have pointed out in various sections of this book, the e-business model has led executives to borrow from commerce models from days gone by. In this instance, the consumer telephoned the neighborhood greengrocer, butcher, fishmonger and drygoods store and placed their daily or weekly order, and the delivery person appeared at the door later in the day with the ordered products in hand. The difference today is that the ordering occurs online, and the consumer is generally absent from home. The e-tailers must establish a mutually convenient time certain to deliver the ordered goods.

A small but growing number of e-tailers are trying to help the modern consumer to relive these bygone days by offering the convenience of same-day delivery. While some try to handle the task themselves, others use outside firms to deliver their product to the customer's doorstep.

Most e-tailers lack adequate facilities or the IT resources necessary to develop fulfillment technology necessary for fast delivery. Many are turning to fulfillment and delivery networks such as Sameday.com. Others piggyback onto the infrastructure of an existing quick-delivery e-retailer.

For example, Mrs. Beasley's (www.mrsbeasley.com), a bakery that provides delicious cakes and cookies with a promise of same day delivery for pre-noon orders. In early 2000 Mrs. Beasley expanded its quick-delivery reach by partnering with Sameday.com, formerly Shipper.com. Mrs. Beasley's has several physical locations in the Los Angeles area that act as depots for products to be delivered and with Sameday.com the e-tailer's delivery footprint reaches into northern California.

The Mrs. Beasley's site takes orders through a central server that analyzes zip codes to automatically fax the nearest store with an order to assemble delivery packages. Orders requested outside Los Angeles but within Sameday.com's delivery range are assembled at noon and taken in a batch to Sameday.com. Sameday.com also accepts orders through its own site for Mrs. Beasley's and electronically submits them to the shop.

Typically, Sameday.com clients interface with the company over the Internet using a proprietary Java application called iShipper. Web merchants with Java e-commerce engines write interfaces to the iShipper APIs. The Sameday.com application is a "many-to-many" command and control system capable of interfacing with several e-business sites on one hand and many sources of supply on the other. iShipper plugs into warehouse management systems using either XML or EDI technology. "Essentially, we're in the rapid response supply chain business," said Sameday.com CEO Alex Nesbitt. Sameday charges a fee per transaction that varies by product characteristics, service level and volume. Nesbitt said the fees are comparable to the shipping and handling fees sites charge consumers.

Sameday.com has a fast-growing list of e-business clients. "If consumers are to leave the malls in droves, they will want the almost instant satisfaction they get by buying goods in person," says Nesbitt. "Droves" may be a bit of an overstatement but otherwise the author agrees with Mr. Nesbitt.

One of the first e-tail sectors to adopt the same day fulfillment model were the online grocers. On an average, the online grocer's customer orders once a week. When online shoppers place an order on most grocer's Web sites, they are given the choice of delivery windows. To hold down costs, many online grocers have delegated much of the order assembly to local bricks-and-mortar grocers, produce wholesalers and other perishable food distributors. If the online grocer has the right LFMS in place, as a customer places the order, it flows into the pipeline going to the online grocer's system, with requests for the relevant items forwarded to its supply chain via a computer link, along with the deadline accompanying each order. Then, once confirmation of product availability is received, delivery trucks, vans or even bicycles periodically swing by the distributors and ferry items back to the main warehouse, where they are combined with other products from the e-tailer's own shelves to complete the order.

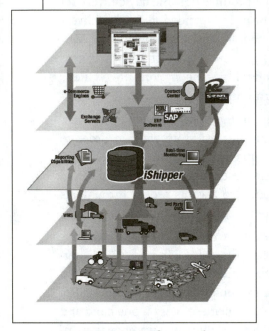

How iShipper works. *Courtesy of Sameday.com*

The optimal system then has the delivery staff perform a quality-control check, reconciling the bar-codes on the totes lined up at their loading bays with the addresses on their route lists prior to delivery.

To provide same day delivery is always more expensive, both for the e-business and its customer. The customer may feel it's a good tradeoff — personal time for money. It also requires a very complex distribution and delivery network. Because of this it must be limited to specific geographic areas (how is an e-business going to cost-effectively give same day delivery to a farmer in the outreaches of Minnesota or a customer in the mountains of New Mexico).

As mentioned previously, Barnes & Noble's (www.bn.com) online store offers same day delivery of in-stock books or music titles to customers who live in select locations at no extra charge beyond its standard ground-shipping rate. BarnesandNoble.com uses an independent courier to make the deliveries up to 7 p.m. seven days a week.

JUST-IN-TIME MODEL

There are numerous ways an e-business could adopt this model. Suppose a FSP ran a network of distribution centers, and each center could ship product for dozens of large and small e-business sites. An e-business could contract with one of the FSPs with multiple distribution centers, giving it a presence in many regional areas. Or perhaps the e-business has one or more of its own distribution or fulfillment centers, it could supplement those using FSPs in areas under-supported by the e-business's in-house fulfillment solutions. Of course, if you're Staples.com you might try to go it alone and still provide your on-line customer base 2-day shipping via ground transport (the least expensive) through strategically located distribution centers.

Using the regional distribution center model also allows an e-business to use just-in-time (JIT) inventory management, thus saving on inventory holding costs, and ground shipment savings. When a business has only one distribution center its products are usually received in large quantities and stored in pallet racks until needed. As items are picked, more products have to be dropped from the pallet racks to replenish the picking area. This receive-store-replenish-pick cycle is a repeated expense, and, if replenishment is too slow, out-of-stock notices may occur even when product is in the building.

If an e-business opts to go with the JIT inventory model through outsourcing, it should look for a FSP that has supply chain management software to accommodate just-in-time shipping; thus allowing products and orders to flow smoothly from manufacturers and distributors to regional distribution centers and finally the customers. Adoption of a JIT model can result in increasing the frequency with which inbound shipments of product are scheduled, but decreasing the lead times and size of these shipments. E-businesses that adopt the JIT model often reduce the number of suppliers and transport companies with which they must deal and select suppliers which are close to their regional distribution centers enabling delivery of shipments with short lead times. In addition, each regional center has only a portion of the e-business's total stock, so it's a simple task to shelve all received product directly into the pick area.

Another reason for choosing this distribution model is that many e-businesses need to give their customers reasonably priced next day or 2nd day delivery. To do this cost-effectively requires that the e-business place inventory in numerous regional centers, thereby increasing its inventory holding costs. However, that increase could be balanced by a decrease in overall shipping costs and an increase in customer satisfaction.

Here's how it works. Normally a business would have one fulfillment center in (let's say) Cleveland, Ohio and a customer in the nether regions of Arizona places an order that could normally be shipped for delivery within the two day time period. But, what if there is a problem (which happens frequently), now the business has to ship "next day" at additional cost (which it has to "eat") to meet the promised delivery date. Now take that same scenario but the business has its inventory in 4 regional centers. The Arizona customer's order is sent to a regional fulfillment center in Nevada; and, even if there is a mix-up, which causes a delay in shipping the product, it can still avoid the expensive air shipment due to the proximity of the fulfillment center to the customer. In other words, with strategically located fulfillment centers throughout the country an e-business can promise second day delivery with more certainty and less cost due to the proximity of the product to the customer, allowing for ground shipment in most cases.

It isn't always absolutely necessary to increase inventory. With the right technology running behind the scenes, an e-business can maximize its normal inventory levels. Take the same scenario: the Arizona customer's order is sent to the Nevada fulfillment center, but that center is out of stock and cannot fill the order. The fulfillment system can seamlessly transmit the order to another fulfillment center and still meet the second day delivery deadline although at times it may need to resort to a more expensive air rather than a ground shipping option. The e-business did not carry extra inventory, but because of its data network it could still adopt the just-in-time model. Although the use of this system, will, at times, require paying premium shipping charges to meet the second day delivery deadline, it will not be the case in every instance.

A good example of the JIT model is eToys, which seems to have its LFMS well in hand, although its cash-flow woes are threatening the e-tailer's viability. That comment is supported by a mid-2000 Forrester's PowerRankings survey in the toys and games category. In that survey eToys was so close to the number one spot held by Amazon that it could dethrone Amazon with only a few simple changes (none having to do with logistics and fulfillment).

eToys has a product line that has always been a friend of the e-business e-tail model — toys and games. In a late 2000 report on online shopping, eToys ranked first in overall customer shopping experience (beating out Amazon). To be honest, the only dark cloud (outside of its lack of cash) in eToys' meteoric rise as an e-business superstar was the 1999 Christmas season — it stumbled, not as bad as some of its competitors, but still...

Even in 1999 eToys was using a scaled-down version of JIT inventory management and shipping. In addition to its own warehouse and distribution centers, it contracted with Fingerhut to help out over the holiday buying season. Nonetheless, as I am sure many of the readers know, thousands of orders (albeit only about 1% of the total) didn't make it under a Christmas tree before the fateful date.

eToys admits that its own fulfillment group was less than perfect, but it does try to place much of the blame on Fingerhut. Of course, Fingerhut (www.fingerhut.com) vehemently denies any wrongdoing stating that 99.9% of the orders forwarded to it for fulfillment were "clear" on Christmas Eve — i.e., those orders had already been shipped.

Early in 2000 eToys built out two new fulfillment centers with JIT shipping as one of the catalysts. Its Danville, VA center was put online to help ensure that shipping will be faster and cheaper to the 70% of eToys' customers who live east of the Mississippi. The Ontario, CA fulfillment operation was located near an airport, which serves as the Southern California hub for both UPS and FedEx. In early 2001 eToys announced the closing of 2 of its distribution centers in an extra-ordinary cost-cutting move in hopes of staying in business.

CONVERGED MODEL

With increased sales, a larger customer database and better customer relationships since adopting an e-business model, the CEO of Sunbelt Sportswear, a leading marketer of men's and women's apparel, only wishes the company could have been on the Internet sooner.

Dan Bennett, CEO of Sunbelt Sportswear, a leading marketer of men's and women's apparel, ventured, "Since launching our upgraded wholesale site (www.sunbeltsportswear.com), we have experienced a tremendous growth in wholesale sales — and significant and steady growth from our new venture retail site (www.sunbeltdirect.com). In just a short period of time — approximately 2 months — we have seen such a positive response and growth rate that our sites are already evolving."

Bennett went on to say, "The response to the sites has exceeded our initial expectations, and based on direct customer feedback we are now prominently featuring sale items on our retail home page. One of the strongest features of our retail site is that it gives us access to customer demographics, shopping habits and preferences — information that was previously difficult to obtain. This feature alone helps us better merchandise to our customers and meet their specific needs."

Numerous click-and-mortars with good brand names actually are doing relatively well against their pure-play competitors. Success is due in part to brand name recognition, but also because click-and-mortars are beginning to leverage the fulfillment and return capabilities of their existing infrastructure.

Bricks-and-mortars are increasingly talking about "convergence" between their multiple channels which may include a manufacturing division, a wholesale division, a retail division, and a catalog with an e-business model servicing them all (plus many times an e-tail division is thrown into the mix). One pristine example is the VF Corp., its Healthtex division has successfully converged its e-business model to incorporate both wholesale and retail customers while optimizing its entire value chain.

Specifically, convergence speaks to the notion of integrating, rather than separating, online and offline distribution and selling channels as a means of maximizing the total business model. Convergence requires working across channels which often means cutting across organization-al and political lines.

There is a genuine opening for the bricks-and-mortars and their online spin-offs to play the convergence card to regain the initiative against their pure-play competitors.

MODEL OF THE FUTURE?

As of this moment, e-business isn't multi-channel by definition. However, according to Gartner Group, "by 2004 we will see . . . true e-businesses begin to emerge. By 2006, many businesses will have made the transition, most likely to a bricks and click mix, and e-business itself will cease to exist. At this point, e-businesses will be completely embed-ded into an organization's business processes." Therefore all e-business will be multi-channel. Period. At least that's what Gartner Group thinks.

Office supplies retailer Staples Inc. acquired the 766,000-square foot fulfillment facility that was formerly occupied by the bankrupt Service Merchandise Inc. to support its catalog, e-commerce and contract cus-tomers. Staples already had four multi-channel distribution centers and currently is in the process of building a new facility in London, OH. "By moving to a multi-channel distribution strategy, we will be able to deliver the highest quality of customer service while reducing our distribution overhead costs," says Joseph G. Doody, president of Staples Contract and Commercial division.

Office Depot used a carefully defined and outlined strategy for launch-ing its e-business model. This included a Web site that was fully inte-grated with its multi-channel distribution and merchandising efforts. Beth VanStory, VP of Office Depot Online (www.officedepot.com) stated that Office Depot wanted its online customer to feel that its Web site was a simple and seamless extension of other Office Depot shopping venues including catalogs and stores.

"We have integrated the Web site into our normal business. We want to make sure that through whichever channel the customer picks, it's the channel that will best serve the customer's needs," VanStory said.

Moving customers to the Internet from catalog and shop-by-phone orders reduces expenses associated with operating a bricks-and-mortar business. Thus, it was vital that the entire Web site be real-time activated, i.e., tied directly into a nearby distribution center's inventory. Officedepot.com customers know immediately if a product is available, which enhances customer satisfaction. "Delivering value and time savings to the people who need them, when they need them is what the site is all about," VanStory said.

It can also take a different turn. Look at Coldwater Creek Inc. (www.coldwatercreek.com), an established catalog business that took the slow route to establishing a full-blown e-tail site by initially offering up a limited number of "gift" items and then once the site started receiving heavy traffic it fleshed out its online product line. Currently, about 25% of Coldwater Creek's revenue is from its e-tail site. "Its percentage of revenue from the Internet is one of the highest I've heard of within the industry," says Kevin Silverman of ABN Amro Inc.

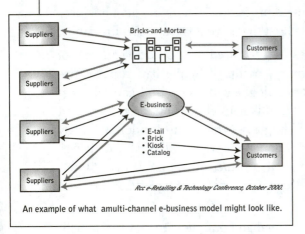

An example of what a multi-channel e-business model might look like.

All the while, Coldwater Creek was moving toward the bricks-and-mortar world, through the slow, deliberate establishment of stores around the country. Coldwater Creek's expansion would have been difficult before the Internet's expanding influence, but in today's environment a retailer can't be just a "catalog," a "Web site," or a "bricks-and-mortar." These days, says Dennis Pence, chief executive of Coldwater Creek, there's a mandate to "multi-channel," the industry buzzword for selling through catalogs, over the Internet and out of stores as well.

In the end the e-businesses that know how to sell through multiple channels, such as Nordstrom and QVC (the champion of multi-channel distribution) are more likely to prosper than those that don't partly due to the inability to share costs among multiple channels. This is a big boon to the multi-channel e-business vs. the pure-play e-business, which won't be able to reinforce their brand or drive customers from one venue to the other and at the same time reduce overall expenditures due to convergence of business processes. By 2005, Jupiter predicts online spending will total $199 billion, yet, the Internet will influence $632 billion in offline purchases.

As Rick Whiting reported in an article for *Information Week*, Home Depot (www.homedepot.com), a bricks-and-mortar business who was late to adopt an e-business model, did finally begin selling products online, albeit to only a few contractors in Las Vegas. Though tardy in its appearance on the Web, it may have an advantage over companies that moved faster since Home Depot designed its Web operations from the start to be fully integrated with its core IT systems.

Eventually Home Depot plans to offer a host of online products to contractors and do-it-yourselfers nationwide through its e-tailer and its 1,022 North American bricks-and-mortars — all offering the same inventory and prices. Ron Griffin, senior vice president and chief information officer at Home Depot, Atlanta, stated that "We're not doing this to maximize Internet sales, the objective is to maximize the relationship with the customer."

Home Depot's fashionably late arrival to online sales means that its IT staff didn't have to deal with the more frequent problem of "I wanted the site up and running yesterday!" This allowed Home Depot to reap some of the benefits of merged systems: improved customer service and consistency in business processes.

Home Depot isn't the only e-tailer out there with a "merged system." Office Depot Inc. operates with integrated systems and many other retailers are beginning to realize that there's something to lose by divorcing e-tail operations from the enterprise. For example, a survey by Jupiter Communications Inc. found that 76% of "converged retailers" (and I use that phrase with some trepidation) could not track their customers across store, online, and catalog channels. "If you're not serving your customers in a seamless manner across all channels, you're effectively giving your best customers a fractured experience," said Jupiter analyst Michele Rosenshein.

J. Crew Inc. is working on a solution to that very problem. The clothing retailer recently disclosed plans to build a data warehouse containing customer, product, inventory, cost, and financial data from its store, catalog, and Web channels. Thus, allowing it to analyze the data to better understand customer demands and conduct targeted marketing. "The big challenge is to have a customer-centric, brand-centric environment," said Mirek Zlotkowski, vice president of business integration at J. Crew. "We want to give customers the same experience through all our channels. The goal is to retain customers for life."

By viewing data from multiple channels, the integrated e-business can create unified pricing and promotions, better allocate merchandise between channels, and improve inventory and fulfillment operations.

At the time this book was being written Borders Group Inc. (www.borders.com) was in the midst of building a 1-Tbyte data warehouse that would enable it to tell whether customers who buy books in the company's bricks-and-mortar stores are the same who buy from its Web site. The system, scheduled for completion around the time this book goes to the publisher, will pull information from multiple databases and provide a consolidated view of customers of Borders Books and Borders Music superstores, Borders-owned Waldenbooks stores, and Borders.com.

Such projects aren't cheap. Borders' data warehouse will cost more than $1 million. Other companies find it difficult to move quickly because of the financial and human resource requirements. A merger last year brought CVS.com (formerly Soma.com) and CVS Corp. together. The online pharmacy is now integrated with CVS's procurement, inventory, and order fulfillment systems. They're in the process of integrating customer service operations. "We want to present one face to the customer, no matter where they shop," said CVS.com vice president and CIO Debra Robinson. However, plans to create a single database by linking the CVS and CVS.com customer loyalty programs are on hold. "It's an enormous project, and we have so many competing priorities right now," said David Zook, strategic alliances manager at CVS.com.

One challenge IT managers with a multi-channel e-business model face is that enterprises frequently run some core operations on older computer systems, while e-businesses are generally built on newer technologies. Many software products can help facilitate data integration, but the effort still involves time-consuming programming work and data conversion.

Click-and-mortar integration isn't the goal for everyone. Some companies continue to run their divisions separately — and successfully. Earlier this year, bookseller Barnes & Noble Inc. spun off its online operation in a public offering, Barnes & Noble.com Inc. And although the parent retains a minority stake, their IT systems are not and were not ever linked although it's playing in the local fulfillment space.

Other retailers, while acknowledging the benefits of integration, seem to be in no hurry to do the work. Kmart Corp. has a database on 90 million households, and its Bluelight.com Internet operation has a database of 4 million customers. There are "plans in the works to see how we can optimize the two databases to create a better shopping experience," according to a Kmart spokesperson; but there doesn't seem to be any timetable for the project.

Business practice issues are another factor. Should customers be allowed to return merchandise bought online to a retail outlet? Breaking down barriers between traditional stores and online operations require a rethinking of policies.

In a couple of years, there may well be a new business alignment where no one is exclusively an e-business or a bricks-and-mortar. There will be a mix and match environment where the strongest elements of bricks-and-mortars, bricks-to-clicks and pure-play entwine to provide what customers really want, where and when they want it. "Customers are going to be free to shop however they choose," says Thomas Weisel Partners LLC (www.tweisel.com) analyst Anne-Marie Lillestrand. "Companies need to be there."

Look at e-tailer Outpost.com's relationship with the retailer Wolf Camera. Outpost runs the Web store for Wolf, and in return it gets in-store promotion at Wolf's and placement of in-store kiosks at Wolf stores where customers can order out-of-stock products for next-day delivery from Outpost. I believe you will see more and more of these partnerships in the future.

A Deloitte & Touche report indicates that a multi-channel distribution strategy, that includes the Internet, will be essential in the future given the competitive advantage it offers to increase sales. All readers should note that the Internet is the only channel of distribution that is expected to grow at a double or triple rate in the coming years.

Offline assets are crucial to lessening some of the online customers' concerns about online purchases. The Mainspring study showed that the top three drivers of repeat purchases were:

- ensuring secure transactions,

- having bricks-and-mortar stores in which to view products,

- making it easy to return goods.

E-businesses that could mix online and offline assets enjoyed superior customer economics compared to pure plays.

Though e-tailers have been commonly viewed as the ultimate winners in the new "e" paradigm, the e-businesses that have adopted first class supply chain management, an LFMS and distribution enablers, will be the real victors in the world of e-business.

Strategizing and Planning for an LFMS

SUCCESS IN E-BUSINESS IS determined more by the
ability to deliver the *right* product to the *right* place at the *right* time rather
than by astute marketing and merchandizing skills. Yes, you do need to get
the customer to your site and have the product displayed that the customer
is searching for. But getting that customer to the site and displaying a
product is not the same as *having* the product on hand *ready* to ship to the
customer in a *fast, efficient, and flawless* manner — err in your performance
of that segment of the business process and the customer waves bye-bye!
Effective fulfillment requires a comprehensive logistics and fulfillment
plan mapping business processes and technology so that they mesh into a
cohesive unit. The traditional business model of functional handoffs
between autonomous business units will not work in e-business.

A practical Logistics and Fulfillment Management System (LFMS) can
handle all processes from the moment the "buy" button is clicked until
product fulfillment is concluded. A viable LFMS ensures that customers
receive the products ordered online in a timely and traceable manner. It
enables the customers to choose the method of shipment and the ability
to track the order status, i.e., seeing when the merchandise has been
shipped and tracking its progress to their premises. An LFMS gives the e-
business's customer service department a 360-degree view of all processes and offers ways to handle post-sale issues such as returns, warranties
and technical support.

Logistics and fulfillment efficiency enable e-businesses to deliver on their promises to their customers. As e-businesses grow to recognize the link between profit and logistics, more are bringing logistics management into the mainstream of their enterprise and value chain. Every day e-businesses face the reality of redesigning and strengthening their logistics and fulfillment infrastructure to move goods in support of online commerce.

Dr. Wulf H. Bernotat, the CEO of Stinnes AG (one of Germany's largest companies) said, "at the end of the day, each commercial transaction on the Internet will have to be backed up by a traditional logistics function." Bernotat went on, "without the backbone of smoothly functioning logistics, e-commerce would remain a utopian idea."

The growing importance and worldwide expansion of e-business logistics is evident at Georgia Tech, which conducts international research and educational programs in logistics. "Our Logistics Institute offers expertise on such [e-business] problems as streamlining manufacturing processes, organizing warehouse systems, scheduling transportation crews and fleets, designing delivery zones and routes, and creating vendor-managed re-supply systems," said Georgia Tech President Wayne Clough.

Although even in the e-business community, you can find logistics and fulfillment management run as a transportation or warehousing unit off to the side of the organizational chart; the clear trend is for logistics and fulfillment operations to be centralized. Logistics management has come a long way from the days when "logistics" was viewed as an upscale moniker for "traffic department," and the logistics manager's duties were limited to moving freight around.

In the Internet Age of the 21st Century, the streamlining of the value chain and its transportation methods through technology will serve to better enable all aspects of commerce, expedite trade and create new global economic opportunities.

LOGISTICS AND FULFILLMENT GOALS

The basis for an effective logistics and fulfillment strategy is an understanding of the e-business's logistics and fulfillment goals. The technical nature of e-business provides a way to facilitate improvements in a company's LFM. Therefore, the business processes, systems, applications and value chain partners that will be integrated into the LFMS' infrastructure must be both known and ready for integration. To implement an LFMS without understanding the e-business's logistics and fulfillment goals or processes is likely to lead to e-business failure. A questionnaire is a good first step in a logistics and fulfillment strategy plan.

The Questionnaire

The purpose of the questionnaire is to formalize an e-business's logistics and fulfillment goals. Once you have a clear picture of the goals, you can understand the scope of the e-business's logistics and fulfillment management schema. Of course, you should target your questions to the characteristics and goals of your specific e-business. However, the following questions will provide a good starting point.

Start within the e-business's executive suite and work your way through the upper management level and perhaps even into middle management to define the e-business's logistics and fulfillment limitations and then goals:

- Who should be on the e-business's logistics and fulfillment strategy and planning team? The team could and probably should consist of at least one member of the e-business's executive suite and the tech solution partner. You should also consider representatives of the value chain members and a logistics and fulfillment consultant.

- What is the role of an LFMS within the enterprise and/or its value chain?

- What are the e-business's strategic options as far as developing a comprehensive LFMS is concerned?

- What will the role of inventory have within your LFMS, such as, inventory management, distribution, drivers of change, facilities planning?

- What are the e-business's customer service requirements?

- What competitive advantage will a comprehensive LFMS give to the e-business?

Once you have your answers in hand, focus on your value chain by performing a transportation management analysis covering the modes of transportation your value chain uses. Then ask the following questions:

- What will the impact of a full scale LFMS have on not only the e-business but also its value chain, especially the financial implications of integration?

- Will the e-business use its LFMS for product modification? If so, how will that affect the value chain members?

- Will the e-business use its LFMS for timing of material flow? If so, how will it affect the value chain?

- Will warehouse systems utilize an automated ID system? If so, which one and how will it be implemented throughout the value chain?

- How does the e-business and/or its value chain plan and schedule distribution? How should it change for efficiency and economy?

- How does the e-business and/or its value chain handle materials management? How should it be changed for efficiency, cost savings and time constraints?

- How will a fully implemented LFMS affect manufacturing processes?

- How will a fully implemented LFMS affect storage of inventory? Will it affect the value chain? For instance, will it be possible to implement Just-in-Time (JIT) procedures?

Next look at how an LFMS will impact the e-business's current systems and processes:

- How will the LFMS fit in with inventory management, warehouse planning, transportation, customer service, marketing, manufacturing/ sourcing, and financial strategies?

- How will the LFMS mesh with your supply chain management including accelerating materials and information flow, materials management, and value-added analysis?

- How will the LFMS deal with payments (domestic and international) including documentation, financial arrangements and security?

- How will the LFMS deal with claim documentation, clearance of foreign customs including import value, value for duty, dealing with foreign customs brokers and consultants, transportation and storage abroad?

- How will the e-business integrate order processing, shipping and transportation, delivery, fulfillment quality control, after-sales service and customer satisfaction into the LFMS?

- Will the LFMS be set up for multi-level distribution channels such as franchise models, catalogs, retail and wholesale, third-party distribution, and such?

- Will the LFMS affect any plant layout and design or warehouse/distribution center/fulfillment facility design?

- What system is in place to keep track of all products as they move from supplier to customer (item by item, not just by order)? Options might include bar-codes and RFID. How does the shopping cart technology link with the warehousing/distribution operation?

- Will the LFMS need to interface with Electronic Data Interchange (EDI) systems or other VANs?

- How will the e-business's financial systems be integrated with its inbound shipping, inventory management, orders entry, delivery and returns information systems?

Then assess how much re-designing of the e-business and/or value chain's systems will be necessary:

- Can suppliers, order entry, inventory management and fulfillment systems, accounting department, shipping department and carriers all seamlessly communicate and share data to trigger coordinated action or will these systems need updating?

- What online "alert" systems exist for replenishment, delivery delays, order inaccuracies, erroneous shipping addresses, incoming returns, etc.? Will they need updating?

- Within the order processing and fulfillment services, can the LFMS efficiently and effectively handle orders, provide a 360-degree view of the processes for customer service systems and other departments that find the data helpful, such as customers and suppliers? Or will these systems need updating?

- Can the LFMS process and deal with pre-determined pricing and contracts, both domestic and international, including inquiries and quotations, credit checks, offers and counteroffers with the current systems and processes in place? Will these need updating or replacement?

- Can the LFMS provide visibility throughout the ordering and manufacturing process for optimal tracking and monitoring, expediting of orders, control of flow and preparation of shipments with the current systems and processes in place? Will these need updating or replacement?

- Can the LFMS handle global logistical needs with the current systems and processes in place? Will they need to be updated, or replaced? Will they be outsourced?

- Can the LFMS easily handle exceptions, exemptions and packaging for export including special labeling requirements and exports' packing checklist with the current systems and processes or will they need to be updated or outsourced?

- Can the LFMS ease export documentation, providing documents necessary for international trade, pro-forma invoices, contractual documentation, commercial invoices, waybills, bills of lading, insurance certification, weight and packing certification, certificate of origin, certificate of quality, carnet, consular invoice, and the like with the current systems and processes? Will you need to update or outsource?

- Can the LFMS handle import documentation, such as, importer number, customs accounting document and customs invoices with the current systems and processes or will they need updating?

- Can the LFMS handle transaction number in bar-coded format, refunds, warranty issues, and other post sale transactions and exceptions with the current systems and processes? If not, will you update, replace or outsource?

When you have the answers (tailored to your specific e-businesses processes and needs), use them as the starting point to begin formulating your logistics and fulfillment plan. The first step for designing, building and implementing of a best-of-breed LFMS is to form your strategy.

Organize what you know and do not know. Do this through sketches, diagrams, concept/mind maps, or flowcharts of the activities, actors, processes, functions, structures, environmental forces, etc. present in your e-business's logistics and fulfillment environment. The objective is to break out of linear thinking and explore both existing and potential relationships. Some ways of approaching this are:

- Map out on a single page your e-business's specific logistics and fulfillment needs.

- Determine the root cause of any problem(s). Look repeatedly beneath surface explanations of problems in the e-business's logistics and fulfillment strategy. Don't be satisfied until you have uncovered a set of relationships that reveal both true problems and opportunities for improvement. It's okay to seek a holistic answer rather than a strictly logical one.

- Solve the problem(s). As difficult as determining root causes may be, you also need to deal with unanticipated problems that are uncovered when an e-business puts its logistics and fulfillment strategy to work. Sometimes these crippling problems arise out of poor implementation or poor planning. One trick is ask "How" five times by examining implementation processes five levels deep, this can help to avoid such problems.

- Determine if there are any problems or major issues standing in the way of implementating a logistics and fulfillment strategy. If so, do they need to be resolved immediately? What will be the impact of resolution on quality, productivity, and fulfillment issues? What will it cost to solve the problem?

- Assess the attitudes of your logistics and fulfillment managers. Are they proactive? Do they anticipate the long-term impact on their business and management systems as a whole? In that regard, what are the likely systems effect on any action in the value chain?

- Anticipate additional information that might be needed prior to drawing up and implementing your logistics and fulfillment plan.

- Estimate how the proposed logistics and fulfillment plan may impact quality, productivity, costs and profits, as well as the creativity and enthusiasm of the value chain.

- What is the trade off financially between outsourcing versus the e-business operating its own warehouse and distribution facility?

- Based on your analysis, what is the best course of action for the implementation of a suitable logistics and fulfillment strategy.

Product and Packaging

You've considered your goals, business processes and systems, and your value chain, now focus on the products and the daily minutia of logistics and fulfillment for your particular e-business model, customers and products. These questions enable implementation of the fulfillment solutions that fits the particular e-business's situation and products.

- What are the physical characteristics of your e-business's products and how do they vary in size, weight, and packaging?

- Does your e-business offer products that will require special handling and/or packaging (breakables that will need repackaging, different size items in one box or a separate box per item, signature on delivery requirement, etc.)?

- Will your e-business offer products that will need a number of different components or accessories to be in the same box (a printer, printer cable and spare ink cartridge or a DSL Modem, a telephone cord, line filters, etc.)?

- Do any of the products require sub-assembly?

- Are any of the products "over sized" or "heavy weight" so that they may require a different carrier from the norm?

- Are any of the products perishable or fragile, requiring a specific transportation mode?

- Do any of the products require special licensing for transport (i.e., alcohol, pharmaceuticals, etc.)?

Average order

- What is the size and value of the minimum, maximum and average order?

- What is your e-business's current volume of orders?
- What volume of orders is expected 6 months, 1 year, 2 years and 5 years from now?

Shipping

- What carriers do your e-business and its supply chain use and what system is in place to track shipments? Is the tracking system easily accessible to everyone including the customers?
- Will your e-business offer online tracking and tracing to customers and its supply chain?
- Will your e-business offer its customers a choice of carriers? Online?
- How will shipping rates be determined? Can your e-business accommodate customers who already have a UPS/FedEx/other carrier account number and want to be billed directly? Is COD an option?
- Can customers ship to multiple addresses from a single order?
- If the e-business ships in branded packaging, will this external branding affect security as far as delivery is concerned (i.e., will it encourage theft)?
- What is the back-up plan if notification is received that a shipment has been delayed/lost/damaged?
- Is your e-business willing to absorb any of the shipping and handling costs? If so, under what conditions?
- What is the acceptable level of shipping costs compared to the order value (from both the customer's perspective and your e-business's)?

Delivery Quality Control

- What is an acceptable time period to get products to the customer?
- What are the criteria for on-time delivery, damage claims, order accuracy, supply availability?
- How will quality checks be performed?

Inventory

- How are orders for out-of-stock products handled? If the product is expected to be available in a short timeframe, will the e-business still take the order and risk having to upgrade the shipping to meet the promised delivery date?

- How much inventory is needed to ensure product availability?
- Can the supply chain respond adequately to a sudden increase in orders?
- How will replenishment be triggered once an item is picked from storage?

Returns

- What is the percentage of anticipated product returns?
- How are returns to be handled (dispose of them, use a secondary market, refurbish and put back into inventory, return to supplier...)?
- What are the arrangements with suppliers for returns?
- How will customers return the products? Do they require authorization or special packaging/labels for return? Are there any return restrictions, and if so, does the e-business have the documentation posted to support that policy?
- Who is responsible for inspection/valuation?
- What information systems determine when ownership shifts to the customer or back to the supplier?
- What records are required to keep track of potential tax write-offs or supplier credit?
- How are tracking records integrated with inventory management and shipping records to produce necessary documentation?
- What financial arrangements are in place with suppliers for return credit?
- What documentation is required from the receiving department?

International Orders

In addition to what was previously covered through the questionnaire:

- Is your e-business selling products for international shipment? If so, how are currency transactions to be handled?
- Who will fill out international documentation? Who will be responsible for duties and taxes/customs clearance?

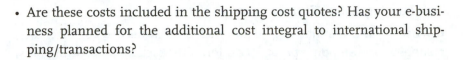

- Are these costs included in the shipping cost quotes? Has your e-business planned for the additional cost integral to international shipping/transactions?

Seasonal Considerations

- If your e-business offers products that are seasonal, how will that affect the warehousing/inventory requirements?

Supply Chain

- Is your supply chain willing to ship direct to the customers upon request?
- Can they ship daily, if necessary?
- Are they willing to change from a "pallet" or "bulk" shipment basis to a smaller count shipment?
- Will supply chain members accept small orders?
- Will your supply chain be responsible for transportation costs to the warehouse/distribution center/fulfillment center?
- If your e-business is using a drop-ship/direct fulfillment model, is your supply chain willing to repackage their product in the e-business's branded boxes and use its branded labels, promotional material, etc.?

Infrastructure

- If outsourcing, how will the e-business send order information to the fulfillment service provider, how often (real-time, hourly or daily) — separately or in batches?
- How will your e-business handle package tracking and provide the information to its customers?
- If outsourcing, how are your e-business order entry systems integrated with the fulfillment service provider's infrastructure?
- If outsourcing, how will your e-business integrate its inventory management, returns management and shipping systems with the outsourcer?
- Do some orders get priority over others, if so, what are the criteria? Are business rules and exceptions in place?

Warehousing and Fulfillment Centers

- What are the warehousing requirements (area needed for inventory, supplies and shipping prep; docks; fork lifts; racking and sorting bins; conveyors; pick-and-pack systems; radio transmitted bar coding; software; shipping and labeling equipment; etc.)?

- Is the inventory storage area designed for easy and efficient order picking?

- What are the preferred geographic locations of the warehouse(s)/distribution center(s)/fulfillment center(s)?

- Is a dedicated facility needed or are the products to be put into a warehouse/distribution/fulfillment operation that others also use?

- Are sophisticated services and space needed or would a direct mail company or public warehousing space be satisfactory?

- How well does the warehouse/distribution/fulfillment facility accommodate multiple carriers for inbound/outbound shipments? Who will handle scheduling?

Insurance

- What is your e-business's policy regarding insurance coverage for loss, damage, and theft? What is the carrier's responsibility and what is the customer's responsibility?

- Is the insurance information clearly posted anywhere on the Web site?

Exceptions

Just as in the traditional sales channel, there is the need for handling exceptions. If an e-business is using the drop-ship model, what does it do when customer's order includes products from multiple suppliers, and one of the products ordered is out of stock or backordered? Or perhaps the e-business handles its own shipping and inventory. What happens when the product is out of stock and the e-business doesn't know when the inventory will be replenished.

- How does the e-business initiate a partial shipment? Hold the shipment for all the items, ship all ordered items that are available and cancel the rest?

- Does it request the customer's input prior to making a decision?

• Does it hold the order until it receives a reply from the customer?

One solution to "exception" issues is to have the e-business's LFMS include event-based triggers that are modeled on specific business rules. To implement such a rules-based system requires that you sit down with the appropriate personnel, suppliers and, if necessary, the fulfillment provider, and correlate the e-business rules.

YOUR LFMS PLAN: WHAT'S INVOLVED?

To reap the benefits of a properly implemented and fine-tuned LFMS requires a detailed logistics and fulfillment plan. Even if fulfillment is outsourced, you still need a plan. A logistics and fulfillment plan lays out the chain of events that must occur to get a product to the customer including the post-sale processes. Everything you've done prior to this leads to your logistics and fulfillment management plan. This plan should be a guide upon which all logistics and fulfillment decisions are based.

A formalized logistics and fulfillment plan will ensure that the entire value chain consider, not only the e-business's requirements, goals and objectives, but also what each player can bring to the table. This will help to ensure that everyone is on the "same page."

Logistics and fulfillment has many touchpoints — raw material, goods, parts, products, orders, information on orders, packaging, shipment and after sale processes — that flow through diverse areas (manufacturers, wholesalers, distributors, shippers, 3LPs, and retailers) all over the globe. This means there are a myriad of points where something can go wrong.

This also means that no single strategy and plan can cover every e-business's needs. The author has written this section to guide readers through the process that they can then apply to their specific e-business model.

Before trying to integrate an LFMS into an e-business's processes and systems and its value chain be sure to:

• Have in hand the e-business strategy plan.

• Keep the value chain members involved throughout the logistics and fulfillment strategy and planning stages.

- Map the complete logistics and fulfillment path of the products. For example, a typical manufacturer operates with a value chain extending from contact with raw material providers through delivery of the finished product to the customer (distributor, vendor, OEM, end-user). An e-tail, B2B distributor/vendor/OEM might start its value chain with the manufacturer and its "product." Alternatively, such a business might start its value chain with component manufacturers (i.e., Dell, Cisco) the value chain then would run through delivery of the end product to the customer, who may or may not be the end-user.

- Decide on what to outsource to achieve optimum logistics and fulfillment results.

- Understand the e-business customers' expectations and how to meet them.

- Utilize new technologies and channels to enhance the LFMS (for example, ASPs, e-marketplaces).

- Understand how the e-business can fulfill orders in a narrow time frame and improve customer satisfaction.

A well-oiled LFMS involves three distinct jobs — planning, execution, and enabling — and each of these breaks down into various other tasks and technologies.

- Planning includes long-term strategy and scheduling so the product is available when needed in a cost-effective, efficient manner. Proper planning requires the value chain's cooperation.

- Execution involves enterprise resource planning, warehouse management, sales-force automation, shipment and customer service some of which an e-business should already have in place and some it will need to tweak or implement.

- Enabling refers to technology — network technologies, workflow management, order processing and fulfillment systems, data warehouses, etc.

3 Stages of E-Business

An e-business can't buy an LFMS, — to date there isn't "one" application or platform that provides all of the necessary technology. For best results the LFMS should be planned, executed and enabled in stages. Within the first stage of this three-prong evolution is the technology that enables long-term strategization and scheduling with critical suppliers, and customers to place orders and get a shipping date. With this capability in place, an e-business has a logical entity that can communicate and share data within an LFMS.

Most e-businesses are either in Stage One, contemplating Stage One or talking to bankruptcy attorneys.

The journey to Stage Two — serious integration and interconnectedness throughout the value chain — is the roller coaster ride where many businesses and e-businesses attempt to put on the brakes. However, they will eventually, in the short term rather than the long term, begin negotiating and implementing so as to have a full-scale LFMS. Only a very limited number of value chains have achieved Stage Two though a few are moving toward it — VF Corp is one such example of an e-business in the midst of Stage Two implementation.

Stage Three is an enterprise that has become a 100% virtual e-business allowing 24 x 7 interaction within the global marketspace. This pinnacle is enjoyed by only a handful of value chains — Cisco and Grainger are among the few in this elite group and even they continue to evolve their best-of-breed LFMS.

Stage One

In this stage the greatest benefit of an LFMS goes to the end customer. Here is where an e-business integrates into its systems and processes the functionality to seamlessly maintain an accurate inventory count, enable the customer to place an order and track it, provide prompt and accurate fulfillment of the order (order processing, pick-pack-ship). The post-sales processes are automated and integrated into the

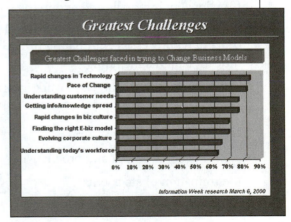

Greatest Challenges

Greatest Challenges faced in trying to Change Business Models

Rapid changes in Technology
Pace of Change
Understanding customer needs
Getting info/knowledge spread
Rapid changes in biz culture
Finding the right E-biz model
Evolving corporate culture
Understanding today's workforce

0% 10% 20% 30% 40% 50% 60% 70% 80% 90%

Information Week research March 6, 2000

LFMS, with customer service given a 360-degree view of the customer data and fulfillment processes.

Although many e-businesses continue to improve in the area of logistics and fulfillment, most haven't totally optimized the processes by which materials and information move through the value chain. Without a totally integrated logistics and fulfillment plan your e-business could be left with bottlenecks that hamper productivity and negate the promised benefits of innovative technology and its ensuing automation.

Stage One e-businesses must continually review their production and information processes for logistical inefficiency. Factors of time, place, distance, sequence, condition, and information accuracy and availability can all have a negative effect. Some common operational inefficiencies include excessive distances and wasted time (plant or warehouse in Chicago, with the main supplier shipping out of Los Angeles) resulting in misplaced or misdelivered material/product, and double handling. In turn this causes poor inventory control and damaged product. Taken together these inefficiencies result in frantic and unnecessary responses (large inventories, rushed shipments), employee confusion ("Where is the product?"), unhappy customers ("Where is my order?"), and ultimately lost sales and a declining customer base. However, proper Stage One procedure will address these negative factors, rooting them out or stopping them before they start.

Stage Two

In this stage the e-business institutes rules and processes for cost-saving functionality internally and within the supply chain. When an e-business is ready to move to the second stage it applies cutting-edge logistical concepts to its processes eliminating unnecessary wastes and delivering significant benefits including:

- reduction in cycle time and work in progress (WIP) inventory
- improvement in customer service
- increased inventory accuracy
- expansion of output and productivity
- elimination of stock-outs
- increased sales

With the right LFMS in place material flow process can be improved through the ability to maintain smaller inventories allowing for reduced cycle times and use of smaller, decentralized storerooms with real-time inventory control. With technology in place, forecasting methods can increase inventory efficiency, reduce WIP time, and virtually eliminate stock-outs.

When implementing the second stage an e-business should start simply; select only a limited number of products within a related product line and chart their actual material flow from receipt of raw material (if a manufacturer) to finished goods to shipment to end-user (if a retailer/e-tailer). This can give an e-business a good look at how far material and products actually travel and why it can take so long to get through the value chain while revealing customer order patterns, which can aid in the forecasting process.

Another important procedure at this stage is talking to the customers, suppliers, partners and other members of the value chain (including production workers so as to better understand the production process) so that there are no gaps in the integrated processes and systems.

Examining customers' needs and analyzing how materials and product flow through an e-business's facility increases the focus on cycle time throughout the process, from purchasing and receiving, through order filling and shipping. (Don't forget to take into account the time a product lays idle.) Once you have completed this exercise, you have the knowledge in hand that can help your e-business keep in close contact with its customers and allow it to respond more quickly to market demands.

The competitive advantages of a second stage LFMS include dramatically reduced inventory investment, improved customer service and response time, lower labor costs, and better product quality.

"Three years ago we were shipping an awful lot of stuff across the ocean but we didn't have any process for doing it," says James D. Molzon, director of AlliedSignal's (www.alliedsignal.com) logistics and operations support group (AlliedSignal merged with Honeywell, which was recently acquired by GE). "Every business and every plant was doing their own contracting with the steamship companies." Therefore the company had diminished leverage with railroads and steamship lines, and little visibility into the distribution pipeline. With the implementation of its LFMS everything began to change and Molzon is now able to leverage AlliedSignal's shipping volumes and create standardized processes for handling both international as well as domestic shipments.

According to Molson, "Our goal is to make shipping a one stop, one phone call process." For international shipment that means using two logistics providers — D.F. Young (www.dfyoung.com) in the United States and HRT in Europe. Once it had its LFMS in place AlliedSignal could link its order entry systems to the logistic providers. Thus, when a European customer places an order, the information is seamlessly sent to HRT, D.F. Young and the appropriate manufacturing plant in the US. Once the plant is nearing completion of the order, it alerts D.F. Young to arrange for shipment. HRT then is responsible for getting the shipment from the European port to the customer.

"It's all done electronically," says Molzon. "Now AlliedSignal can tell a customer exactly where their shipment is. This visibility provides us with the opportunity to reroute a shipment, if necessary."

In the past, redirecting a shipment in-transit took a series of phone calls. "The electronic linkages weren't there," says Molzon. "The plant would handoff a shipment at the US manufacturing location and it would disappear into the black hole of the ocean until it emerged on the other side."

This lack of visibility into the distribution pipeline often led to costly delays. "We had instances where a container had been sitting on the dock in Europe for weeks," says Molzon. "No one had been notified it was coming off. It wasn't cleared and was just sitting at the dock. That kind of thing doesn't happen today." AlliedSignal's goal is to receive an ocean shipment at the dock, clear it through customs and get it into a warehouse and ready for distribution within 24 hours.

Molzon's group has adapted this single-point of contact strategy for domestic moves as well. For example, AlliedSignal once used up to 100 flatbed trucks, but has consolidated everything for Landstar Systems (www.landstar.com) to handle. AlliedSignal has culled the ranks of its less-than-truckload carriers to around twelve — with one primary LTL firm and one back-up for each geographical region. It has also cut a sizable carrier pool to one — Chemical Leaman Tank Lines.

AlliedSignal is also leveraging its shipping volumes with the railroads and has consolidated all of its rate negotiations, standardized its rail shipping process, and improved communication links between its manufacturing plants and the railroads. This resulted in better equipment utilization and has allowed AlliedSignal to reduce its railcar fleet by 15% while growing its rail traffic over 20%.

AlliedSignal implemented a rail fleet management system as a subset of its LFMS, which lets it pinpoint the location of every railcar it uses. It also issues exception reports so AlliedSignal can head off bottlenecks and delays. "If a car hasn't moved in 24 hours, we'll get a message," says Molzon. "That will allow us to proactively go after the customer and say, 'Do we need to divert this shipment? Do we need to send it on a truck?' Now we can advise instead of being on the defensive all the time."

AlliedSignal's integration of its transportation partners into its LFMS provides the transportation provider information on an order as soon as AlliedSignal gets it. This allows the transportation provider to immediately begin integrating AlliedSignal's needs into their planning process. With that kind of vision and effort, AlliedSignal/Honeywell/GE can smooth the flow of goods throughout all of its business units (once they quit merging).

Value Chain Management within a Properly Implemented LFMS: While the mighty pull of the Internet is getting stronger by the minute, many e-businesses lack the technology, information and skills to lug their value chains into the digital age, according to an early 2000 report from the Economist Intelligence Unit (www.eiu.com) and Meritus Consulting Services (www.meritusllc.com). There are innumerable e-businesses that are still within Stage One that desperately need to begin their move to Stage Two.

The report, entitled "Moving the Supply Chain into the Digital Age: Integrating Demand and Supply," is based on responses to a detailed survey of senior executives in Fortune 500 companies with responsibility for supply chain management. Few of those surveyed doubted that the Internet would have a profound affect on value or supply chain management.

"Quite a few people don't measure the performance of their supply chain," said Lars Ljungdahl, vice president, integrated supply chain management at Meritus. Enterprises use different measures to determine how effectively various business processes link up internally and externally, "often they don't tie them together," he said. Therefore, many (even Fortune 500 businesses) are ignorant of how well their integrated supply chains perform. Almost one-third of the respondents interviewed were unable to estimate their supply chain performance.

According to the report, performance measures (i.e., the number of defects per million units) are common and well defined in manufacturing, "the same type of performance measurement is rarely used in the evaluation of the supply chain." According to Ljungdahl there are a number of readily available ways to evaluate supply chain performance that are underused. "Inventory is not used enough," he maintained.

Ljungdahl explained that e-businesses "need to be able to capture the information from the end customer and drive it all the way in near real-time mode to the raw materials supplier." As the information moves through the supply chain, it must be converted into meaningful data for the various trading entities involved.

Some inconsistencies highlighted by the report can be shown by this tidbit: 53% of the executives surveyed expect their suppliers to deliver as requested 96% of the time but only 22% meet this standard with their own customers and only 4% of the executives surveyed believe that their customers are completely satisfied with their enterprise's fulfillment performance.

Ljungdahl pointed out that if the lack of coordinated cooperation isn't addressed, these same companies will struggle to meet the very high customer expectations that are a part of Web-based trading. "They had better wake up," he warned.

The survey also points to the establishment of efficient information flows across the value chain that is becoming more critical as enterprises adopt the e-business model. The traditional model for definition by a core competency that should be kept in-house, such as manufacturing, is giving way to the model developed by companies such as Dell, Cisco and Grainger that require these functions be outsourced.

As more functions are outsourced, e-businesses will rely more and more on efficient communications within the value chain. The survey found that among the typical kinds of value chain exchange, such as, inventory data, requests for quotations and tracking information "saw the greatest increase in digital communication."

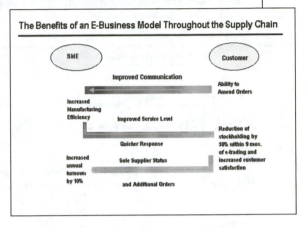

The Benefits of an E-Business Model Throughout the Supply Chain

But Ljungdahl did make the effort to stress that "e-commerce is a far sight more than just the supply chain." He explains that the supply chain is one leg of a three-legged stool, the other two being customer needs and a restructured enterprise that functions as a e-business model. "If you do the supply chain and don't think about the other two, your execution will be good but you may not get the customers," he said.

An integral part of most second stage LFMSs is value chain management of which supply chain management is a subset. Defining a strategy for value chain management is crucial for many e-businesses' success. How products are being marketed and distributed is continuously changing and e-businesses need to find answers to the following questions:

- Is your e-business's logistics and fulfillment approach consistent with your overall vision and goals?

- What is the best way to distribute your products to improve customer service and reduce costs?

- What is the worth of your value chain services, and how can you improve it?

- Is logistics and fulfillment a core strength, or should it be outsourced? And if outsourced, who should you use?

- How does your logistics and fulfillment service differentiate your e-business from its competition?

- What technology should the e-business consider that would improve its value chain management performance?

- Should the e-business enhance its value chain management services via acquisitions?

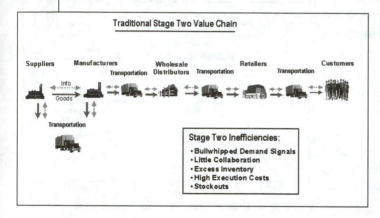

Once an e-business has the answers to these questions, and has instituted the processes and systems necessary to effectively meet the issues raised, it can move to Stage Three.

Stage Three

The new millennium brought with it real-time e-commerce — a demand for goods delivered faster and more cheaply than through bricks-and-mortar channels. E-businesses must expand their value chain to include additional suppliers and trading partners that can help achieve the necessary efficiencies to respond to this demand. This is what a state-of-the-art LFMS is all about.

To accomplish this an e-business needs real-time, collaborative links throughout its value chain. As a result, new Web-based supply chain tools that can deliver an efficient communication stream (and planning and forecasting capabilities) to a value chain are racing in, leaving proprietary systems and traditional client/server offerings eating their dust.

Real-time collaboration allows a value chain to improve its planning capabilities and reduces the lead-time in getting product to market.

Without an e-business model in place, an enterprise is forced to communicate via telephone (teleconferences, faxes, voice mail) and e-mail. This requires data to be relayed and re-entered, resulting in errors and delay.

Essential in the third stage of an LFM plan are Web-based collaborative planning and forecasting tools, such as, Datasweep Advantage (www.datasweep.cpm), Logility Inc.'s Demand Chain Voyager (www.logility.com), Manugistics' NetWorks S/Collaborate (www.manugistics.com), SAP APO (www.sap.cpm) and Webplan (www.webplan.com). These can reduce a value chain's planning cycle from one month to about a week. Although traditional client/server supply chain management software from software firms such as i2 Technologies (www.i2.cpm), Manugistics, and SAP can help an e-business to streamline its internal operations, the new Web-based tools are making it easier and more cost-effective to include the entire value chain.

A crucial piece of a third stage LFMS in Web-based supply chain technology is the enabler, which should become a standard element for doing e-business. Through a browser (Microsoft's Internet Explorer or Netscape), a B2B manufacturer could browse permission-based areas of a suppliers' systems, allowing it to check on inventory and production capabilities. For example, a B2B manufacturer could match demand for the its products (Cisco). At the same time the suppliers could be doing the reverse so they can match demand of their production and this can dribble down the entire value chain (Grainger). Thus the value chain members can always be on alert for potential bottlenecks or backlogs and can work together in real-time to sidetrack potential problems.

But Web-based supply chain systems don't stop there. They also allow value chains to collaborate on forecasts in real-time or let sales reps tap into permission-based systems to check on production schedules and logistics information, letting them keep customers apprised of order status.

As a value chain begins to share critical production, scheduling, inventory, forecasting and logistics information in real-time, e-businesses can respond more accurately to their customers' demands. Factor in the economics gained with a Web-based supply chain system versus a proprietary system or EDI and many e-businesses will see a win-win situation.

With a Web-based supply chain system, suppliers don't need to guess what's needed, they know exactly when an item in their inventory or a service they provide is needed by a member of the value chain (Wal-Mart and P&G is a good example).

With visibility up and down the value chain it's possible to see seasonal demand and it also allows the value chain to react to trends. Remember a lit-

A Stage Three E-Business	
Internet Applications: **Achieving the "Network Effect"**	
Internet Applications	**"Network Effect"**
E-commerce	Diversity of Products/Service
Employee Self-Service	Customization/Personalization
Customer Care Support	Improved Customer Satisfaction
Virtual Manufacturing	Accelerated Time to Market Dramatic Margin Reductions Just-in-Time Manufacturing
Virtual Close	Empowerment
E-Learning	Productivity and Talent
E-Convenience	Anytime, Anywhere Access

tle thing called Furbies — a whopper of a trend. But, with a Web-based supply chain system in place, as consumer orders escalate, and the snowball starts rolling — first to the distributor and then to the manufacturer and finally to the component suppliers — no one would be caught by surprise, everyone could be ready and there would be no roadblocks.

There are obstacles to getting the value chain to embrace an open and extended value chain. You will have businesses that will worry about security ("Oh no! I'm putting my critical business information over the Internet."). Then there is trust. Most members of the value chain are use to a practice of discouraging any kind of sharing of key business data ("You want to look at WHAT?!"). Finally, there is the archfiend itself — modification of business processes to embrace the e-business model ("What do you mean the old way isn't good enough?"). Nevertheless, members of the value chain must deal with these issues if they want to remain competitive and the Web's role in all of this should give reluctant businesses a jump-start.

According to the consulting firm, AMR Research Inc., revenues in the SCM market are projected to soar to $18.6 billion in 2003. What do you want to bet that much of that $18 billion will be spent on Web-based solutions?

Some e-businesses may want to deploy a new system in-house before hooking up other members of the value chain. Over time it can introduce the new system to key members of the value chain, replacing EDI links currently in place, since the new systems bring more flexibility and interactivity than EDI and save the costly EDI link charge.

Allowing customers to have real-time input via Web-based supply chain tools helped Eastman Chemical (www.eastman.com) better identify and time

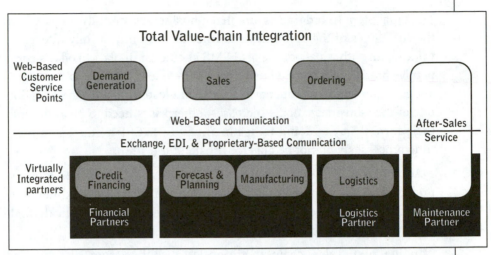

Total Value-Chain Integration

demand. "We recognize we need to do a better job of satisfying and supply-ing what [customers] need when they need it," adds John A. Hewson, Eastman's manager of global forecasting. "The Web lets us do that without seriously impacting our cost structure, without having to hold higher levels of inventory and without flying product around all over the country to meet customers' needs."

Hewson anticipated encountering trust issues

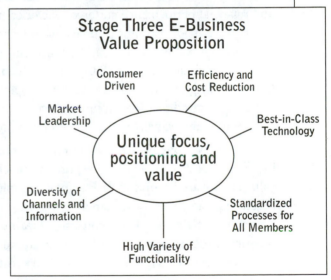

and realized he must find a common comfort level with regard to infor-mation exchange. Eastman's approach was to modify business processes so the value chain could actually take action based on the Internet-enabled, real-time exchange of data. Hewson speculates, "It's no good having a fast interface if once data arrives within the walls of an enter-prise, you don't have the equivalent speed with which to take action."

<u>The Final Step</u>: In order to assure that e-businesses are fully prepared for the challenges of the 21st Century's Internet economy, a fully integrated value chain with a state-of-the-art LFMS should be in place. Today's competitive pressures require e-businesses to provide visibility into their operations, order status, product availability, and lead times. As the adoption rate of the e-business model increases, enterprises need to be aware that their current way of doing things (manual- EDI- ERP-systems and planning processes) will not be able to withstand the strain.

According to research company, META Group, "Companies must be prepared for the pressures that selling through exchanges and net markets will place on their core supply chain processes or risk quickly finding themselves uncompetitive."

In the past, value chain inefficiencies resulting from disconnected processes could be concealed through inventory buffers although operating and financial performance suffered. Factories maintained higher inventories to offset poor planning and lack of forward visibility, and assets were not fully utilized, with labor and equipment either bottlenecked or idle. Thus, rescheduling and expediting became the norm rather than the exception, with a significant negative impact on operating efficiency. Sometimes enterprises found that the wrong product had been produced at the wrong time, consuming valuable capacity needed to produce the right product.

In the new e-business environment, it's futile to try to conceal these inefficiencies. Global visibility exposes value chain weaknesses. But also value chains are becoming increasingly complex — outsourcing of manufacturing, logistics, and other processes creates interdependencies among the chain members requiring a seamless, effective, collaborative planning process linking all value chain members. E-businesses that can profitably receive customer orders and/or create demand via an integrated value chain and plan their operations with all value chain members as a single integrated chain will prosper, i.e., Cisco, Intel, and Dell.

Prior to adopting an e-business model, large enterprises had implemented some form of integrated business processes such as ERP to support internal operations but most haven't brought these processes to the Web. The main reasons are that numerous internal business processes don't have the Web capability, and upgrades are unlikely to provide forward visibility into potential problems or to support "what-if" planning for evaluation of potential alternatives, much less, the ability to support real-time planning.

An e-business implementing a third stage LFMS will rely on a new breed of planning tools that can cope with an increasingly complex and demanding business environment. Depending on a specific e-business's needs, it can implement, within the LFMS planning, solutions

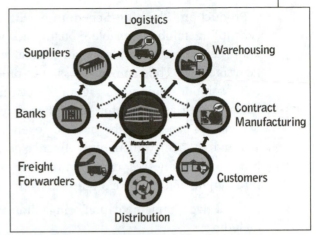

There are numerous touch points with many-to-many collaborative interactions once an e-business begins implementation of a Stage Three LFMS.

that address one or more of three major planning areas — demand planning, supply planning, and production planning/scheduling.

Demand Planning: Effective demand planning solutions enable e-businesses to anticipate and influence future customer demand. They include collaborative forecasting tools that provide consistent demand data and information throughout the value chain so as to optimize supply chain responsiveness. By implementing an effective demand planning process, e-businesses can achieve notable increases in their value chain performance.

Supply Planning: Effective supply planning solutions enable e-businesses to determine what goods and/or material are required and when they are needed, as well as optimizing the distribution of the same, through a careful matching of internal and external sources of supply with prioritized demand. In some multi-source, multi-distribution center value chains, effective supply planning solutions will typically determine which demands will be supplied by which trading partner and/or which distribution center, as well as where to stock specific inventory quantities to support customer-service objectives. An effective supply planning process supports global visibility and coordination among trading partners, rapid response to change, and reduced working capital requirements.

Production Planning/Scheduling: Effective production planning/scheduling solutions enable e-businesses to ascertain what to produce and when to produce it, based on calculable capacity controls and material availability. Thus an e-business with production and planning/scheduling solutions built within its LFMS can manage labor and equipment loads as well as determine time-phased future material requirements. Scheduling can be on the hour- or even on the minute-level of detail. Through the achievement of an effective production planning/scheduling process, e-businesses can significantly reduce inventories, increase throughput, and improve on-time delivery performance.

Third stage implementation brings dramatic benefits for an e-business including:

- A 20-30% reduction in raw materials inventories, attributable to reduced lead times, improved supply planning, and supply chain integration.

- A 5-10% increase in throughput resulting from improved scheduling and material planning.

- A 25-35% reduction in WIP inventories due to improved coordination of materials and capacity.

- A 15-25% reduction in finished goods inventories arising out of improved forecasting, reduced lead times, and improved inventory planning.

- A 5-15% increase in customer service levels due to identification of realistic delivery commitments based on true capabilities and forward visibility of potential problems with sufficient time to respond.

Vender Managed Inventory

Another benefit of a third stage LFMS is that an e-business is in the position to adopt vendor-managed inventory (VMI) within its e-business model. An extended value chain with the proper technology and partnerships in place can realize savings of as much as 35% in their distribution and order processing costs through the introduction of the VMI model. However, before a VMI model can be instituted, the vendor's customers need assurance of a reliable supply from the vendor and its partners. In the past, this has been addressed by physically locating a substantial amount of inventory on the customer's premises. Thus the benefits arising from a shorter supply chain and reduced paperwork were lost due the increase in inventory required to assure the customer of a steady supply of material. The challenge is to maintain an adequate level of inventory at the lowest possible cost.

A VMI vendor that has adopted an e-business model with a fully implemented and integrated LFMS can determine:

- Shipping costs that are incurred whenever a shipment is made between two locations.

- Holding costs that are incurred continuously whenever inventory position of an item at a location is positive.

- Backorder costs that are incurred continuously whenever inventory position of an item at a location is negative.

To compute the optimal replenishment policies the LFMS must be able to look at all the different replenishment options simultaneously. Such as balancing the cost of expediting and alternative transportation modes against the cost of inventory while simultaneously considering the many shipment alternatives.

Note that traditional methods for calculating safety stocks don't consider routine expediting rules. Advanced inventory planning techniques select a plan based on cost incurred whenever:

- A shipment is made between two locations (shipping costs incurred).

- Whenever inventory position of an item at a location is positive (holding costs incurred as a continuous cost).

- Whenever inventory position of an item at a location is negative (backorder costs incurred).

The vendor needs an LFMS that can:

- Compute the cost of a restock plan (the sum of the shipment cost, the cost of the buffer stock, and the expediting and repositioning that occur when the plan is executed).

- Optimize inventories (allocate the inventories to minimize runouts and either calculate the amount of inventory required, or allocate a given amount of inventory as efficiently as possible).

- Take into account expediting rules since inventory is simply one alternative for protecting against runouts.

Advanced Inventory Planning

Many e-businesses can profit from advanced inventory planning, i.e., trading working capital for better planning. However, the key is developing a logistics and fulfillment plan that integrates manufacturing and distribution and then executing the plan through a fine-tuned LFMS.

A best-of-breed Stage Three LFMS extricates profit from its value chain, although this can only be achieved if an LFMS can properly process the inherent variability of demand, transportation, and manufacturing. For example, safety stocks of inventory are normally maintained at one or more locations but safety stocks provide only one way to insulate the system and value chain from disruptions.

Advanced inventory planning capability must answer the questions: How much inventory is needed and what combination of safety stock and expediting rules is most cost effective in guarding against uncertainty? Look at the entire distribution network simultaneously to compute the effects of demand variability. This allows an e-business to select a plan based primarily on the cost drivers that are basically the same as for VMI — shipping costs, holding costs, and backorder costs.

Key features include the ability to impose inventory targets by a group of locations, balance the cost of expediting and alternative transportation modes against the cost of inventory, and to consider the entire distribution network as an integrated entity.

Typical Quantified Benefits from Integrating the Supply Chain	
Delivery Performance	16%-28% Improvement
Inventory Reduction	25%-60% Improvement
Fulfillment Cycle Time	30%-50% Improvement
Forecast Accuracy	25%-80% Improvement
Overall Productivity	10%-16% Improvement
Lower Supply-Chain Costs	25%-50% Improvement
Fill Rates	20%-30% Improvement
Improved Capacity Realization	10%-20% Improvement

SECURITY

By its very nature the integration of an e-business's value chain into its LFMS requires the involvement of multiple parties with differing levels of technical expertise. When creating online business processes each type of technical sophistication must, to some degree, be catered to with functionality designed to facilitate the exchange of data.

When trying to implement security the entire value chain must realize that security is a chain that is only as strong as its weakest link. The security of any value chain is based on many links and because people are people, they won't all have the same level of security within their systems.

Security is a subject on which volumes could be written. The author's advice to an e-business adopting an LFMS is to hire a security expert to evaluate your systems and ensure that an annual security audit is performed on all of your systems. However, some of the many questions that an e-business pulling its value chain into a Web-based relationship must respond to are:

- How do I know the person/entity with whom I'm dealing over the Internet is who they say they are?

- How can I know that the information received actually came from a member of the value chain rather than someone masquerading as that person or entity? And how do I know the message wasn't changed along the way?

- How can I make the value chain confident they are dealing with a reputable vendor and not an impersonator just trying to get their credit card or private business information?

- How can I keep prying eyes from seeing the value chain's electronic messages?

The contact made by one person with another on a network, whether on a small local area network or the Internet, is an electronic contact. One assurance of identity is a public key infrastructure (PKI), which is a secure infrastructure that allows trust within a value chain. The terms "digital signature," "Registration Authority," or "Certification Authority" are used to describe elements of the PKI.

An enterprise PKI will enable an e-business to be much more certain of who is using its computers even where such access is over open channels like the Internet, and it will give the e-business the ability to grant access rights and take them away when necessary.

SPECIFICITY IN THE LFMS DESIGN

As demonstrated throughout this book, one size does not fit all in the e-business community. Here are some other issues, systems and processes that individual e-businesses may want to consider:

Customized Procurement Processes

In industries with complicated products, procurement requires increasing degrees of customization. When creating processes that apply to a broader market, B2B suppliers and buyers need to take a close look at the steps and information required before completion of a transaction. For example, a bricks-and-mortar buyer and seller will have customized forms to record the information needed to complete a transaction.

The value chain will exchange the right information to allow the online transaction to fit into processes developed with customized information, the complexity of which will vary from industry to industry. For B2B manufacturers that are direct sellers, the standardization of forms that will service the value chain can be a challenging process.

Certain members of the value chain might require that information be transportable into proprietary formats used in the procurement process (EDI for example). To provide this flexibility will bring challenges to everyone. It's best if you can find some common ground for all members.

During the last decade, the business sector has been increasing the efficiency of procurement processes through implementation of costly EDI systems. These systems originated in proprietary formats that were unreadable by any business without an existing relationship with the EDI owner. During the last 2 or 3 years, however, compatibility between varying EDI systems has been developed. A B2B and its value chain may want to consider leveraging the enormous investments previously made in EDI systems through a method of hooking and layering information-sharing technologies on top of the existing EDI systems.

Real-time Procurement and Forecasting

Increasingly, technology is providing the ability to monitor pricing fluctuations responding to demand and supply curves. This allows B2Bs that manufacture and/or procure based upon forecasts to have better opportunity to control cost efficiencies; however, this responsiveness can have a trickle down affect upon product pricing, and distribution processes.

B2Bs may find it advisable to integrate into the value chain JIT solutions providers, as manufacturing upon-demand continues to shift market dynamics.

A good, scalable LFMS must have integration capabilities so it can mesh well with existing systems and applications, support flexible business rules, provide multiple workflows across the value chain, support Web-based technology and not hinder the automation and implementation of the e-business model across the value chain.

Although the logistics and fulfillment needs of the different e-business models vary, they all have some aspects in common. The majority of the pure play e-tail models don't have any system integration in place. This can make it easier to implement an LFMS, although the legacy systems within a value chain may present a challenge or two.

On the other hand the B2B model, due to its converged nature, usually does have portions of its systems integrated, not only in-house, but with certain members of its value chain. You would think that would ease the implementation of an LFMS — no way! These systems can include just about everything: flat-file databases, mainframes, mini-computers, EDI and ERP systems, to name just a few. The question these e-businesses must wrestle with is what systems to leave in place, what to replace, and what new systems should be implemented. Of course all of this entails an unwieldy conglomeration of software, middleware, customized solutions, and the human resources to make it all happen.

E-Tails and Buy-side B2Bs

E-tail and buy-side B2B e-businesses have their own logistics and fulfillment demons. For instance, execution at the order fulfillment level, as indicated by fill rate, on-time product delivery, accuracy, or any number of other typical performance criteria, often fall far short of the mark. Many B2Bs are struggling just to find the right method for taking and delivering orders. You read daily about e-businesses that have experienced substantial operating losses since their inception — many of these losses can be tied directly to the inability to gain control over their LFMS.

There are exceptions, a case in point is SimonDelivers.com, a pure-play, full-service online grocer with scheduled home delivery, based in suburban Minneapolis, MN. It fulfills numerous orders involving thousands of SKUs daily.

SimonDelivers.com's distribution and fulfillment center initially operated out of a limited space and thus, inventory turns had to be high and the work well organized to avoid disastrous congestion. Its logistics and fulfillment plan, which drove many decisions from the outset, included establishing an outstanding level of customer service, a guarantee that all orders would be filled 100% complete (no exceptions), and a commitment to informed communication with the customer at every stage of the process.

From the beginning it sought to build a top-notch management team and utilize its strengths. First it took small steps to prove concepts before investing heavily in assets and it designed everything as scalable as possible while at the same time using the Internet and information systems to full advantage for both sales and distribution. CEO Simon Foster established a number of performance goals, such as large and average order sizes, high customer density within service neighborhoods, and ongoing attention to product mix. This worked to give SimonDelivers flexibility so that it could, wherever possible, avoid structures that limited change.

With strict attention to these goals, SimonDelivers was able to immediately succeed in areas where other e-businesses struggled — accurate picking, packing, shipment, and delivery of individual orders to customers within a promised time window, i.e., LFM.

Foster decided that to reach his set performance goals, he should focus on his strengths — acquiring and retaining customers — and use outside experts for other critical tasks like warehousing and distribution. High on his most-wanted list was a distribution system that was cost-effective, efficient, accurate, flexible, and most important, easy to change (scalable).

SimonDelivers.com first identified and built relationships with reliable suppliers who could handle the expected growth, compliance requirements, and the merchandise mix. This is where the right management team was essential.

Foster then sought outside assistance to support its inventory model and to augment his staff. Realizing that an online grocer had specific LFM needs, Foster looked for a logistics and fulfillment partner who wouldn't be applying a boilerplate solution and that was willing to work with him. In his words, "to plan and execute a 'plan-to-learn' facility, rather than a more traditional operational plan that would have committed a lot of money to fixed assets before the details and 'best' solutions were worked on. Our focus was on developing the best plan, period."

Foster placed particular emphasis on his two-phase approach. "In a start-up business, we couldn't afford to do otherwise. And it worked. Despite all the skepticism out there, all major assumptions that went into this project were correct (deliver to 40-plus percent of our households a day, find customers for less than $50 each, and retain 90% of all customers annually). With limited finances, we couldn't afford to make mistakes. We needed to be able to show people that we could be profitable and that there was a substantial demand for the service."

Foster understood after an arduous 18-month learning period that obtaining orders online would be a snap compared to the challenge of retaining those hard-earned customers by meeting their service expectations. "Every aspect of each delivery is critical to earning the customers' trust, so it's imperative that we not only fulfill orders accurately, but also that we deliver to customers within the promised time window, come rain, sun, or snow," Foster says. "Plus, we also guarantee all customer orders to be 100% complete. These are challenging requirements for any distribution operation. In our business, it's a necessary core competency for an organization to succeed."

Simondelivers.com's plan-to-learn was a two-phase distribution strategy. The first phase was a low-cost, manual distribution and warehouse system, which was used to develop and refine a fast, cost-effective method for fulfilling orders. In this phase there was testing of alternative methods to gain accurate and rapid access to inbound product and to minimize material handling, and throughput, and techniques that new hires could readily learn, speeding their assimilation into the process.

The standards proven and wisdom gained in the first phase then were applied to highly automated, capital-intensive systems that could scale to accommodate large sales volumes without diminution of quality or throughput.

Many e-businesses mistakenly assume that traditional distribution systems are suitable for their new business model. They're wrong. Systems that work for a bricks-and-mortar can actually impede an e-business, especially a pure play. Foster described SimonDelivers' phase-one logistics and fulfillment center as "more like a giant sandbox" where staff members could continue to move things around until they found the right layout and methods.

Each component of the system was highly flexible, allowing everyone involved to test, analyze, and if necessary, reconfigure almost any component of the operation, from the layout and capacity of coolers to the position of pallet racks any the location and flow of products. "The whole approach early on was to design with relatively low-tech systems and techniques that supported business goals and direction," SimonDelivers.com's fulfillment partner, TZA (www.tzaconsulting.com) president Tom Zosel explained. This strategy freed up the majority of SimonDelivers' capital for marketing and delivery. "Fortunately, we were able to outfit the entire operation with second-hand equipment," says Foster. His total initial equipment investment for the entire operation was well under $500,000 — surprise, surprise!

Foster's goals include present and future product and material handling along with information systems that can facilitate rapid, accurate, and efficient unpacking, restocking and picking of product by locating each item strategically. That means optimizing its location by considering its physical characteristics (size and weight), its popularity (demand), and its environmental requirements (temperature, fragility, and so forth). This minimizes handling and ensures consistent stock rotation.

However, when considering design issues, thought was given to the need for easy vehicle access. When properly implemented, the system made the delivery driver's efforts more efficient by grouping all parts of an order in a logical fashion. Shipping containers optimized space. Once orders were picked, packed, and ready to go, they could be dispatched for delivery within 12 hours of the close of orders the night before. Orders could be delivered directly to customers or left "unattended," in totes and insulated coolers deposited either at the doorstep or in the garage. Empty totes from previous deliveries could be picked up at the same time.

SimonDelivers.com's new phase-two logistics and fulfillment facility reflects the lessons learned during its start-up phase. The final design showcases appropriate automation consistent with proven need and affords it both high performance and low risk. "Not only are we basing the design of SimonDelivers' [logistics and fulfillment center] on a proven model, but the new system [is] larger, faster, and better able to accommodate much greater business growth," Zosel says.

Just-In-Time Logistics

As e-businesses continue to explore Cyberland's commerce possibilities, they will discover and implement better control over their purchasing systems. Where traditional purchasing systems consisted of a never-ending paper chain, with the new breed of LFMSs, e-businesses can facilitate just-in-time delivery of spare parts and raw materials needed for production, freeing up the cash that is currently tied up in surplus, redundant inventory.

In the high-volume automobile industry, parts and materials are gathered from hundreds of vendors and delivered to a few manufacturing plants. Continuously throughout the day trucks rumble out of a Michigan factory bound for a nearby cross-dock warehouse, laden with automobile parts destined for new Toyota cars. At the warehouse the parts are combined with shipments of numerous other suppliers and then the consolidated shipments are hauled off to Toyota assembly plants throughout North America — you say "so what."

Here comes the remarkable part — the shipments are timed to arrive at the plants within 15 minutes of a set delivery time and are unloaded in precise sequence. When this "warehouse ballet" has been played out, the assembly workers have the right parts at hand when a specific Toyota model rolls onto the assembly line and Toyota has saved millions because it has an LFMS that allows it to operate with a minimal parts inventory. That's state-of-the-art just-in-time (JIT) delivery in the automobile industry.

Toyota annually purchases more than $8 billion worth of parts and materials from a list of over 500 vendors and delivers the products to 10 manufacturing plants throughout the US and Canada. Its LFMS, which incorporates JIT delivery, is not unique. It's an example of how a properly integrated value chain can squeeze inefficiency throughout the supply line allowing manufacturers and suppliers to virtually eliminate inventory costs while shippers shuttle parts between suppliers and manufacturers on daily "milk runs" thus achieving maximum utilization of their vehicles and staff.

Although many companies employ some version of JIT logistics, automakers are the acknowledged leaders. This is one of the main reasons you don't find many analysts downplaying the importance of Covisint, the planned automotive e-business trading exchange, supported by General Motors, Ford, DaimlerChrysler and latecomer, Renault/Nissan. Covisint's goal is to allow OEMs and suppliers to reduce cost in their respective supply chains and bring efficiencies to their business operations.

JIT logistics is designed to give customers what they want when they want it. The system "is not all about price. It's about service and value. Other industries do it [JIT logistics], but not with as much standardization and discipline," said Todd Ericksrud, vice president-automotive at Schneider National Trucking (www.schneider.com). Schneider is one of Toyota's core carriers and has formed its own Freight Velocity Center to transport parts and materials for automobile manufacturers in the Midwest.

Like all automakers, Toyota has worked to shorten the time it takes to manufacture a car after the customer places an order. It is attempting to compress its order-to-delivery schedule through its revamped logistics system that it has introduced throughout North America.

The system described herein helps Toyota, as well as its vendors, to level their production throughout the day, and guarantees truckers full loads. Like most automobile manufacturers, Toyota sources parts and materials from hundreds of outside vendors. Engine parts, batteries, oil filters, brake pads, ventilation hoses, crankshaft pulleys and wire harness brackets are just some of the components that pass through the cross-dock distribution centers every day.

However, a JIT logistics model isn't only for the big guys, smaller operations such as Mitsubishi Motor Manufacturing Corp., with its one US plant, sources parts from more than 350 vendors and also gets value from a JIT system. Mitsubishi uses GATX Logistics to coordinate the movement of products through its cross-dock facility across the street from the plant. "The Mitsubishi plant was built around JIT logistics," said Russ Dixon, director of marketing communications at GATX Logistics (www.gatxlogistics.com).

GATX Logistics also manages an even smaller JIT system for five hospitals in New York City. Medical products are consolidated at a facility in the Bronx, and daily deliveries are made to the hospitals.

It's an entirely different story in the e-tail and retail industry. Take the retail giant, Wal-Mart, which imports thousands of containers from Asia through a single cross-dock facility operated by Distribution Services Ltd. in South Gate, Calif. The merchandise is transloaded and shipped to hundreds of stores across the country. "This is all basic stuff," said Cobb Grantham, managing director of Distribution Services Limited. "What you want to do is get the freight to the final destination with the least amount of handling," he said. But convincing all participants in the value chain to cooperate so as to initiate a JIT system would be challenging, Grantham added.

Click-and-Mortar Synchronization

In the October 30, 2000 issue of the *New York Times* there was an article that discussed Kohl's, a department store chain that dealt with the click-and-mortar synchronization issue, i.e., putting everyone's logistic and fulfillment operations and system in sync with each other. Rather than scurrying to put all its LFMSs in synchronization with its Web sales it anticipated the problem before it occurred. To ensure that it didn't suffer the typical logistics and fulfillment nightmare of so many e-businesses, Kohl's built a state-of-the-art distribution center. This would allow it to find, pack and ship an item within hours after an order came into its Web site — prior to launching its Web initiative.

To deal with the synchronization issue Gap, Nordstrom and the Container Store are putting up new buildings to meet their multi-channel logistics and fulfillment needs. And you can find click-and-mortars, such as HomeDepot.com, using their bricks-and-mortar counterpart as their warehouse and distribution hub. Then there are e-tailers like Kmart's Bluelight.com and WalMart.com that have farmed out their logistics and fulfillment needs to fulfillment partners. Why? Well, according to Alex McNealey, Bluelight.com's director of operations, "It takes 9 to 12 months to bring a new warehouse to full utilization, and it'll take longer than that to know what items our Web customers will buy."

Home Depot, a relative latecomer to e-tailing, has a Web site that will only accept orders from people with zip codes near Las Vegas and these few lucky online customers have the choice of whether to pick up goods at the Home Depot stores or have them delivered.

Home Depot does expect to roll its Web-sales program out nationally before the end of 2001. Home Depot has stepped out of the box a bit because even in 2002 Web customers will only be able to order items that are stocked in their local stores, and their orders will be filled from those stores. This probably means the online customer must type the zip code in before attempting any ordering or maybe even browsing activities. "Our customers really want the Internet to be a version of their store, online," Ron Griffin, Home Depot's chief information officer, told the *New York Times*.

Many e-businesses that have an in-house catalog-based operation find that the warehouses that served the catalog division are often too small or too reliant on legacy systems to process orders in the nanoseconds demanded of an Internet-based operation. "Internet customers place an order, then run to the door to see if the UPS truck is there yet," said Elaine Rubin, the chairwoman of Shop.org.

Synchronization hasn't been an issue with J. C. Penney's multi-channel entities, at least thus far. Although it has struggled with the front-end, due to its catalog experience it has always had a handle on the logistics and fulfillment end of its e-business. Dennis Radabaugh, director of logistics, told the *New York Times* that the company's five catalog fulfillment centers have enough capacity to absorb the Web orders easily. "There really isn't a need to differentiate between a phoned-in order or an Internet order," he said.

Another old hand at catalog fulfillment is Eddie Bauer and its move to an e-business model doesn't seem to have taxed its 1.5 million-square-foot catalog fulfillment center. Although Eddiebauer.com's customers are given the option of paying extra to have orders delivered in 24 hours, few do so, there is no overburdening of its fulfillment center's systems due to the crush of rush orders. "Internet customers are even more sensitive to delivery price than they are to delivery speed," said Mark Staudinger, Eddie Bauer's vice president for interactive media. (The readers may want to re-read that last sentence!)

Until recently, the Gap filled Web orders from a 270,000-square-foot warehouse in central Ohio, but that warehouse could no longer accommodate the growth in Web sales so Gap leased a nearby warehouse while it built out a massive new distribution center. "If we do it ourselves, we know that our customers are not in line behind some other retailer's customers, waiting to be served," said Kellie Leonard, a Gap spokeswoman.

Then there is the Container Store (www.containerstore.com), an e-business that sells home storage products and currently handles all logistics and fulfillment for its stores, catalog customers and Web customers from one center in Dallas. "Our customers have never insisted on unreasonably fast delivery," said Kip Tindell, the company's president. But, due to the growth in its online sales, Container Store has found itself running out of space and has been forced to rent a second all-purpose center while it builds out a new fulfillment and distribution center. "We were growing anyway, "but Internet sales were the straw that broke the camel's back," Tindell told the *Times*.

LFM HAS "ARRIVED"

It is impossible to implement the right LFMS for a specific e-business without professionals in your camp to lead and guide you. Ten years ago, it would have been difficult to find the executive talent necessary for such an undertaking. Today, logistics and fulfillment management has moved into the mainstream. MSAS Global Logistics, now known as Exel, (www.exel.com), launched a trade-finance program that is a blend of physical logistics, insurance and finance.

Many e-businesses have wrapped procurement, logistics and financial managers into one team focused on managing an e-business's capital, said Bill Payne, vice president of trade finance at MSAS Global Logistics, a third-party provider. Payne went on to explain, "logistics is evolving to the next step, it's all driven by finance, as companies seek to increase their return on assets." Shareholders and investors look for e-businesses with superior operating statistics and therefore e-businesses are being pressured to find ways to improve operating ratios, particularly return on assets. "With a major part of a company's assets tied up in inventory, it's the first area scrutinized," Payne said.

"Electronic commerce is reshaping our process, our people, our products and, of course, most importantly, it's changing our customers' expectations," Jim Kelly CEO of UPS said at a February 2000 executive forum, entitled Delivering E-Commerce: Logistics and the On-Line Revolution, that focused on both B2B and e-tail commerce. Kelly went on to surmise, "E-commerce is also the catalyst behind a trend that I believe will transcend virtually every business and policy issue we will face in the coming decade. That trend is the convergence we're seeing today in the goods, information and funds flow of commerce."

To further illustrate just how important logistics and fulfillment management has grown, H. Lee Scott, logistics manager of Wal-Mart Stores Inc., was named chief operating officer — a promotion that puts him in line to succeed David Glass as chief executive of the world's largest retailer. "From logistics manager to chief executive is the new career path. The path was laid out because of the contribution logistics makes to the prosperity of the firm," Jim Stone, president of Stone Management Consultants of Chicago explained to *JOC Transportation News* (www.joc.com). Stone went on, "the logistics manager gains the same kind of experience as a chief operating officer, chief executive, or general manager. Logistics ties together all the elements of the company."

Links with Banks

Another development of the logistics and fulfillment upsurge is that banks have begun to work directly with logistics companies. According to Bill Payne, vice president of trade finance at MSAS Global Logistics, a third-party provider, it makes sense. Banks finance the bulk of the trade that goes on between members in a value chain. The logistician has all the trade documents and collateral. Payne explained that "the logistics company can insure the cargo and physically manage the asset. This reduces the risk to the bank." But also, Payne ventured, "More than ever, there are greater pressures on logistics, procurement and the finance arms of a business to all share in the responsibility of better managing the company's assets, resulting in an improved return on assets."

Jim Kelly, CEO of UPS supported Payne's assertions in his presentation at a February 2000 executive forum, entitled "Delivering E-Commerce: Logistics and the On-Line Revolution." Kelly speculated that this "morphing" or "streamlining" of the transportation, technology and financial service industries should better enable all aspects of commerce to expedite trade and create new economic opportunities around the world.

Improved Efficiency

For example, MSAS Global has a just-in-time inventory program that allows e-businesses to delay taking possession and paying for the goods until they need them for manufacture or sale. "The cost of doing this is less than their cost of capital and it allows companies to deploy their assets into other aggressive growth areas," Payne explained.

Today an increasing number of e-businesses are using economic value added (profit less capital charge) to measure financial performance. "Improving efficiency improves the overall economic profit of the company. This allows [an e-business] to sell more at the same price," according to Stephen Timme, president of the consulting firm, FinListics Solutions Inc (www.finlistics.com). He opined that more-efficient e-businesses have higher asset turnover and "the supply chain is affecting the velocity at which money flows through a company."

Dell Computer has worked to cut costs by putting tighter controls on inventory. "Dell is using logistics as a strategic weapon to drive volume. The key is not just to save money, but to grow the business and to get to market a week faster than the competition," Timme pointed out.

Take a gander at Dell's archrival, Compaq. In its configure-to-order industry, Compaq was faced with not only competitive market pressures to increase service levels, but to also provide quick and reliable delivery commitments. Through the establishment of an effective planning solution, responsiveness increased significantly and on time delivery performance improved to 95%.

Siemens AG (www.siemens.com) implemented an effective demand and supply-planning process within its LFMS that improved forecast accuracy resulting in improved customer service while reducing overall inventories by 66%.

Robert V. Delaney, vice president of Cass Information Systems (www.cassinfo.com), a provider of payment and information services for financial, accounts payable, transportation, logistics, and utility needs, said logistics and supply chain management has been noticed by the financial community. "Investors are looking at companies able to achieve a higher return on assets. They also are looking at e-commerce as an attractive area."

LOGISTICS AND FULFILLMENT MANAGERS

Individuals employed in the field of logistics plan and schedule the delivery of products and services to customers all over the world. "Logistics professionals manage and coordinate activities in this global pipeline to ensure an effective and efficient flow of materials and information from the time a need arises until it's satisfied and beyond," states the Council of Logistics Management. Just a smattering of some of the managerial staff necessary for a first-class logistics and fulfillment strategy are listed below.

Analyst — uses analytical and quantitative methods to understand, predict, and enhance logistics processes. The analyst is responsible for assembling data, analyzing performance, identifying problems, and developing recommendations that support the management of logistics. A transportation analyst's duties revolve around a specific logistics activity, while supply chain analysts are responsible for a broad range of activities. Analysts are employed by carriers, logistics services providers, manufacturers, or other supply chain members.

Consultant — works with client organizations to enhance logistics performance though strategic planning, process re-engineering, and/or information technology implementation. Among other responsibilities the consultant develops and manages a wide range of projects including global supply chain optimization, software selection and development, strategic sourcing, and logistics network design. A consultant helps the client develop the logistical tools, processes, and knowledge base needed to create customer value, build competitive advantage, and boost profitability worldwide.

International Logistics — works closely with manufacturing, marketing, and purchasing to create timely, cost-effective import/export supply chains. The international logistics manager is responsible for handling the technical details of international transportation-multiple modes, complex documentation, and varying customs regulations, developing distribution strategies, and building relationships with logistics intermediaries. The international logistics manager also serves as a troubleshooter, dealing with the problems inherent in moving freight long distances and holding inventory in multiple countries.

Materials — manages raw materials and/or components inventory needed for manufacturing. The materials manager is responsible for inbound inventory levels. The manager coordinates with purchasing, manufacturing, and suppliers to ensure reliable, cost efficient delivery of the raw materials to create a production plan. The materials manager is often responsible for receiving, warehousing, scheduling, and inbound transportation.

Production — supervises production in a manufacturing setting. These managers are responsible for manufacturing engineers, production associates, machine operators, and other plant equipment operators. The production manager coordinates production scheduling, quality control, labor requirements, materials requirements, and finished goods inventory. The production manager also manages costs within the production department. Success as a production manager may lead to the position of Plant Manager.

Purchasing — directs the buying activities for a company, government agency, or organization. They are responsible for identifying global sources of materials, selecting suppliers, arranging contracts, and managing relationships. The purchasing manager coordinates with materials management and manufacturing to ensure timely delivery of the proper materials. The purchasing manager provides analysis to increase levels of service at reduced costs.

Plant — directs and coordinates all manufacturing activities to obtain optimum efficiency and economy of operations and maximize profits, while cost-effectively adhering to adequate quality standards and delegating and controlling the areas of production, maintenance, and planning. The plant manager is responsible for the development of plant policies in congruence with the agenda or goals of the company or division, and executes them at every level of the manufacturing operation. He or she calculates manufacturing schedules as a function of market demand and plant capacity. Using the chain of command, the manager interacts with product R&D programs, process engineering and specialized equipment procurement, as well as regulating inventory, production costs, and all aspects of the BOM (bill of material) from receiving to shipping.

Transportation — directs the effectiveness of private, third party and contract carriage systems. These individuals manage staff and operations to assure timely and cost efficient transportation of all incoming and outgoing shipments. The transportation manager plans and assures adequate equipment for storage, loading, and delivery of goods. The transportation manager is responsible for scheduling, routing, budget administration, freight bill presentation, and contract negotiations. These managers work with international carriers and freight forwarders to streamline the flow of goods across international boarders and through customs.

Roger W. Lowther, vice president of transportation at USCO Logistics, has determined that the corporate mind-set is difficult to change. Logistics managers in today's marketplace, he notes, are looking for a crystal ball to answer how they should manage the changes. The problem is that logistics and fulfillment is seen as something that happens in the back-end of the supply chain. That has to change, Lowther asserts.

"If the logistics manager is not involved with the procurement, marketing, and financial departments on the front end of product development, all the planning in the world won't mean anything."

A FINAL FEW WORDS

Outsourcing logistics and fulfillment is also gaining popularity with those involved on the inbound supply chain side of the equation. For instance, companies such as network maker Cisco Systems, passive-component manufacturer BCcomponents, and chip vendors National Semiconductor and V3 Semiconductor have signed outsourcing contracts that will enable them to dedicate more resources to developing products and technology.

"Companies want to focus on their core competencies," says C. John Langley, a logistics professor at the University of Tennessee. "The growth of the supply chain as a business practice means putting more focus on the needs of the customer," and many companies lack, or choose not to put up the resources or capital necessary to invest in comprehensive logistics and fulfillment expertise.

The idea of drop-shipping packages directly to the end user is also appealing to companies looking to streamline the delivery process, said Bob Moncrieff, a director in the Mountain View, CA, office of management consulting firm Pittiglio Rabin Todd & McGrath (www.prtm.com). And, as more companies post inventory, shipment tracking, and product-availability information on the Web, the drop-ship process gets easier because the necessary data is easy to find and access.

Subscribe to Art Avery's newsletter (www.elogistics101.com) covering logistics and fulfillment issues. Mr. Avery is a recognized leader in the field of e-commerce order fulfillment and gives good, common sense advice. For more information also visit www.entrepreneur.com where Juanita Ellis answers questions on "e-commerce fulfillment," and www.about.com, which has an informative section entitled "Logistics/ Supply Chain". Of course, there are www.joc.com, www.supplychainbrain.com, and www.elogisticsmagazine.com; if you don't already have them bookmarked, do so now. There are many more sites and publications that I am sure many of you already know about. I mention the ones above because I felt they might have been overlooked by many readers.

Fulfillment: In-house or Outsource?

AS DEMONSTRATED BY THE complex fulfillment models outlined in Chapter 7, e-businesses are falling back on the tried and true, or adopting entirely new fulfillment models in their quest to solve a Web-generated logistics and fulfillment dilemma.

The Gap, Nordstrom and Kohl's are building out new distribution centers to meet their logistics and fulfillment needs generated by the adoption of the e-business model. Others, such as Home Depot, Circuit City and UK grocer Tesco are making their stores perform double duty as warehouses and distribution hubs. And many, including Kmart and Wal-Mart, are temporarily farming out the entire fulfillment process.

The B2B side is just as inventive: Cisco's suppliers ship directly to the end customer; Safeway keeps most processes and services in-house including much of its shipping; and some e-businesses, such as GE and VF Corp., use every strategy in their race to get the end product to the consumer.

Some e-businesses, such as Bluefly and SkyMall.com, embrace the "virtual corporation" vision. This means outsourcing logistics and fulfillment needs, including outbound distribution, delivery and transportation, and extending to returns and call centers.

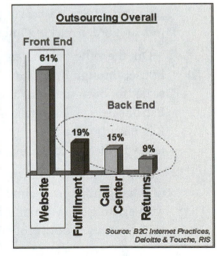

Outsourcing Overall

Front End: 61% Website

Back End: Fulfillment 19%, Call Center 15%, Returns 9%

Source: B2C Internet Practices, Deloitte & Touche, RIS

As the reader has surely come to realize, there is no simple answer to the in-house or outsource question. The e-business's decision regarding how it will handle its logistics and fulfillment obligations rests mainly with its willingness to form partnerships with third parties and its ability to oversee partner relationships. It's not an "and/or" decision. For instance, an e-business may have an in-house fulfillment operation but still need order processing management due to a host of drop-ship relationships; or an e-business may outsource some fulfillment to enable JIT shipping; or perhaps the e-business requires a fulfillment partner to handle only returns and/or customer service issues. There are numerous situations where an e-business will find itself seeking a logistics and fulfillment partner.

The Bain & Company/Mainspring Analysis referred to throughout this book offers some statistics that may be of use in the decision to outsource: Warehouses become scale-efficient beyond about 15,000 transactions per day or about 250,000 square feet. If an e-business's order fulfillment strategy requires four warehouse locations, it would only be cost-effective to build its own facilities if it anticipates over 60,000 total transactions daily or requires roughly a million square feet. Even Amazon.com has only 33,000 transactions per day. The next largest, CDnow, has 23,000, and PlanetRx has only 4,000.

The small- to mid-sized pure-play e-businesses typically will outsource allowing an economy of scale by being one of many in a managed warehouse, distribution or fulfillment operation. If the IT is right, an e-business can achieve cost savings and still provide customers access to inventory and order tracking information.

On the other hand, an e-business with mail-order competency in-house, through integration of its catalog and online operations, has the scale to own and enhance order fulfillment assets cost-effectively. Established catalog retailers Lands' End (150,000 transactions per day), L.L. Bean (125,000) and J. Crew (95,000) have e-tail sites that are consistently in the top 50 of any rating survey concerning e-tailers.

Any e-business, no matter the size, will find that state-of-the-art logistics and fulfillment technologies are expensive and difficult to integrate with existing IT systems. At the same time, logistics companies such as UPS with its 4,000 programmers and technicians are in a position to offer their systems to e-business customers on a pay-per-use basis. For example, currently UPS tracks approximately 13 million packages daily. Customers can access that information on their computers, phones, or PDAs. In addition, UPS has moved into the world of electronic funds transfer with a cash-on-delivery program and customer services (running a call center on behalf of Nike.com).

For many e-businesses — whether to keep services in-house or to outsource — is a loaded question. In-house capabilities could allow the company to provide better customer service as illustrated by PlanetRx.com's in-house fulfillment center that enables the e-business to add "surprises" to each package before shipping — something they might not trust to an outsourcer. However, the jury is still out on whether profits will follow in the wake of PlanetRx's innovative techniques.

Consider KBkids.com. KBkids.com was a joint venture between Brainplay.com and Consolidated Stores (K-B Stores) and as such could have been recipient of an existing distribution system. Instead, it took a page from Walmart.com and decided initially to stay with Brainplay's fulfillment service provider (FSP), Keystone Internet Services (www.keystoneinternet.com). This decision allowed KBkids.com to investigate options and take its time in building out a viable fulfillment center to service its online customers.

In early December 2000, KB Toys Management and Bain Capital purchased the KBkids toy division from Consolidated Stores. As reported in *Information Week* at the end of 2000 KBkids.com transformed a 300,000 square foot facility in Danville, KY from a bricks-and-mortar fulfillment center to an Internet-only operation. Inside, KBkids.com has installed Logistics Pro from Intrepa LLC (warehouse management system) (www.intrepa.com), and an order management system from Smith Gardner & Associates (www.smithgardner.com). KBkids.com has also added hardware to increase its online scalability and stability. KBkids.com links its customer service system that contains all of its customer information (including where an ordered item is in the fulfillment process), with its Danville fulfillment operations providing it with a 360-degree view of all order processes as they move through the system.

Hopefully, this will help KBkids.com when the next Forrester's

PowerRankings survey of the leading e-commerce sites in the toys and games category is announced. Prior to the institution of the in-house fulfillment system, KBkids.com did beat out its click-and-mortar competition (mainly due to its quick e-mail responses), but it came in dead last when compared to its pure-play competitors, mainly due to problems like poor order-tracking capabilities. Improvement should be dramatically visible with the next survey.

If your e-business has a best-selling product (such as hand-painted ceramic Princess Diana replicas), it isn't always cost-effective to hire someone else's staff to encase your figurines in bubble wrap and box them for FedEx pickup. This is the dilemma of many e-tailers. What's the most efficient way to deliver orders into the customers' hands? The answer lies in the decision you make regarding when to outsource order fulfillment and when to bring it in-house.

Online customers expect delivery on the promise of ease, speed and convenience when making online purchases. The e-businesses (pure-plays in particular) have seldom been able to meet these expectations because of their inexperience in picking, packing and shipping one and two item orders.

The solution? Educate the online shopper. Let them know that online shopping has its advantages, but also keep them apprised of the reality of the commercial world.

As e-businesses put more products online and offer a wider array of products per site, logistic and fulfillment issues must be dealt with head-on if e-business is to ever become "business as usual."

MEET THE CHALLENGE

Set out a plan and follow it to the letter to meet, within reason, customer expectation. According to John Hagel with McKinsey & Co. www.mckinsey.com), a 75 year old world-famous consulting firm, "too many companies started with the assumption that the challenge was getting people to buy things, when, in fact, the real challenge is getting it to them." Although a host of e-tailers perform impressively there are too many that do not.

There are still e-businesses with order processing and fulfillment processes that are chock full of inefficiencies. For example, it's common for an e-tailer to accept an order without knowing if the product is available. The e-business then sends an e-mail informing the customer that one or more items that they had ordered is out of stock or will be shipped at a later date — not a good way to build customer confidence or loyalty. Once a customer has been disappointed when finally informed that the eagerly anticipated grape festooned plastic serving set will not be available for Easter dinner, he or she quickly loses enthusiasm for shopping with that e-business.

There comes a time when every e-business that sells a physical product must decide how to pick, pack and ship that product to its customers — there is no margin for error. So what should an e-business do?

- Integrate the e-business's Web site so that real-time communication occurs throughout the logistics and fulfillment process, whether handled in-house or otherwise.

- Install a real-time inventory management system so that inventory is constantly verified. If a customer sees a product on the Web site, it should be in stock and available.

- Process and ship products the same day that the customer's order is received. If a B2B's (operating under a buy-side fulfillment model) or an e-tailer's customer places an order by 5:00 p.m. (local time), it should be out the door the same day. All orders received after 5:00 p.m. should be shipped within 24 hours of their receipt.

- Incorporate bar-code and pick-to-light technology in the fulfillment center as well as quality checks such as weighing the order after the pick-pack process to insure complete picking accuracy.

- Offer special low rates on 2nd day shipping to the customer if an order will take more than 2 days in transit, (i.e., fulfillment center is in Vermont and customer is on the Arizona-Mexico border).

- Apprise the customer of his or her order status throughout the fulfillment process through the judicious use of e-mail.

- Send an e-mail to the customer after the e-business receives delivery confirmation to verify that the customer received and is satisfied with the product.

- Include a return label (bar-coded, if possible) and return documentation within every package to provide the customer with ease of return.

If all of this can't be done effectively in-house, then outsource. Re-visit the situation regularly and when the return on investment (ROI) shows it's feasible, bring the process in-house with all of the necessary technology, personnel and facilities in place.

In an effort to retain the customers that they so expensively sought out, many e-businesses that originally outsourced have begun to take more control over the entire fulfillment process by moving the operations in-house. To handle fulfillment effectively in-house requires an expensive high-technology warehouse, distribution center and/or fulfillment facility (for simplicity, hereinafter referred to as "fulfillment center"), which can take more than 36 months to build out. Many e-tailers (especially the pure-play) don't have the time or money. Therefore, many have opted (at least for the short term) to contract with a third party fulfillment service provider such as Keystone, Marketing Out of the Box (www.motb.com), Fingerhut (www.4fbsi.com), and a host of other fulfillment providers to handle their order processing, fulfillment, shipping and returns.

Before an e-business jumps on the outsourcing bandwagon it should realize that outsourcing isn't the nostrum many e-businesses thought it would be — integrating the e-business's back-end with the fulfillment center's technology takes a small army of people, a good bit of time, and cooperation all around.

Online customers are a savvy group and they want real-time inventory reporting. This means a Web site has to provide the customer with access to information about product availability and shipping status. To do this the fulfillment centers (third party or in-house) must be faultlessly integrated with the e-business's Web-based systems; so that every "purchase click," can flow through the "pipeline" to provide real-time availability information to the customer.

When a fulfillment center receives a new shipment of inventory, the Web site also must be informed — not just receive data but seamlessly provide accurate updates to the e-business's back office systems. The e-tailer and its fulfillment end (third party or in-house) must have systems in place to quickly and efficiently deal with "out of the box" issues such as shipping to numerous addresses from one order, gift wrapping, signed card, engraving, and so forth.

Have you ever looked at Amazon.com's plain vanilla Web site, no bells and whistles whatsoever, and wondered why is it always among the top 10, week after week? It's because Amazon owns its customers from the time they walk in the door. How?

Mainly due to what its customers don't see — a rapid and efficient ordering and fulfillment process that's sweating blood in the background. Amazon has ful-fillment centers strategically placed through-out the US, which means that 60% of its US-based orders can be delivered within one day using inexpen-sive ground shipping (a per-fect example of JIT shipping).

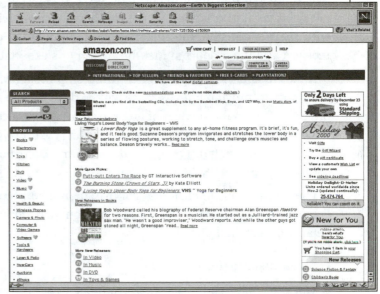

Just as Amazon understands the importance of logistics, it also knows that time-ly order processing, immediate notification of unavailable items, real-time order tracking and status information, state-of-the-art billing and inventory-tracking procedures are also key to customer satisfaction. And it understands that in the end a loyal customer base is bought with the flawless underpinnings of its e-business, not just "pretty pictures."

When an e-business has a properly integrated, well-oiled LFMS, then its back-end systems and processes can take center stage. Order and ship-ping confirmations should be common practice; they should be seam-lessly delivered to the customer's e-mail in-box at the time the order is processed. The purpose of e-mail is to keep the customer apprised of where their order is in the pick, pack and ship process.

Provide order confirmations that contain enough data to keep the customers from questioning whether or not their order will arrive on time or ever arrive at all. Once the e-business has confirmation that the order is on the way to the customer (it's in the hands of the shipper), it should follow with an e-mail to its customer. This e-mail needs to say something like "Just thought you would like to know that your Order No. XM146LZ is on its way." (Also provide the shipping and tracking information plus a link to use if they want to check on the status.) Then when the e-business obtains confirmation that the package has been delivered, follow-up with another e-mail to the customer verifying that the correct order was received and the product(s) met the customer's expectations.

If the e-business has opted for the drop-ship model without an integration process, providing this service will be difficult and time consuming, but do it. Obtain the services of an order management company (as mentioned previously in this book) — OrderTrust (www.ordertrust.net), Netship (www.netship.com) and Dotcom Distribution (www.dotcomdist.com) — to help with the process.

The "Holy Grail" of customer confirmation is to keep the customer in the loop by providing written confirmation that outlines their order's details. This should include:

- a personalized greeting

- the order number and summary with charges

- estimated shipping and arrival date

- bill-to and ship-to addresses

- customer service contact information

- special request information (gift wrap/gift messages, special delivery instructions)

- links to order status and order history

- links to return information

The shipping confirmation should include all of the above information plus tracking numbers (when relevant) and links to the e-business's package tracking service.

Get the Tech Partners Involved

As discussed in Chapter 5, tech partners bring rich consulting, design and development skills to an e-business while understanding the intricacies of LFM, real-time inventory availability, value chain integration and legacy systems. Many also provide comprehensive e-business advisory and management services and offer comprehensive solutions.

Integrator, Organic Inc. (www.organic.com) has the right idea — have a logistics expert at the first client meeting. However, Organic does find some of its e-business customers surprised to find logistics experts at the table. Why? Because in many instances marketing and sales people are in charge of the initial Web initiative. According to Dan Lynch, president of logistics for Organic, "They're taken aback a little at the thought that, yeah, they're going to have to answer e-mails, get an 800 line, and get goods to their customers. Surprisingly often, logistics [and fulfillment] are still an afterthought. But overall, the industry is becoming more sensitive, especially after what took place last holiday season [1999]."

If 1999 was the midterm exam for many e-businesses, 2000 was their finals. If an e-business's LFMS failed the course, they're operating on borrowed time. "Customer expectations are incredibly high and tolerance is slim," says Mark Layton, CEO of outsourcer PFSweb (www.pfsweb.com. "In the consumer's mind, we have had plenty of opportunities to learn what the infrastructure requirements are, and I don't think people will be tolerant of slow Web sites, slow deliveries, broken promises or non-real-time inventory interfaces that don't allow them to see what's in stock and what's not. This is the year dot.com companies are going to have to cut bait. This Christmas [2000] is going to be the finish line for a lot of start-up dot.coms."

Even after all of the hype about the need for the 3Rs, providing good customer fulfillment is still, in some ways, a thankless task. If you do it well, you don't get kudos, but if you do it poorly, you get bad press and lose customers forever. Tony Blasetti, a supply chain consultant in e-business for KPMG Consulting, took this a bit further in an interview with *VARBusiness* in June 2000. He acknowledges that if an e-business does attend to the 3Rs, "it gets an overall neutral reaction from the customers in terms of whether or not they come back, because customers assume they will get excellent service. But if the order arrives five days late or the order is incomplete or they bill incorrectly, in most cases the customers never come back to that site. There's limited upside experience but very severe downside potential."

Jean-Gabriel Henry, a senior analyst with Jupiter Communications Inc. declares that tech solution providers should go out of their way to perform the proper due diligence on FSPs for their e-business clients. Whether taking the outsourcing route or going in-house, it seems as if many e-businesses and their tech partners have gotten the message. Numerous tech solution providers are working on e-business fulfillment. For instance, Organic is currently helping an e-business in the apparel indus-try to establish a failsafe LFMS that integrates incoming orders with the warehouse database, as well as with the call center system in case delivery problems arise.

Logistics and Fulfillment Experts

Bringing in a qualified logistics and fulfillment expert (LFE) should be among the first steps an e-business and its tech partner(s) take when struggling with logistics and fulfillment issues. The Internet provides the e-business with a global customer base. The smart e-business will view this customer base as a way to service a worldwide market in a cost-efficient manner. That's where an LFE can provide specialized guidance.

According to Ford Cavallari of the consulting firm Renaissance Worldwide, there are legions of e-businesses that have an almost endless list of instances where they can fail within the logistics and fulfillment realm. A good LFE will take inventory, analyze systems and present the e-business with a report laying out the deficiencies, quick fixes and a strategic plan for a well-structured LFMS.

Cavallari pointed out that a common failure occurs in systems that permit an order to be modified after the buy button has been clicked. Another common failing is that many e-businesses don't even have a zip code database set up that can enable automatic verification of a zip code in a shipping address. As we all know, courier services will not accept a package without the proper zip code; the lack of this resource results in costly hand checking and re-keying of the correct zip code, and/or mis-shipped packages.

The improper integration of databases can have an adverse affect on logistics and fulfillment. It's not just the small e-businesses that are struggling with getting all "their ducks in a row" for the proper integration of their back-end systems to provide reliable fulfillment to the end-user, large international e-businesses also have problems. A case in point is when one of the author's dear friends, Cliff Perciavalle, suffered through an order mix-up by Nissan, which almost caused him to pull out his more than abundant hair trying to get everything ironed out to his satisfaction. Perciavalle is the proud owner of a new Nissan Xterra and as most proud owners are wont to do, he surfed over to Nissan's Web site and ordered some spiffy accessories for his new SUV and paid for them with his credit card.

The problem arose because due to improper integration of its databases (I assume) Nissan evidently wasn't fully set-up to accept different "bill to" "ship to" order processing although they offered the option in their online form. When Perciavalle saw the "ship to" option, (being among the overworked populace) he went for it, requesting that his order be shipped to his place of work. However, due to a snafu in Nissan's back-office order processing systems, UPS (Nissan's shipper of choice) didn't get the message — it delivered (or at least tried to deliver) the package to Perciavalle's home address.

After numerous e-mails and telephone calls by Perciavalle and his representatives, Perciavalle did receive his order, was not overbilled and he still has a full head of hair. But not before he and others had wasted valuable time solving the problem. Perciavalle stated that he's now a bit more wary about online ordering.

A manufacturer adopting an e-business model and facing the necessity of re-fitting its warehouse(s) and/or distribution center(s) to meet the demands of its new e-business model may want to engage the services of a firm such as KMG Enterprises (www2.prosavvy.com/affiliates/kmg) that "focus[es] on providing practical solutions to client problems, without consultant jargon and one-size-fits-all alphabet soup-du jour systems."

Another consultancy with a "logistics and fulfillment bent" is Management Information Consulting (www.micinc.com), a systems integrator and information technology consulting firm that specializes in not only ERP packages, Web application and custom software development, but also e-business order fulfillment, and end-to-end project management solutions. Also look at Avery & Associates (www.elogistics101.com), an e-commerce distribution and logistics consulting firm.

Fulfillment Service Providers

A FSP at the most basic level provides an efficient nation-wide distribution facility where its employees pick-pack-ship merchandise belonging to a cadre of merchants, in this case, e-businesses. Initially, if an e-business does not handle logistics and fulfillment in-house it will need to partner with some type of FSP. The FSP's first goal in working with the e-business and its expert partners (LFE and/or tech) is to help the e-business determine how long it should outsource its logistics and fulfillment needs and when it should take the entire LFMS in-house. "The make-versus-buy decision is critical," opines JT Kreager, president and COO SubmitOrder.com, a FSP for e-tail models.

A click-and-mortar may already have substantial infrastructure devoted to fulfilling orders for individual clients. Therefore, expert partners may recommend development of some or all back-end fulfillment in-house. For pure-plays trying to grow rapidly enough to establish themselves as the leading e-business in a particular vertical market, outsourcing is usually the way to go when first starting out.

When outsourcing fulfillment, an e-business's tech partner(s) has an important role in aiding that e-business and its LFE (if there is one) in finding an FSP that will deliver on the e-business's fulfillment promises to its customers. For example, when Organic was working with one of its e-business clients it went through a thorough RFP process with more than 50 third-party fulfillment providers, building a list of the top 25, then it sent engineers and operations experts out to examine the infrastructures of the would-be providers.

"We found some really good providers out there and some providers with existing legacy challenges who were just slapping an e-commerce sign on the door in hopes of attracting business," Organic's Lynch says. "You never know their strengths until you have an opportunity to go out there and see them."

TAKING IT IN-HOUSE

Whether hosting your own fulfillment center or choosing to outsource your fulfillment services, an established enterprise that adopts an e-business model will, out of necessity, make changes in its distribution efforts. Fulfillment centers, distribution centers and warehouses should implement state-of-the-art systems that allow them to keep pace with the e-business model. But do it right, don't do it "bass-akward." First, upgrade your database management systems and put in state-of-the-art tracking and bar-code systems. Then, once those improvements are operating as needed, take on the task of building Web-enabled systems.

If the e-business is still in the first growth period and has expectations of a huge growth spurt within the next 6 months — outsource. However, if the grow is projected to increase steadily over time and the in-house staff is still adequately managing the fulfillment process, then there is time to build a proper in-house fulfillment infrastructure that can scale as the order volume increases.

Amazon.com was at one time the "king of the drop-ship models," but Amazon.com realized that it couldn't continue to rely solely on outsourcing if it was to reach and maintain profitability. As its business grew, it began to take the majority of its fulfillment in-house. In addition to its fulfillment centers throughout the US, Amazon also has a cutting edge warehouse outside Reno, Nevada that is approximately 6 times the size of a football field. This facility enables Amazon to provide real-time inventory data, accurate order fulfillment and speedy delivery to its customers. The bottom line: Outsourcing became expensive as the number of its online orders mushroomed.

Two years ago, Reel.com was a basic garage-based operation, filling orders from a collection of 8,000 hard-to-find videos stored in an old car dealership in Berkeley, CA. Two distributors drop shipped the remaining 52,000 titles listed on Reel.com's Web site. However, as Reel.com grew and after competition reared its ugly head when Amazon.com opened its online video store, Reel.com felt it must do more to stave off the incursion by cutting delivery times and expanding its product line. Unfortunately, its distributors couldn't always keep pace so Reel.com took the next step — full in-house order fulfillment — and leased a warehouse. Although it now has better control over its entire logistics and fulfillment processes, Reel.com still hasn't managed to translate it into a profit. But it has boosted its gross margins through cutting out the middleman (the distributors) and through shrewd negotiations with those same video distributors when purchasing videos and DVDs.

University of Nevada, Reno's professor of supply chain management, Dale Rogers, teaches that fulfillment is where the critical turf wars in e-business will be decided. He states, "It's fairly easy to put up a pretty neat storefront on the Web, but you need a good supply chain behind the store. And that is difficult. Order fulfillment is where a lot of the battles are going to be fought in the future." Ask what caused the downfall of Pets.com, Furniture.com, Garden.com and numerous others and you will always find at the top of the list logistics and fulfillment woes.

Many e-businesses, after evaluating the reluctance of their distributors to take on the fulfillment burden, have come to the conclusion that the best way to fix their logistics and fulfillment problems is to invest in their own facilities. Although logistics and fulfillment is in all probability not within most e-businesses core competency, the successful ones understand that by establishing an all-inclusive, in-house LFMS they gain a competitive advantage (Amazon). This isn't news or you wouldn't be reading this book.

I believe that all enterprise-size e-businesses receiving around 10,000 orders per day should bring their e-commerce fulfillment in house to leverage economies between existing and online channels, and give more control of the operations and customer service.

Upgrading an Existing Warehouse, Distribution or Fulfillment Center
In this section I will just touch on the issues an e-business will face dur-

ing the build out of a warehouse/distribution center/fulfillment facility. I must admit that the technology I've chosen to discuss is what interests me, but I've tried to give the reader a feel for what is involved in constructing and fitting out a distribution facility.

An enterprise's existing warehouse, distribution center or fulfillment facility (for the sake of brevity, hereafter "fulfillment center" although I realize there are real differences between the three facilities) will quickly feel the burden when an e-business model is adopted. As online orders increase (e-tail or B2B) the e-business will quickly see the inefficiencies and inadequacies of its traditional fulfillment center(s).

The first step in assessing technology needs for a fulfillment center is to understand what objectives must be met. E-businesses need to look at what technology is currently in place, what they need to meet their current needs and what they might need in the near future (within three years). But read what Scott Stratman wrote in his colmun in *ASA News'* (www.asa.net) September/October 2000 issue wherein he explains that too often the concept of being paper-less and "going electronic" isn't given enough thought prior to implementation. He also asks some pertinent questions the readers should heed:

- How is the warehouse laid out?

- Are there clearly marked aisles, bins, and racking and bulk storage areas?

- Do the item locator strategies coincide with the layout scheme?

- Is the pick ticket printing routine consistent?

- Does the warehouse have adequate "road signs" for the pickers when they are using their "road map" (the pick ticket) to pull products?

- In receiving, are item locator tools consistently used to restock?

- Are there primary and secondary bin locations, with easy to find bulk storage areas?

- Is it easy to find everything owned within the warehouse?

Stratman goes on to advise that the key element here is that most of the personnel are working as fast as they can. Without some order to the warehouse layout and multiple road signs to follow, they will get lost. Worse yet, the e-business's assets will get lost.

PlanetRx.com was one of the first pure-play e-tailers to solely operate its own fulfillment center, providing the company with the opportunity to streamline the fulfillment and distribution process. Its facility incorporates advanced technologies such as automated tote movement, paperless picking, and automated dispensing technology in the pharmacy.

Chris Newton, an industry analyst on supply chain management for AMR Research, a consulting and research firm, says, "The idea is to streamline ... to move through distribution facilities with as little handling as possible. Companies are attempting to attract customers by lowering costs, which are derived from streaming distribution activities." That's where automated warehouse management comes in. It allows an e-business handling its fulfillment in-house to streamline operations, increase responsiveness, and reduce costs through elimination of labor and space-usage inefficiencies, for example, in order to further improve performance. What I've described is commonly known as a Warehouse Management System (WMS).

A best-of-breed WMS gets product or material in and out of the door faster, for less money and with fewer errors.

Today's Web-enabled WMSs provide real-time control over the resources needed to fill the orders generated by an e-business. The WMS can determine the best place to store inventory, the most efficient sequence of picking inventory from the warehouse/distribution center/fulfillment facility, as well as determining the best method of packing the inventory for shipment. For instance a WMS can generate summarized pick lists that combine several individual pick lists, thereby minimizing the number of trips made in retrieving items and can even choose the most efficient carton size in which to ship the picked order to the customer.

Benefits of a WMS include shortened order turnaround times, higher inventory accuracy, increased order fill rates, and improved shipment accuracy. For example, productivity can be increased by 20 — 30% and inventory and shipping accuracy rates can usually be found to exceed 99%. Most e-businesses will also see cost-efficiencies through better utilization of their fulfillment center's floor space, inventory reductions, fewer data entry errors, and reductions in the amount of inventory lost to shrinkage.

An enterprise-size e-business might opt for a WMS that can determine movement of items from one location to another based on quantity on-hand and fluctuations in demand. And also facilitate cycle counts virtually eliminating the need for costly physical inventories. WMS vendors are creating new ways to make warehouse operations as efficient and cost-effective as possible. "It's gone from 'put away,' and 'find it,' to the science of managed 3-D space against the fourth dimension of time," says Loraine Waybourn, senior consultant with the manufacturing enterprise group of Symbol Technologies Inc.

AMR Research states that there are currently about 300 WMS vendors. AMR's Newton explains that it's common now for some of the traditional WMS vendors to act as ASPs, renting or leasing software to e-businesses instead of selling them a license. Newton goes on to explain, "Instead of system implementation, it's basically a rental agreement. Traditionally the costs are a lot lower than the huge up-front costs of owning and maintaining the system." Some companies that provide ASP-based WMS applications include:

HK Systems formed a wholly-owned subsidiary called irista (www.irista.com) that has moved into the ASP business through a partnership with Exodus Communications. Its WMS application is a highly engineered, built-to-order application that targets no specific industries.

Radcliffe Systems (www.radcliffesystems.com) made its move to an ASP model with its ROC, an innovative WMS. Radcliffe will host an e-business's data along with ROC on a special server farm. Customers make no commitment to a capital expenditure because Radcliffe buys the server and RF hardware and supplies the entire system for a monthly usage fee.

TRW (www.trw.com) began Web-hosting its MARC-CS warehouse management system this past year. TRW maintains the WMS software on its own equipment and rents access on a user-fee basis. It's offering the service through a partner, US Internetworking.

Other WMS providers are expected to follow suit and adopt an ASP model of their applications soon.

For those e-businesses in the market for their own WMS there are many out there, some specialized for certain industries and others that are generalist. A few to get you started are:

Amplexus (www.amplexus.com) provides wholesale distribution software with an e-commerce order entry system.

Catalyst International Inc. (www.catalystwms.com) provides WMSs specifically designed for Automotive, Consumer Goods, Industrial Technology, Process Goods, Retail and Internet Fulfillment markets.

DSA Software (www.dsasoft.com) develops and implements robust WMS, including seamlessly linked RF and EDI applications.

Montego Systems's (www.montego-sys.com) WinWhere is a WMS that is Windows NT-based and utilizes radio frequency portable terminals and bar-code technology.

Royal 4 Systems' (www.r4-wise.com) WISE is a rules based, Internet enabled WMS.

For more information on the many warehouse management systems available go to any search engine that allows exact phrase searching and type in "Warehouse Management System."

An e-business that manages its logistics and fulfillment in-house may want to use technology to further automate the system through use of bar-code readers, voice-recognition software and wireless appliances. All can help an e-business shave the "minutes" by optimizing its logistics and fulfillment services in the race to the customer's door.

Web-enable Data-collection Terminals

The consumer-electronics retailer, Crutchfield Corp. (www.crutchfield.com), has begun using a new technology wonder that can help an e-business's logistics and fulfillment department to speed product to the customer — the "Web-enabled" data-collection terminal. Crutchfield uses the terminals that contain bar-code scanning micro-Web browsers to help its staff store and pick products. When the fulfillment staff scans a bar-code, the scanned information is placed in the appropriate field on a form that is transmitted to the Web server, where the transaction is processed.

A number of bar-code equipment makers have just released or have plans in the works to offer Web-enabled data-collection terminals. These terminals display the scanned bar-code as well as the information in HTML. Web-enabled bar-code tools make it easier for e-businesses to integrate data into their operations and take advantage of tools developed for the Internet.

For example, Symbol Technologies Inc. (www.symbol.com) announced that all of its terminals can output data in HTML format including its PPT 5100 pen terminal that combines bar-code scanning, a rugged design and optional wireless LAN connectivity. Psion Teklogix (www.psion.com/tek-logix) says all of its terminals can provide HTML emulation, including a wireless system.

Intermec Corp.'s (www.intermec.com), model 2415 is an economical, ergonomic and reliable Hand Held Data Collection Computer that can grow as needs change. For example, with an internal PC Card slot an e-business can start with a batch 2410, and upgrade to the 2415 RF later.

Or start with the OpenAir radio today and upgrade later to the new 802.11 radio and future RF developments as they occur. The 2415 can be configured for terminal emulation today, and tomorrow upgrade to client/server or even Web-enabled for integration into HTML applications. By the time this book reaches the readers LXE Inc. (www.lxe.com), and Handheld Products (www.handheld.com) should have Web-enabled products ready for shipment.

What is the advantage of automatic identification equipment makers taking the HTML route? For starters, HTML provides richer content providing more than the straight text of an ASCII terminal, i.e., forms with check boxes and image maps. Scanned output then can be placed directly into a specific field on forms, like purchase orders.

Web-enabled data-collection terminals make it possible for distribution departments to implement so-called network-centric computing where the data and applications are centralized on a server. The terminals simply carry client software, such as Web browsers, that lets them interact with the servers. Paul Liska, data collection product manager at Intelligent Instrumentation Inc. (www.instrument.com) points out "Web-enabled systems will become the norm for firms to collect data and provide information worldwide. Ethernet data collection terminals already provide a natural interface to the Internet [and intranet] environment. More and more Web functionality is the wave of the future."

Web-enabled terminals can run Java applets that are transmitted from a server to the terminal. The applets are then used to reconfigure the terminal to read new bar-codes.

For example: Web-enabled terminals allow e-businesses to track goods throughout the supply chain via the Internet. When a shipment is received at a warehouse, the worker scans a bar-code and then transmits the HTML data via radio waves to a computer gateway connected to the Internet. The bar-coded information then could be posted on a Web site. Authenticated value chain members could go to the e-business's Web site to check on the receipt of the specific item at the warehouse.

Crutchfield uses Symbol's Portable Pen Terminal (PPT) Model 4640 Web-enable terminals, which are radio-equipped touchpads that uses a Spectrum24 wireless network. The terminals can exchange information with a server via radio waves. The browser on the PPT displays a form with fields for input. When the worker receives a pallet of merchandise for storage, he or she first scans the pallet's bar-code. The scanned product's data then is placed automatically into the appropriate field in a templated form. Next, the worker scans the location where the pallet is stored placing it in the correct field.

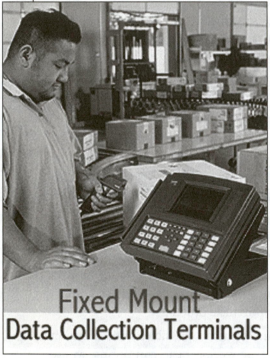

Fixed Mount Data Collection Terminals

The future is bright for fixed-mount data collection terminals that keep up with the advances in technology. *Photo courtesy of Intermec Technologies Corp.*

"A form is just a Web page that has input," explains David Dierolf, Cruchfield's vice president of information technology "and the input fields can take scanned data." The data captured is sent via radio frequency to a server that is linked to a database that maintains an up-to-the-minute list of inventory in the fulfillment center.

Crutchfield's fulfillment center staff also uses the terminals for cycle counting. The warehouse manager can determine the items for cycle counting after viewing data within Crutchfield's systems, then a worker goes to a location and counts the items by scanning in their identity. The terminal displays direct the worker where to go and which items to count.

In addition, Crutchfield's fulfillment center uses a specialized Web form to direct product picking. The computer sends a pick list to the terminal, telling the worker the location and the quantity of the items to retrieve.

The readers might also be interested in:

The Dolphin with Image-Capture Handheld Computer (www.handheld.com) which incorporates a low-power, high-resolution digital camera to capture airbills, damaged cartons or any other image in a rugged mobile data collection terminal.

Intermec Technology Corporation (www.intermec.com) offers a complete line of data collection hardware, network devices, mobile computing systems for inventory control, ERPs, mobile computing, WMS and data collection systems, radio frequency, data collection/ID, pen-based computers, networking systems, scanner and input devices, hand-held terminals (stationery and vehicle mount).

Peak Technologies (www.peaktech.com) is a good source for data collection terminals that can best fit an e-business's requirements. It carries numerous models and configurations, including hand-held, pen-based, wearable, and fixed mounted. Among the equipment it offers are bar-code printers and verifiers, bar-code scanners and readers and data collection terminals.

Dolphin with Image-Capture Handheld Computer.

Another item of interest in the laser scanning sector is Symbol's PDF417, a two-dimensional bar-code technology that uses lasers to scan items. "Think of it as a data file that travels with goods. If you use my goods, you don't have to also pay for a host computer system to track them. We provide the technology that enables you to use these applications," explains Loraine Waybourn, senior consultant with the manufacturing enterprise group of Symbol Technologies Inc., a provider of inventory management technology. Symbol's PDT 6800 Series provides a rugged, lightweight portable data terminal combining mobile computing and optional wireless communications with comfortable, well-balanced "forward-scanning" ergonomics.

A real-world example of how technology is used is Boise Cascade Office Products Corporation. It installed a turnkey, reliable wireless solution that includes LXE's rugged 2280 RF handheld computer, LXE's latest 1380 RF vehicle mounted computer, LXE's 6200 RF backbone and PSC scanners along with Haushahn VIAWARE Warehouse Management System software (www.haushahn.com).

In discussing the decision, a Boise Cascade spokesperson explained, "In Boise's business, it is crucial to understand both business processes that affect operations and the other inter-departmental processes that blend together to get a customer order out the door. To meet customer expectations of timely, accurate deliveries, Boise must effectively manage its inventory. Boise can meet this objective by working with companies such as LXE and Haushahn to control operational and internal processes on the warehouse management system." Joe Comeford, Project Manager for Boise, adds, "Boise expects to benefit tremendously by acquiring leading edge technology with LXE's wireless communications that interface with Haushahn's VIAWARE Warehouse Management System software. This type of investment will produce positive results ranging from improved customer service to a good ROI."

Wireless LAN

J.C. Penney Company, Inc., like Crutchfield, has installed Symbol Technologies' Spectrum24 wireless LAN at a number of its fulfillment centers. This enables Penney to implement a number of automated features at their centers meaning "no surprises" when it comes to products and inventory control, order flow, and out-of-stock early warnings. Add an

Advance Shipping Notification (ASN) and high-tech distribution and transporting systems that get the products out fast and accurately, and you have the backbone of a state-of-the-art fulfillment facility.

Symbol's wireless technology is used for narrow-aisle picking, at pick-to-light stations, as well as in shipping and receiving. Fulfillment center staff armed with Symbol hand-held and vehicle-mounted computers can know instantly which items to select or put away in the facility by communicating via the Symbol Spectrum24 network to the fulfillment center's host computer. "We expect quick payback on our investment through enhanced accuracy and productivity, which results in better service to our customers," said Tom Schmitt, systems and controls project manager-Distribution Center Development, J.C. Penney.

Auto ID Technology

An e-business that institutes an auto ID technology in its fulfillment center is taking a big step. Before introducing this technology, ensure that there is a standard policy in place wherein the e-business's warehousing, pick-pack-ship facilities, suppliers and customers work from the same set of rules. The policy should set out what the e-business wants on its labels, when to use the labels, and which bar-code standards or RFID to adhere to. The e-business should also have a procedure to follow if and when problems arise.

Bar-codes: A bar-code is a symbolic representation of alpha/numeric information that is machine readable. A bar-code scanner reads the bar-code and translates it into a machine readable alpha/numeric (ASCII) format. You will find three common bar-code scanning technologies: laser scanners, wands or pens, and charged couple devices. The most pop-

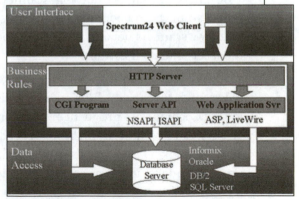

The Spectrum24 Web Client supports the three-tier client server model for quick application development and deployment. *Graphic Courtesy of Symbol Technologies.*

ular is the laser scanners (the most expensive of the three) since they offer high performance and are available in many different configurations. The wands and pens were the first devices in common use mainly because they are the least expensive products that can read and translate a bar-code. The charged couple device works on the same principle as a camera in that it takes an image or picture of the bar code to be read, and decodes it into the alpha/numeric format.

Bar-code technology is a boon for time-pressed warehouses, fulfillment facilities and distribution centers. But this new technology isn't just for the e-tail community. Thomas Pipe (www.thomaspipe.com), an enterprise that is methodically adopting a B2B e-business model, built a state-of-the-art distribution facility in Baton Rouge, LA that houses more than 55,000 tons of pipe. When a new shipment is received, each piece of pipe is bar-coded with critical information including size, origin, grade, heat number and exact length. "Our goal was to design a unique system that would drastically impact the time required to accurately process and load a customer's order," said Jay Roccaforte, Thomas Pipe president and CEO. Thomas' fledgling LFMS, in tandem with its new distribution center, allows its customers to access the company's inventory via the Internet. Sometime in 2001 Thomas' customers will be able to place orders, check order status and download invoices online.

Scanners: When considering scanners look for ruggedness, greater range, accuracy and portability. But that's not all. Now imaging technology allows scanners not only to read bar-code labels, but also to photograph the labels and their cartons.

Some e-businesses may be in the market for a digital camera version of the scanner technology. Why go with a digital camera version? According to Jack Cochran, vice president of sales for Accu-Sort (www.accusort.com), "Lasers can't read at as high of a speed as imagers can. A laser gives between 500 and 1,000 reads per second, while a digital camera can take up to 10,000 pictures in a second." In a big warehouse or distribution center such an increase in the read rate is significant.

One such device, the Dolphin terminal with in-built bar-code scanner and digital camera, provides the latest image-capture technology. This allows images of items such as damaged goods to be visually captured and stored electronically together with the bar-code for identification.

Cybex International an enterprise that's in Stage Three of its e-business integration, installed bar-coding technology for its shipping process of equipment and service parts. Cybex boasts that with the adoption and implementation of its e-business model, it has seen over a 30% increase in B2B revenue and at least a 10% increase in its e-tail customer base. A spokesperson speculates that these impressive improvements have grown out of its ability to reduce lead times and order backlog up to 50%, resulting in a marked improvement in on-time delivery and order tracking.

An e-business might want to emulate Zuellig Pharma's (www.zuellig-pharma.com) Canlubang, Philippines distribution center, which operates in a paperless environment. It makes full use of bar-code technology in receiving stock, order picking and checking of stock. The bar-code scanners are wireless and linked to the system through a radio frequency transmitter for portability and flexibility of use throughout the facility. This also ensures fast information transmission countered by eight checking systems for improved order fulfillment accuracy (a weight-check scanning device validates the orders picked based on their manifest weight). Comprehensive bar-code labeling is also used to identify and validate that the warehouse staff are storing and retrieving inventory into and from correct storage locations. This system ensures a higher degree of accuracy in its operations and assures that the correct items (and in the right quantity) are delivered to your customers.

There are numerous bar-code technology and service companies ready to assist an e-business. Go to your favorite search engine and type in "bar-code scanning" and the returns will keep your browser hopping for quite some time.

RFID: Radio-frequency identification (RFID) tags may be the right technology for an e-business's warehouses, distribution and fulfillment centers. RFID tags can read in random orientation at significant distances, without requiring a change in processes, allowing an entire pallet load of goods to be read with one quick scan. RFID includes benefits such as:

- RFID tags can be embedded in boxes or pallets and still be readable.

- Scanners don't need to have an RFID tag in sight to correctly scan it.

- No operator intervention is required to read an RFID tag.

- RFID tags allow an operator to read several items at once.

- In many cases, RFIDs also have read/write capabilities, which allow users to change and update data on the fly.

RFID tags come in two major formats: active and passive. Active tags have an on-board battery that allow long-distance reading. These cost from $5 to $50 per tag. Passive tags don't contain a battery, remains inactive until activated and have a typical range of three to ten feet, depending on the frequency of the tag, but these costs only $2 to $3 per tag.

Escort Memory Systems (www.ems-rfid.com) one of the leaders in Radio Frequency Identification (RFID) Tags, Antennas and Controllers for industrial applications, proudly announced that its FastTrack Tunnel Antenna and Disposable Radio Frequency Identification (RFID) Tags have been introduced into the USPS for large postal and material handling applications. Mark Nicholson, CEO of Escort Memory Systems made this forward-looking statement: "We anticipate that our post office installation will serve as an RFID model, as more material handling applications adopt our RFID solutions over traditional data capture systems."

Also check out Symbol Technologies (www.symbol.com), Zebra Technologies (www.zebra.com), Avery Dennison (www.averydennison.com) and Texas Instruments (www.ti.com/tiris/default.htm) for the latest updates on RFID technology.

Carousels

A carousel promotes high throughput and flexibility by bringing specified items for picking to the picker, making the process far more efficient. As Ed Romaine, director of marketing and e-commerce business development for Remstar International (www.remstar.com), a leading provider of automated storage and retrieval systems, points out, "The carousel market is growing exponentially with the impact of e-commerce and the need for providing faster deliveries, more efficient returns, order customization and the increasing demand to ship [ones and twos], not cases or pallets." He added, "Using clusters of carousels provides the fastest throughput possible, and the horizontal carousel provides the most cost-effective cubic inch of storage available."

The majority of carousels are categorized as vertical or horizontal; each with its own advantages and disadvantages. Greg Chaffee, vice president of sales at Diamond Phoenix (www.diamondphoenix.com), a leader in the design, manufacture, integration and installation of innovative solutions for automated materials handling, argues that "vertical and horizontal carousels are very different products." He adds, "horizontals are much more common to distribution centers." The advantage of horizontals as a storage and retrieval system is they provide high-throughput and flexibility with low maintenance and cost. White Systems' (www.whitesystems.com) Rick Frye, vice president of sales and marketing advises, "Typically, you can eliminate two-thirds of the pickers you'd need with horizontal shelving. You can usually see an ROI within a year." White Systems is a leader in designing, developing, implementing and servicing automated solutions for staging, sequencing, storing and retrieving.

New FastTrack Tunnel Antennas and Disposable Passive RFID Tags keep USPS's Priority Mail on Track. *Photo courtesy of Escort Memory Systems.*

Vertical carousels bring an added advantage when you include them in your storage and retrieval systems. They can be enclosed to allow access only via the pick window, which reduces pilfering. Verticals are best when the SKU physical profile can accommodate it, and when the cost of square foot of floor space is significant. The greatest advantages of vertical carousels include ergonomics, maximizing the vertical cube and providing static control.

A horizontal carousel waiting for merchandise. *Photo courtesy of Diamond Phoenix Corporation.*

A carousel should be designed to integrate easily with the other equipment, processes and systems in an e-business's fulfillment center. According to Romaine, horizontal carousels, pick-to-light, shelving and racks can fit together easily as total solutions. "Depending on the SKU profile, this equipment can be organized into a universal workstation," he says. "This integrated workstation incorporates multiple tech-

Vertical carousel in action. *Photo courtesy of Kardex Information and Material Management Systems (www.kardex.com).*

nologies by matching SKU profile, order velocity and profile to determine the best solution."

Romaine advised that an e-business could expect to pay in the range of $17,000 for a single installed carousel with basic controls. For an entire workstation with pick lights and software, the cost could run up to about $56,000.

Pick-to-Light: A very productive computer-aided enhancement to any distribution system that uses carousels is the pick-to-light system. This type of system sends the pick list to the slots, which are lighted where picking is needed. Then picks are arranged in order, which speeds up the picking process through the reduction of operator movement.

Pick-to-light can be refined for vertical carousels through depth position-indicator lights along with multiple-partition bins. Thus allowing workers to pinpoint picking locations and specific items, which can speed up the picking process and improve picking accuracy. The growing need for picking accuracy is why many e-businesses should opt for the pick-to-light technology in an in-house fulfillment operation.

An e-business should have its in-house fulfillment center designed so that every pick is automatically checked. For example, pick-to-light bars on carousels and flow racks, light bars on the batch table, or a conveyor scale that checks carton weights, can all enhance the accuracy rate in a fulfillment center's pick-pack-ship activities.

Hand-free Picking Technology

Hands-free picking technology is a convenient alternative. For example, you can find voice recognition devices for product picking at Drugstore.com's fulfillment center. Thousands of Motek's (www.motek.com) RF Voice Picking units are in use at Wal-Mart and Kroger grocery operations. Actually, hands-free picking

PCC's Lighting Pick pick-to-light system delivers speed and accuracy to an order processing and fulfillment operation. *Photo courtesy of PCC (www.lightingpick.com).*

seems to be emerging as a viable technology in grocery and foodservice operations. Pickers do not have to interact with a computer screen, keyboard, or scanner. They can "walk and talk" at the same time. Industry studies show picker productivity increases 5%–10%, while delivering pick slot replenishment timing and pick accuracy levels comparable to wearable or hand-helds with scanners.

Voxware's VoiceLogistics (www.voxware.com) can speed up processing in a fulfillment center that has picking operations that require hands-free processing. However, Voxware also has been diligently working on applications that can support receiving, putaway, cycle counting, and other procedural and directed operations. It has implemented its technology in a [so far unnamed] returns center operation. SyVox, Inc. (www.syvox.com) is another company that provides speech solutions for fulfillment center personnel.

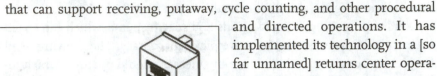

The Doran Pop-Up Scale (www.doranscales.com) is an alternative to an in-line checkweigher. It interfaces to automation controls, printers, and PCs without modification to an existing conveyor. *Graphic courtesy of Doran Scales, Inc.*

Technology Issues

The deciding component of an e-business's success in building an in-house fulfillment system will be its willingness to view the entire fulfillment process as a realm without borders. An e-business cannot restrict its view to internal operations alone. When an e-business optimizes its fulfillment processes it must examine everything from the customer's initial product order to its actual delivery to the customer's door.

The biggest problem all e-businesses face is that there doesn't seem to be a "single" solution available that can help integrate all back-end order processing operations. Even with a good logistics and fulfillment plan, the building out and integration of a reliable logistics and fulfillment infrastructure involves a mess of thorny specifications including:

- taking care of credit-card authorizations or handling purchase orders and pre-contracted orders

- routing one order to multiple suppliers

- routing status updates from those suppliers to customers

- handling order cancellations and product returns

- keeping up with the availability of inventory and the forecasting thereof

- shipping specifics, and so on

The dilemma is that all of these applications have no *de facto* communication standards. One solution might be to bring an extensive library of pre-built connectors into play; the connectors could reside at the e-businesses hub, speaking the language of and translating between the various applications that must communicate with each other. However, a customized, comprehensive integration project can be a long, resource intensive process.

Many e-businesses will recognize that developing the needed expertise internally is not cost-effective. For most, the faster, more efficient option will be to contract with one of the new breed of tech solution providers, as discussed in Chapter 5, to help forge a trail through this technological briar patch. But first the e-business must assess its current logistics and fulfillment needs and capabilities and compare those with its long-term goals (perhaps with the help of a LFE). Then, determine what is missing in terms of operational and functional processes, strategic direction, technology and organization. Once everyone has a good grasp of that they can then set out the tactical steps that need to be taken to fill in the missing pieces and begin moving toward complete implementation. Sometimes the easy part is agreeing on a strategy and identify what is missing with the sticky wicket being definition of the tactical operational requirements. If an e-business can set out a feasible plan where it's possible to really get down to the nuts and bolts of the process, then it has a fighting chance.

E-businesses that are willing to do their homework will succeed faster. Once work has begun, everyone on the team should be available for daily or thrice weekly conference calls to avoid duplicated effort and to assure that everyone is adhering to the logistics and fulfillment plan and timetable(s).

Unhappily, there is no cookie-cutter solution. Every solution will require at least some custom development. My best advice: stay focused on the unequivocal requirement that a LFMS must be flexible enough to grow over time.

Other In-house Fulfillment Considerations

One way for e-businesses to bring fulfillment in-house is to look for either a direct-to-consumer competency buried somewhere in-house (such as a small catalog operation) or, if it has deep pockets, buy a logistics or fulfillment firm or a competitor with e-business fulfillment capabilities already in place. Either option can make it easier to implement technologies to handle basic e-procurement or elementary e-commerce tasks. But this course won't give an e-business complete integration of internal and external systems across the entire value chain. Custom solutions must support real-time two-way flow of information throughout the value chain (i.e. the entire supply chain, customers, internal applications, and financial systems).

Another consideration for bricks-and-mortars: From a tax and economic standpoint, many traditional bricks-and-mortar businesses need to keep their Web-based business separate from their traditional business to enable them to keep track of tax liabilities incurred along with attribution of costs. If the Web-based business experiences early losses, the parent bricks-and-mortar business will need to keep these losses separate on its financial statements.

OUTSOURCING

In Patricia Seybold's keynote speech at a National Retail Federation conference in February 2000, she advised e-tailers who don't have fulfillment resources in place to investigate outsourcing instead of trying to develop capabilities in-house in time for the next holiday shopping season. The same still holds true today. You need a minimum of a year to get an in-house system up and running flawlessly. Seybold goes on to state, "Get hooked up with outsourcers now because Internet shoppers want next-day and in many cases same-day delivery," she said. "If you blow it... they're not coming back."

Partnering with an independent FSP to store product and provide fulfillment services is the correct move for many pure-plays. Click-and-mortars are courting fulfillment providers as well. In fact, demand is so great that some companies have stopped accepting new customers. "The issue isn't capacity," says John Buck, president of the fulfillment division of Fingerhut Business Services. "I could bring on more clients, but I'm saying no for performance reasons."

A click-and-mortar's in-house fulfillment requires that not only its back-end legacy systems be prepared for the hits that a Web site will bring, but also its warehouse systems. There is also a need for specialized systems, build out of a fulfillment center within the existing warehouse space (or a new facility), that provide the facilities, equipment, and manpower neces-

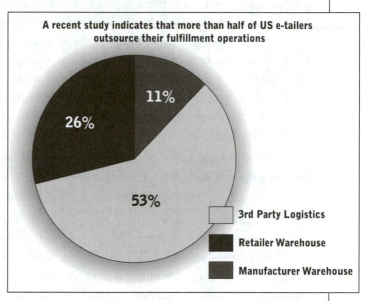

A recent study indicates that more than half of US e-tailers outsource their fulfillment operations

- 3rd Party Logistics
- Retailer Warehouse
- Manufacturer Warehouse

sary to service all these functions. For most e-businesses, once the decision has been made to move on line, speed to market becomes a critical issue.

Let's say, after numerous strategy planning sessions, it's been determined that the e-business will build its own fulfillment operation and (by some miracle) that it can be completed in time for the upcoming holiday season (i.e., less than a year). It will still be nearly impossible to find the warm bodies necessary to staff a fulfillment center and a call center to handle the increased volume of customer e-mail and voice inquiries within the time

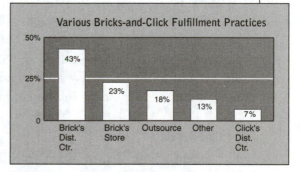

Various Bricks-and-Click Fulfillment Practices

limitations you face. You will be going against everyone else that's searching for labor during the fourth quarter. Outsourcing allows an e-business to let someone else worry about it.

If your e-business finds it difficult to conclude whether an in-house or outsource solution is the answer, look at the current volume of orders and project what the volume is expected to be in 6 months, 1 year, 3 years and 5 years. With figures in hand, take a long hard look at the e-business's current staff — can it really handle the workload. If online orders take off and the workload exceeds the staff's capacity, an e-business's customers won't be happy with the poor service that they may receive from a harassed and overworked staff. The e-business may have jeopardized its hard-earned success with the wrong fulfillment decision.

If an e-business's online order volume is low and inventory requirements are not onerous, then it's probably better to handle fulfillment in-house until the volume justifies a more formal order fulfillment procedure.

Consider the e-business's core competencies, fulfillment may not be one of them. To stay on top of fulfillment issues, as the business grows, it will need to re-evaluate. Before making a rash decision, get a pencil and paper out and compare the costs of adding more staff and facilities (including automation) with the cost of delegating the fulfillment process to an outside company. That being said, if the e-business has a large volume of orders now and is not prepared to handle that amount in-house — then outsource NOW. However, at the same time an e-business can and should put an in-house solution on the drawing board.

A pure-play e-business that expects to handle a substantial volume of orders from the get-go and does not have a warehouse and staff in place, might find that in the beginning it could be more cost-effective to outsource its fulfillment processes to a FSP. In any case, all e-businesses should ensure that they have a back-end built with scalability to accommodate a move to in-house fulfillment processes when the need arises.

Some FSP Facts

Fulfillment is the "heavy lifting" of e-business — it's not virtual, its bricks-and-mortar. No matter how virtual the online experience, there's no way to get around the need to pick and pack orders, ship them to the customer, and then to manage the cumbersome returns process. It's dirty, backbreaking, expensive work, but someone's got to do it.

Increasingly, that someone is a third party fulfillment services provider. This route is definitely not cheap. Pricing for outsourcing your fulfillment starts at around $8 per package before shipping charges. Costs go up from there, depending on extra services such as inventory management, returns processing, call center facilities, engraving, gift wrapping, and so forth.

While an e-business can find FSPs that price fulfillment on a percentage-of-sale basis (usually about 10%), it still must budget a large start-up expense for the integration of its infrastructure with the FSP's systems. These expenses range from $2,000 on the low end, to $200,000 at the mid-range, and up to $1 million at the high end.

The integration process requires at least a few weeks, with the FSP personnel doing most of the work. As expensive as you might think the start-up costs are they are minor compared to the cost of building your own fulfillment center.

The decision to outsource an e-business's logistics and fulfillment needs isn't an easy one to make. The e-business is, after all, handing off its customer's online experience to a third party that might not understand the e-business's vision, corporate culture, and product related idiosyncrasies. Your new FSP will not know your products or your customers at the outset. Nevertheless, flawless fulfillment is the goal.

According to a Mainspring and Bain & Co. report titled "Order Fulfillment: Delivering on the E-Promise," for all except the home-based e-businesses, up until the time that orders reach around 15,000 a day [the author says 10,000] it can be more cost-effective to outsource fulfillment needs rather than build a warehouse and distribution operation. But e-businesses that opt to take this route must choose their FSP carefully.

Lately FSPs have flooded the market from all directions. They range from traditional fulfillment houses (such as Keystone, Kohl Packing and Fingerhut with years of experience) and transportation companies (such as USFreightways and UPS that know logistics inside and out) to the new FSPs that have recently hit the e-business byways (SubmitOrder.com, Mindthestore.com, for example), touting superior technology and easy integration. These newcomers claim they're the best because they don't have the excess baggage of legacy systems that the traditional FSPs must carry. In some ways these "young Turks" are right. Because of legacy data formats, traditional FSPs generally have a harder time integrating their back-end systems into the e-business's Web sites. However, these "Johnny come lately's" don't have the experience of the traditional FSP.

Effective Fulfillment Outsourcing

FSPs each have their own strengths and weaknesses. Companies like Fingerhut and HanoverDirect (www.hanoverdirect.com) have "a wonderful infrastructure set up, so they're the closest to being ready to handle this dot.com fulfillment business," Organic's Lynch told *VARBusiness* in June 2000. "They're now two of the most sought after organizations in the game."

On the other hand, Lynch points out, startup organizations have had the luxury of starting from scratch, adopting some of the newer technology and without many legacy computer system challenges. Lynch listed PFSweb and SubmitOrder.com as two of the more successful new Web fulfillment houses.

But hold your horses, there are also e-tailers like eFANshop.com, an online sports store, which entered into an agreement with logistics provider Sameday.com and Federal Express for the fulfillment and delivery of eFANshop products. Sameday.com will provide end-to-end distribution, fulfillment and technology solution services to eFANshop customers, while FedEx will handle delivery. Sameday.com provides a range of supply chain services to e-tailers and B2B clients and specializes in high-speed fulfillment and delivery of online commerce orders.

Finding an effective fulfillment partner begins with the kind of thorough qualification process that Organic conducts. "It's not like moving freight where this week you can use Yellow Freight, next week Roadway," Carl Young, a principal with Arthur Andersen commented in an interview with *VARBusiness's* Peter Jordan. "Defining the scope of work, doing the hand off, and dealing with transition issues take months and months of work to get a third party integrated into your environment."

In addition to the kind of on-site visits Lynch and others recommend, the e-business and its expert partners need to perform due diligence on the short-list FSPs. "It seems as if every outsourcing firm gives you three reference accounts," Jupiter's Henry explained to *VARBusiness's* Jordan.

"I would ask for five that have not been references for anyone else in the last three months. They all claim hundreds of satisfied customers. If they have hundreds, they can give you five."

KPMG's Blasetti advises his clients to consider two- or three-year contracts that allow the e-business to decide at the end of the contract term whether to bring fulfillment in-house, contract with a different FSP or continue the arrangement.

"Most of these dot.coms are trying to be almost exclusively virtual," Andersen's Young says. "They don't have inventory. When they get a sales order, they cut a purchase order, then delegate the inbound logistics responsibility back to the vendor. A given is that you've got to have leading-edge supply chain technologies. You have to have the ability to electronically communicate not only with your customers, but also with your suppliers. The dot.coms should have the ability to watch the logistics flow from the time it leaves the manufacturer's dock until the time it's in the hands of the consumer."

Real-time inventory is essential, meaning the e-business (and its customers) need to know exactly what's in the warehouses and available for shipping at any time. IT systems must not only deal with shipping but also with receiving and with the many returns that are endemic to e-business as practiced today. Lynch says, "If you have to manually receive all of those goods, you end up getting into a bottleneck. You have three categories: products going out the door, replenishment coming in, and then returns being processed," all very labor-intensive activities. The more those are automated, the more efficient everyone will be at crunch time.

Effective fulfillment outsourcing depends on training. Much of the customer's shopping experience will be dependent upon the employees of the FSP. Therefore, those employees need to be continually trained to act as extensions of the e-business. "If you don't spend a lot of time training the outsourcing company, it's guaranteed they will do an exceptionally poor job servicing your customers," Jupiter's Henry says. "That's what a lot of dot.coms overlook; they don't spend a lot of time on the outsourcing firms. And you carry the risk that if they lose a person you've trained, you've got to go back in and train them again." Well-trained employees, even if they work for a FSP, should be a positive force for the e-business.

Branding also can happen at delivery. SubmitOrder.com's Kreager says, "We take branding to the nth degree. The process starts with planning with a new client. We take time to understand their business plans and goals then have a sit-down with their executive team. We ask what the brand means to them and what the experience is. We have sent some of our team to work in customer stores and had store personnel come to work in our operations so we all understand what the new experience is going to be. We focus on having the same product knowledge and philosophy as the people in any given store."

Vertical Specialists vs Generalists

Whether FSPs that specialize in verticals (servicing only a specific market, i.e., hanging apparel, sporting goods, bath and beauty products) are superior to those that say they can store, pick and ship almost anything, is a matter of debate. Kreager says that SubmitOrder.com can handle everything from clothes to electronics, from fragile items like china to bulky items such as surf boards. At present the company doesn't handle perishables or pharmaceuticals, but otherwise SubmitOrder.com will take over the fulfillment of almost anything an e-business's customers order.

But Andersen's Young and other e-logistics experts say a vertical focus is the way to go: "The players that are going to win are the guys that focus on industry verticals instead of trying to service on a generic basis." A FSP that specializes in receiving, storing and delivering clothes on hangers will build an expertise in that kind of processing that will be difficult to transfer to the skills needed to pick and pack fragile glassware. But the bottom line is, whether they line up partnerships with vertical specialists or generalists, every tech solution provider needs to put logistics on the front burner for their e-business clients.

It's time to get into the game. KPMG's Blasetti says, "companies have to start working at Internet speed. They can't spin their wheels. In our business, in the past, if you were developing a supply chain strategy, it would be a 10- to 16-week process, but we're now being asked to do it in four weeks. The reality is, instead of a high level of due diligence, we have to work collaboratively with our clients [the e-business] to make assumptions and develop solutions that are a 90 percent fit, because speed to market is everything."

The Outsourcing Plan

Where should an e-business begin its search for the right logistics and fulfillment solution? How does it decide the number and locations of its distribution centers and warehouses? Should it depend on ground transport or air freight to move products to and from the customer? And what happens when the product doesn't please — the rose encrusted ceramic vase is just like the one Aunt Rose gave last year — what returns process best meets the online customers' needs?

First know your customer, this will give you a starting point for estimating customer expectations of delivery time, cost, and returns handling.

FSPs are well aware of customer service issues and most offer services that integrate well with the e-business's infrastructure. That being said, FSPs differ widely on the variety of options they provide and the type of client they serve.

Finding the right fit for an e-business requires in-depth research. Once the research is completed and the information compiled, it will be possible to price out the most cost effective and efficient method of getting the products to the customer while maintaining an adequate profit margin.

Keep in mind that an outsourcer (FSP and/or drop shipper) will be an integral part of an e-business's operations. Therefore, find an outsourcer that not only offers the services the e-business needs, but is also a com-

---

FSP SERVICES

Besides the basic pick-pack-and-ship services, individual FSPs might offer:

- Call center operations
- Real-time inventory
- Bag and hanger services for apparel clients
- Refrigeration for clients with flowers and various food items for shipment
- Product assembly
- Engraving
- Gift wrapping and signed gift cards
- Special packaging needs
- International shipping

FSP QUESTIONNAIRE

- What system will you use to manage inventory so the customer is confident the product is available and the Web site can cross-sell, if necessary?

- Will you offer multiple shipping options?

- How will you track orders (so the customer can always be kept informed)?

- By what rules and systems will you handle returns and disputes?

- What types of product does the outsourcer currently have in stock for other clients?

- What is the minimum volume the outsourcer will handle? Is that minimum per month or averaged over a set period?

- How does it handle the packing? What type of packaging material is used. How will the box be labeled? In other words, is only the e-business's brand used or is the outsourcer's brand included as well? Don't dilute the e-business's brand.

- Determine if the outsourcer requires an exclusive contract to fill all of the e-business's product orders. The e-business may want the flexibility of processing some of its orders in-house or to hedge its bets with a secondary FSP or drop-shipper.

- Is there a setup fee? If so, how much and is it a one-time fee?

- Does the outsourcer offer special services such as gift-wrap or sub-assembly? Will the outsourcer include the e-business's catalogs or other branding materials or special offers in the shipments? If so, what are the fees?

- How quickly will orders to be filled? Is there a guarantee?

- What volume of orders can the outsourcer reasonably handle and how scalable is its capacity?

- How will the e-business's infrastructure be integrated with the outsourcer's systems? Will special hardware and/or software be needed? If so, what? What support does the outsourcer offer for the integration process?

- What credit cards and alternative payment methods does the outsourcer accept?

- How are sales taxes handled?

- How does the e-business get paid and how quickly? (drop-ship model)

- How will the e-business and its customers track orders?

- How will the e-business be able to monitor and replenish inventory?

- What reports does the outsourcer provide?

- How will returns and disputes be handled?

- Does the outsourcer offer customer service support?

- Does the outsourcer handle international orders? If so, how and are there extra costs involved?

- What shipping arrangement does the outsourcer have, and is there flexibility in that arrangement to allow for the use of other shippers if they have better rates?

- What account servicing does the outsourcer offer?

fortable fit in other ways — location(s), product aptitude, IT capabilities, customer service, parcel management, mission statement, financial wherewithal — all part of a thorough due diligence. To determine whether a prospective outsourcer meets an e-business's requirements, an outsourcing plan is needed. This should be an addendum to your logistics and fulfillment plan.

First determine the services the e-business needs and expects from a fulfillment provider and what they will need to know about the e-business — this isn't easy. A starting point is to review your carefully drawn up logistics and fulfillment plan.

Your Product

Look at the products offered for sale via your Web site. If the answer is "yes" to either of the following two questions then the decision to outsource is a no brainer.

1) Do your products require special handling, i.e., fragile, sensitive to temperature changes, or special licensing requirements (alcohol, perfumes, pharmaceuticals, etc.)?

2) Will the majority of the product orders include multiples of different products? This makes the picking and packing more labor intensive.

With a yes answer, a FSP should be found that will accommodate the specific product needs and still allow the e-business to earn a profit.

However, if it isn't possible to find an FSP to provide the special services required, an e-business has two choices: to outsource all fulfillment except the products requiring special handling, which will be handled in-house, or to keep all fulfillment processes in-house.

IT Capabilities

Although it's possible for an e-business to send its customers' orders via e-mail or FTP directly to the FSP's warehouse facility. The optimal FSP is one that can enable an e-business to integrate its systems with the FSP's back-end systems so that there is real-time exchange of information including inventory data. The FSP should offer continuous technical support to assure that the operation runs smoothly from both ends; but the e-business needs to be sure it's clear who is responsible for what and who will pay for specific costs. An e-business should keep in mind that the FSP selected will become a partner within its value chain and as such an essential arm of the e-business's operation.

Due Diligence

As with all potential partners, you must perform due diligence on any perspective FSP. Carefully investigate such issues as financial health, union related issues, stability of management, the customer list, references, the physical plant (lease, ownership, condition of building, equipment, etc.). One critical question to answer: have they seen battle — has the FSP been through at least one Christmas season? It's imperative that your fulfillment partner has been there, done that and lived to tell the tale.

How automated are the provider's operations? Do they have reporting systems so you can tell what is selling or what is in stock? Do they have to re-key any of the information that is transmitted to them? An e-business, no matter what size, needs to find a fulfillment partner that is Internet-savvy with a solid infrastructure for reporting, and fully automated so there is no re-keying of data.

Does the provider meet the e-business's unique needs? If you're an e-business that caters to the insomnia crowd, can your FSP keep pace? What happens when you are suddenly flooded with orders for your vibrating footrest because you bought a 30-second ad to air every 10 minutes during a Charlie's Angels festival on late-night cable?

Does the FSP offer real-time inventory status? If not, you are going to have some very unhappy shoppers when customers get a backorder e-mail notice two days after they placed an order for your cute set of matching plastic placemats, cups, saucers and paper napkins that they were planning on using at next Wednesday's bridge club.

Does it support multiple ship-to addresses (with the option of gift-wrapping each)? Are its service-level guarantees (such as same-day shipping on all orders received before 6 PM and reshipping at no cost if the order was initially fulfilled incorrectly) acceptable?

As many e-businesses' search for the perfect FSP partner there are numerous roadblocks, such as:

- Many will not service an e-business unless it has a certain volume of orders.

- If an e-business has an inventory that consists of a large variety of products, it will in all likelihood only find a handful of FSPs that will provide the necessary services at a bearable cost. It's more costly and time-consuming to prepare packages that contain different combinations of items than it is single-product packages.

- Some FSPs will only respond to inquiries regarding the status of an order while others will provide full product support.

- The level of services in warehousing and inventory management may also vary from company to company. In some cases, the FSPs will order stock directly from the manufacturers while others will expect the Web site to ship the products to their main warehouse for packaging and delivery.

- The drop shipment option may result in multiple shipping charges for some orders.

- E-businesses using drop shippers may have to deal with customer confusion due to packages arriving at different times from different shipping locations and possibly without your e-business's brand anywhere on the packages.

- The drop shipment option requires complex tracking and returns procedures compared to FSP shipments.

Order fulfillment is the link between the e-business and its customers. Don't expect to throw fulfillment over the fence and not look at it again. No matter which provider you go with, you must monitor the customer's experience closely. One way of doing that is to place one or more of the e-business's staff at the FSP's operations. According to Mainspring's Morrison, "Don't think you can dump your merchandise and walk away. You need to keep people there in the warehouse to assure quality control."

See for yourself. Going on site to evaluate the FSP's operations is a crucial part of the vendor selection process. How else will you find out that the provider is really entering orders into the system by hand?

Listen to the potential FSP's customers. Ask for customer references and call all of them, not just the top three. Ask what kind of products the outsourcer handles for them and how well it delivered on its obligations.

Ask them if they have any complaints or reservations about the outsourcer. Question them about their plans to renew the contract when it comes due. Another reason for wanting the customer list is to determine if there is a conflict between your e-business's product line and others that the outsourcer handles. Plus, the customer list will alert you to any large clients that may compromise the outsourcer's resources, especially during a busy holiday shopping season.

Identify your priorities up front and stick to them. However, when time is of the essence — compromise — some of the items farther down on the e-business's fulfillment "want" list may have to wait.

Indulge.com contracted with SubmitOrder to provide fulfillment services but found it impossible to manage and train its dedicated SubmitOrder team on the unique qualities of its inventory from a distance. Realizing that Indulge.com's employees had an intimate understanding of its inventory, Indulge.com's management made the decision to have its own employees on site to inspect and process returns. The theory was that an outside employee might not notice that a returned Ultimate Indulgent Gift Set was missing one of its seven products, for example.

If it's not feasible for the e-business to have an employee on-site, insist on a single point of contact at the FSP. Helwig Industries, LLC (www.wigjig.com), an online jewelry tool business has made a point of having a specific contact at its FSP, Kohl Packing Inc. (www.kohlpacking.com). That contact knows Helwig's inventory inside and out. Now when Helwig receives a complaint relating to order processing and fulfillment an employee can zip off an e-mail to the Kohl contract, who will investigate.

The Partnership

Will the FSP be a true partner? Choosing an FSP partner is a crucial decision for any e-business. Both businesses' fortunes are tied together in a very real way. Gerry Brunk, vice president of operations for Indulge.com hit the nail on the head when he stated, "we needed people who felt an ownership stake in growing our business." Brunk went on to say that he found "that wasn't in the culture of some of the more established vendors."

It's important to match your style with the FSP's. If the little things are important to your company, you want them to be important to your FSP, too. MuseumCompany.com pays a lot of attention to detail. Whether it's the categorization of products, the navigation of its e-store, the products it selects, or the quality of it wrapping paper. So it went looking for a FSP with the same mindset — the details.

Let the customer's needs also guide your FSP choice. Some e-businesses will find that their customers are more concerned with speed of delivery (a gourmet shop) and others with a super-easy return process (a children's clothing store).

Whatever partnership an e-business makes, it must choose wisely because its online fortunes are tied to how well its FSP performs. Mainspring analyst Morrison was unusually pithy when he stated: "E-fulfillment is the most important thing in terms of delivering on your promise to your customer."

Issues Specific to a Small E-business

FSPs that cater to the small e-businesses allow even the busy home-based Web site to take advantage of the latest cost and time saving techniques, such as supply chain management software, and orders sent directly to the fulfillment center floor for picking. But keep due diligence in mind, since if the FSP falls down on the job during a peak selling season, a small e-business might not be able to recover and could easily lose its entire business.

Some businesses, even small e-businesses that ship only a small number of orders may not want to fill those orders in-house. But, especially for the smaller e-businesses, outsourcing to an FSP makes good financial sense ONLY when the e-business has more money than time. When an e-business needs every penny, it should handle its fulfillment processes in-house. While the cost per order is significantly increased when an FSP is brought into the picture, if it has been determined that over the long haul the e-business can make a larger profit by outsourcing, then by all means outsource.

The only caveat is to find a FSP that caters to small e-businesses. It may make economic sense to hire an LFE to aid in the planning, search and decision-making process.

How Much Does It Cost?

The cost of outsourcing to an FSP is dependent upon which services the e-business require and the volume of orders it forwards to the outsourcer since many of the fees or commissions are set on a sliding scale based on volume. On the average, you will pay an FSP a monthly fee for warehousing the products of around 3 cents per small item, or $15 for each pallet of products. An inventory count is usually performed monthly and the fees are assessed on the products the e-business has in the FSP's warehouses at that time. The FSP also charges a handling fee for each package and for incidentals, such as mailing labels, boxes, packing material, and then, of course, shipping.

Drop shipping is a bit less complicated. There are no outright, up-front expenses involved with the drop-ship model. The drop shipper usually pays the e-business a commission that can range from 10% to 25% per order shipped.

The Contract

Once a decision has been made to go with an outsourcer, the next step is to ask the attorneys to draw up a contract. The contract should specify that the e-business can have its representatives at the fulfillment provider's place of business learning as much as possible about how fulfillment works so the e-business can make an informed outsourcing decision at the end of the contract term.

E-businesses should have, KPMG's Blasetti explained, "an on-site presence. We firmly believe that makes for better operations. Not only does it give you eyes and ears on site, but it also gives the third party provider a conduit for information." He went on to spell out that an e-business should "look at pricing and the contractual agreement itself to make sure you capture the performance information you can use to judge performance. It's not all about pure cost per unit; it's also about services provided. We typically put in place a compliance or performance measurement system that helps our clients monitor performance and work collaboratively with the third party to make sure all service levels are achieved." The FSP typically gets bonuses for exceeding performance levels in any negotiated contract.

Contracts with the fulfillment providers are crucial, agrees Jupiter's Henry. "You've got to monitor them, and you have to have very, very clear service level agreements about what is acceptable and what is not acceptable as well as who owns the information on your customers. You have to own the database," he says.

The contract should clearly outline each business's expectations, services to be provided and fees — give your legal representative the logistics and fulfillment plan and the outsourcing plan to use as a guide. Keep in mind that both the e-business and the outsourcer want to maximize revenues, so it's important that everyone agree on a compensation rate that is fair to all. The contract that is ultimately signed should be for a limited term since outsourcing with a specific outsourcer is a choice that will need to be revisited again and again throughout the business relationship. However, the contract should be a definitive document laying out the specific services and responsibilities of both the e-business and the outsourcer.

Once the contract or agreement is signed, the next task is integrating the e-business's systems with the FSP's back-end in such seamless execution that the customers won't know the difference.

Technical Issues

You've signed your contract now you have to start working on getting your systems to talk to the FSP's systems. Your expert partners know and should have stressed to you that the most important criteria in the selection of any FSP partner is its IT systems and support. "In evaluating these providers, we've found that almost all of them are making investments but most aren't quite there in terms of IT support," KPMG's Blasetti warns.

While off-the-shelf solutions exist to solve some pieces of the fulfillment and integration problems — relational databases and shopping-cart applications, for example — no turnkey packages currently exist to provide complete integration with FSPs. Know that the e-business is responsible for setting up product/inventory master synchronization, pricing, inventory status, invoicing, and final reconciliation. There are many challenges that an e-business faces when it builds and manages infrastructures that interact with third parties.

There are many points throughout the order processing where an FSP could come into play. For instance, if the FSP is handling credit-card settlement for the Web-based commerce site, then the charge to the customer's credit card is authorized and settled for the order amount. The products are then shipped to the shipping address using the selected carrier. If a product requested by the customer is not available, the customer's order is placed on hold (backorder), until inventory is replenished.

Until the customer actually receives the order, the customer must be

THE ORDER CAPTURE PIPELINE — A SCENARIO

Once the customer order has been received, it's dropped into the "order capture pipeline." From there the Web site must send each product to the correct fulfillment provider(s) (the right FSP(s), the right drop-shipper(s) and maybe even the in-house fulfillment center), who assume responsibility for delivering the products to the customer. Even if that sounds simple, it's not; the system must contain business rules to determine which fulfillment provider(s) to send what portion of the customer's order to. An example of rules:

- Use the same fulfillment provider for all the products, if possible.
- Use the fulfillment provider that can give the customer the lowest per unit cost.
- Check in-house inventory before using an outsource solution.

Remember, if more than one fulfillment provider is used, then the customer will receive separate shipments (more shipping expense). Then, sometime during this process (it varies with systems and is dependent upon whether all the fulfillment providers support real-time inventory queries), the e-business composes an XML message and transmits it via secure HTTP to the appropriate outsourcers. If the e-business has outsourcers that do not support real-time inventory queries, then the site will need to rely on daily supplied inventory profile data.

This is where it gets real sticky and where sometimes there is a need for consultants and programmers. For each of the interactions with the entire system the outsourcer requires mapping data from the e-business's order management system (and pipeline) into messages that can be understood by the fulfillment providers' systems. First the data has to be represented — the way that is handled is dependent upon the outsourcer's systems. For example, it might be an EDI X12 format to represent the transaction, then other FSPs might have proprietary batch-file data formats, and there are some who have their own "special" crafted variety with their own key-value-pair grammars to represent information.

kept informed as to the order status. In addition, it's desirable that the customer be able to go to the e-business's Web site and bring up the order history and request a real-time order status query. If it's supported, the site communicates with the outsourcer via secure HTTP and requests the status. The response message should include details of all shipments, cancellation, backorders, and other transactions that have taken place while processing the order. Or perhaps with the right interface the cus-

The next step in the order process is the collection of the customer's shipping address and shipping instructions. Depending on decisions made upstream in the pipeline, the available shipment options are determined by the outsourcer(s). If multiple outsourcers are involved, then a shared shipping carrier is usually used to ship the order. If a single outsourcer is involved, then the e-business queries it for current delivery options. Other complications at this stage can include support for multiple ship-to addresses for the same order (for example, Christmas time, Mother's Day, Graduation season, etc.) and gift wrapping and messages.

Now we are at the payment stage where the credit card information is entered or retrieved from the customer database, and the credit card is authorized for the order total. The e-business interacts with a credit-card clearinghouse to validate the credit card and to determine whether there is sufficient credit available. Communicating with a clearinghouse normally requires a dedicated line and transmittal of the requests using the clearinghouse's proprietary protocol.

Once the credit card has been approved and the customer (yes, all of the above should have occurred within seconds) has clicked on the confirmation button, the order is accepted by the e-business's order management system. At this point, a few options exist depending on the site's policy and outsourcer(s) capabilities. If the site offers the customer the opportunity to cancel the order within a specified time frame, the order is not immediately transmitted to the outsourcer(s). If the outsourcer doesn't support a real-time protocol, then the order will be transmitted during the next batch-file generation cycle. If the outsourcer supports real-time order processing, then the site can transmit over secure HTTP (as discussed previously) data containing all of the information necessary for an outsourcer to process the order.

tomer is invisibly transferred to the FSP for direct communication.

Many outsourcers send nightly, via FTP or encrypted email, order status files that describe all of the day's order activity. By law, an e-business can't charge (settle) a customer's credit card until the order has been shipped. So, the order information returned to the e-business by the outsourcer(s) must be verified for accuracy before the credit-card information is processed.

Without valid information, the e-business can't post a shipment invoice to the order management system. Settlement tasks run periodically to process shipment invoices that need collection. The settlement process communicates with the clearinghouse to charge the buyer's credit card (note that when the order was originally placed, funds were only allocated [authorized] but not disbursed). If the site and the outsourcer(s) don't agree on order details, customers may be charged the wrong amount. Once the order details are squared away between the FSP, the merchant credit processing bank, and the e-business, the information is transferred from the order management system to the Web site's financial system for purchase order generation, accounts payable, and so on.

Then, once the products are in the customer's hands, the e-business and the outsourcer need to have in place a system whereby they can jointly handle any post-purchase activity such as returns or exchanges, and perform transaction reconciliation.

Drop-Ship

The vision of the "virtual corporation" was dependent in large part upon the drop-ship model being a success. It's true that with the drop-ship model an e-business doesn't need a warehouse, and in some cases, it doesn't even carry any inventory. As explained previously, using drop-shippers allows the e-business to source multiple manufactures and distributors but own and hold none of the inventory — that's the job for the drop-shipper. The e-business's job is to sell the products and collect the orders. Adoption of the drop-ship model allows the e-business to pass order information including the customer's shipping instructions to its distributors.

The drop-ship model does present one huge problem: the e-business is limited to working with vendors, distributors and suppliers that have the ability to ship "ones and twos." Many good potential partners are large manufacturers and distributors with warehouses set up for pallets and truckloads not the individual package — thus causing fulfillment delays.

Logistics can be convoluted unless the e-business's drop-ship supply chain makes substantial investment in their back-end systems. Think about it — how will the drop shippers and the e-business exchange information in a real time manner on issues concerning inventory and shipping status, without integration of sophisticated systems? To avoid costly upgrading and integration expense, an e-business can take advantage of order processing management services such as those offered by the aforementioned OrderTrust, Netship or Dotcom Distribution. Another option is EDI. E-businesses that have opted for the drop-ship model (whether for all products or not) will find that a number of their drop shippers will have strong IT capabilities and/or the means to support EDI standards.

Check out GDI (www.globaldataintegrators.com), its EPIC service allows Web-based commerce sites to exchange EDI data via the Internet. The service is geared for low volume EDI users who do not have the traditional EDI infrastructures and VAN accounts in place but who have the need to support EDI within their supply chain. Or perhaps Edi Exchange (www.ediexchange.net), its subscribers can make use of their sophisticated software to conduct business with the Web-based commerce site's supply chain via the Internet.

A possible solution for the "let's not integrate crowd" is OrderTrust.com. Its centralized network allows Web-based commerce sites to seamlessly exchange order information within their supply chain. According to OrderTrust.com it can connect hundreds of Web-based commerce sites, their suppliers, banks, distributors, with call centers and each other. Another advantage of using OrderTrust.com is it provides the technical know-how to connect a Web-based commerce site with its supply chain and the OrderTrust's systems giving everyone the means to exchange data in almost real-time.

Another small problem for the majority of e-businesses using the drop-ship model is that drop shipments work better for single item orders than they do for multiple item orders. However, many e-businesses do use drop shippers so they can offer their niche market items that would be impractical for the e-business to handle itself.

Then there is the "returns" curse that all e-businesses must deal with. With the drop-ship model, the customer, in all probability will turn to the e-business when a return is contemplated. The e-business would then turn the customer over to the drop shipper (bad for branding), or take the returned product and forward it to the drop shipper (cost intensive).

If coordinating between one Web store and several distributors sounds daunting, imagine working with more than 100 distributors. That's what SkyMall.com does everyday, with the help of OrderTrust.com. SkyMall.com is the "click" to SkyMall, the catalog too many of us have thumbed through during a "tarmac flight delay" while crammed into one of the oh so many cattle-car air flights in operation today. Like its parent, SkyMall.com collects placement and transaction fees in return for selling merchandise from well-known merchants such as Frontgate and Hammacher Schlemmer. However, SkyMall.com has grown well past its parent — the print catalog offers at most 2,000 items — SkyMall.com lists around 25,000 and is still growing.

SkyMall's logistics and fulfillment needs are complicated; among it's supply chain are a small select group of distributors that don't handle their own shipments, and then to handle its international orders it must lease space in strategically located distribution centers in Scotland and the Philippines.

When an order comes in, SkyMall conveys the data to OrderTrust, which disseminates it to the appropriate vendor or distribution center and sends status reports back to SkyMall. SkyMall.com's LFMS (which includes OrderTrust) is a wonder to behold — allowing it to grow to more than 30% of the parent company's overall revenue, although like many children, SkyMall.com did push its parent into the red, for the short-term. "We needed to spend significant dollars to put together a highly reliable system that will stand up to demand and allow us to scale dramatically in capacity and [shrink] our time to market," a spokesperson stated in defense of SkyMall.com.

Management Information Consulting, Inc. (www.micinc.com) was approached by Many-Thanks.com to build it a Web site with a transparent order fulfillment process specifically for the drop-ship model. Management Information Consulting (MIC) customized Many-Thanks' back-end so that each of its drop-ship vendors would be automatically notified when an order was placed and would receive the correct information for personalizing and shipping each gift. Besides online credit card validation and billing, MIC also implemented an e-mail notification system that informs the customer about the status of his or her order.

Outsourcing Wrap-up

Despite the advantages of using a FSP and/or drop shipper, there are a few potential downsides. Putting someone else between an e-business and its customer can be a risky proposition. And there are significant data integration issues. When sorting through these issues, it pays to see what others have done — get out there and talk to everyone you know that is using or has used an FSP and/or drop shipper.

Whatever decision an e-business makes concerning its fulfillment partnership(s), issues will arise. What happens when the busy and ever important Christmas season arrives and it comes time to decide between shipping an order for a smaller company (maybe like your e-business) or shipping an order for The Children's Place? Which one is the outsourcer going to choose? It's a given, the big guy will get the attention.

An e-business can protect itself to some degree by establishing a detailed service-level agreement to ensure performance (get the legal department involved). A series of coordinated steps is required to bridge the gap between (1) a customer clicking the buy button, thus sending the order to the shopping cart software and into the "pipeline" and (2) the customer receiving the products. Ad-hoc solutions to handle the communication with a FSP and/or drop shipper(s) can be put into place that may be sufficient for an e-business with low sales volume and limited inventory. However, if sales increase substantially, then even a small e-business must deal with the lack of standards for data representation and transmission requirements. This means dealing with the API issues or taking the EDI and XML approach for communication between systems so as to be able to interact with each outsourcer (FSP and/or drop shipper). Eventually, the "string and sticky tape" method will fail and proper integration will become essential.

Where and how should you begin your search for a FSP especially if you aren't availing yourself of the services of a LFE? I've given the readers three Web sites that should give everyone a good start in their search for the perfect fulfillment partner.

1. www.lycos.com > Business and Careers > Business Services > Distribution and Logistics > Distribution > Internet Order Fulfillment.

2. www.digitrends.net/digitrends/dtonline/features/sections/fulfill-ment/listing1 or go to www.digitrends.net, on the left hand side of the site you will see a Search Site link, click it, then type in "E-Fulfillment Directory," click, and then use any of the links that say "listing" except the top one.

3. www.yahoo.com) > Business and Economy > Business to Business > Marketing and Advertising > Fulfillment. There are 58 companies listed, of which at least 40 are relevant.

The Internet is a great equalizer. With the right FSP and the right integration between the FSP and the e-business, all e-businesses can do business on the same playing field with the same type of equipment and the same type of personnel.

RETURNS

On the e-business side, the process by which returns are accepted and processed must be considered. The time to do it is when you are considering how you are going to handle your fulfillment. Issues such as repairs, refurbishment or reconditioning of the product, decisions whether to issue a full credit, partial credit, and the logistics of return shipping must be resolved. An e-business should consider the return question from both its customer's and its systems' perspective.

Get serious about managing returns. You'll save money while meeting the needs of your customers. Although the numbers are all over the place, it seems that retailing industry research firms and trade groups estimate that by 2002 the e-tail model will have $11 billion in returns and $1.8 billion to $2.5 billion in losses from these returns. Currently, e-tailers only receive approximately 17% of retail value back on returned items and on average, wait six to 18 months for any cost recovery, and even then, they usually receive only a small fraction of the original sale.

Brian Hudock at Tompkins Associates (www.tompkinsinc.com), a firm that designs warehouses for Fortune 500 companies, sees the return problem up close, "It's chaos. Nobody ever focuses on it in retail. Their primary goal is to get product out the door."

E-tailers write off millions of dollars each year when they process returns. As the reader will grow to understand, the return statistics are murky — the US Postal Service's research indicates that about 25% of all goods sold online were sent back.

Returns are bad news for e-tailers. It can take up to 18 months to put salable returns back on store shelves. Often, by that time the product will have lost up to 90% of its value, according to Jeffrey Rogers, co-founder and chief financial officer at ReturnBuy.com.

Even without factoring in the time, expense and hassle that goes into handling refunds, credits, repairs and exchanges, the most devastating cost to the e-tailer will be its loss of hard-earned customers. Even Forrester is mystified when it trys to estimate how many customers are at risk by incompetent return processes. But Hudock bravely estimates that it's as much as 5%, which is about half the number of customers who typically return products to a bricks-and-mortar. Don Gilbert, senior vice president of information technology for the National Retail Federation (www.nfr.com) speculates that returns in the bricks-and-mortar retail industry averages around 10%. But Gilbert qualifies his statement, "It depends on your business model and strategy."

Gilbert explains that many e-tailers in the three main e-tailing markets — click-and-mortars, e-catalogers and e-tail pure-plays — are looking to handle returns in-house. "It's early in the game. A lot of people are still trying to figure out which strategy makes sense," he asserts.

For example, according to Gilbert, retailers that spun off an e-tail operation as a separate entity may encounter tax problems. If the e-tailing enterprise allows products to be returned to physical stores and does not collect the mandated sales taxes that the bricks-and-mortar store is responsible for, tax authorities may decide that the e-tailing side is not a separate business and is taxable.

Barnes & Noble isn't intimated by the "tax collector." It's baby sibling

BarnesandNoble.com's customers enjoy the convenience of being able to return books and music CDs purchased at BarnesandNoble.com to any Barnes & Noble store. Customers who take advantage of the returns program will receive merchandise credits at Barnes & Noble stores.

When Gilbert wrestled with the "what percentage of online purchases are being returned" question, his answer was a non-answer. He stated that such previously mentioned anomalies, combined with the complex mix of retail channels that are now available to buyers, make it difficult to pinpoint what percentage of Web purchases are returned. Where he didn't waver was the issue of dealing with returns in an efficient and seamless manner, which he felt was a major issue for the entire e-business community.

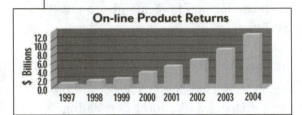

Projected growth of returns by online purchasers. Figures taken from Forrester Research documentation.

As GATX Logistics (www.gatxlogistics.com), Tom Scanlin, vice president e-logistics initiative pointed out, anything the logistic house can do to reduce the time products spend in return channels and make the ordering process as accurate and reliable as possible will help e-businesses improve their bottom lines. These services are becoming more important as the cost of acquiring online customers grows.

According to Shop.org, a consulting group, customer acquisition costs as a whole increased by 15% last year to $38 per customer. For pure e-tailers the cost was so much higher, averaging $82 per customer. The product return experience is a crucial part of a customer's decision whether or not to keep using an e-tailer.

Many customer satisfaction and retention problems are centered on the e-business community's returns dilemma. With around 20% (the numbers fluctuate quite a bit) of all online purchases being returned or exchanged, a major challenge surrounding e-businesses — especially those without a bricks-and-mortar presence — is how to make that process as non-traumatic for the customer as possible. Although the current number of online customers who actually return items purchased online is small and little customer defection has occurred due to dissatisfaction with the return process, it can grow to be a problem for e-businesses if not taken in-hand now.

According to the Yankee Group, among factors that limit consumers' online purchasing, concerns about the difficulty in returning goods rank fourth, behind shipping costs, the inability to discern product quality (affecting an e-business's returns ratio) and concerns about site legitimacy. Fully half of all online customers cited returns as a "very" or "somewhat limiting" factor in their overall online shopping experience. Similarly, Jupiter Communications states that 37% of online buyers say they would purchase more if they were assured of easy returns.

"Minimizing the rate of return is obviously desirable for any e-tailer, if the mechanism used to lower return rates is making the process harder than it is already, customer satisfaction is sure to wane. That already appears to be the case for some online purchasers," commented Mary Brett Whitfield, principal consultant and director of the E-Retail Intelligence System at PricewaterhouseCoopers (PWC), in discussing its late 2000 survey of 500 online customers on the subject of returns.

According to the PWC survey, while only 4% of online purchasers reported returning their most recent online purchase and only 29% have ever returned a non-business product purchased from an e-tailer, 41% have wanted to return a product purchased online. Why didn't they go through the return process — it was too much of a hassle. The numbers also indicate that while online customers are not at the present making the effort to return unwanted products, the stalemate cannot continue forever. It's important that e-tailers understand the reason for product dissatisfaction, with so many online customers in possession of merchandise that they are unhappy with and want to return. It seems that the majority of online purchasers returned or wanted to return a product because it simply didn't meet their expectations. This suggests there are plenty of opportunities for e-businesses to make advancements in realistically representing the products they sell.

When the PWC surveyors asked the respondents to identify the three biggest problems associated with returning online purchases, two-thirds identified having to pay a return tariff. Nearly half of respondents stated the inconvenience of returning an online purchase because it required a trip to the post office, UPS or FedEx pick-up location. Not being able to return products to a store came in as the third biggest problem, demonstrating the inherent advantage enjoyed by multi-channel retailers.

"The leading problems mentioned by respondents point to two primary culprits — money and time," comments Whitfield. "To enhance customer satisfaction with the return process, online retailers should aim to make the process cheaper and quicker/easier."

Nearly half of respondents expect e-tailers to provide the option of returning products to a local store, especially if it isn't a pure-play. This points out that the inability to return a product to a bricks-and-mortar store is clearly a major problem for some online purchasers.

A late 2000 study by NFO Interactive (www.nfoi.com), a market research firm, confirms that online customers often keep items they might otherwise return because they do not want to pay the return shipping costs. About 20% of online customers surveyed told NFO they've kept products purchased online rather than pay for the return.

Also, almost one-fourth of the respondents told NFO they had returned an item purchased online in the past six months with 89% sending the item back post paid, 45% paying for return shipment and 7% returning the item at a bricks-and-mortar location (multiple responses allowed).

The good news for e-tailers is that more often than not the customer making a return was not so dissatisfied with the return process that it adversely affected future shopping behavior with the specific e-tailer. In fact, over half of online customers who have returned products indicated that their return experience(s) had no influence on their future shopping behavior with that particular e-tailer. However, one-third did say that they were less likely to shop at that specific e-tailer — so there is some customer dissatisfaction coming to the surface due to return policies.

For the click-and-mortar, the option to allow the customer to return a product by hand to its bricks-and-mortar establishment may be an easy solution. But are systems in place that can process the return? If an e-business has installed an automated merchandising and inventory system, it must be able to integrate all types of returns. Note that returns can take up a significant amount of time when handled manually.

Offering incentives such as providing labels for post-paid returns are a good way for e-tailers to build loyalty. "I think it says a lot about the respect they have for the customer," stated Ann Green, vice president of e-commerce and retail at NFO Interactive. Once a company decides on a return policy, however, "they'd better stick to it," she added. "It's an important part of their business model and their bottom line."

Solutions

Another industry has been born to serve the e-business community — Reverse Logistics Providers. Reverse logistics is the process of managing the flow of returned goods and excess inventory from the customer to its final disposition. Most e-businesses have synchronized their supply chains to cut costs, but the supply chain does not operate efficiently in reverse. This is where reverse logistics providers get into the act. They work with the e-businesses to develop and implement reverse logistics strategies that optimize the entire reverse logistics value chain.

There are a number of solutions that promise to give e-tailers more control over the problem. "The first order of business is to try and avoid the return in the first place," said Tom Scanlin of GATX Logistics', a reverse logistics provider. That means more sophisticated ways of presenting and describing products to consumers.

Kevin Sheehan, president and CEO of reverse logistics specialist USF Processors (www.usfprocessors.com), voiced his opinion that the shift toward single-package e-tailing makes return logistics more complex. The Web has changed the ground rules. In the logistics market the direction is toward smaller and more frequent shipments with the Internet as both the enabler and the driving force. In traditional bricks-and-mortar retailing, returns are processed at the store, "and the goods are sent in bulk to a return center," he pointed out. But in e-tailing there is more emphasis on processing returns individually, rather than in bulk within their returns center, thus adding to an e-business's return processing expense. As Sheehan explains, "there is more reliability when receiving goods from the store than from individual consumers."

This means more work for logistics providers such as USF. "When a consumer sends something to us directly, we are the ones who get involved researching it based on the data provided to us by the e-tailer," he said.

The lack of a technical fix for the problem also makes it difficult, adds Keith Biondo, publisher at *Inbound Logistics* magazine (www.inboundlo-gistics.com), which tracks logistics companies. "Most are trying to do it [reverse logistics] on their own. About 20% use third parties. There's certainly room to grow. We call it the undiscovered country."

NFO's Green suggested that e-tailers could bring down the number of returns by ensuring online descriptions accurately reflect the product being advertised. "The closer they can get to what it really is, how it looks and feels, the lower these returns are going to be," she said. Still, meeting that goal may be easier said than done. While new technologies can provide clearer pictures, some might be "too sophisticated for the average user," with long download times, turning off potential buyers, Green judged.

A GATX client in the hunting and fishing business recommends the type of clothing a buyer should wear for a particular situation. For example the e-tailer's Web site can show the buyer "what the clothing looks like in the eyes of the deer," Scanlin explained. Some retailers are even experimenting with holographic scanning booths.

If some readers feel all this seems to stray a bit from the nitty gritty of returns, it doesn't, at least according to Scanlin. He believes that the reverse logistic providers need to broaden their product portfolios to become more service oriented. "For one of our customers we are building a photo lab in our facility," he said. The lab will enable the GATX's client to produce better images for its Web site. GATX has licensed Web site technology to enable it to help e-businesses develop more effective e-tailing sites.

A few merchants such as JCrew.com and Amazon.com have streamlined their return process; but most e-tailers are still in the technological dark ages when it comes to return processing. Hudock claims, "they still look on it as a manual process. They don't use voice recognition or automated processes. The technological investment is still way behind the curve."

Some of the reverse logistics start-ups are taking the simple approach of providing a link from an e-business's commerce site to their return page. When a customer submits a return through the reverse logistics provider, it records the data, checks that data against purchase history from the e-business, and then take an appropriate course of action — either processing the return or rejecting it.

The Return Exchange (www.thereturnexchange.com) is trying a new gambit. One of its services, titled "Verify-1," is proprietary return authorization software that tracks returns from every angle. For on-line transactions the system is a Web-based application that is accessed by the customer from the retailer's Web page. Customers "click" on the "Return" icon on the e-business's Web site to bring up the electronic return form. This technology allows all concerned to determine whether a product being returned should go back into inventory or be sent to an alternative channel such as a liquidation auction. "We are taking data and trying to make the decision earlier," said Mark Hilinski, The Return Exchange's vice president of marketing and sales. The service uses a national database of customer return histories to decide where a product should go before the customer actually returns it.

Hilinski theorizes that returns are a problem for e-tailers because of their rapid growth and the logistical complexities inherent in on-line sales. For these e-businesses, processing returns can be unwieldy, and improper handling of returns can create customer service problems. He states that Return Exchange's unique returns management system allows an e-business to earn money (versus losing money) on every return.

> Three questions to ask when pondering the "returned merchandise" predicament:
>
> • Do you anticipate a high return rate?
>
> • Where will you process returns in-house or out-of-house?
>
> • Do you intend to offer free shipping for all returned products?
>
> An e-business should base its return policy decisions and its return management solutions on the answers.

Linking up with other specialists to extend their product reach is also an option for FSPs handling e-business returns. Eager to establish such alliances are companies such as The Return Exchange, which provides a comprehensive solution to the returns problem. Its aim is to "bookend" its services with fulfillment and reverse logistics businesses. More e-businesses have begun to outsource their return processes due to the complexity of the task, according to Hilinski. "Since the second quarter, we've gotten a lot more reception," he added.

An e-business might want to check with its current logistics partner, numerous major logistics companies have opened a returns division. Outsourcing proponents and the vendors themselves say this will yield better customer service and reduce the internal work needed to integrate back-end and Web systems.

Naturally, some e-businesses don't want nor need an outsourcer to manage their returns. But others say working with a vendor is easier than setting up return infrastructures.

For example, customers who buy branded apparel, collectibles and home decor at coca-colastore.com will have the option of making returns at kiosks at Mail Boxes Etc. franchises. Return.com, a joint venture launched by Mail Boxes Etc. and fulfillment services company, Innotrac Corp., developed software that connects e-tailers' order management systems — including those of coca-colastore.com — to Return.com's return processing system.

"The whole purpose of getting involved with Return.com obviously is customer service," said Andrew Lelchuk, manager of business development and e-commerce at Coca-Cola Co. "It makes it that much easier to keep the customer happy," because the return process is straightforward.

Designer-bag merchant Timbuk2 Designs (www.timbuk2.com) is working with The Return Exchange. Timbuk2 installed a link from its site to The Return Exchange server that hosts TimBuk2's HTML return form. The form is consistent with pages on the Timbuk2 site. Customer data is analyzed in The Return Exchange's returns engine against rules supplied by Timbuk2 that determine whether it grants refunds.

The Return Exchange's system compiles a history of online and in-store returns for merchant customers. At the moment, there is no direct IT systems link between the two companies' respective ordering and return systems. When The Return Exchange gets products back, it uses e-mail to notify Timbuk2. In the future, Timbuk2 will consider giving The Return Exchange direct access to its order processing system, said Timbuk2's vice president, Jordan Riess.

The Return Exchange charges on a per-transaction basis for its returns management service. Cost varies by product type and volume, but generally runs between 25 cents and 50 cents per transaction. Other services that The Return Exchange (and other reverse logistics providers) offer are refurbishing, repackaging and handling of product returns, as well as product liquidations via online auctions.

Another new offering comes from ReturnCentral.com, a company that began operation in mid-2000. ReturnCentral's Web-based Virtual Returns Desk applies the e-business's specific returns rules, generates return mailing/shipping labels, issues advance shipping notifications, and tracks returns through each stage of the process. Customers go to an e-business site to make a return and the e-tailer brings up their personal order history. When customers select the item they want to return, they're invisibly linked to ReturnCentral's returns processing system, which includes a Return Merchandise Authorization wizard that's linked to the e-business's Web site.

ReturnCentral gains access to the systems of its e-business clients through an XML gateway that facilitates integration with order management systems or through ERP systems such as SAP's R/3. In a typical deployment, the ReturnCentral system will use this XML link to obtain the payment method, shipping address and other information needed to process a return.

ReturnCentral charges an undisclosed up-front licensing fee, plus per transaction fees that vary by product category.

Another new vendor, Return Store, which states it's designed to serve the online and offline merchants and their customers in handling product returns, is slated to debut about the time this book is published. Return Store has announced that it has already contracted to operate from a number of Winn-Dixie Customer Service Centers in 14 states.

According to the Return Stores' brochure, it will have a network of stores conveniently located throughout the US. Customers who have made on-line purchases will be able to visit one of the affiliated locations and return or exchange merchandise or gifts; receive prompt, courteous, friendly and intelligent service; and not be required to package and wrap merchandise for shipment. The Return Store's mission is to adhere strictly to the e-business's return policies. At the time this book went to the printers, you could view a demo of The Return Store at standpipe.com/returnstore/home.htm.

Although reverse logistics is an old industry it brings new opportunities for companies wanting to break into the market of returns management for the e-business community. I give the readers a small sampling of outsourcers that have customized their services for the e-business.

Newgistics (www.newgistics.com) brings to the e-business community and its customers its ReturnValet, a fully integrated returns management system for e-businesses. The system is designed to make it as easy and efficient for customers to return products to e-tailers as it is to return them to a bricks-and-mortar store. Newgistics has assembled a national network of return centers where customers can easily return products they've purchased from e-businesses. With the ReturnValet service, customers receive quick credit, and the face-to-face service they would expect from a bricks-and-mortar.

ReturnValet helps the e-business complete the returns process by consolidating and shipping packages to its centralized processing center that sends returns back in bulk rather than the inefficient process of individual customer returns. The merchandise can be restocked, shipped to a retail outlet, liquidated or disposed of, as specified by the e-business.

ReturnBuy (www.returnbuy.com) offers a leading-edge technology-based process that is touted to net e-businesses more than 60% higher revenues on returned items, expediting payments, and ensuring repeat sales through customer satisfaction and loyalty.

ReturnBuy can handle the entire returns process for an e-business. It's solution is simple — instead of shipping a product back to the e-business, the customer sends the item to a ReturnBuy warehouse. Using its own technology-based process, ReturnBuy then evaluates a product's condition and, if in the proper condition, resells it through a variety of Internet channels. ReturnBuy's take on the returns issue eliminates a substantial part of the traditional supply chain interaction usually necessary with any returned product. Egghead has decided ReturnBuy has the solution to its return quandary. Norm Hullinger, SVP of Sales and Operations for Egghead.com stated just before the 2000 holiday season, "With the holiday season fast approaching, we have engaged ReturnBuy's services to help us process returned products even more efficiently and economically."

ReturnBuy and the aforementioned ReturnCentral have formed a strategic alliance to manage the entire returns process from the time a consumer requests a return authorization through the physical processing of a returned item in preparation for a customer credit or refund. E-businesses can integrate into the Web site ReturnCentral's Virtual Return Desk to give them more control of the returns process.

David Hommrich, founder and CEO of Return Central, pronounces, "By combining our unique front-end solution with ReturnBuy's state-of-the art warehousing technology and returns processing, we can offer a comprehensive solution that manages the entire reverse supply chain efficiently and cost effectively."

ReturnView (www.returnview.com) provides a complete returns management solution designed to facilitate an e-businesses returns process from beginning to end through its suite of services. Upon implementation of its FlexRMA software the e-business's returns are automated, providing the e-business with a solid, updateable and easy-to-communicate return policy, including automated return merchandise authorization processing, inventory tracking and auditing, standard and custom reporting. ReturnView's ServiceNet program eliminates an e-business's overhead involved in physically processing returned product. This includes direct labor, warehousing space, warranty service and customer support needed to receive, inspect, repair (if necessary) and ship the returned product. ReturnView's service centers manage returns according to the e-business's guidelines and operate on its behalf. And finally, ReturnView's CapTrak service resells the products into secondary channels.

In-House

Most e-businesses have yet to work with a returns vendor, and some say they have no reason to. A robust infrastructure that's already in place can make working with a partner unnecessary. Sears.com has all the goods it sells online returnable to its bricks-and-mortar locations, and it has tied its existing systems for managing returns directly to its Web site, according to Dennis Honan, vice president and general manager of Sears Online. Although the Sears method doesn't involve total integration, it has found a way to work within the limitations. If customers lack a receipt or shipping invoice, sales associates at the retailing giant's stores can call a central call center that accesses purchase data across Sears's sales channels to determine whether a refund should be accepted.

United Parcel Service (UPS) thinks it has the solution to the return puzzle. An e-business can use the new Web-enabled version of UPS' Authorized Return Service (ARS) to let customers seeking to return goods print out mailing labels using their own computer and printer. Several e-tailers, including Buy.com, have been testing the ASP system, which should be ready for eager e-businesses the first quarter of 2001.

Andy Tibbs, director of electronic commerce for UPS, told RetailTech.com that online ARS can turn a problem into an advantage. "Returns are a fact of business. They can either be your weakness or your strength," he said. And Tibbs went on to explain that not only can the UPS system save time for customers, it can slash the costs of returns for the e-business while getting goods back into inventory more quickly.

According to RetailTech.com, the Web-based ARS system works this way: When a customer decides to return goods to, say, Iwantcandy.com, he or she logs onto the Iwantcandy.com site and pulls up the customer profile, which is protected by a password. From the buying history, the customer selects the item to be returned. After answering a series of questions (including the reason for the return) the return is either accepted or declined, based on Iwantcandy.com's return policy.

If the return is accepted, the customer's profile is used to generate an XML document and ARS return label. Once the label appears on screen, it can be printed out. Instructions for shipping the goods back are provided, including a hot link to the UPS drop-off locator. In addition to those locations, the package can be given to any UPS driver. And even after the package is sent off, the customer can track the order (using a tracking number from the label) on the Web right up to the time it arrives at its destination.

Both UPS and Buy.com have utilized the system for more than six months and speculate that the savings will be huge. Tibbs estimates that each customer response at a call center costs a minimum of $1.75 (I say $5), while the Web-based system costs mere pennies per use.

Tom Wright, vice president of operations for Buy.com, told RetailTech.com that his company didn't even bother to calculate a ROI before implementing the system. Wright feels that already the savings are more than Buy.com spent. He noted that queries handled by Buy.com's call center fell a significant percentage. Wright also confirmed that Buy.com's costs are more than the $1.75 per call Tibbs estimated. Therefore, call center savings over a full year would be in the "hundreds of thousands of dollars." Also according to Wright, there were no major problems with implementing the system, "it's a pretty darn simple way of handling returns."

Wright admitted that returns for Buy.com are less than half those encountered by most e-tailers — accounting for less than 4% of sales — but the e-business certainly doesn't ignore them. "The perception of customers still makes it important," Wright stated.

Wright noted that Buy.com's customers like the system because it gives them choices of how they want to return a purchase. Customers can still use the old phone-based system, or, through the Web system, can choose how they want to send out the package — taking it to a UPS location or having a driver pick it up.

Buy.com is handling the physical aspects of the returns in-house. Wright confirmed that although the company uses 15 fulfillment partners to create a "virtual supply chain," it decided the best solution for returns was to create a specific returns center. Buy.com did look at other potential partners for the logistics, such as the US Postal Service, but UPS won out, at least partly because most of Buy.com's shipping is done with UPS, making integration of the new system easier. UPS hosts the hardware and software that powers the online ARS system in an ASP arrangement. "This is very significant. Every customer I work with has some type of IT constraints. So we've designed the system so they can implement it quickly," claims UPS's Tibbs.

As Buy.com searched for a solution to its returns problem, the company asked itself, "How do you come up with a returns process that's more elegant and simple than taking goods back to a store?" All pure-plays should pay heed, and pose the same question.

A couple of young start-ups offer ASP solutions for the e-business handling returns inhouse. You may want to check these out:

e-RMA Corporation (www.e-rma.com) provides a set of Web-based return management solutions delivered through an ASP model that can lower an e-business's cost of processing the return of online and offline purchases. Designed for the larger e-business, the e-RMA solutions minimize or eliminate manual handling of returns throughout the supply chain, ensure smooth service for customers, and provide detailed reports on return patterns that e-businesses can use to identify problems.

The e-business can view all return activities and reports from its private Customer Center on the e-RMA Web site. The e-business's customer service representatives or other authorized users can issue a return authorization number, reject the request, request additional information or perform related functions

The e-RMA return management solutions run with any accounting or ERP system, requiring no system integration for basic functionality and offering value-added features when integrated with an e-businesses' legacy ERP system. Using e-RMA's solutions an e-business can customize easy-to-use forms that allow return requests to be submitted over the Internet. The system automatically generates e-mails advising customers of the status of their requests as well as real-time reports on the products, reasons and sources of returns.

The e-RMA solutions can be integrated with an e-business's ERP system, utilizing XML technology. This enables return requests to be screened based on user-defined business rules, return authorizations to be issued without manual intervention, and special promotions or cross-selling recommendations to be offered directly to the customer during the return process. Integration also allows credits and purchase orders for replacement products to be performed automatically by the ERP system when the return is authorized, further reducing manual processing. Return reports can also be customized when full integration is selected.

For the enterprise e-business the e-RMA solutions provide usability by all partners in the supply chain, including manufacturing, fulfillment houses, refurbishment facilities, distributors, resellers and others.

returnrite (www.returnrite.com) is in the process of Web-enabling its returns management system, RMS, to create a seamless B2B return and recovery network for e-businesses including manufacturers and e-tailers of branded consumer products and their asset recovery partners. The RMS system consists of an integrated suite of applications that provide inventory, order fulfillment, process management and financial information. The RMS system seamlessly restores the inventory record into a stand-alone warehouse management system during processing to automate redistribution into primary and secondary markets. Since the applications are table driven, customization is accomplished through simple administrative tasks. The technologies employed to automate the system include an Oracle database, bar-code data collection, RF connectivity for mobile workers, Intel-based stationary workstations, and mobile and stationary bar-code scanning stations. Business rules are defined at the Universal Product Code (UPC) level to insure maximum flexibility and floor control. returnrite offers its system on an ASP basis and supports the technology with complete training, systems preparation and maintenance.

THE BOTTOM LINE

When determining which logistics and fulfillment capabilities should be owned and which should be outsourced, the main issues involved are avoiding service failures and developing a winning strategy in a "profit effective" manner. In doing so the e-business satisfies its customers' order fulfillment needs and delivers acceptable profit margins.

No matter what fulfillment model you go with, remember that the majority of e-businesses are burdened with systems that are designed to move out a pre-manufactured supply of goods to asset-intense stocking locations. Suppliers "push" goods towards customers and then respond to orders.

But when an enterprise adopts an e-business model and goes the full distance with the proper business processes, system upgrades and integration, it can adopt real-time customized interactions throughout the value chain, giving far better information about what the customer wants (customer pull) and what is on hand. Dell is a perfect example of customer pull. Its computers are supplied to meet the individual customer's specifications be it one computer for the author or 200 computers for CMP Publishing. Dell set the standard and in doing so captured the lead in the PC market — through real-time collaboration — allowing its supply chain partners to provide the goods necessary to assemble a computer to individual specifications and ship it on the same day.

Whatever capabilities and infrastructure an e-business puts in place now, it will in all probability, need to evolve over time to a less asset-intense, more IT-intense system. Eventually there will be less emphasis on inventory and more emphasis on a "build-to-order" or

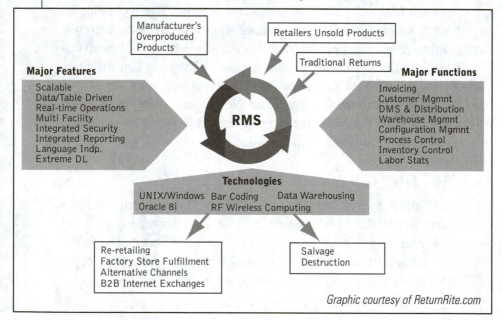

Major Features
Scalable
Data/Table Driven
Real-time Operations
Multi Facility
Integrated Security
Integrated Reporting
Language Indp.
Extreme DL

Major Functions
Invoicing
Customer Mgmnt
DMS & Distribution
Warehouse Mgmnt
Configuration Mgmnt
Process Control
Inventory Control
Labor Stats

Manufacturer's Overproduced Products

Retailers Unsold Products

Traditional Returns

RMS

Technologies
UNIX/Windows   Bar Coding   Data Warehousing
Oracle 8i   RF Wireless Computing

Re-retailing
Factory Store Fulfillment
Alternative Channels
B2B Internet Exchanges

Salvage
Destruction

Graphic courtesy of ReturnRite.com

just-in-time approach, particularly for high-specification items — look at Cisco.

The traditional business model that's been around for years — the supplier-push model — will not ride off into the sunset — the three Staples.com entities: Staples.com, Quill.com, and StaplesLink.com are a good example of that. That e-business group and others will continue to have a healthy supply of inventory on hand at all times to provide the service their customers require.

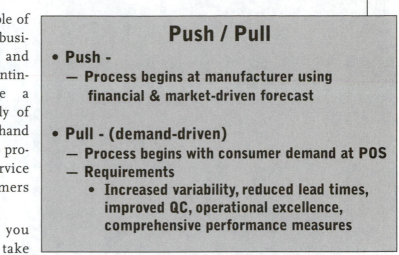

Push / Pull

- **Push -**
  - — **Process begins at manufacturer using financial & market-driven forecast**

- **Pull - (demand-driven)**
  - — **Process begins with consumer demand at POS**
  - — **Requirements**
    - • **Increased variability, reduced lead times, improved QC, operational excellence, comprehensive performance measures**

Whether you decide to take some or all of your logistics and fulfillment operations in-house or outsource them, don't underestimate what will be required or you and your e-business are lost.

Exploiting Logistics and Fulfillment Technology

WHAT TRULY DIFFERENTIATES AN e-business from the rest of the pack is its ability to deliver finished goods faster than its competitors. The only way to do that is to have the value chain's back-end processes in sync with an e-business's Web front-end so it can provide the 3Rs through a fully integrated and implemented LFMS. It's this emphasis on the interconnected e-business commerce value chain that strikes a common chord.

The individual e-businesses need to understand the structural barriers that exist before a viable LFMS can be implemented. The problem is that many enterprises have an IT infrastructure that is hampered by the heritage of its previous traditional business implementations

The E-Business Model Challenges the Value Chain	
Fulfillment Players	Fulfillment Challenges
Suppliers	New channels and customers, tighter demand forecasting and replenishment schedules
Warehousers	More intense operations — labor, equipment, and IT systems, expansion of local warehouse centers
Parcel Delivery Carriers	High growth, electronic integration with customers, new demands for large items and delivery appointments

Source: Norbridge, Inc.

that has grown to a level of complexity which is hard to manage, especially given the speed of change in today's e-business environment. But, automation and technology that are capable of significantly accelerating the implementation of the 3Rs are a must for the e-business model. A cutting-edge system creates seamless connections from the beginning to the end of the order process — order intake, pick-pack-ship, inventory management, and quality assurance such as a built-in bar-code or RFID (radio frequency identification) systems. The viable LFMS combines software, order fulfillment automation and bar-code technology (or its equivalent) in every fulfillment center within the value chain resulting in improved efficiency, high labor productivity and lower production fulfillment costs. Along with that comes the control of value chain member activities such as supplier lead times and shipper performance.

In many of today's enterprises, relevant logistics and fulfillment information is often hours old and can be weeks old when it has finally made it through a traditional value chain's communication network since there can be members that don't have electronic data sharing capabilities. Therefore, an enterprise might find that although it has adopted an e-business model, it still suffers from massive inefficiencies.

In the past enterprises were protected from disconnects through time and inventory buffers. However, with the advent of the e-business model, an enterprise and its value chain need fulfillment processes that are based on the e-business model and its Internet-based connectivity if they are to effectively compete in the new paradigm.

Long-term profitability through efficiencies due to connectivity enabling real-time data sharing and elimination of waste is not the only goal for adopting an e-business model. Causing even more urgency is that the e-business and its supply chain members are finding that their customers have become accustomed to operating at "Internet speed" and are increasingly impatient with poorly synchronized, long lead-time fulfillment processes that provide little flexibility and even less visibility. These Internet savvy customers are increasingly seeking e-businesses that operate on cyber-time, characterized by agile, high-velocity systems and processes.

Anyone can post a product catalog on the Web, but very few will go down the path to the adoption of a Stage Three e-business model where an enterprise can achieve true efficiencies resulting in real cost-savings. This means that today there are only a small number of e-businesses that can create personalized delivery experiences that optimize the flow of goods and information throughout the value chain in a cost-effective manner. However, its quickly changing. Consider the e-business adoption rate taking place in the gigantic "old guard" enterprises — General Electric, Grainer, VF Corp., to name a few.

Before the upsurge of the e-business model, the primary means of systems integration across the value chain was on a point-to-point basis (i.e., bilateral file copying and batch EDI) and most interfaces were hard-coded. This resulted in a long fulfillment cycle and asset gobbling inventory while ERP systems or something even worse produced their typical batch file or paper report — not suitable in the Cyberland environment.

The e-business community and its customers value quickness and speed. Yet, traditional integration architectures and fulfillment systems are a handicap. E-businesses and their value chain have increasingly found that most of the information needed to manage high-speed logistics and fulfillment processes resides in external systems that are often in formats and semantics that cannot be understood by external data gathering applications. This means that the needed data, once received, is often incomplete and dated. Throughout the value chain, members' business processes speak another language and make it next to impossible to dynamically engineer an external relationship due to lack of a shared meaning, data context, or common set of design principles. Then add to that systems that are transaction-oriented based on a monolithic data model focused on the enterprise and the e-business and its value chain has a "cat by the tail" when it comes to integration so as to share information dynamically.

Most legacy systems (many sitting on mainframes) cannot integrate and interoperate in a high-speed Cyberland environment. These same legacy systems are also ignorant of process flows and events-based applications that flow in a value chain context. This means that most legacy systems can't provide the visibility necessary to track the movement of goods and information across the value chain, much less user-defined, exception-based alerting. And just forget about personalized views of relevant information, it won't happen with legacy systems because no matter how much "tweaking," meaningful dynamic e-business-based collaboration with concurrent decision dialogues are impossible.

Knowledge sharing requires changes in processes and technology. Remember that legacy systems were designed to optimize the internal management of an enterprise, not to act as outward-facing applications. Therefore, an e-business and its value chain are compelled to find a way to adopt and implement cutting edge technologies that are architected to be deployed across a value chain in a far-flung high speed environment, allowing cooperation and collaboration. An e-business's and its value chain's systems and processes have to be configurable into numerous, unique client-oriented systems. They need to have the ability to adapt to new and changing product and service demands and thus require a new architecture.

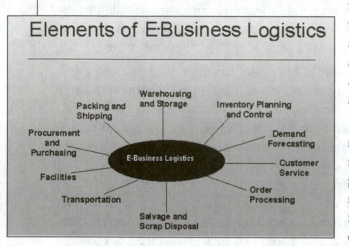

Elements of E-Business Logistics

Today's e-business systems and processes should capture, integrate, analyze, and present information residing in applications and databases toward the four corners of the world and encompass wireless and mobile devices. At the same time these systems and processes need to master the languages and dialects of a distributed computing environment that also incorporates complex, hard-to-predefine business processes and data flow. They also should be designed for real-time data sharing, i.e., as soon as data is received it's immediately available to any other authorized systems and/or users. Thus everything is compelled to be event-based and workflow-enabled — point-of-sale data automatically triggers a purchase order or a shipment release. A proof of delivery can trigger the order processing and financial systems to start their chain of events.

That's just the tip of the iceberg, the e-business-based systems and processes ought to provide an outward-facing view (that is unique for each value chain member) allowing for real-time alert capabilities and management of dynamic and complex business dialogues and integration scenarios that are singular to each member.

Next is the dynamic optimization for the speed to market type planning necessary for many e-business models. An e-business's systems and processes must be designed to integrate with its value chain's systems and needs to be built to embrace external data, processes, and applications. At the same time they need to provide transparency of data and events to authorized value chain members.

Among the technologies that an e-business will need to adopt is an architecture that can accommodate high-speed, multi-source connectivity and supply chain visibility within a dynamic environment. This will enable an e-business to build a high-performance LFMS that can handle both inbound and outbound product flow visibility and real-time decision support capabilities.

Enterprises may note that the new systems and processes required by their e-business model isn't just about connectivity among the value chain, it's also about adding intelligence throughout the value chain, creating new services, new revenue streams, and new efficiencies based on the data exchanged. As the value chain becomes accustomed to shared resources and collaboration, interoperability will be the "business" of e-business.

To manage a value chain in real-time requires an architecture that includes real-time source data collection and advanced e-business integration. Collecting data and dropping it in a pipeline in real-time to authenticated value chain members can ensure a high level of data quality and timeliness. In numerous warehouses, distribution centers and fulfillment facilities, the implementation of wireless devices that can capture data in real-time, through RFID tags, bar-codes, Web forms, and wireless technology, are becoming the norm.

Most importantly, enterprises should realize that Stage Three e-business integration means adding intelligence throughout the value chain, JIT inventory management, giving the value chain visibility that enables everyone to proactively respond to problems before they impact the end customer. For example, real time service failure avoidance, which leads to customer service improvements. Ponder the automobile industry, Cisco, Dell and the semiconductor manufacturers, discussed in this book.

Consider the massive amount of data that can and will be shared between value chain members. Think of the power that ensues when an individual user within the value chain can personalize his/her/its information. A fulfillment and logistics manager may want to know what is being delivered within the next 24 hours so he or she may plan accordingly. A manufacturer may rely on alerts that are received when a crucial product is not going to arrive on schedule, allowing it to reconfigure its assembly line or put in action a search for the goods through other channels. An e-tail customer service department can be kept apprised in real-time of its courier service deliveries. If there is 17 inches of snow in Memphis and the shipper has a main hub there, the customer service department is alerted and can be prepared for an onslaught of calls or send out pre-emptive e-mails. An appliance repairperson can be advised when needed parts are shipped to the customer and can schedule the installation of the part to coincide with delivery.

A world-class LFMS is the command and control center for an e-business and its value chain, enabling the monitoring and control of numerous activities that touch upon one or numerous members within the chain. By utilizing value chain visibility, an e-business and its partners can have real-time visibility into the movement of goods and data across the value chain, synchronizing all of the disparate systems and activities over a neutral data network — the Internet. This is what allows Stage Three e-businesses like Cisco to ship directly from its suppliers' warehouses to its end user.

The vast majority of e-businesses have implemented one system after another in their goal to serve their individual customers. But what these enterprises end up with is a mish-mash of systems, little connectivity, basically no data sharing, and minimal visibility across the value chain.

E-businesses with the capability to adopt a Stage Three model today, can reinvent systems and processes, value chain relationships, create new businesses and revenue streams, and reshape entire industries. The key is to embrace technology that gives connectivity, visibility, and dynamic optimization across the value chain.

Another issue that many executives in and out of the tech field are grappling with is Web commerce deployment — not just an e-business strategy or a Web presence — actual Web-based commerce. Numerous enterprises are still struggling with the decision of whether it's cost effective to use the Web to sell products and provide customer service information to its value chain. Once the decision is made, the tactical question becomes, "How do I set up a Web storefront?"

It's not a simple answer. The answer to this question must consider the range of technology involved if an e-business wants a first-class online commerce offering. Then take a gander at the technology vendors and technology partners that will be necessary for most enterprises to become a true Web-based commerce entity.

A BALANCING ACT

After an e-business has chosen its tech solution provider, the team (the e-business's staff and the tech solution provider's personnel) still has many options and decisions to consider. For example, whether it should build a custom solution, use ERP system vendors or best-of-breed e-commerce software vendors, and/or providers of Web-enabling platforms and development tools. E-businesses will find that their options will range from commerce modules from ERP vendors, to custom building a storefront to everything in between. Even in the face of all the technology choices, an e-business should make technology a secondary consideration. What do I mean? Continue reading and I will explain.

An e-business should keep its focus on customer satisfaction (the 3Rs), and how to best sell products via the Internet. That is why you find the sales and marketing departments intricately involved in most enterprises' online commerce moves. However, there must be a balance between sales and marketing, the executive suite's concern with costs, and the technology department that oversees and manages the implementation. Bob Parker, e-commerce service director for AMR Research (www.amr-research.com), an information technology advisory firm, puts it succinctly, "Once the core business strategies are well thought out, they map back in a fairly straightforward manner to the technologies."

In an interview with Manufacturing Systems (www.manufacturingsys-tems.com), Parker laid out four basic components for a sell-side Web storefront:

- personalization, which is the ability to tailor site content to the interests of individual users

- order/catalog management

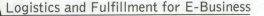
- product configuration

- channel management, which addresses dealer network activities like warranty programs and financing options

Parker opined that the relative importance of any one function ties back to an enterprise's e-business model. For example, for a manufacturer of complex products, Internet-enabled product configuration may be the key storefront component.

Once an e-business understands the components necessary in the Web storefront software it chooses, it then must successfully build out and integrate all back-office systems so there is a serviceable Web-based commerce model. This is where LFM comes into play; however without a fully integrated back-end an e-business cannot implement an LFMS. Effective integration with back-end ERP and legacy systems is why many enterprises pay lots of green to tech partners and vendors so the deployment issues are dealt with effectively. In fact, such diverse enterprises as Cybex International, Boise Cascade, U.S. Electrical Motors and General Electric list effective integration with back-end systems as a key driver in their Web storefront projects. Another issue that all e-businesses consider when deploying a Web storefront is the ability of the tech vendor(s) and partner(s) to quickly implement a solution, while also having the resources to keep up with rapidly evolving Internet technology.

THE BIG GUNS — ERP

In bygone days before the Internet was a household word, the darlings of the business software set wrote mammoth programs to help businesses with various processes such as accounting, human resources, data and inventory management and order tracking. With the ascendancy of these software packages — called enterprise resource planning (ERP) — came the huge enterprises like SAP (www.sap.com), Baan (www.baan.com), PeopleSoft (www.peoplesoft.com), and others to advise, implement and service this technology.

More than 60% of the Fortune 1000 companies have implemented some type of ERP application. The enterprises that bought and implemented these incredibly complex (and often highly customized) ERP tools now find that integrating their systems with their Web sites can be a huge task, but it must be faced and done right or the entire e-business venture will suffer.

Web-based ERP has gained significant attention within the logistics and fulfillment community due to its ability to integrate the databases used by LFMSs and other key business processes. The integrated databases enable various departments to more easily share information and communicate with each other (a necessity for an LFMS to work effectively).

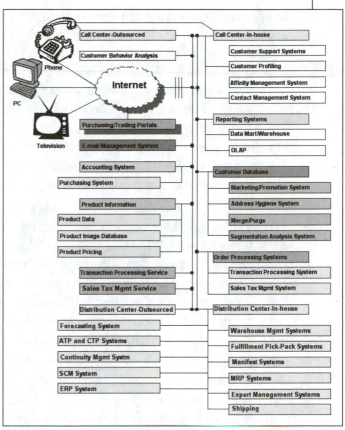

The mapping of a typical best-of-breed e-business back-end systems will look something like this. Notice how the systems necessary for a first-class LFMS link with the other systems.

Logistics managers view Web-based ERP as an opportunity to make better and faster decisions, to more effectively trade-off lower information costs against higher inventory costs, and to reduce information processing costs and cycle times. Estimates of the potential inventory savings achievable through better capacity utilization, compressed cycle time, and reduced inventories range as high as $150 billion in the US alone.

Despite the opportunities, Web-based ERP implementation has posed a major implementation challenge for most e-businesses. A survey by the Standish Group (www.standishgroup.com), an independent research and advisory firm examining enterprises with revenues over $500 million, reported astronomical cost and schedule overruns with ERP systems, not to mention functionality deficit where one in five implementation efforts are scrapped as total failures. The cost of ERP implementation and potential failure can be quite high, as the average total cost of ERP implementation is approximately $15 million with some companies spending more than $100 million. But ERP is here to stay and when integration and implement goes smoothly, it's a wonderful technology. "It's hard to ascribe a value to providing better service to your customers," says Frank Buchheit, electronic commerce business manager of SAP America in defense of ERP.

Today, the same ERP vendors hawk their wares using the new buzzword "Web-enabled." What that means is a browser interface added to a jazzed up ERP system that allows the applications to be accessed via remote Web browsers. However, "functionally they represent little more than a screen scraping of existing ERP applications," at least that is what a report from Zona Research (www.zonaresearch.com), which provides research and strategic consulting for the Internet industry, stated.

Vendors like J.D. Edwards (www.jdedwards.com), SAP and Baan will continue to webify more aspects of their applications as time goes on, businesses will follow suit and plug more of their core business logic into their Web sites. As the e-business community becomes more populated, it becomes increasingly crucial that the legacy back-end systems (including ERPs) achieve full integration with the Web-based systems.

Gartner Group released a report in mid-2000, which indicated that as much as 70% of e-businesses launch a Web site that is *not integrated* with their bricks-and-mortar business processes. In most click-and-mortars Gartner found, "data is being manually pulled out of one system and re-entered into another system. Very few enterprises are even attempting to integrate into ERP systems at this time."

But to have the attitude, "just build a Web site now and we'll worry about back-end integration later" results in poor service, inability to provide the 3Rs and in all probability brand damage and customer disaffection. Not to mention the inability to leverage the e-business model into an efficient cost-saving Web-based enterprise.

A February 8, 1999 article in *The Industry Standard* (www.thestandard.com) provided the shinning example of Antioch (www.antioch.com), a manufacturer of bookplates, bookmarks, journals, diaries, photo albums and scrapbooks. The article pointed out the real savings in overhead that might be

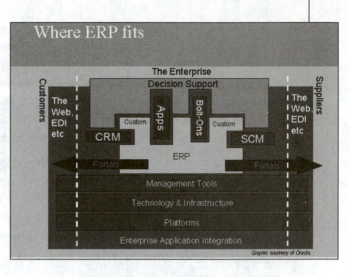

achieved with a Web site that is fully integrated with all of the e-business's processes and systems. Antioch worked with systems integrator, Waterstone Consulting (www.waterstone.com), to integrate its Web site with the SAP R/3 system it uses for managing suppliers, order fulfillment, distribution and shipping. Joe Bly of Waterstone told *The Industry Standard* that 25% of Antioch's orders come from its Web site; and handling those orders requires 25% less staff than those taken through conventional channels thanks to the integration of the online systems with Antioch's ERP systems. And Antioch saved another 15% by having better information about its inventory, reducing the chance that it will unexpectedly run out of items. Additional advantages of fully integrated online and offline systems are that Antioch ships more efficiently, reduces errors and thus achieves greater customer satisfaction in addition to cost savings.

You can find numerous software applications that have been developed specifically to help link elements of an ERP system to a Web site. Look at Ariba's (www.ariba.com) Operating Resource Management System (ORMS) that automates the purchase of supplies and services. For example, Ariba provides links to Cisco's legacy PeopleSoft and Oracle systems, eliminating the need to re-key information. Cisco Systems has linked 16,000 employees to Ariba's ORMS.

Caroline DePalmo, business design manager at Cisco, says, "If there's not a good buying process in place, employees will go out and buy stuff that's too expensive. We have all of our preferred suppliers on the Ariba system (in an extranet). There are tremendous cost savings if you get everybody to buy from discounted providers rather than retail. We now enjoy faster and easier access to information. This makes our company very efficient. That ultimately comes back to the customers and shareholders."

Con-Way, a division of CNF Transportation (www.cnf.com) an outsourcer of warehousing and transportation services for small businesses has taken another approach. As the aforementioned article in *The Industry Standard* pointed out, Con-Way has used its legacy ERP systems to manage order flow, warehousing and billing, a transportation system from i2 Technologies (www.i2.com), and a financial system from Oracle (www.oracle.com).

"We're enabling our customers to have a supplier management and order fulfillment system that they normally could not afford," Tom Ryan, Con-Way's director of technology told *The Industry Standard*. "This will empower them to compete with the top-tier businesses that can normally afford such systems."

Each customer transaction has about 40 interactions, which begin with the initiation of an order and follow through to completion. Multiply the 40 interactions per customer by 200 — 20 warehouses that each support 10 customers — and you have a highly complex business that would be impossible to run without automation.

According to *The Industry Standard*, Con-Way (www.con-way.com) has extended its reach to customers online, through a messaging system, DeliveryNet.com (sold by Descartes), which is a platform for communicating logistical information. Specifically, DeliveryNet enables electronic data interchange (EDI) over the Internet. EDI is a set of standards for transmitting purchase orders, invoices, payments and other trade documents electronically.

The DeliveryNet software plugs directly into Con-Way's ERP software, residing between the company's legacy systems and its Web site. The software translates information from the ERP systems into Internet format, and vice versa. Con-Way says the approach will give customers options they didn't previously have by enabling EDI over the Internet.

Now this network, accessible by Con-Way's customers through DeliveryNet, provides a platform for communicating logistical information. Con-Way expects EDI to be a moneymaker. "Our corporate parent has IT departments ranging from 50 to 300 people, and a large portion of that is directly related to EDI communications," Con-Way's Ryan was reported as saying. "But I have an IT department of three because of this technology. My revenues will equal my investment in the technology," which Con-Way says ran into the millions of dollars.

Linking and integrating a large enterprise's data to e-commerce software can be problematic. Lawrence York, portfolio manager at WWW Internet Fund (www.internetfund.com) told CNETnews.com in March 2000, "There may be over-expectations that a company will be up and running in a quarter or six months. But the task is suddenly monumental when you try to automate and tie back to the data stored."

A groundswell of software development companies and shrewd integrators are marketing back-office applications with tools and hooks that can leverage existing business logic. In this chapter I've attempted to provide the reader with a balanced sampling of the many different types of software, tools, middleware, messyware and applications he or she might want to look into to help bridge the gap between back-office systems (whether current or legacy) and Web-based applications. Such software tools are used to build systems that handle Web transactions, track inventory, or collect other business information.

Even before the Internet explosion, the fastest-growing software companies produced massive programs to help enterprises run critical parts of their business, like accounting, order tracking and human resources. As stated earlier, the rise of these "enterprise resource planning" software packages created huge companies such as PeopleSoft, SAP, J.D. Edwards and Baan. But these four have lots of company. For example, fulfillment processes must be structured to meet the ever-evolving requirements of Internet-based commerce; demanding that many e-businesses take their enterprise optimization software to a Web-based format. This is a major change for many ERP companies using traditional technology; but it must be done in order to increase speed, ease-of-use and to offer integration with e-commerce engines, storefronts, order entry, and LFMSs.

Here are a few examples of vendors an e-business can turn to for guidance as it ventures into Cyberland.

Baan's (www.baan.com) BaanInternet Configuration is a commerce server that's integrated with the vendor's legacy ERP products. Baan's Web strategy also includes development of a new Java-based Web interface for all Baan applications, new workflow-based capabilities, and the creation of a suite of standalone Web applications that can run with any ERP software. Costs are $29,000 per seat, plus an additional $8,500 per concurrent session.

Commerce One's (www.commerceone.com) Commerce Chain solution automates procurement. It consists of BuySite for internal processes and MarketSite for supplier interactions. MarketSite ranges from 25 cents to $2 per transaction. BuySite can cost from around $500,000 to $1 million, depending on the number of users. Singapore Telecom Group deployed Commerce One's BuySite Electronic Procurement Application to all of its major SingTel Group companies for the procurement of goods and services. Commerce One is also the power behind W.W. Grainger's Web-based catalog of MRO supplies.

Descartes's (www.descartes.com) Energy Supply Chain Suite provides an enterprise a clear view of its supply chain. Multi-Marques Inc., the largest wholesale bakery in Quebec, Canada implemented the Energy Suite as a global solution for its order-to-delivery operations in its numerous production facilities and distribution centers. Descartes's Energy Suite is also popular among the soft drink crowd, it's one of Coca-Cola's preferred vendors for automated route planning and fleet vehicle dispatching for the company's bottling divisions and operations worldwide. And Buffalo Rock, one of the largest Pepsi distributors in the US is making good use of the Energy Suite. Pricing begins at $500,000 but varies depending on the number of points of contact with customers.

Industrial & Financial Systems (IFS) (www.ifsab.com) offers its e-business ERP solution that includes Internet-based ERP applications (with 50+ERP modules), plus front-office applications such as CRM. IFS e-business components provide storefront Web kits for do-it-yourself portal creation. "All aspects of the IFS ERP and e-business solutions are fully integrated, providing companies seamlessly integrated front- and back-office operations," states Brian Johnson, chief technology officer. "IFS uses third-generation component technology which makes it easy and cost-effective to add new e-business modules and capabilities that span the entire supply chain. eVolve is an IFS initiative that takes companies step-by-step from their present operations — even if they are using older, legacy systems — to being a full-blown dot.com company, in their own timeframe, by adding the pieces as their business requires them," Johnson interjects. IFS also adds one nice little perk to its repertoire, it understands that many enterprises know they need an e-business strategy, but don't understand how to get from where they are to the world of e-business. As a result, IFS helps educate them, so they can determine what their vital requirements are and what aspects of 'e' technology they don't need yet. IFS's US clients include National Semiconductor Corporation, Gold Eagle Co., Willamette Valley Company and BlueBolt Networks. Pricing was not available.

J.D. Edwards offers 4,000 different ERP modules — grouped into five major suites — all of which are Internet enabled. PlasticsNet.Com told *InformationWeek* (www.informationweek.com) that it chose J.D. Edwards as an ERP partner not only because the vendor offers superior integration tools, but also because of its willingness to work closely with the company to develop interfaces to other systems, such as a proprietary online procurement front-end and a messaging hub that exchanges data with suppliers. "Integration is one of three or four technology pillars of our organization, says Justin Dye, director of operations at PlasticsNet.Com. ERP module pricing was not available. However, keep an eye out for its new offering — OneWorld Xe. Xe stands for extended enterprise — it should be interesting.

Macola (www.macola.com) offers a modular, mixed-mode manufacturing and distribution ERP system and is currently the only ERP vendor that offers Microsoft Visual Basic for Applications (VBA) integrated throughout its product, meaning the ERP system can be customized according to user needs, not developer needs. Cable-Link, Inc. has a legacy Macola ERP system that it is putting on the Web through the help of Fourth-Channel (discussed later in this chapter). "We have a catalog, a listing of all our inventory, that comes out of our Macola ERP system," says company president Brenda Castle. Pricing was not available.

CPN International, manufactures instruments that measure soil density and moisture, and it opted for Macola Software's Progression Series 7.5 to provide the accounting and manufacturing capabilities it needed. Today CPN uses accounts receivable, accounts payable, general ledger, bill of materials, purchase order, inventory management, production order processing and bank book modules that make the inputting of information much less cumbersome. CPN also gets better information out of the system. It can keep track of margins on products more easily and the system has streamlined manufacturing reporting, and bill of materials.

Oracle (www.oracle.com) offers more than 45 modules for financials, human resources, manufacturing, supply chain and front-office automation that are Web enabled. For example, at Micros Systems Inc. (www.micros.com), a supplier of restaurant point-of-sale and hotel-property management systems, an Oracle ERP system offers its 500+ employees and customers a browser-based view to vital business information. Because its customers can see for themselves the ship dates, carrier numbers, even a link to the FedEx page, they are less likely to ask routine questions, points out Micros Systems CIO Robert Moon. "In less than three years, we've gone from the Web being a novelty to a critical application. It's now our main focus, adds Moon." Oracle pricing was not available.

PeopleSoft's 100+ ERP applications have all been reinvented for the Internet to make them accessible anytime, anywhere through a Web browser. In addition, PeopleSoft 8 includes 59 new e-business applications and is an upgrade to its flagship ERP suite with a completely reworked code base. The result is purely browser-based applications that a company spokesperson says can improve the ease of use and deployment. The JPM Co. (www.jpmco.com), a manufacturer of cable assemblies and wire harness for OEMs, selected PeopleSoft Global Manufacturing System to facilitate the integration of its numerous worldwide manufacturing facilities as well as remote sales, engineering, and distribution locations. Green Mountain Coffee Roasters, Wisconsin Technical College and even the US Mint are among PeopleSoft users. Costs run about $100,000 per module.

QAD's (www.qad.com) MFG/PRO Web-enabled core enterprise software provides midsize and multinational companies with full-function, integrated solutions that include manufacturing, distribution, and financial applications within an open system environment. It's available in 26 languages and can support multiple currencies including the Euro. MFG/PRO also supports centralized, client/server, and thin-client configurations. In addition, QAD offers e-business software solutions that enable companies of all sizes to acquire raw materials, transform them into top-quality products, and deliver them to customers within the shortest possible time. A.G. Simpson Automotive Systems, Inc., a leading supplier of bumper systems, metal formed products, and related metal processing services in North America chose QAD's products to support its aggressive international expansion. Add to that A.G. Simson's introduction of new products and processes, such as laser welded blanks and value-added services and QAD had a job on its hands. Today, A.G. Simpson is among a growing list of full-blown Second Stage e-businesses.

Brocade Communications Systems Inc., a leading storage-area-network (SAN) gigabit switch provider needed to replace its nonscalable ERP system, and to integrate disparate applications running off-line. "We chose QAD because of its short implementation cycle time and the breadth of business processes supported by QAD," said Carl Lee, Brocade's chief financial officer. MFG/PRO replaced our current system in three months, one month sooner than originally planned. Excellent consulting support from Ernst & Young, L.L.P., helped us achieve the short implementation time," Lee eulogized.

With MFG/PRO, Brocade was able to integrate its sales orders, inventory control, shipping and receiving, manufacturing, and purchasing functions. Within a month after implementation of MFG/PRO Brocade had accelerated the order cycle time and shortened its month-end close. QAD's MFG/Pro pricing starts at around $4200 per seat and an average installation will cost around $260,000.

SAP's R/3 line of products has been Web enabled since 1996. The 600-module suite includes procurement, supply chain management, human resources, accounting and Web development. SAP's clients include the Universities of Nebraska and Toronto, the Cities of Alberta and Phoenix, and numerous Fortune 500 companies. Pricing varies widely, but for $2 million you can get a 1,000-user installation, with

400 of them active, 400 read-only and the remaining 200 as enterprise office users.

SCT Corp. (www.sctcorp.com) is an ERP vendor that offers a suite of B2B e-commerce applications including Web-based order entry. But it offers products that also allow users to drill down to quality and catch-weight data. This enables customers to adjust plans based on the characteristics of actual shipments, not just on due date information. SCT's documentation states that it has 2500 clients in 34 countries. Pricing was not available.

For the companies that buy them, implementing these incredibly complex ERP programs is a long, painful process. Integrating the systems with Web sites can be equally difficult.

Here is a real life example: Suppose a customer bought something online, only to be told 24 hours later that the item was out of stock. That problem unfolded recently at the online store run by the apparel company J. Crew when orders jumped so sharply that the e-business couldn't keep up. Brian Sugar, media director at J. Crew, said the problem stemmed from the way orders moved from the Web into the mainframe. "The actual count that we think we have in our supply bins might be different than what the mainframe thinks it is," Sugar admitted. "We get thousands of items in stock, and it's easy to miscalculate." Sugar confessed that the J. Crew Web site was not connected to the mainframe in real-time, nor does it have electronic integration with its suppliers, distributors and shippers.

According to Sugar, J. Crew's "ERP software isn't integrated with the site. The same thing happens in [our] mail order and direct marketing — and that piggybacks online." Sugar admits that integrating the company's ERP system with the Web — a process that could cost up to $1 million — isn't a high priority. Notwithstanding its recent order snafu — Sugar feels the site's order-taking failure rate is minimal.

J. Crew's attitude about Webifying its core ERP applications is typical. Up to 70% of traditional enterprises that launch a e-tail or B2B site haven't integrated their "click" with their "bricks" business processes. There are many e-business executives fooling themselves — they have not achieved an e-business model.

When an enterprise makes the decision to build a Web site now and worry about back-end integration later, they take a huge risk. The results of such a foolhardy decision will not only negate the substantial cost-savings that an e-business model can bring to an enterprise, it most likely will end in poor service, damage to an established brand and the likelihood of customers flocking to the competition — online and offline.

LINKING ERP SYSTEMS

A recent study by Cambridge Technology Partners (www.ctp.com) found that many IT executives expect their ERP systems to drive new revenue and business. Cambridge research reveals enterprises believe they will derive value from their expensive ERP installations. "Our study shows users are implementing ERP backbones and are now extending them," says Sandy Strauss, a vice president in Cambridge's ERP practice. Almost one-third of the executives interviewed plan to integrate their ERPs with e-commerce systems. After all, "overall, the ERP market boom is over," says Strauss. The focus now will be on e-commerce systems and decision support systems that will use ERP back-ends. The front-end solutions will come from the traditional ERP vendors and an exploding market of Internet-savvy entrepreneurs.

There is a burgeoning third-party industry of add-ons to Webify traditional ERP systems, offering systems ranging from e-commerce, supply-chain automation, sales-force automation and customer relationship management. The common ground is that they all interface with ERP back-ends. For example, the previously mentioned Ariba's Operating Resource Management System automates the purchase of supplies and services and can link legacy PeopleSoft and Oracle systems.

Enterprise application integration (EAI) specialists insist ERP vendors lack one quality they say is essential to the integration game: neutrality. "What is impossible for an ERP vendor to supply is independence," says Kate Mitchell, senior VP of marketing and business development at STC (www.stc.com), a global provider of e-business integration solutions.

Mitchell says STC has a library of more than 500 adapters for mainstream applications, including those from Baan, Oracle, PeopleSoft, SAP, and Siebel Systems. STC sees its job as connecting any and all applications. Whereas ERP vendors, Mitchell says, will naturally put their products at the center of any project. Fred Meyer, VP of product management at Tibco (www.tibco.com) pipes in, "We are the Switzerland of software companies; we work with everybody."

TIBCO Software Inc. is one of the leading providers of real-time e-business infrastructure software. TIBCO's product line enables e-businesses to integrate their enterprise applications, interact with other e-businesses

---

ENTERPRISE APPLICATION INTEGRATION (EAI) IS THE INTEGRATION OF BEHIND-THE-SCENES SYSTEMS.

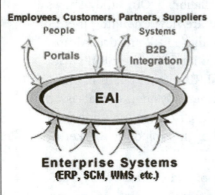

The first benefit of EAI is that it makes businesses more efficient by letting internal applications work together and automating routine processes.

The second benefit of EAI is that it improves the way businesses interact with the outside world by enabling interactive portals and B2B connections.

Graphic courtesy of Tibco Software, Inc.

---

and efficiently deliver personalized information through their corporate portals. TIBCO's patented technology, The Information Bus, or TIB enables the real-time distribution of information. The TIB technology was first used to digitize Wall Street and has since been adopted in diverse industries including telecommunications, e-business, manufacturing and energy. TIBCO has a global client base that includes Cisco Systems, Yahoo!, Ariba, NEC, 3Com, Sun Microsystems, GE Capital, Philips, AT&T, Pirelli and AOL/Netscape.

Unfortunately, for many e-businesses the ROI in ERP integration, upgrade and Webifying will vary widely given the limitless diversity that can be found in the software. Cybex International, a manufacturer of fitness equipment, installed its ERP vendor's eStore module as its Web commerce solution. And, along with the PeopleSoft eStore Cybex also installed PeopleSoft's Supply Chain Management application to enable contact

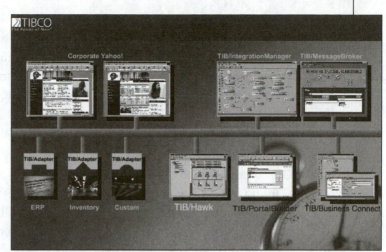

Tibco in acton. *Graphic courtesy of Tibco.*

management, demand management, supply chain planning, replenishment, Web-based selling, and other functions that helps Cybex manage its value chain. Cybex customers can log onto its Web site to place and track orders, get status information on accounts and shipments. Internally, visibility has improved enterprise-wide, and planning and forecasting have improved. Prior to the upgrade, data and reports were kept and held by individual managers, which reduced collaboration.

Thor Wallace, Cybex's CIO, declared PeopleSoft's ability to demonstrate effective back-end integration was a major factor in going with eStore and other PeopleSoft modules. "The customer self-service aspect of the project hinges on being able to securely expose information from the ERP database. Based on this requirement, we did a risk assessment of who could integrate ERP system information best, and there was no one more qualified than the ERP vendor in doing that."

Fourth-Channel Inc. (www.fourthchannel.com) is one of dozens of companies offering Web-to-ERP systems. Fourth-Channel's software is a Web and application server for supply chain management. CableLink launched a Web site selling refurbished cable TV equipment worldwide that was built by Fourth-channel Inc. Fourth-Channel has formed alliances with a number of ERP vendors, including J.D. Edwards, Macola Software and

QAD. "People are finding that ERP vendors cannot do this fast enough," says Fourth-Channel president Jonathan York. "Also, when you extend these business systems beyond the firewall, the user interface and the usability become much more important." It charges an up-front fee of $25,000 to $35,000, plus ongoing software management fees. Or the software can be installed for a flat fee of $50,000.

In an *Information Week* article, VF Corp. said it turned to a middleware specialist to tie together its various SAP, i2 Technologies and Logility systems. "Our approach is to choose the vendors that are best at what they do," says John Davis, VP of supply chain at VF. The ERP vendors "should do more to make their products more open and be willing to cooperate with other vendors that are represented in their installed base." VF uses integration tools from New Era of Networks (www.neonsoft.com) to manage the complex interconnections required to take and fulfill orders as well as replenish its customers' supplies.

Working with ERP Vendors and their Partners

The ERP Vendors are proud of their products and support them wholeheartedly. Baan and Oracle say EAI vendors such as STC and Tibco fill a different niche — they offer integration tools for their own applications. "We're in the business of selling apps that integrate very well with both Baan and non-Baan apps," says Rocky Gunderson, senior VP of product management at Baan.

Oracle is friendly with the EAI crowd. It incorporates application adapters from STC and Mercator's (www.mercator.com) data transformation product to round out its own offering. It also maintains a close relationship with EAI provider Vitria Technologies, Inc. (www.vitria.com), named one of *Business Week's* "New Software Whizzes."

According to *Information Week*, Baan customer, Phillips Plastics Corp., a manufacturer of industrial molded plastics, found that tools to ease ERP integration couldn't come soon enough. The company worked with consultants to tie its Baan manufacturing and accounting suite to custom-built bolt-ons, PeopleSoft payroll and human-resources applications, a quality-control package, and an EDI suite from Harbinger (now a part of Peregrine Systems) (www.peregrine.com). Craig Mey, VP of manufacturing services at Phillips, voiced concern that the more custom coding and third-party interfaces he adds to the Baan deployment, the harder it will be upgrade the suite. "If there were tools to ease that and help us stay on top of the upgrade path, we'd certainly look at them," Mey told *Information Week*.

SAP, PeopleSoft and J.D. Edwards have integration strategies to improve the routes in and out of their applications rather than introducing new middleware tools to the market. "We have no intention of selling EAI tools," says Robert Res, director of e-business technology at SAP. "It's partnering we're interested in, because the EAI market is already well-established." J.D. Edwards, PeopleSoft, and SAP are working industriously to make their systems interoperate more easily with third-party software, focusing for the most part on adding more APIs and building support for standard messaging formats such as COM/DCOM, CORBA, and XML into their software.

Whether ERP vendors can address an e-business's integration needs may depend on how central ERP is to the enterprise. 3Com's (www.3com.com) chief technology architect, Klaus Schultz, says ERP may not be at the heart of every operation and remains unconvinced that ERP providers can offer truly independent middleware to such companies. "ERP vendors are all making a mistake by trying to fill niches that other companies already do really well."

CPFilms (www.cpfilms.com), a manufacturer of window treatment films, deployed a B2B Web storefront application designed for use with MFG/PRO, the ERP system from QAD. Its e-commerce software package — Trading Partner Transactions (TPT) — from ISS Group (www.iss.net) is what allows CPFilms to give its distributors near-instant access to ERP system information, and manage their orders on-line.

A key benefit of the site is an MFG/PRO module that processes customer releases using a set of scheduled shipment dates and quantities, rather than discrete sales orders. "In the past, distributors would fax or phone-in with changes. For one distributor, there might be 50 changes, resulting in the need to generate 50 orders. By Web-enabling customer schedules, distributors will be able to modify what they want, when they want to," says Tony Morgan, CPFilms' IT manager. "They also will have access to inventory levels, and can check their invoices and statements. This should greatly reduce customer-service overhead."

When CPFilms adopted an e-business model, it did so because, as Morgan so aptly put it, "the Web will free our order fulfillment team to work more closely with distributors to identify which products sell best, and to help them build up markets for our products. For our distributors, the Web will bring them closer to relevant information, and empower them to control their orders, order more products if they wish, and more clearly see what's going on in the market."

ISS Group built TPT using Progress Webspeed, a Web-based transaction development environment from Progress Software (www.progress.com), a database vendor. Webspeed provides the transaction management function that sits between the Web server and the back-end ERP database connecting the two. "CPFilms runs MFG/PRO on a Progress database, making the use of Progress technology naturally," says Morgan. "ISS developed TPT with MFG/PRO in mind, and it's built with Progress technologies, so it doesn't seem at all like a foreign layer of software," he adds. "Besides, I'm a bit suspect of an ERP vendor trying to develop everything itself."

Best-of-Breed Vendors

If an enterprise finds itself stuck with back-office systems that don't have a vendor-specific "Web fix," they can look to the hordes of new tech firms that are making inroads into back-office applications. Many have nifty software tools that can leverage existing business logic to bridge the gap between the back-office and the Web.

Listen to what Dave Patterson, CEO of FutureNext Consulting (www.next-future.com), an IT consulting firm, told ManufacturingSystems.com: "ERP vendors' Web storefront capabilities generally aren't as advanced as those from best-of-breed vendors. Today, you get meat-and-potatoes e-commerce capabilities from ERP vendors. If you believe e-commerce is a strategic part of what your company is and does; then your company is more likely to cross into needing a best-of-breed solution."

IBM WebSphere Commerce Suite (formerly IBM Net.Commerce) allows an e-business to take their online presence beyond buying and selling to effectively and efficiently create a dynamic e-marketplace that reduces sourcing and transaction costs. Thus leveraging relationship marketing, streamlining purchasing processes and integrating the Web site with back-office systems such as inventory, order processing and shipping (i.e., an LFMS).

Infobank (www.infobankinc.com) specializes in providing products for Web-based procurement and delivery systems. Its InTrade commerce system for B2B Web-based transactions provides an end-to-end online commerce solution using Web-based technologies to integrate purchasing, electronic catalogues and back-office systems, enabling e-businesses to significantly reduce supply and process costs as well as simplify their value chain.

Intershop's (www.intershop.com) Enfinity is a complete XML-and-Java-based, sell-side online commerce application that offers advanced selling features tightly integrated with existing business systems, while providing the extensibility to grow into a rapidly evolving e-commerce business model. Intershop avers that Enfinity's pipeline architecture and support for industry standards including Java and XML, can give an e-business the tools to sell anywhere, integrate everything, today and tomorrow.

Ironside Technologies Inc. (www.ironsides.com) is a leading supplier of sell-side B2B commerce solutions for the manufacturing and wholesale distribution market. Ironside Solutions include the Ironworks product suite and the Ironside Network service offering. The Ironworks suite provides an e-business's value chain sophisticated transaction and order-management capability while integrating into existing enterprise business logic to deliver real-time information.

Ironside provided the central component for Cacique's, an industry-leading Hispanic cheese manufacturer, online strategy. John Cotcher, Cacique's director of information technologies eulogized, "Ironside provided the leading-edge technologies, proven industry experience and strong partnerships to ensure that [we have] a rapid and successful implementation. Any e-commerce initiative that touches our mission-critical enterprise systems must be bullet-proof. Ironside has proven that it can rapidly deliver a best-of-breed e-commerce solution without disrupting our business."

Ironside's system will reside on Cacique's AS/400 server, tightly integrating with Marcam's (www.marcam.com) PRISM ERP system. Ironside's application-level integration taps directly into Cacique's ERP system's existing business logic, rather than data, ensuring that information is always current and consistent with the enterprise system. Thus allowing Cacique customers to place orders and conduct inquiries online, with full access to current pricing and inventory information — everything that a world-class LFMS should offer.

Derek Smyth, a senior vice president with Ironside Technologies, says the fundamental difference between Web-enabled ERP modules, and a true Web storefront solution, is that storefronts bring together several functions. "There should not be one log-on for order status checking, and another to check accounts receivable information, and yet another site to go to for parcel tracking. Companies moving to the Web should look for a solution that allows them to provide access to all key functions within one consistent user interface."

NetVendor's (www.netvendor.com) software solution enables manufacturers and distributors to manage their online customer relationships. The E.MBRACE solution enables manufacturers and distributors to streamline sales and distribution channels within new and existing markets. It addresses the unique business requirements of enterprises with broad product offerings, multiple sales and distribution channels, and complex products. For example, suppliers can offer their customers real-time, 24 x 7 access to their products, services, and people. Customizable interfaces, simple navigation, configure-to-order, design-to-order, and advanced search capabilities make it easy and convenient to do business.

E.MBRACE is the Web-based commerce solution that DESA International, a manufacturer of zone heating and specialty power tool products, chose when it decided to provide Web-based customer service support to its dealer network, and allow on-line ordering of service parts. DESA's reasoning was very simple as Jake Miller, DESA's vice president of materials and systems points out, "With the first wave of cold weather, we get a lot of technical service calls, service parts orders from customers without EDI, and customers calling with questions. The e-commerce solution will relieve some of the pressure on our technical support personnel, as well as on our parts service department."

There must be properly integrated systems if a fail-safe LFMS is to be introduced and E.MBRACE offers that and more. E.MBRACE can enhance an e-business's current services by supplying its customers with self-service access to their orders and accounts 24 x 7 with real-time status on their orders and credit. E.MBRACE provides a single point of contact for order management and status, fulfillment support, information access, and help facilities as part of its complete supplier enablement solution.

E.MBRACE provides the Web user interface, search mechanisms and tools for security and integration to DESA's homegrown, AS/400-based enterprise system and passes Web-based transactions to DESA's ordering processes to avoid re-keying service parts orders. Although E.MBRACE does support a full-blown e-tail solution, DESA states that it isn't looking to circumvent its established selling channels.

Yantra Corporation's (www.yantra.com) PureEcommerce solution delivers a scalable online commerce operations platform that results in a superior buyer and seller experience, flawless execution, decreased operational costs and increased profitability. A Yantra spokesperson brags that PureEcommerce's "scalability, extensibility and real-time inventory management capabilities will drive significant competitive advantage."

The PureEcommerce solution offers an infrastructure that connects and manages the critical elements of the Web-based transaction lifecycle. It manages complex transactions between sellers, suppliers, distribution centers, drop-ship vendors, logistics providers, shipping companies, value-added services and the buyer. At the same time it can deliver real-time transaction visibility, continuous workflow, and business rules management that will allow greater efficiencies in completing the e-commerce transaction. All of which is necessary for a viable LFMS.

Linking the LFMS

Some ERP vendors point out (and rightly so) that e-commerce solutions could fall short if they can't drill-down to customer-specific pricing information, or integrate with a feasible LFMS. "In process industries, customers want to know more than the status of a shipment, they may want exact information about quality, or catch weight," says Michael Taylor, a vice president with ERP vendor SCT.

With vendors like SAP continuing to Webify more aspects of their applications it's hopeful that enterprises will follow suit and plug more of their core business logic into a Web-based system allowing for a meaningful LFMS. Yet, as demonstrated throughout this book, enterprises are continuing to launch and operate Web sites that don't have real-time communication with core applications in their bricks-and-mortar's back-office — purchasing, manufacturing, inventory, sales, shipping, accounting and human resources (everything it takes to have a viable LFMS). (Notice I said "enterprises" not "e-businesses".) In the 1990s many enterprises took pains to integrate all of their systems into one large, customized package. As previously discussed, the makers of these "customized packages" are releasing Web-enabled versions of their wares. For enterprises to hold a full membership in the e-business club, they must dish out the moola to fully integrate. How they do it is up for grabs.

Another way enterprises use the Internet to achieve supply chain efficiencies is through specialized Web-based logistics and fulfillment packages. ShopLink Inc. (www.shoplink.com), a $14 million online grocery delivery service in metropolitan Boston, has installed an Internet-based logistics and routing tool from Descartes Systems Group Inc. to bring efficiencies and knowledge sharing capabilities to its supply chain. This software enables ShopLink to confidently offer on-time and accurate delivery as well as a personalized shopping experience.

"We are judged by our customers in fairly simple ways — if we deliver on time and if we deliver 100% of the products ordered," says John Icke, chairman and CEO of ShopLink. Eighty percent of ShopLink's customers place a weekly order averaging $100. Web-based supply chain management is a key tool that ShopLink uses to satisfy its customers and to keep logistics and fulfillment costs within reason.

Descartes' DeliveryNet.Home fulfillment package, customized for a home-delivery business enables ShopLink to optimize routes, prevents drivers from getting lost and performs dynamic scheduling to reroute deliveries, due to traffic congestion or inclement weather.

There's more — ShopLink embraced the whole enchilada. About the time this book hits the shelves it should be installing handheld, wireless devices in all its trucks which will let its drivers tap into its central Oracle databases. This will allow them to access key customer information such as delivery preferences as well as input fresh data including additions such as which household has a new baby or pet, this enables ShopLink's staff to suggest additional targeted products and services (maybe an industrial size box of paper towels!). "The new products will help us improve operational efficiencies, but they also provide us with a broader set of tools to gain customer intimacy," explains Icke.

The desire for effective back-end integration has led some e-business-bound enterprises to go back to their original ERP vendors for logistics and fulfillment solutions — US Electrical Motors (www.usmotors.com) is a good example. "The main advantage of going with an ERP vendor's solution is that you can be fairly sure the integration to the back-end system is in place," said a spokesperson for US Electrical Motors, a division of Emerson Electric Co. that manufactures motors, gears, and drives. Consequently, US Electrical Motors' distributors can access real-time inventory information and place online orders. Today, according to a US Electrical spokesperson, they sell a significant portion of their products through their online channel. "Our fundamental strategy is to make it easier for existing customers to do business with us, and reduce our support costs."

Datasweep Advantage (www.datasweep.com) a Web-based supply chain management tool is aimed at enterprises in build-to-order/just-in-time industries such as high tech and telecommunications. These industries build highly customized products and rely heavily on contract manufacturers. According to the vendor, the Datasweep tool suite replaces existing pencil-and-paper shop-floor systems or client/server applications, giving e-businesses a browser-based, real-time window into what's happening on their own shop floor as well as on those of their key suppliers. These tools are designed to improve time to market, flexibility, collaboration, and ultimately — customer service. "The trend of build-to-order, customized manufacturing is breaking existing shop-floor or legacy systems, which were set up to build 1,000 units, not to track custom units across an extended supply chain," explained Matt Holleran, Datasweep's vice president of marketing.

For example, Datasweep tracks work orders at the unit level for individual customers in real-time. It can flag and manage product shortages, manage change orders and provide "as built" records to all parties in the value chain to control quality, and also monitor production throughout the product's lifecycle.

The software incorporates an integrated data mart to filter data into leading ERP and advance planning software such as those from i2 Technologies and SAP. Datasweep, built on Microsoft Corp.'s DNA (Distributed interNet Architecture) for manufacturing platform, works with Microsoft SQL Server 7.0 or Oracle 8.0.

Acma Computers Inc. (www.acmacomputers.com), a custom computer systems manufacturer, tapped the Datasweep suite to improve on-time delivery to customers and track and analyze quality information during the production cycle. Since implementation of the software Acma heralds some very impressive numbers. It has increased on-time delivery of custom units from 78% to 96% and improved final test quality from 90% to 97%, as Allen Lee, Acma's president noted.

Rentway Limited (a division of Trimac Corp.) (www.rentwayltd.com), a truck leasing and fleet management consulting company, is leveraging its deployment of Descartes' EasyRouter Web-based routing and scheduling software as a new business service. Customers with such *cutting-edge equipment* as a browser and a phone line can tap into the tool to dynamically route their leased vehicles. Rentway then charges the customer a monthly fee for the software for each truck along with a transaction fee each time a route is optimized.

"By offering the Descartes system, we've gone from a 'narrow service offering' to 'broadening our footprint of influence.' That differentiates us from competitors in the leasing area, adds tremendous value to existing clients and provides us with an additional revenue stream," explains Scott McRorie, national business development manager for Rentway.

SMTC Manufacturing Corp.'s (www.smtc.com) use of WebPlan's (www.webplan.com) e-Supply Chain suite is key in how it promotes itself to its high-tech customers like Dell Computer Inc. SMTC produces circuit boards and other components that manufacturers use to assemble finished goods configured to their customers' specifications and thus is a major outsourcing partner for many high-tech firms. This enables Dell and other customers to work within build-to-order and just-in-time models, which is more cost efficient than maintaining inventory.

For example, one e-Supply Chain module, the OrderIT Web-based tool, allows SMTC's customers to "peer" into its factories to check on the status of orders, which in turn allows SMTC to provide better information to its customers. At the same time the supply chain can access SMTC's master production schedule enabling everyone to better respond to dynamic customer demand. Soon SMTC will require its suppliers to use WebPlan's SupplyIT module so all customers can have the same visibility into SMTC's extended supply chain. "We're aiming to be the supply chain integrator for our customers. The Web-based initiative is truly to integrate customers so they can talk to us and our suppliers in a quick, reactive fashion," said Phil Woodard, SMTC's senior vice president of enterprise development and integration.

In October 2000, J.D. Edwards unveiled its OneWorld Xe line of products that allows enterprises to easily connect to diverse systems built by other makers. J.D. Edwards' OneWorld Xe products and XPI technology, which focuses on products that allow enterprises to integrate buying and selling, not only integrates different systems within an enterprise, but also hooks into the various applications of other makers. In this way, enterprises can pick and choose the best software applications and connect them without concern that they might not work together.

Gordon Food Service (GFS) (www.gfs.com), an enterprise ranked 71 on the *Forbes* Private 500 list in 2000, chose Manugistics' supply chain solutions (www.manugistics.com) when it decided it was time to optimize the distribution of its inventory to not only 70 retail stores but also schools, hospitals and restaurants. With the implementation of the Manugistics suite of products, GFS maintains customer service levels of over 98% while meeting the needs of seasonal patterns for customer product demand. Additional savings were achieved through improvements in inventory visibility, turns, mix planning, exception management and distribution center-to-vendor communications. "Manugistics is an integral part of our growth and logistics strategy," said Scott Hicks, business process manager at GFS. "Manugistics helped us to improve our distribution and logistics processes to 'best practice' allowing us to be more responsive to customer demands in very competitive food service channels."

E-COMMERCE PLATFORMS

A growing number of ERP vendors are using e-commerce platforms such as the Site Server 3.0 Commerce Edition from Microsoft and WebSphere from IBM. For example, PeopleSoft's eStore is built on the e-commerce capabilities of Site Server, rather than built from scratch.

ClearCommerce (www.clearcommerce.com) provides e-businesses with transaction payment, processing and reporting technology with advance technology and safe practices that give e-businesses a more secure marketplace in which to operate. Along with Visa and Mastercard, ClearCommerce spearheads the Secure Electronic Transaction (SET) initiative to develop security standards for credit card transactions online. The ClearCommerce Merchant and Hosting Engine system provides online customer credit card authorizations, order and payment processing, automated tax and shipping calculations, order tracking and status and internet fraud detection devices. *Information Week* says the company's "Internet StoreManager is a breeze to run for the non-technical user." *Internet Computing* picked ClearCommerce a "Net Best" because, "of its powerful fraud protection module, extensive sales reporting features, SNMP support, along with APIs that link to fulfillment and accounting databases."

Cyclone Commerce Inc. (www.cyclonecommerce.com) provides an open platform for "instant-on" B2B commerce. Cyclone's products are Java-based trading engines that joins an e-business's business processes over the Internet in a way that is fully transparent — platform, database, translator, and security-framework independent. "This allows companies to form, join, and manage dynamic trading communities with their suppliers, partners, and customers with unprecedented speed," explains David Bennett, founder and chief technology officer of Cyclone. Its Cyclone Interchange is available in two editions — one for organizations with multiple trading relationships and another for those with single-partner trading.

Great Plains Software (www.greatplains.com) (now a part of Microsoft) offers a comprehensive e-business solution that tightly integrates with a back-office engine. Lynne Stockstad, vice president, brags, "it will transform all the key business processes within a business across managing, selling, purchasing, and servicing." Great Plains delivers a host of e-commerce solutions for a wide-range of customers with all kinds of pocket books. The company also offers a number of self-service solutions, including e.Requisition, e.Employee, and e.Service Center. Their e-commerce solutions offer an end-to-end process for selling goods and services through a Web storefront by integrating critical information, such as item names, pricing, availability and customer information, into the process.

Hitachi's (www.hitachi.com), TradeLink is a global electronic commerce suite that includes its ERP Back-end Legacy Module. The TradeLine Internet Commerce Software is a modular package of software products, which provide a complete solution to enterprises wishing to adopt an e-business model. TradeLink provides one-to-one marketing capabilities and is designed to expand existing sales channels, while offering integration with legacy and ERP applications. Each module costs from $15,000 to $40,000; the average implementation costs $100,000, depending on the items selected.

i2 Technologies (www.i2.com) is the leading provider of supply chain optimization and intelligent e-business solutions. Its RHYTHM Customer Management is a comprehensive, scalable solution that enables intelligent e-business transactions by tying together front-end electronic commerce functionality with Internet-based demand fulfillment capabilities. Customer Management not only integrates workflow across different functional silos, different geographies and multiple enterprises, but also provides extensive customization and personalization capabilities. Its customers include Frito-Lay, Lipton, E&J Gallo Winery, The Andrew Jergens Company, Johnson and Johnson Medical, 3M, and Whirlpool.

IBM's (www.ibm.com) new platform, WebSphere, is a lot more than just an e-commerce platform. It includes development tools and

Commerce Integrator — a piece of middleware that connects Web store-fronts to back-end systems — and delivers more than 60 discrete application components, according to Dave Liederbach, an IBM vice president. He told ManufacturingSystems.com that "we deliver application code in the context of [WebSphere]. If you want to move quickly in deploying search functions, integrated ordering and payment management, or customer registration and tax calculation, there is a fair amount of these functions that you get right out of the box."

Service Graphics Inc. (SGI) (www.servicegraphics.com), a distributor of marketing materials that also performs kitting and light assembly work, is using WebSphere as the basis for a B2B Web storefront. For instance, Steelcase, a dealer of office furniture manufacture, uses the site to order marketing materials. Although SGI initially built its online presence using a freeware development tool; due to rapid growth and other circumstance, it became necessary to rebuild. SGI opted for WebSphere to facilitate the rebuild. Forrest Adam, SGI's CIO said, "we wanted to go with an e-commerce application with some support behind it, and IBM and its partners certainly provide that. It also integrates with our back-end system better than the previous technology we used, and provides more pre-built features."

Logility's (www.logility.com) Voyager Solutions suite version 5.4 for B2B commerce includes two new Internet-based applications. The first is Logility Voyager XPS (eXtensible Planning Solution), which enables a value chain to collaborate on sales forecasting and replenishment plans. The second is Logility Voyager XES (eXtensible Execution Solution) that allows viewing of processes such as order status, purchase order payment status, load tendering and freight payment over the Internet. The latest release also includes enhancements to Demand Chain Voyager, Inventory Planning and Replenishment Planning, Manufacturing Planning, WarehousePro, Transportation Planning & Management and Spreadsheet Import.

Netfish Technologies, Inc. (www.netfish.com) is a leading supplier of XML-based B2B commerce solutions, and highly scalable XML-based B2B integration solutions. Its products provide a complete end-to-end B2B solution that enables automation of a wide spectrum of business processes ranging from procurement and order fulfillment to billing and payment. Netfish products and solutions can be found in use by some of the world's top e-businesses — Cisco Systems, NTT Communications and Sun Microsystems — to enable B2B commerce within their value chain. Netfish Technologies supports all major XML protocols and EDI messaging standards and provides complete back-end integration into ERP and legacy systems. It enables automation of a wide spectrum of business processes ranging from procurement and order fulfillment to billing and payment.

The Netfish XDI system supports all major B2B industry standards, such as RosettaNet, the BizTalk Framework, commerce XML (cXML), CommerceNet's eCo, and major EDI standards in XML, so it can communicate with any other open B2B XML solution.

The Netfish system is a 100% Java application, designed for extensibility, scalability, fault-tolerance, and mission-critical failover in a high-volume B2B transaction environment. These benefits translate into a more tightly integrated and automated value chain, dramatically improving efficiency and reducing operating costs in vital business functions.

OTHER SOFTWARE SOLUTIONS

Phillips Chemical Company's Plastics Group (a division of Phillips Petroleum Company) wanted to reduce inventory costs and compress cycle times. In aid of its goal, it took a close look at its manufacturing/distribution cycle and decided that re-tooling its order fulfillment processing systems was the answer. According to a Phillips spokesperson, "the challenge was to have the right product at the right location at the right time [the 3Rs!] to better manage our supply chain." The objectives were clear: reduce inventory, improve the forecasting process and distribution planning, decrease response time.

Aspen Technology's (www.aspentech.com) MIMI supply chain solution from its Chesapeake Supply Chain Division was chosen for the project. Aspen MIMI became part of Phillip's business decision support system while leaving in place the scheduler, inventory manager or strategic planner. It meets Phillips' technical standards and has the capability to integrate with any database or ERP system. It's a tool for "what-if" analysis that allows Phillips to quickly analyze multiple constraints and other factors that could never be done with a spreadsheet or pencil and paper.

Supply chain planning at Phillips involves balancing the capacity across their production and distribution network in monthly time periods. With the Aspen MIMI Phillips can simultaneously optimize its production and distribution plan and decrease response time to business and operational upsets. Supply/demand balancing is done in daily time periods using Aspen MIMI's scheduling functionality.

Fill rate (the ability to fill customer demand on time and with the requested volume) is one product line that has seen an increase of more than 20% since using Aspen MIMI. The key to this increase is an improved forecast and the ability to optimize the feasible production schedule.

Eighteen months into the project, Phillips switched from extracting data from an Oracle database to SAP. Because of Aspen MIMI's versatility and open architecture, this change had little impact on the existing models' functionality. Furthermore, Aspen MIMI enhanced the business value of Phillips' SAP R/3 implementation by providing a means for data verification and analysis. For example, the Aspen MIMI models received all the orders, inventory, and distribution data during the SAP start-up. Aspen MIMI reports were used to detect and summarize data issues. Getting these reports to Phillips' business units quickly had a very powerful impact. A Phillips spokesperson stated that the volume of data in SAP is just so massive that having Aspen MIMI reports, which have been filtered to provide the exact detail we need, has made it easier to react quickly and fix data problems.

Some readers may be interested in Ariba's Operating Resource Management System (discussed previously). It automates an e-business's procurement and management of non-production goods and services, which includes automation of the entire acquisition cycle. It also provides access with a Wizard-based approach that can eliminate need for extensive training sessions. One "neat" feature is that it can automatically subscribe to supplier managed catalogs and aggregates all catalogs into a single user interface. Ariba offers APIs for integration with ERP software like SAP, J.D. Edwards, Oracle, and PeopleSoft, as well as a toolkit to ease the integration. Another added benefit is that captured data can be modified through changes to XML. Sonoco, a leading global manufacturer of packaging materials for industrial and consumer markets, recently began installation of Ariba ORMS. Pricing starts at $750,000.

E.piphany's (www.epiphany.com), e.4 System uses a data mart to integrate customer information in an enterprise, linking the front-end with the back-end, and connecting relevant information from the supply chain and other third-party sources. The e.4 System interfaces with packaged applications such as ERP, sales force automation, call center, e-commerce, and with legacy applications and information stores. Its clients include BellSouth, Boise Cascade, DaimlerChrysler, Emerson Electric, Staples, and Thomas Cook. Pricing for modules begin at $200,000.

Industri-Matematik International Inc. (www.industrimatematik.com) provides high-performance fulfillment and customer service software solutions for supply chain management. The company specializes in pull-driven supply chains with complex logistics, information-rich high transaction volumes, and rigorous demands for customer responsiveness that's emerging in the e-commerce world. The company has strong technical expertise in global logistics management from its 30 years in the industry. It counts among its satisfied customers, British Airways, Campbell Soup, Canon, Carlton and United Breweries, Hartz Mountain, Kellogg's, Canadian Tire, Skyway Freight Systems, VWR, Warner/Elektra/Atlantic, and Starbucks.

Intelisys (www.intelisys.com) was formed by Chase Manhattan Bank and BVR. Its IEC-Enterprise is an Internet-based procurement system that networks buyers with suppliers focusing on intranet purchasing, it integrates requisitioning, ordering, acknowledgments and payments. The IEC-Enterprise can also provide seamless integration with ERP legacy systems, standardize product/service searches across suppliers,

incorporate XML for product/price comparisons, and receive electronic invoice back from a supplier to settle transaction. Pricing is customized for each client.

Intrepa's (www.intrepa.com) (now a part of Manhattan Associates, Inc.) Logisticspro, a supply chain management software solution, is available on Windows NT and AS/400. It's geared for small to mid-market e-businesses and integrates warehouse and transportation management capabilities. After installation of Logisticspro in the Nissan Motor Company's distribution centers, its spokesperson, Tim Henderson stated, "One of our biggest achievements is that we have eliminated most of the paperwork used in the parts distribution centers to handle receiving. We are approaching real-time response in our put away processes that make our inventory available to our customers faster."

Lawson Software (www.lawson.com) offers Lawson Insight Series as it's flagship product. According to Lawson's own documentation, "Gain a clear competitive advantage by conducting e-business with anyone, anywhere, anytime, through any device. The lawson.insight 8 Series makes it possible. Lawson delivers the power to extend your business far beyond B2B transactions to fully automated, fully integrated 360-degree e-business solutions." Enough said.

Manhattan Associates, Inc. (www.manh.com) is a global provider of technology-based solutions that operate on the AS/400, UNIX and NT platforms. These solutions enhance distribution efficiency and effectiveness through the integration of: pure-plays and multi-channel manufacturers; distributors and retailers with the customer; infomediaries; trading exchanges; and transportation providers. This results in enhanced collaboration and synchronization among all value chain participants. It offers a suite of value chain execution solutions that allows fulfillment operations to successfully manage high order volumes, achieve high inventory and shipment accuracy and meet the specialized demands of the e-business's customers. One of its customers is Staples Contract and Commercial fulfillment centers which service Staples' contract, catalog and e-commerce customers.

Optum, Inc. (www.optum.com) offers software solutions that are pure Internet applications. They utilize an open architecture design to help a value chain share real-time data. This allows e-businesses to monitor inventory positions across their enterprise and their extended value chain. Optum's TradeStream aggregates actual inventory information including consumption, movement, and status, such as — Where is it? When is it needed?

Webvan (www.webvan.com) plans to use Optum's e-fulfillment software at all future distribution centers. Currently it is using the software at its distribution facility in Oakland, CA. Optum software provides the e-fulfillment engine to Webvan, enabling high-volume, reliable fulfillment services for products ranging from grocery items, non-prescription drugs and chef-prepared meals to best-selling books and pet shop supplies. "Webvan and Optum share a common vision for e-business fulfillment," said Peter Relan, senior vice president of technology for Webvan Group, Inc. "We partnered with Optum because its software is highly configurable and is easily integrated with our proprietary automated distribution and material handling systems. Optum B2C e-fulfillment capabilities support high-speed mass customization of large order volumes and are helping Webvan manage its order accuracy and inventory levels."

It's a simpatico relationship — David J. Simbari, president and CEO at Optum explains that "Webvan operates what is probably one of the most highly automated fulfillment facilities in the world, in the ultimate high-speed environment. It has conquered the last mile to the customer and relies on Optum software to deliver the right products to the right customers, every day."

VIT's (www.vit.com) SeeChain "e-supply chain" performance measurement applications allow business managers to view the performance of the entire value chain from any Web browser, as well as to collaborate within the value chain. By leveraging XML and Java technology, business managers can drill down into detailed information, and even receive alerts when performance strays outside acceptable levels. SeeChain can quickly diagnose problems and pinpoint opportunities. When performance goes outside of acceptable levels, SeeChain automatically alerts business managers so they can take corrective action. VIT's SeeChain applications leverage data from SCM, ERP, and legacy systems, because it's Web-based, users can access information anytime, anywhere, from a standard Web browser.

Lighthammer Software Development's (www.lighthammer.com) Illuminator Plant Information Portal provides immediate access to plant information for all appropriate users in the value chain. Lighthammer's CTO says, "Illuminator improves decision making by providing real-time access to key performance indicators such as asset utilization, production efficiencies and yields, inventory levels, order status, and quality and traceability data — all through a standard Web browser." Illuminator's Web architecture and XML interface make this information available to all in real-time, giving a value chain the information needed, when its needed. Illuminator is a Web server-based application that uses both Java and DNA technologies to extract data from plant-floor systems, aggregate it at a Web server, transform it into business information, and distribute it to appropriate users through a standard browser. Currently, Illuminator is in use at over 50 enterprises in a range of industries, including chemical, pharmaceutical, biotech, semiconductors, utilities, food and beverage, mining, and many others.

EDI

Electronic Data Interchange (EDI) is a methodology used to transmit business instructions and documents from the computer of one organization to the computer of another, either directly or indirectly, through a third party "network" which communicates with both parties (a value-added network or "VAN").

E-business and the ability to exchange information over the Internet appear to be slowly overtaking EDI as the preferred means for performing business transactions. However, at the moment there is still an interesting split between the use of EDI and the Internet.

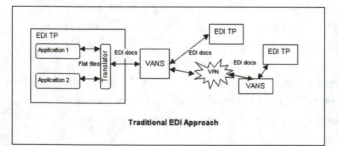

Traditional EDI Approach

The Internet is the communication vehicle of choice when performing non-financial transactions such as placing purchase orders, marketing, or customer service. However, enterprises rely much more heavily on EDI when performing financial transactions such as accounts payable, billing or fund transfers. In financial transactions, very few enterprises are currently using the Internet. For instance, of the enterprises that are engaged in some sort of electronic communications in a trading environment, more than 50% use EDI to some extent or the other. This is mainly attributable to the relative security of EDI and its standardized formats that better facilitate financial transactions between multiple parties and financial institutions.

To help illustrate this point, the industry giant Dow Chemical, although it's an equity partner in several e-marketplaces, still does 90% of its business over EDI links.

IPNet Solutions (www.ipnet-solutions.com) enables its customers to leverage the Internet while extending the capabilities of their legacy systems and proprietary networks. "IPNet's Enterprise eCommerce software allows companies to support all value chain transactions including traditional EDI, Internet EDI, Internet-based buying and selling, as well as SCM solutions — including vendor-managed inventory and business data-object exchange," explains Kian Saneii, senior vice president, world-wiide marketing, for IPNet.

A champion of EDI is Wira Logistics (www.wiralogistics.com), which specializes in providing modern integrated logistics, third party warehousing and distribution center services to manufacturers, distributors, wholesalers and large retailers. Wira believes that there are mutual benefits for all parties in the logistics business cycle that adopt e-business EDI technology. Wira states that e-business and EDI provide a strategic advantage in both the distribution and the transportation sectors of today's competitive market. The logistics specialist is of the opinion that the joining of e-business and EDI is a partnership whose time has come.

One option for EDI users is the service provided through a partnership between Kleinschmidt Inc. (www.kleinschmidt.com) and Prime Advantage (www.primeadvantage.com). This service offers a B2B demand-aggregation e-marketplace within the industrial manufacturing industry. These two have partnered to develop XML translation services for that market. Prime Advantage will further expand its e-marketplace by using Kleinschmidt's 'best-in-class' translation services to automate B2B communications using both XML and EDI.

"Many leading members of the industrial manufacturing industry are using EDI today to conduct B2B data exchange," said John Sprouse, CIO, Prime Advantage. "Using Kleinschmidt's XML to EDI and EDI to XML translation services allows Prime Advantage to rapidly add buyers and suppliers to its net based e-marketplace."

Harry Gaples, president of Kleinschmidt Inc. says, "providing translation services is one of Kleinschmidt's core competencies and we expect to see continued growth in requests for EDI to XML translations as XML usage becomes more widespread." Kleinschmidt Inc. began providing EDI-related services in 1979.

Upside magazine named Fourth-Channel, Inc. to its "Hot 100" list of private companies with exceptional potential. Fourth-Channel, Inc., discussed previously in this chapter, added Internet EDI capabilities to its profitbuilder e-business selling suite. With this enhancement, e-businesses can easily exchange EDI standard documents as part of their B2B selling and collaborative relationships. The addition of EDI capabilities makes Fourth-Channel one of the first Web-based selling and configuration solution providers to manage the full range of human and automated B2B transactions, including catalogs, auctions, EDI and XML exchange.

"As e-business evolves, the focus is not only on uncovering new selling opportunities but also on building and nurturing long-standing relationships," said Jonathan York, Ph.D., Fourth-Channel chairman and CEO. "The addition of EDI provides our customers with yet another way to deepen relationships with current customers while creating incremental revenue opportunities with prospective customers who require their suppliers to be EDI-enabled."

The Yankee Group estimates that EDI will account for $541 billion of the nearly $2.8 trillion in US B2B transactions by the year 2004. "Fourth-Channel's support of both structured and unstructured information exchange advances the more collaborative approach to B2B transactions required by an ever-increasing number of companies," said Greg Runyan, senior analyst with the Yankee Group's B2B Commerce and Applications Planning Service.

However, any e-business that uses an EDI system must ensure that its system can provide ASNs (advance ship notices) and UCC128 bar-coded carton labels. An ASN is a notice sent to a customer from a vendor indicating what merchandise has been shipped. With an ASN, a receiver can electronically identify the contents of a package, without having to open the package.

THE LANGUAGES OF E-BUSINESS

For a bricks-and-mortar making a move to the Web, one of the early steps it takes is to integrate its back-end systems. Until joining the Cyberland community, the only integration issues that most enterprises had to deal with was limited to the applications residing within their own domain. However, logistics technology requires that integration now extend outward toward the four corners of the world and application program interfaces (APIs) and XML are the passports in this Cyberland journey. Most e-business systems have APIs but they vary widely in capability. Then there are the legacy systems that an e-business needs to integrate with that also have APIs with varying capabilities. Not to mention the custom-built legacy systems without APIs. However, there is usually a way to work around these varying bits of technology to directly use an e-business system's APIs.

If it's determined that taking the API route is too pricey or inadequate or maybe even risky, the next course to take is EDI and XML, both can provide communication within a value chain. EDI is a well-established standard — the EDI messages are normally transmitted between businesses via Value-Added Networks (VANs). Extensible Markup Language ((XML) is an

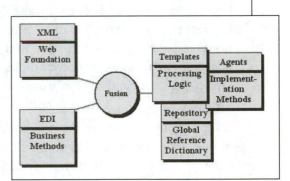

XML/EDI the fusion of Technology. *Graphic courtesy of the XML/EDI Group*

emerging standard for describing information and can be transmitted directly between e-businesses over the Internet, but translation will be required between the legacy system and the e-commerce system.

There is an openness in Cyberland not found in the closed environment of LANs, WANs, VPNs, VANs, and extranets. This détente has created a bit of a predicament in the global e-business community — what language are they to converse through? Without a basic vocabulary for the common exchange of data of the "everyday e-business" processes, the massive migration to the e-business model would come to a screeching halt. Moving different types of data across disparate systems was nearly impossible in the ecosystem of the traditional world of the 20th Century but that changed with the introduction of a computer-based patois.

Due to Cyberland's Tower of Babel, there is a need for new platforms, technologies, languages and translators that ease the burden of communication so there can be an exchange of data by any system, anywhere, anytime. With the arrival of new communication vernacular, the exchange of data through the integration of computer systems and processes opened the communications highway of e-business commerce. It's one of the driving forces behind the explosive growth of the Internet and its e-business community.

I am not talking about programming structure, but the basic vocabulary for conducting business in the everyday e-business environment. The terms HTML, XML, BizTalk, VBA (Visual Basics for Applications) and Java are the "languages" of e-business. "Which language [to use] is a number three or four consideration, after determining how to satisfy the needs of your end customer. The first question to ask is how to accomplish your goals easily, quickly, and in a timely fashion," says W.B. (Bill) Lipsin, president and CEO of Ironside Technologies Inc.

In this Internet age, an e-business's selection of technology must also comprise one or more of the new enabling languages that may not have been around long but designed specifically for the task at hand and the open environment of Cyberland. Lipsin suggests, "It's no longer about its use within the four walls of your organization, but about being deployed within the four walls of every single existing and future customer you have."

According to Lipsin, "the first layer is the interaction or transaction layer, where protocols such as TCP/IP (transmission control protocol/Internet protocol) exist. This is the 'must have' area dealing with information infrastructure, protocols, and routers."

The second layer, out of necessity, involves the choice of language or more precisely a dialect, which could be, as suggested by Lipsin, "VBA, BizTalk, XML, or another — but they should not affect the operability of the underlying infrastructure."

When you get to the third layer, the implementation layer, you actually construct the specific content being presented. "Everything changes in the Internet very fast," observes Yobie Benjamin, chief of global strategies for Ernst & Young LLP Consulting Service (www.ey.com). "What is essential to remember is that you cannot write or construct a system that takes 12 years to build — like the traditional ERP systems. The choice of e-commerce systems must be open and easy to integrate, because time is of the essence."

XML is at the moment clearly the dominant language in Cyberland (somewhat like English is in the Web community) and "HTML and XML are complementary," says Marcus Schmidt, industry manager for e-commerce at Microsoft

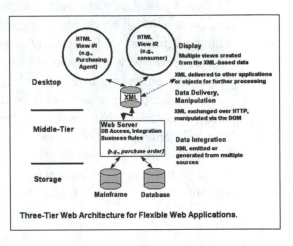

Three-Tier Web Architecture for Flexible Web Applications.

(www.microsoft.com). Then why worry about learning other languages or dialects? Read what the experts have to say.

"What BizTalk adds is a set of guidelines on how to build XML schema. It culled out certain key things to increase the ability for trading partners to use XML," stated Schmidt. According to Schmidt, BizTalk allows software applications to talk to one another in a more businesslike way.

Joe Dugan, managing director of the e-business solutions practice of AnswerThink Consulting Group (www.answerthink.com) wades in to say, "BizTalk is a product that we will see more and more of. To me, BizTalk is really a toolset for the front-end. Microsoft is definitely a player, so when Microsoft gets behind a product, it will be used, whether it's through Microsoft front-ends or not. Because of the investment being made, and because of the plug-and-play features that are a part of other Microsoft releases, BizTalk will be very powerful." Schmidt admits, "Some have been concerned that this is something proprietary we are doing. We are trying to accelerate the acceptance of XML — there is nothing in BizTalk that hasn't already been submitted to the W3C standards. It's all based on 100% open standards." According to Microsoft, any application or computer system, which understands XML, can converse also in BizTalk, thus allowing easy data exchange regardless of the underlying technology.

But it's not a clear road, Denny Michael, vice president of marketing for AlphaCONNECT (www.alphaconnect.com), advises that his company has filed for a patent on its software programming language, Network Query Language (NQL), which was designed to enable applications to easily manage information throughout Cyberland. Michael explains that "NQL was designed with the same objectives as structured query language (SQL), a standard language used to interrogate and process data in a relational database. It provides software developers with a scripting tool to create applications that acquire, analyze, filter, convert, and deliver data across the Internet and corporate networks." He clarifies by saying that e-businesses are beginning to rely on transparent technologies, such as intelligent agents called infomediaries, to broker for products, services, and information on their behalf. NQL will be one of the languages spoken by these agents.

HTML and HTTP

HyperText Markup Language (HTML) is the native language of Cyberland's Web community and was the standard that elevated Cyberland from text-only data to what is available today. It's used to create documents served over the Web by defining the structure and layout of the document through the use of tags and attributes thereby determining how documents are formatted and displayed. HTML has the remarkable ability for various parts of a hypertext document to link to, or follow a specific thread or concept, other than the topic under discussion. You can't talk about HTML unless you also mention its kissing cousin, HTTP (HyperText Transfer Protocol). HTTP defines how messages are formatted and transmitted throughout Cyberland and what actions Web servers and browsers should take in response to various comments.

Java

Java is Cyberland's gift from Sun Microsystems. It's a high-level object-oriented "true" programming language similar to C++ technology and was designed primarily for writing software that can be positioned on a Web site and downloaded over the Internet (Java Applet). It also moves media content across networks of heterogeneous devices and offers the capability to move "behavior" with the Java Applet along with the content. The Java 2 platform provides a comprehensive, end-to-end architecture for building and deploying network-centric applications for the value chain.

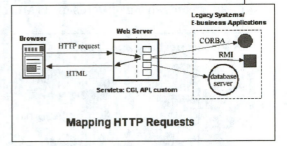

Mapping HTTP Requests

BizTalk

As previously discussed, Microsoft's BizTalk is a technology framework that allows software to speak the language of e-business. BizTalk is a dialect that advances the capability of XML, it's a framework based on new XML schemas and industry standards that describes common business documents. This enables application integration and data exchange throughout Cyberland, regardless of platform, operating system or underlying technology.

XML

The XML standard is in the hands of the World Wide Web Consortium, known as the W3C. The current standard, 1.0 was approved in February of 1998. XML provides a generic way to process data on the Internet. It is also viewed as a very efficient way to transfer structured data between applications. And that is why e-businesses should care about the health and well-being of XML. Note the word 'structured' in that last sentence. Combine it with 'flexible' and 'extensible' and you have everything that traditional EDI is not.

XML is fast becoming the dominant "language" of Cyberland. XML isn't a "true" language, it's a meta-markup language and as such provides a format for making precise descriptions of data to enable a meaningful exchange of data across multiple platforms. It's a family of technologies that gives structured data flexibility which is accomplished by placing the data (documents, spreadsheets, address books, financial transactions, technical drawings, etc.) into text files that are transformed into objects.

If you're still confused, Ernst & Young's Benjamin clarifies, "It's important to note that it's not a language, but a way to code, a way to describe data or objects in context. XML data can act upon other data. It's hard to act upon a string of words in HTML, but XML will tell me what this string of data means, so it can be acted upon." He explains that what is missing is a transaction engine. "This is where the battleground will be, with regards to who gets to define the vertical spaces — the middleware, so to speak — that mediates between the two."

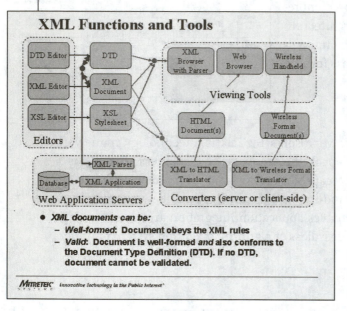

Lipsin's take on XML is enlightening, he says, "when they get down to thinking about the technology, XML is emerging as a very strong language or 'alphabet' where a lot of e-commerce functionality will revolve around. Where there will be variances among vendors is in the way they take that alphabet to put words and sentences together. Think about the number of words and sentences within a character set, an alphabet, and that is analogous with how XML works. However, it does give great flexibility and evolutionary capabilities in a common character set, and that is why so many have gravitated to it."

In addition, according to Alex Zatuchny, executive vice president of The Revere Group (www.reveregroup.com), "The language has to integrate with a company's current platforms and support infrastructures and be on track with long-term insourcing or outsourcing strategies." Internally, Zatuchney says, this could be any language or a combination of languages, "but for external exchanges, XML seems to be the clear leader. What we are seeing is a more homogenous output. There are going to be a number of standards dictating what the output is, to facilitate integration with other companies. The language used has to fit those standards."

Lipsin does add though, "you shouldn't look first at technology, but at how it will affect or enhance the company's strategy. The key is not necessarily what technology you choose, but whether or not it will translate into usage for the lowest common denominator of the business's customers." However the main issues in this area are scalability and the amount of data transferred to the users' display screen.

XML is coming into play in the integration of Web sites with order entry processing systems. Unlike HTML, which just marks up text, XML lets developers write custom tags to identify objects. Beyond using XML to solve its interoperability problems, an e-business can reengineer its processes to be XML-centric, i.e., to build code components that can be easily combined or reorganized. In this way an e-business can use XML as a way to bridge the gap between its entire value chain's systems by sharing XML definitions and access points with members of the value chain. This allows everyone to perform systems integration on a much more rapid time line, independent of the systems or platforms that are being interfaced.

Legacy integration is a puzzle for e-businesses that have customer data scattered across different databases in far-flung locations and want to get a single view of a customer's business with them. XML might be the answer.

One of XML's primary uses is as the "glue" to integrate applications, as GM is doing, says Joshua Walker, an analyst at Forrester. This is true not only for individual companies but also for entire industries. Wall Street, for example, is looking to XML as a way to

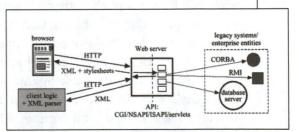

Serving XML to allow programmatic access.

simplify electronic communication among brokerage houses, banks, and other financial institutions.

XML promises to bring simplicity and speed to electronic content. As more information in Cyberland is labeled with XML tags, searching for specific data will become easier. XML offers capabilities that go far beyond those of its relative, HTML. A proposed XML standard called Xlink, for example, will bring greatly enhanced capabilities to hyperlinks. Among other things, clicking on an Xlink hyperlink will let you choose from a list of possible destinations instead of taking you directly to another Web page as HTML links do.

But where XML will see heavy use — and one of the places where it's catching on most rapidly — is in the e-tail and B2B arena. Vendors such as Ariba Technologies Inc., Commerce One Inc., and Concur Technologies Inc. (www.concur.com), and others are already using XML to simplify the process of matching up RFPs and purchase orders over the Web. The boom in B2B has fueled the rush to XML.

Regardless of whether they're exchanging credit information, purchase orders, or anything else, before two e-businesses can share data, they must agree on a common language. One of XML's main advantages and main disadvantage is that it provides a simple way to do this. XML stores the definition of tags relating to specific industries in files called Document Type Definitions (DTDs). The files — often referred to as dictionaries, vocabularies, or schemas — serve as a uniform source of data definitions, so organizatiions using the same dictionary don't have to match up their data every time they want to do business.

A disadvantage of XML is that disparate individual unique dictionaries, each with its own alphabet, are springing up everywhere. Each dictionary can cover practically any subject. Commerce is one, of course, with cXML; but there are also dictionaries for mathematics, astrology, astronomy, telephony, music, air traffic control and so forth. However, each one of these "dialects" are unreadable by any system outside the members of the dictionary's organization. This may present problems for e-businesses that are members of or communicate with the different organizations utilizing different XML dictionaries.

Also, XML is not for every e-business process. For example, if an e-business is using a OLTP/high-transaction type systems, XML isn't necessarily that e-business's best choice.

Although an e-business's choice of technologies will vary, certainly for applications, Java will continue to dominate the landscape. But with regard to integration and content management, XML will play a major role. The challenge will be making sure one XML standard can easily talk to another. That is where BizTalk comes in and other common schema formats. Ernst & Young's Benjamin agrees and states, "certainly XML is going to be dominant. One way to prove this theory is the fact that Internet Explorer 5.0 and Netscape 5.0 are both XML-enabled."

But read closely Microsoft's Schmidt's caveat concerning XML: "With XML you will want to encrypt your data for additional security, add digital signatures, or a secure channel. Inherently there is nothing that speaks to security in XML, but companion security measures are available. Fundamentally we think XML is the way that people will do business-to-business commerce. It enables an elegant yet simple exchange of information between trading partners."

XSL

Extensible style language (XSL) is a companion to XML that combines the formatting advantages of HTML with object-oriented intelligence. It denotes the style sheets that work in conjunction with XML data to format the electronic information at runtime. In the future XSL will enable the generation of HTML without complex scripting. XSL is a transformation language that defines rules for mapping structured XML data to HTML (or other display formats) using an XSL Processor.

A group of rules defines a style sheet and then XSL allows data to be transformed into a presentation structure different from the original data structure. This lets data elements to be formatted and displayed in multiple places on a page, rearranged or removed. Thus, numerous style sheets can exist for one data set, describing various delivery platforms or output devices. Microsoft has released an XSL processor for developers to experiment with and provide feedback for the further development of the technology.

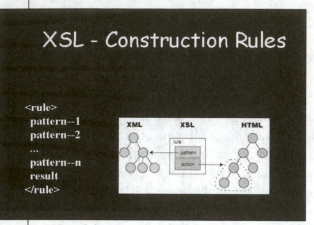

XML and the automation of Web Information processing. Yannis Papakonstantinou (UCSD).

XHTML

This eXtensible HyperText Markup Language is a proposed XML-compliant version of HTML 4.0, which can make it easier for Web pages to be displayed on handheld Internet appliances, such as PDAs, cell phones, and other outlets besides the laptop or desktop computer. The semantics of the elements and their attributes are defined in the W3C's recommendation for HTML 4. These semantics provide the foundation for future extensibility of XHTML. Compatibility with existing HTML user agents is possible by following a small set of guidelines.

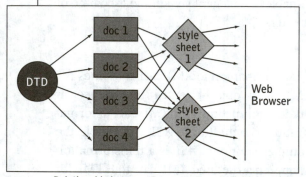

Relationship between Document Type Definitions (DTD), XML documents (doc), stylesheets (XSL or CSS) and information received by the browser

ebXML

You might say ebXML is one of the alphabets of XML. According to Netfish (a strong supporter that has been actively involved in the ebXML Initiative from the beginning), ebXML's applicability is highlighted by three models of B2B communication: point-to-point, hub-and-spoke and federated. The ebXML Initiative was formed to create an XML-based framework for e-business globally.

As stated previously, the most common data exchange technology currently available is EDI. EDI is expensive and for most e-businesses, difficult to implement, particularly if it's a smaller enterprise with more limited resources. ebXML can overcome these obstacles by making the

STANDARDS COMMITTEE

In general, a Standards Committee is a task force comprised of key individuals from all business areas whose activities are impacted by a specific technology. The responsibilities of the committee includes analysis, communication, corrective strategy development and deployment and testing and certification of all related products and internal and external services.

established conventions available to the public at a significantly lower cost. ebXML is a set of specifications that together enable a modular e-business framework. The vision of ebXML is to enable a global e-business marketplace where enterprises of any size and in any geographical location can meet and conduct business with each other through the exchange of XML based messages. ebXML is a joint initiative of the United Nations (UN/CEFACT) and OASIS, developed with global participation for global usage.

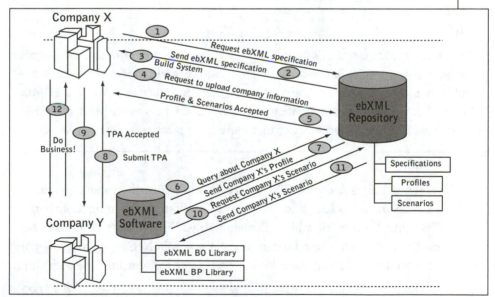

"ebXML provides a platform on which to build standards without requiring users to use idiosyncratic software tools. The combination could lead to standards that are developed faster and yet supported by a rich set of software tools. "

—The Gartner Group

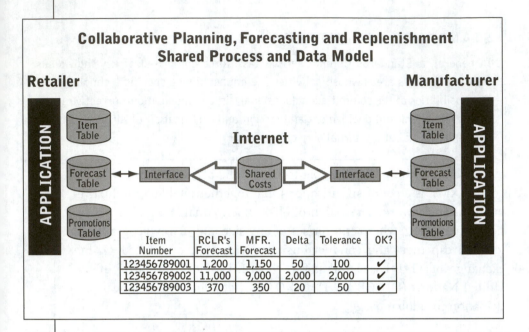

Collaborative Planning, Forecasting and Replenishment Shared Process and Data Model

Item Number	RCLR's Forecast	MFR. Forecast	Delta	Tolerance	OK?
123456789001	1,200	1,150	50	100	✔
123456789002	11,000	9,000	2,000	2,000	✔
123456789003	370	350	20	50	✔

OASIS

The Organization for the Advancement of Structured Information Standards (www.oasis-open.org) is a non-profit, international consortium that creates interoperable industry specifications based on public standards such as XML and SGML. OASIS members include organizations and individuals who provide, use and specialize in implementing the technologies that make these standards work in practice.

CPFR

When writing a book about logistics and fulfillment, there can't be a discussion about technology and "languages" without mentioning Collaborative Planning, Forecasting and Replenishment (CPFR) — a set of industry standards for B2B Web-based communication. RosettaNet, (www.rosettanet.org) another industry standards initiative, has agreed to come into line with CPFR.

The hottest commodity is information — information that allows goods and services to be moved quickly and more efficiently — that is where CPFR comes into the piicture. As Ron Ireland, explained to Lynne Bairstow in an article she wrote for e-comadvisor's "News and Trends" (www.e-com-advisor.com), transportation companies, manufacturers, suppliers, distributors, brokers, wholesalers and retailers all must use the Internet and sophisticated software to exchange information about their needs and CPFR is the conduit. The author notes that Ireland is the acknowledged grandfather of CPFR and became its champion in the 1990s when he worked as strategy manager in the information systems division of Wal-Mart Stores Inc.

According to Ireland, "the companies with a .com after their name are going to be demanding this kind of business-to-business communication soon." He went on to speculate, "With technology, we are able to manage with a much lower level of detail. We can go all the way down to the consumer level of demand. The ones who invest in that technology are going to be the leaders in the future."

The basic idea behind CPFR is to have demand forecasting that is as accurate as possible for all the parties involved. Through a value chain's cooperation CPFR can deter the practice of "safety" stocks, erratic ordering cycles and other unnecessary costs and hassles.

With CPFR, everyone has input into the demand forecast — an e-tailer that knows it's running a special promotion can advise manufacturers that it will need more stock. A carrier that would find it much cheaper to deliver a week earlier or a week later than usual can negotiate around that knowledge. A manufacturer with inbred intelligence of how its products sell can add its input. This type of communication has always been desirable. The Internet has evolved to where software can conduct these conversations almost completely automatically.

As reported in a September 7, 2000 *Wall Street Journal* article, Kimberly-Clark has been a leader in making CPFR an industry standard. Chris Sellers, president of Syncra Systems commented that Syncra (www.syncra.com) is "committed to helping Kimberly-Clark deliver CPFR benefits to its community of retail trading partners. By using open Internet-based B2B technologies, such as, Syncra Ct, Kimberly-Clark will continue leading the industry in building a win-win network of trading partners."

Costco has adopted the VMI model in its dealings with Kimberly-Clark. This means that Costco provides detailed information on sales and inventory levels in each of its nearly 300 locations, and Kimberly-Clark takes responsibility for restocking the shelves. Thus, Costco saves money not only on staffing its inventory department, but also on warehousing and inventory holding costs. Before Kimberly-Clark began managing Costco's inventory, it kept about a month's supply of Kimberly-Clark products in its warehouses. Now, Costco needs to keep only a two-week supply.

"Kimberly-Clark is using Syncra Ct to automatically compare forecasts for specific stock codes and individual retail locations with its customers' volume forecasts. This automated comparison will greatly increase supply chain efficiency," said Larry Roth, senior consultant at Kimberly-Clark. "There are far too many codes to compare manually. What used to take more than two days of an employee's time each week will now take only 15 minutes," he explained. "Syncra Ct gives us the opportunity to maintain a tighter customer inventory so we can increase inventory turns and achieve a double-digit increase in in-stock percentages.'"

Another benefit is that Syncra Ct can identify significant discrepancies in Kimberly-Clark's and its customers' forecasts. Business analysts then resolve the discrepancies, ensuring that business plans for both partners remain synchronized. In an initial pilot program using the software, for example, Kimberly-Clark and a major national retailer identified and resolved discrepancies in forecasted promotions, resulting in increased revenue for both trading partners.

"We chose Syncra Systems because of its leadership position in CPFR and the value it adds to our efforts to strengthen relationships with our customers," said Bruce Olson, vice president — supply chain logistics for Kimberly-Clark. Through the coordination of business planning and forecasting processes and data sources, such as point-of-sale, Kimberly-Clark and its value chain can create the most efficient supply chain possible. Kimberly-Clark CPFR pilots conducted with partners like Kmart have lowered costs and increased revenues. "By deploying Syncra Ct over the Internet, we can now apply these benefits to many of our customers," opined Olson.

Whether an e-business has a spanking new B2B commerce system or legacy systems, it needs an easy and cost-effective platform to link into, and enough capacity to enable its value chain to communicate effectively. Lipsin clarifies, "Don't be shortsighted in how people will be interacting with your information. Be prepared to provide your information no matter how it will be viewed."

There are many changes just over the horizon in Web-based communication making collaboration and the sharing of information across value chains a reality. The technology exists now that allows all of this, although still a little bit bulky, but just wait....

AN OPTION

The most intense headache for some large e-businesses is not linking with the biggest partners, but with the smallest. PlumRiver Technology Inc. (www.plumriver.com) offers a set of software and services that could help ease that pain. It launched PlumLink, a Web-based order fulfillment system that helps large manufacturers automate the process of exchanging information with small dealers and retailers. According to various experts, the system could help eliminate paper-based ordering processes that currently make it expensive to deal with smaller channel partners.

USA Footwear International, during a testing phase of PlumRiver's service, offered the opinion that PlumLink definitely can enable electronic communications with small dealers. Since, according to Robert Moore, USA Footwear's president, "the high cost and complicated nature of selling to low-volume, high-margin dealers has left many of them underserved by large manufacturers. PlumRiver's business model will help the footwear industry service the numerous smaller independent dealers that are very important to our industry." PlumLink is available for a monthly fee, which varies with the features selected and the number of partners involved.

Many small enterprises just cannot afford software and services such as EDI that would allow them to order products from large manufacturers electronically. As a result, these small enterprises still place orders via phone and fax, forcing manufacturers to employ large numbers of customer service representatives in a process that can be not only costly but much more error-prone than EDI. This may result in the manufacturer dropping this cost-intensive customer from its customer base. Although some enterprises have continued to service the small order customer and offset the cost of doing so by adding a surcharge to that customer's transactions.

"Our research has shown that it costs between $40 and $65 to process each paper order, and that assumes no mistakes are made," said Henry White, PlumRiver's CEO. "Mistakes may cause that figure to be multiplied by a factor of 10 or 15." However, with the installation of the Web-based PlumRiver software, an enterprise can service its small customer for about $5 per order. The software allows enterprises to map their EDI systems to the Web, where one and all can access it with the right ID, password, a Web browser and a phone line. In addition, PlumRiver can plug in its customer relationship management tools and services that, for instance, enable an enterprise to upsell based on the customer's previous buying patterns.

As mentioned above, some large enterprises actually charge their small cost-intensive customers a surcharge. Although sometimes they only penalize the small order customer for any order placed via phone or fax, which incrementally increases that small customer's cost of doing business making it harder for the "little guy" to compete. However, with a system such as PlumRiver, new opportunities for enhancing revenue streams on both sides of the equation come into play.

Here is another technology the reader might find interesting. Optum's TradeStream. It will be brought to the Internet by USinternetworking (www.usi.com) through their USi AppHost Program and will be sold as a subscription service, said a spokesperson for Optum. TradeStream is an integration layer and analytic tool set, which combines information from multiple layers, such as, warehouse and transportation management software applications, enterprise software suites and advanced planning software applications, into one layer that can then be accessed over the Internet. This layer enables users to access the information in a meaningful way, for example, performing track and trace or checking key performance indicators.

TradeStream can track goods over the Internet down to line-item detail. The integration piece, connecting TradeStream to the Internet, has been standardized for all data sources associated with orders and inventory, not just software produced by Optum. Optum thinks that e-businesses can reduce inventory by up to one-third with TradeStream. "The traditional fulfillment system is not built for today's reality. We have moved to a fulfillment model requiring fast-moving piece-pick operations. We didn't envision customers placing orders almost daily five years ago," an Optum spokesperson explains.

Larry Clopp, an analyst with The Gartner Group, describes TradeStream as a natural evolution for Optum and feels that it "brings a lot of functional knowledge and capability that should show up on the Web." He tempered that statement by pointing out that Optum needs to overcome "old applications operating in batch," which goes against the real-time capabilities of the Web.

Capstan Systems (www.capstan.com) focuses on international trade logistics and international supply chain execution management and is another software company that has introduced a hosted version of its software. Steve Zocchi, Capstan's chief marketing officer said Capstan is focused on "global shippers mostly in economic perishables — high-tech, apparel." In other words, it "creates all the documents needed" to move goods across virtually any border, such as, commercial invoices, bills of lading, pre-entry screening, audit and export compliance. The Capstan hosted software offerings doesn't stop there, it also provides collaboration capabilities, workflow management, messaging and alerts.

Capstan has also lined up a variety of logistics service partners (such as MSAS Global Logistics (Exel), Optimum Logistics, freightquote.com, Savi Technology (www.savi.com), and i2 Technologies) which allows B2Bs to offer a full solution for their customers.

At the moment Capstan's focus is only on the international market. According to Clopp, with its supply chain software Capstan doesn't have many competitors, as "most service providers focus on domestic, like Celarix and Descartes. Optum also focuses on domestic supply chain execution. But I think customers will drive them to do international as they have more international requirements."

Clopp thinks that the integration between marketplaces and logistics service providers is the wave of the future since he projects that most B2B transactions will be within marketplaces or similar structures. A marketplace "is just another customer" for supply chain application providers, voiced Clopp.

Clopp holds that application integration with other applications and the Internet is a driving issue along with "trying to get the data and information out of the four walls of the enterprise and integrate that in an intelligent manner" with data from other e-businesses. Many companies are using "private Internets" [VPNs, extranets] for transferring information, said Clopp, who predicts that marketplaces will establish technical, and perhaps settlement and contract requirements for members.

EXE Technologies (www.exe.com) and i2 Technologies, Inc. are among the leading companies in supply chain execution and intelligent e-business and marketplace solutions. These companies have extended their strategic relationship to provide a combined fulfillment solution for e-tail and click-and-mortar Internet marketplaces. As a part of the relationship, EXE Technologies is interfacing its EXceed eFulfillment System (eFS) into i2's TradeMatrix Fulfill solution. The combined solution integrates optimal inventory positioning, intelligent order promising, fulfillment execution and delivery capabilities to B2B marketplaces.

"EXE's EXceed makes it possible for companies to see beyond available inventory to fulfill orders with inventory they don't yet have in stock, but plan to produce or receive from suppliers," said Ray Hood, president and CEO, EXE Technologies. "It's a great way to maximize customer loyalty and profitability at the same time."

With this advanced fulfillment execution capability added to i2's TradeMatrix Fulfill, e-businesses can instantaneously notify customers if their order is in stock, and if it's not, notify them when it will be and when the order can be delivered. When a customer requests a delivery quote before purchasing an item through TradeMatrix, the combined solution determines availability, pricing and delivery capabilities. When the order is booked, Fulfill broadcasts the plan to the EXceed WMS (warehouse management system), a component of EXE's EXceed eFS solution. EXceed WMS then provides the capability to pick, pack and ship the order according to plan. EXceed WMS also feeds real-time as well as forward-looking snapshots of inventory to the TradeMatrix Demand Fulfillment engine, giving users the ability to promise orders based on inventory not yet in stock.

"A solid supply chain management and execution system is critical to the strength of a marketplace," said Michael Ellis, senior vice president of Business Development at i2 Technologies. "With this advanced fulfillment capability added to TradeMatrix, companies can position their supply chain to meet forecasted demand, promise and capture orders intelligently and execute and monitor all deliveries."

There is a caution though. "We're going to see many exchanges fade away this year. The exchanges that remain in competition will be the ones who understand and have in place the necessary supply chain and order fulfillment infrastructure to support the potentially massive amounts of transactions in the digital economy," said Steve Banker, director of Supply Chain Solutions, ARC Advisory Group (www.arcweb.com).

E-procurement has become a buzzword among the distribution and supply chain set, and now even Tech Data (www.techdata.com) has joined the fray. The distributor is helping solution providers and integrators leverage Web development infrastructure with a new back-end procurement solution called SupplyXpert. This new back-end procurement solution is part of Tech Data's new focus on accessibility, proactive initiatives, e-business commerce and supply chain management.

Tech Data's customers can set up an online storefront using the distributor's infrastructure. Price profiles and bundles can be set up for specific customers with the tool's dynamic pricing catalog. End users can make purchases via the storefront and those orders flow directly to Tech Data for fulfillment. According to Tech Data, this will save time and take costs out of the order process. Tim Lowe, vice present of business development at Tech Data says, "you really have customers filling out the paperwork for you. "It's a full-blown e-procurement solution" and a perfect timesaving digital tool.

TECH MUSINGS

The supply chain is many e-businesses' lifeline. Much of what e-business and their customers expect from the supply chain depends on how well data can be retrieved from the back-end systems. Anything clouding visibility into supply or demand information can disable a manufacturing line or, worse, make the e-business miss a deadline in bringing a product to market.

There is a high price to pay for inefficiencies in a supply chain. Talk to Kmart Corp.'s new CEO, Charles Conaway, he has publicly stated that Kmart's sagging profits were due, in part, to a weak supply chain infrastructure. He further said that Kmart expects to spend about $1.5 billion over a two-year period to update Kmart's technology, including systems for coordinating with suppliers. Also ask Revlon Inc. why it has been forced to slow product shipments? It will candidly tell you it was because store shelves were backed up with older inventory.

Also high on the list of things all e-businesses look for when adopting their new e-business model are order processing and shipment tracking, on-time delivery capability, customer support, and product availability. It's important to develop systems that can handle increases in orders, offer product availability information, and be managed in a Web environment and at the same time introduce cost-cutting efficiencies.

E-businesses face the issue of setting up a platform that allows the value chain to retrieve information about the demand picture, forecasts, delivery dates, shipment tracking, and other data necessary for planning their business suggestions. I call this a "logistics hub." Disparate systems must be integrated. Then with the right technology in place that uses a repository of different languages and dialects, buyers, sellers, manufacturers, distributors, suppliers and transportation providers can tap into this "hub." From there they can pull data from its ERP and other systems, and receive order tracking alerts and notification of potential problems. Everything should work in tandem with other platforms being used for customer service management, inventory and warehouse management, manufacturing planning, and business analysis.

In the end, the back-end system is what drives e-business — and logistics and fulfillment is all about the back-end.

If e-businesses don't address logistics and fulfillment issues, they will find orders that are late or never delivered, delivered to the wrong address or billed incorrectly becoming the norm and not the rare exception. These recalcitrant e-businesses will also find that backorders are common, and there isn't a system in place for prompt notification of such backorders — internally or to the customer. In discussing this common e-business problem, Rick Burghli, director of Internet fulfillment solutions for i2 Technologies, voiced his opinion that "many systems take orders on-line for product that is not available. Then, as an afterthought, they discover the problem and try to fix it. These orders shouldn't even have been accepted in the first place."

Successful communication between front- and back-end systems often involves a middle layer that allows the value chain to integrate planning and visibility to support Web-based promises of delivery dates. Thus, the server notifies fulfillment engines of real-time inventory availability, resources, and materials to complete the order. Then, according to Burghli, "For more elaborate make-to-order products, the system checks component availability, labor, and logistics data." The server should also include an allocated ATP (available to promise) engine, which can offer a multidimensional response, such as, "You asked for 10. We can give you three now and the remaining seven by next week."

Even with promise dates, many businesses are unable to follow through due to lack of integration, poor visibility, and errors in sourcing and allocation. These problems can seriously harm an e-business's reputation for customer service and fast response, not to mention its overall affect on market share and profits.

To synchronize order fulfillment, e-businesses must have the back-end infrastructure in place and must incorporate demand and other capacity constraints. The "back-office" subsystems of e-businesses — the ones that provide the link between the value chain and/or e-tail customer and the actual physical delivery of product — continue to be a challenge and often prove to be more difficult to put in place than the construction of the Web site itself.

It's All About the Customer

COMMERCE IN THE E-BUSINESS community must place the customer at the center of all activity. The online customer aided by smart search engines can view, compare, and price products in a few clicks of a mouse. The result is a fully informed customer armed with multiple choices with which to make the buying decision.

At a Strategic Technology Conference sponsored by *Traffic World Magazine* (www.trafficworld.com) and KPMG Peat Marwick (www.kpmg.com), Jeff Crowe, the chairman, president & CEO of Landstar System (www.landstar.com), offered this advice: Don't get "too caught up in the hype. The customers that you have today are where you must focus. Learn where your customer intends to lead you. Figure out where the core values are and continue to deliver deep, long-term relationships." He closed by emphasizing, "From the cradle to the grave it's all about the customer." He is so right!

CUSTOMER RELATIONSHIPS

The nature of e-business has put the customer in control with the ability to peer into the depths of the value chain. An e-business must accommodate the new "push/pull" customer paradigm. In the traditional business world the company "sold" (push) the product to the customer. With e-business the customer approaches multiple online commerce sites and demands information and product (pull).

In a customer "pull" environment, it's of little note whether the e-business owns everything from raw materials to finished goods, or if it's dependent upon service providers and contract manufacturers. Nor does it matter whether the e-business is operating under a build-to-order, JIT, or VMI model, because its distribution channels are still evolving.

Customer care is tied directly to LFMS. In his 2000 COMDEX keynote speech, EDS chairman and CEO, Dick Brown, outlined a set of imperatives for success in the digital economy: eliminate boundaries; collaborate in new ways; continuously seek improvement; and establish trust with customers, partners and colleagues. He nailed it — because he was basically talking about customer care.

In the Internet community, Brown's philosophy means literally turning an e-business — and its entire supply chain — over to the customer (collaboration). Good customer care also entails gaining a customer for life through interactive dialogue (improvement), not simply a transaction. While the goals of customer care are straightforward, its implementation can be another matter. When a customer steps through a properly implemented e-business model, he/she/it must be able to see and navigate throughout its entire supply chain (trust) — a big step for an e-business and its value chain. Given the reality of e-business, customer care must now extend beyond customer relationship management to value chain relationship management.

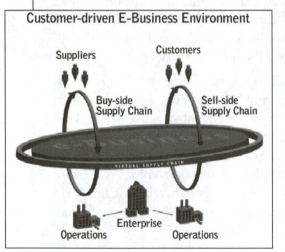

Customer-driven E-Business Environment

Suppliers

Customers

Buy-side Supply Chain

Sell-side Supply Chain

VIRTUAL SUPPLY CHAIN

Enterprise

Operations

Operations

E-business is shifting the power from sellers to buyers at a time when manufacturing and distribution companies are looking downstream to improve efficiencies. *Courtesy* of QAD, inc.

As more enterprises adopt the e-business model, a power shift in global markets is taking place. Armed with networked information technology, the customer has grabbed the power and in doing so has become a fully informed, never satisfied customer who determines what is to be made, when, where, and at what cost

— today's e-business customer wants it all. Whether it's buying an MP3 player, office furniture, beauty supplies, spare parts, financial services, or auto insurance, customers want complete care throughout the product/service's life cycle. The online customer demands the best — product, price, service and support.

Brown states, "You must see the big picture, work to improve everything you touch and be there when you're needed. Better yet, [you must] anticipate what consumers want and be there before you're needed." Today's successful e-business knows it's about gaining customers for life.

In idealized days, when a customer walked into a store and engaged in conversation with the staff, the content of their dialogue shared know-how — not just concluding a transaction. That is where today's e-business should be headed — only they will be doing it digitally and not face-to-face.

Bob McCashin, an EDS corporate vice president, put it better than I ever could. He said, "we are entering a new era — or perhaps it's the rebirth of an older one — in which the individual customer is central. It's an era of understanding or intimacy with the people we serve — even when they live on the other side of the world. It's a time when we can know hundreds of thousands of customers *well* — particularly our best customers. And we can show them that we appreciate their business in meaningful ways. It's called 'enterprise' because market leaders today realize that all forms of interactions with their customers — whether through sales, service, or delivery — affect their customer relationships. These interactions can help you acquire the right customers, retain them by meeting their individual needs, and maximize the lifetime value of the most profitable customer relationships. "

In a study released in September 2000, the Gartner Group stated that, based upon two August 2000 surveys, there is overall customer dissatisfaction with the online commerce experience. One of the surveys showed that 24% of online customers were extremely dissatisfied with their online experience, exhibiting concerns about online security, shipping costs and timely delivery. The other survey found that of the top 50 e-tailers, not one was rated "good" or "excellent" for online customer service. It's time to get to work!

Bain & Company Inc. (www.bain.com), one of the world's leading global business consulting firms and Mainspring (www.mainspring.com), one of the leading eStrategy consulting firms, copublished an Online Retail Service survey that I have referred to throughout this book. A number of participants in the survey stated that they did not receive exactly what they thought they had ordered, they were not made aware of the total price when they placed their orders, product delivery was late or poor, and return policy and service commitments were not met. The results of that survey (which polled over 17,000 online consumers) point out that improvements in order fulfillment and dependability can have a huge impact on an e-business' customer loyalty ratio. In spite of these grim statistics, another surprising outcome of the survey is that customers visit their favorite Web sites far more often than they do their favorite bricks-and-mortar business.

The Internet Simplifies Life?

One of the many great benefits of the Internet is its potential to broaden and to simplify our lives. Unfortunately, it remains to be seen when e-business will begin to live up to that potential. For example, in a July 24, 2000 article in *Internet Week* entitled "Lessons On How Not To Run an E-Business," David Yackelson related a personal tale that represents not only poor fulfillment services but also poor customer service. "One online vendor of executive gifts, after accepting my order, shipping and billing information, sent the gift to my house instead of the intended recipient. Calls to resolve the problem took several days and involved several people — none of whom could find the same order history. This experience resulted in a maddening conversation with an employee who asked me if I would return the now opened food gift (hey, my wife thought it was for her). Ultimately, a new gift was sent to the appropriate recipient 2 weeks after its intended arrival date. I won't be back."

Mr. Yackelson's second story demonstrates how poor fulfillment issues can be ameliorated through excellent customer service. He relates, "A second online vendor also lost an order, but a call to customer service resulted not only in the gift being shipped immediately but also at a 20 percent discount. I will be back. The implication here is you'll lose customers if you don't have systems in place to resolve issues quickly."

I refer again to Julie Bort's article penned for microtimes.com entitled "Even With E-com's Gains, Caveat Emptor," wherein she related her frustrations in using the technologies offered by the Internet to lift some of her "time gobbling" errands. One such item is gift giving, which out of necessity must be dealt with thoughout the year for holidays as well as birthdays, anniversaries, christenings, and graduations.

In her article Bort stated that "My secret weapon would be the Internet. I'd easily order my gifts on time, since I'd merely sit at my computer and type in a mail-to address. No running around to malls. No scavenging around my home for giftwrap and postal boxes. No trip to the post office. This year, shopping would be as easy as sending e-mail. So I was completely unprepared for the near-disaster my e-shopping would provoke."

According to Bort, finding the right online gift was just as problematic as a trip to the local mall. She adds, "Although I had no parking problems on the Web, getting a good idea of what was available, and how much it would cost, turned out to be tougher than I would have guessed. In all, I spent about three hours that evening shopping and zero time buying."

However, Bort was not one to give up easily — she was determined. So within a couple of days she was back in Cyberworld on a gift-buying mission. This time she felt she had hit pay dirt since after a two-hour search she found (in Bort's own words) "a store that could accommodate all my desires — fresh gift ideas, a recognized brand name, low prices." After (I imagine) a lady-like victory yell, she checked the "buy button" for three separate orders to be shipped to three different addresses. Then, came the first hint that all was not well in Cyberworld — the nationally known catalog merchant she was dealing with couldn't give her the option of enclosing a card or any type of message. But not to be thwarted, and being a very smart person, she put "Happy Birthday" or "Happy Anniversary," as the case may be, as the first name on the packing slip and then put the whole name in the last-name slot. Once she received an e-mail confirmation for each order she wrote, "I leaned back in my chair, feeling pretty darn smug with myself. The experience wasn't as smooth as I had expected it to be, but at least it was done."

Soon though, Cyberworld had her racing along its cyber byways as anxiety flowed through her system. Bort was told that shipment would take 10 to 14 days and sure enough, when she checked on the 10th day, the customer service representative informed her that the orders had left the warehouse on the 9th day, leaving Bort to wonder "what took them so long?" She wasn't kept in the dark long, for the next day, she found out that the e-tailer had shipped two gifts for each single order she had placed and charged her twice for everything. Even worse, according to Bort, "for some reason, the two identical gift orders were entered on different days, making it appear that I had actually placed these orders."

Bort called the e-tailer's customer service department to explain the problems. The unnamed e-tailer had a first-rate call center (probably because of much practice), and the agent quickly promised to deduct the charges from her credit card, adding that she wouldn't need to return the merchandise. He went on to knowledgably explain to Bort that the e-tailer logs orders from its Web site into a central file and then, the next day, a clerk manually enters them into the e-tailer's main order-entry system. In error, the clerk didn't delete Bort's orders after they were entered, so they were entered again the next day.

In the end, Bort only lost some of her valuable time and added a notch or two on her personal stress meter, because the e-tailer quickly agreed to take a loss on the cost of the second set of presents including shipping costs. Both sets of presents did arrive, albeit a little late, and the recipients were delighted with the gifts.

The moral of these stories is that e-businesses must make online purchasing easier by integrating their back-end systems and incorporating foolproof checks and balances.

As Bort so aptly put it, "Consider that in a virtual world, once you lose customers, you will probably never get them back because you'll never be the only shop in town." She ends the article with "As for my mother? This year she got a card and a check." Now my question is, will Bort go back and try again? If so, how long will she wait before she decides cyber-shopping can save time, offer convenience and provide products she is looking for?

MANAGING THE CUSTOMER EXPERIENCE

Managing the overall customer experience is an important ingredient in the sales process. As I have stated throughout this book, customer service goes hand-in-hand with a good LFMS. E-businesses that want to increase revenue per transaction and the number of transactions per customer must integrate the cost of logistics and fulfillment (including customer support and management) into the overall cost of sales.

Time — A Valuable Commodity

The e-business revolution is driven, in part, by the cost of time. Time that the customer has in short supply and time that eats into the profits of e-businesses. The modern populace has less time available for the simple maintenance of their lives let alone for leisure, while the changing dynamics of today's workplace put the employee's time at a premium and create pressure on the corporate structure to save every minute possible.

As Greg Drew, CEO of 800.com stated, "People have less time than they have money. If they can get online and save the drive to the mall and back and having to wait in line there, they prefer it." But only if they know they can save time by going online for their purchase.

Moneyed, time-starved, value-seeking, proactive consumers drive the Internet's economy. They're distinguished by an ethic of self-empowerment and a willingness to settle for nothing less than the best value for their money. Longer work hours and shrinking leisure time means many consumers have more money and less time to spend it. It has been estimated that by 2010 upwards of a staggering $65 billion in business will be done outside regular business hours. Hey guys, get your house in order so you can benefit from this predicted 24 x 7 onslaught of business.

One factor contributing to the predicted continuing upswing in e-business growth is simply that today's tired, overworked, overwrought consumers spend most of their limited free time at home, and that time typically revolves around "unwinding" and "getting away from it all." Once entrenched, they loathe leaving their self-styled cocoon. The goal of e-business should be to win the confidence of the consumer so they will "click the mouse" rather than "grab the car keys."

LFMS: Your Map to Great Customer Service

The e-business community must pay close attention to and protect the fragility of its customer relationships, for the success of any e-business is dependent upon the goodwill and loyalty of its customers. However, deliv-

---

A FIRST-CLASS LFMS ALLOWS AN E-BUSINESS TO:

- Improve customer service while reducing costs by providing a 360-degree view of each and every customer transaction.

- Put the customer in control by providing self-service and solution-centered support via a Web-based system that can provide information, support, maintenance, warranties, upgrades, tracking and status.

- Segment customer behavior one-to-one to individualize goods and services bringing in data mining and personalization tools.

- Earn customer loyalty to gain a lifetime of business through the 3Rs.

---

ering exceptional customer service and faultless fulfillment is both a science and an art. The first step in developing and maturing this symbiotic relationship is the implementation of an integrated customer service solution with an e-business's LFMS.

When strategizing and planning your LFMS, remember that the Internet has changed the processes an enterprise uses for customer acquisition, procurement, pricing, and customer satisfaction. The focus is now on the customer, who wants to buy products anytime, anywhere, and quickly. An LFMS must be in place to meet these demanding requirements.

In many ways the e-business with its customer-centric processes is entering a new age of marketing enabled by the implementation of a top-notch LFMS. Instead of making a product and finding customers for it, today's e-business finds the right customers, learns what they want, sells it to them, and services all their needs, doing it in a fast, cost effective, efficient manner. Personalized customer care, which requires a full integration of its back-office systems including LFM, makes sense if a customer's lifetime value sufficiently exceeds the cost of building the relationship.

The Gartner Group has espoused its views on this subject: "As enterprises make the transition to customer-centric business models, all organizational functions must have access to a consistent picture of the customer relationship." Customer-facing processes include cataloging, order entry, customer support, and overall customer relationship management. Supplier-facing processes include maintenance and repair operations and supply chain procurement, tracking, logistics, and collaborative supply and demand planning.

The goals of superior customer care are simple, but designing and implementing them can be another matter. Two central problems must be solved:

1) The e-business's information and the customer's information must be integrated into a unified whole, not scattered around and locked away in many departmental silos.

2) New kinds of customer behavioral information must be captured and processed.

These are exciting times. Every day new technologies are introduced into the market that change the way e-business is conducted. Among these are numerous technologies to help e-businesses better manage their customer relationships. These tools fall into three categories: sales-based customer service, post-delivery service including fulfillment issues, and post-sales service including returns, warranties and technical service. They all help to automate and facilitate the various aspects of your customer relationship management.

Many of these technologies make it easy for e-businesses to offer superior customer service with self-service tools. These include lists of answers to frequently asked questions, knowledge databases, and message boards. Customer evaluation and segmentation technologies help companies develop customer profiles so an e-business can identify its most profitable customers.

Thus, once an e-business has come to terms with the two key issues for online success — logistics and fulfillment — many turn their focus toward customer service. Some of the features on the top of many e-businesses' customer management strategy list are 24 x 7 customer service support, postage-paid packaging for returns and advisor services. Taking the 3R philosophy to the customer service arena, the e-business that comes out the winner will be the one that can service the *right* customer at the *right* time, through the *right* channels.

According to a report from the market analysis firm Datamonitor (www. datamonitor. com), poor online service cost e-businesses, in particular e-tailers, a combined $6. 1 billion in sales during 1999, a price that and could balloon to more than $173 billion in 2000 once all the figures are in. "The average company could have improved its online sales figures by almost 35% last year if it had provided better online customer service for potential customers," said Datamonitor consultant Steve Morrell. "This will be particularly important for new dot-com companies who are now realizing that they have to produce a profit, and soon."

While study after study show that a customer management strategy that marries customer service with logistics and fulfillment is a key part of a successful e-business, many e-businesses just don't seem to get the message. Just look at the delivery and stocking problems experienced by both B2Bs and e-tailers throughout 2000.

For an e-business to build a good customer service and LFM strategy it should ensure that its customer service department, which includes the call center, knows how to handle every aspect of a customer's transaction. The customer service agent needs to access and manipulate all the information involved in a customer's order, including tracking the status of an order through the fulfillment process until it reaches the customer's premises. If possible, the customer service agent should be able to communicate with the customers via e-mail, the telephone or online direct-connection software (chat) — all of which are within the budget of the majority of e-businesses.

Customer Care

Forrester defines the e-business standard for customer service as "consistent, high-quality customer support across all communication channels and business functions, based on common, complete information shared by employees, their customers, and business partners." The Web will be the first place a customer will choose to go among the many enterprise touchpoints. However, without the proper integration of LFMS and customer care, the customers may choose to return to the "mega mall" rather than order from the "inconvenient" convenience of home.

Make it a priority to define what customer care systems are and why they are so important to the bottom line of a business. Once you've examined the processes underlying the e-business model and its technology architecture, begin to optimize and integrate these processes and systems so as to provide optimal customer care.

These processes apply to all kinds of businesses: manufacturing, distribution, retail or services. In any industry where an enterprise is located in a value chain, it buys goods and services from suppliers, adds value, and sells to customers.

Customer-facing processes include cataloging, order entry, customer support, and overall customer relationship management. Supplier-facing processes include maintenance and repair operations and supply chain procurement, tracking, logistics, and collaborative supply and demand planning.

Too many times a large global enterprise may be unaware that XYZ's Zander division is buying products from its own Yalta division. As e-businesses begin to document its value chain's relationships and contracts, records that are established and maintained in multiple, often disparate, information systems across the value chain can be centralized, integrated and secured. Once that is done, this information can be extended to the Web for convenient value chain access based upon specific business rules-based access criteria.

When an e-business takes advantage of the fully interactive nature of the Internet, relevant information and intelligent support processes all can be marshaled in real-time and available 24 x 7. From tracking orders or shipments, to searching a knowledge base to solving a problem, these processes can support an increasing array of useful and intelligent services. Online help, education and training, knowledge bases including

FAQs and newsletters, technical support including product and service upgrades can be just a click away.

Much of the large enterprises business processes are embedded in legacy, ERP, sales force automation, customer relationship management, and client/server systems, but e-businesses can't afford to think of customer management-enabling technology as a cost center — visualize it as a strategic weapon. It contributes to overall enterprise cost reduction, improves service throughout the value chain and optimizes efficiencies for all.

Getting a value chain member's problem solved in one shot, cross-selling and up-selling, or gaining valuable feedback (complaints included) can generate metrics that count when it comes to measuring success in overall enterprise relationship management. Customer care initiatives cannot be evaluated unless they can be measured, and companies wanting to succeed must design and implement appropriate measurement strategies.

By constructing solutions from best-of-breed e-business application components, an enterprise can arrange, rearrange, and reuse the components as requirements dictate. An e-business must build business-specific applications to provide its customers with Internet-based access to the information they require. This requires adopting an infrastructure that can deliver enhanced services in a controlled and effective manner. Simultaneously, an e-business must look at leveraging legacy and common components that will allow it to reduce costs and complexity for building, managing, and delivering Internet-based information, systems and applications, throughout the value chain.

A Forrester survey of executives from the Fortune 1000 companies points out that large e-businesses risk poor customer service daily due to the grab bag of independent applications they use to support their customers. "While this problem has existed for years, it will soon end as the Web becomes an ever-stronger force and high-quality self-service becomes a competitive differentiator. In the Internet economy, high quality customer service is an absolute requirement. And the current haphazard approaches to customer management will destroy a company's future."

Another requirement for many customer service departments and call centers is that they must wear many different hats when interacting with a customer. Take an instance when a customer calls in about their modem, saying it's going bad because page feed is much slower on their machine than other people's computers. After a bit of interactive conversation, the agent suggests the customer trade in their 33k modem for a 56k which will allow a faster download speed. In this instance the customer called in for technical support and after the agent realized the problem was ineffective equipment rather than "broken" equipment, the agent put on his or her sales hat and began singing the praises of the 56k modems. One moment the agent was a support person and the next, a salesperson, tools are needed that allow employees to easily respond to customer interactions and opportunities.

The customer service department also needs complete visibility over all of the customer's interactions within the e-business, including orders, service calls and other contacts. By having a comprehensive 360-degree customer view, agents can solve customer problems more quickly; but also they can proactively work with customers, for example, assisting with complex order fulfillment, calling or e-mailing customers to advise them of problems or changes in their orders, and cross-selling and up-selling.

Making integrated customer service and LFM systems a cornerstone of your e-business strategy will enable your business to acquire, develop and retain customers more profitably and manage the complete lifecycle of customer relationships in the Internet age.

A good example is Zurn Industries, Inc. (www.zurn.com), which has grown to become a leading provider of building products for the specification, residential and retail do-it-yourself markets. Zurn's order processing and fulfillment engine (Industri-Matematik's VIVALDI software — www.industrimatematik.com) manages its complex logistics requirements and diverse customer preferences to coordinate, monitor and measure the physical movement of goods across the supply chain. "With VIVALDI Advanced Order Management software, we can decrease our order fulfillment cycle times while also improving service levels for every customer," said Marla Longoria, vice president of information systems at Zurn. "The system improves how we source products by matching product availability with customer proximity to fill orders faster and save transportation costs. Additionally, we have gained the ability to rapidly analyze orders and inventory, allowing us to identify more profitable sales opportunities."

Zurn's order management software is integrated with Calico Commerce's eSales Configurator software (www. calicotech. com), enabling Zurn's sales staff to configure its range of complex building products with full supply chain visibility, including current inventory status and exact delivery date. This allows Zurn to offer its customers accurate substitutions for unavailable items, but at the same time ensuring that the full product configuration remains precise as new components are added. Also, it helps Zurn better manage follow-up shipments. If a contractor orders a full roof drain but wants the components delivered incrementally, the correct products are supplied in each shipment. This combination provides Zurn with the automatic translation of a proposal into an electronic order, managing the complete cycle from bid to invoice.

Though marketing is often mentioned as Amazon's (www.amazon. com) and Dell's (www.dell.com) primary reason for success, it would never have become a reality without the exacting attention they give to their back-office systems. An LFMS and a tightly integrated customer service platform are what allowed these pioneers to benefit from high customer retention rates and repeat customer purchases. Amazon is one of the best at keeping in touch with customers and consistently shipping products as promised. Amazon and Dell both realize that though their well-turned, integrated customer service and fulfillment platforms makes them leaders today, it isn't enough to sustain their lead in the future. To keep ahead of their competitors, Dell and Amazon utilize an ongoing improvement strategy for their back-office operations enabling them to continue to fulfill orders at the lowest cost possible.

Toysrus.com publicly stated that the primary reason for its agreement to a 10-year partnership with Amazon. com is to compensate for Toysrus. com's weakness in the areas of on-line customer service and fulfillment. And this may be the first of many such partnerships. Bernard Elliott, a senior research analyst specializing in call centers at Gartner Group, Inc., said he expected other e-commerce companies to turn to established direct marketers for help in providing customer service and fulfillment. Speaking of Amazon's end of this new partnership, he goes on to state, "This is an example of how providing great customer service not only brings you customers, it brings you partners. It isn't just having a Web site and making a sale, it's having good customer service that starts with the order and helps the customer all the way through to completion, and if they want a return as well."

Even the third party fulfillment providers realize the pluses of a customer service and logistics and fulfillment partnership. Look at Fulfillment PLUS, Inc. (www.fulfilllmentplus.net), a provider of turnkey e-commerce fulfillment solutions, which provides an interactive customer service and fulfillment solution for e-businesses. According to Fulfillment PLUS, its customer service and fulfillment partnership offering is designed to enhance customer loyalty for "dot-com" merchants. Its technology-based solution provides online order fulfillment and personalized customer care. Through the integration of Web technologies, automated business processes and customer service, it offers a comprehensive back-end solution that is capable of handling the scale and complexity of the Web. Add to that its real-time order fulfillment software system and management of the physical logistics of delivering merchandise to customers, and you have a comprehensive system for managing a high volume of orders daily, along with the ability to manage inventory, track shipping and handle returns.

Another third party fulfillment provider that got the customer management message is Precision Response Corporation (www. prcnet.com). In early 1999 it launched a new division, prcnetcare.com, to meet the burgeoning "demand from large corporations for Internet and e-mail-based customer care." According to Precision's own announcement, its first prcnetcare.com offering, InfiniteAccess, integrates clients' Web-based "customer care and commerce initiatives with our existing customer service and fulfillment services." It goes on to state that "Infinite Access provides customer service and Web-based fulfillment services for large corporations operating in such industries as information services, telecommunications and healthcare."

Customer Service Strategies
Customer service defines much of the strategy that's going on behind closed doors throughout the e-business community. An e-business must

be able to commit product availability, price, and delivery date at the time the customer clicks the buy button. If the product isn't immediately available to ship, the e-business must have the ability to know when it will be available and to allocate it to the customer through a Capable-to-Promise (CTP) process.

Know your customer. There is a wealth of information that can be captured and gathered to provide meaningful ways to maintain a complete view of current and potential customers. The previously referred to Forrester survey of executives from the Fortune 1000 companies was telling. Less than half of these companies use customer data collected from the Web. Of the customer information they do capture in their various systems, only a little more than half of the respondents felt they do an adequate job by synchronizing customer data (usually via batch interfaces and manual re-keying of printed reports).

This can't be the basis for a real-time customer dialog. The same Forrester survey further revealed that although these companies expect the Web to be the dominant approach to customer service by 2001, few integrate online customer behavioral data with other contact channels. So how do they think it will happen — by osmosis?

Forrester points out how far today's enterprises have to go before they have a truly viable e-business model. Many are simply not set up to manage information across the enterprise, much less the value chain. Therefore vital information, which could reduce costs in the long run, often remains invisible or unavailable to the greater enterprise and its value chain since it simply stays with those to whom it was given. There is no mechanism for properly disseminating it.

Customers and employees must share a common knowledge base with a more holistic view of both the e-business and the currently disjointed customer information dispersed throughout the enterprise. Customer care means providing transactional data like order and account tracking and customer history information. A robust e-business platform with customer care and LFMS in place can enable new kinds of interactions, new kinds of information, and comprehensive access to all customer and enterprise touchpoints, allowing joint problem-solving, convenient self-service and self-selling. If an e-business can give its customers and its entire value chain the information they need, customers can go a long ways toward selling to themselves and servicing their own information needs.

Customer needs change over time. By blending sales force automation with customer self-service, a new generation of marketing strategy can be implemented for a competitive advantage. And since the customer and the sales force can have a 360-degree view of each other, true customer partnerships can be forged. In many ways the customer has become a partner in development and production of the desired product. Many e-businesses are finding this type of thinking difficult, because they've focused their business processes and systems on improving time to market and view their customers as end targets rather than partners. To succeed, e-businesses must look at their customers as partners.

Is your e-business getting the bookmarks? If not, create and/or integrate your workflow, customer service, and an LFMS to optimize the movement of product through your distribution center efficiently, or partner with a third party provider that can offer these systems. Devise packing and handling standards to make sure products arrive in top condition. Ensure that returns processing proceeds without hassle. Implement forecasting systems that optimize inventory so that product is available when customers order it. And, of course, have an implementation strategy that will allow the e-business to make these changes in such a way that its costs are kept low and revenues and profits can reach stratopheric levels.

The only way to prevent becoming embroiled in constant price wars is for an e-business to differentiate itself. The speed, accuracy, and completeness with which orders are picked-packed-shipped could be the answer. For a value chain to operate at such high levels of performance and efficiency demands a revamping of how an e-business operates. Rather than managing multiple processes within the e-business, multiple enterprises are managed with one collaborative process enabled by a Third Stage LFMS. The e-business acts as the demand center, coordinating and ensuring that the entire supply chain is focused on serving the customer. This requires full visibility into supply chain inventories including purchase order status, transportation status, and alert and workflow processes.

Bookmarks

While it's true that the Internet empowers online customers through price and service comparisons, currently many online shoppers don't take advantage of these features — there is just too much information to process. Instead, a significant number of online customers use the bookmark feature provided by their Web browser. This allows the customer, once they have visited a site that has provided a satisfactory experience, to return at the click of a mouse. For many online users, this usage pattern is highly addictive and the successful e-business, whether it's e-tail or B2B, should exploit this benign but potentially lucrative addiction. **But** today's customer insists upon ease of use, convenience, reliability and strict attention to the 3Rs if they are to bookmark a Web site for repeat visits.

Call Centers

"Virtual" e-businesses may consider a strategy of outsourcing some or all of their call center operations. Dan Lynch, president of logistics for Organic, suggests that some of their customers retain at least partial call center operations in-house to maintain control of critical customer contacts. JT Kreager, president and COO SubmitOrder. com, disagrees, stating that a split operation can result in the right hand not knowing what the left hand is doing. He usually recommends that as much as possible be done under one roof to prevent conflicts and duplication.

I'm not going into the ins and outs of operating or outsourcing a call center. Readers who are interested in optimizing, building or outsourcing their call center operations should pick up Brendan Read's excellent, book, <u>Designing the Best Call Center for Your Business</u>.

Keep It About the Customer

All over the world enterprises are struggling with the monumental task of developing corporate portals. Those who have had the greatest success have learned that it's not a singular proposition, it's plural — portals. Pioneering e-businesses are establishing relationships where none had ever existed — with customers, suppliers, and trading partners. The "old guard's" value chain — material producer to supplier to manufacturer to distributor to customer — is going by the wayside. Instead more and more customers are gaining control and turning the producer-to-customer relationship upside down.

Armed with the Internet, fully informed customers come close to meeting one of the doctrines of pure competition — perfect information. To say that this is a paradigm shift is no exaggeration, and e-businesses that will win in the 21st Century markets should have already begun their journey. Additionally, the customer label has become somewhat unclear. In many B2B scenarios customer versus supplier is a function of role, not entity. In some transactions, the same entity plays multiple, simultaneous roles of producer and customer.

My best bit of advice is to attack your customer management issues head-on and invest in state of the art customer service and logistics and fulfillment solutions so as to provide improved customer experience. You will find your e-business soon becoming a popular bookmark entry, in many online customers' Web browsers.

The 3Rs Go Global

GLOBALIZATION WILL OVERPOWER existing relationships as enterprises adopt the e-business model and gain access to different channel members such as suppliers, distributors, shippers, wholesalers and retailers (to name a few). This enables the e-business to procure new items and bring down prices. Where an e-business places the balance between the maintenance of relationships and the exploitation of new technology shows the impact of the Internet on logistics and fulfillment.

Most e-businesses have a dismal track record when it comes to global logistics and fulfillment. To get your adrenaline flowing, I am going to state a few cold, hard, but fascinating facts. Forrester Research (www.forrester.com), a leading independent research firm that analyzes the future of technology and its impact (What would the e-business world do without Forrester?), observes that e-tail sites, starting on day one, routinely get 30% of their traffic and 10% of their orders from outside the US. They also routinely turn away half of the international orders that these potential customers attempt to place.

According to a BizReport (www.bizreport.com) dated May 4, 2000, in 2000 the number of Internet users topped 375 million in 51 countries. Much of the growth in Internet users is taking place outside the US, with Asia rapidly catching up on the US in market share terms. The US accounted for just 36% of total Internet users at the end of 2000 — down from 46% in 1998 and 55% in 1996.

Here is additional evidence of this powerful trend. Nearly 50% of the Web sites in North America and the Asia-Pacific regions are e-tail. Only 25% of European sites and 33% in other regions are e-tail. A full 50% of the European sites are B2B. Only 35% of North American sites and 25% in Asia-Pacific, and 31% in other parts of the world are B2B.

Now, are you ready to tackle the thorny issue of globalization, internationalization and localization? I hope so.

As everyone has heard numerous times, and it's true, the Internet has expanded the marketplace. "Companies that were traditionally domestically focused in their fulfillment operations have now become *de facto* exporters as they've opened up their e-commerce sites," states Martha Urscheler, director of marketing for Syntra Technologies (www.syntra.com), now known as Clearcross. "The Internet knows no international boundaries and creates international companies by simply providing buyers and sellers with access to other buyers and sellers. The tools developed for the optimization of domestic operations need to be rethought to manage the regulatory, financial, and logistics constraints inherent in the global procurement and fulfillment process," espouses Urscheler.

"No longer is it just company versus company — now it's global supply chain versus global supply chain, competing not on price alone but on speed and quality of service. Success in such a market demands supply chain excellence," says Paul Albright, CEO of SeeCommerce (www.seecommerce.com), a software company that provides Web-centric applications.

Carolynn Sherby, director of analyst relations for Extricity Software (www.extricity.com), a provider of B2B software products, adds, "The Internet has enabled businesses to be tightly linked with those of their partners, suppliers, distributors, and customers — providing a quantum leap in competitiveness."

Harry Wolhandler, VP of Market Research at ActivMedia (www.activmediaresearch.com), an authoritative source for custom and syndicated market research about today's rapidly evolving e-business climate, explains, "Two in five online companies attribute greater geographic presence to the Internet, and all acknowledge its power to impact total company sales. A similar two in five also rely on the Net for business management support to knit together far-flung operations and collaborative partnerships. This is particularly important in B2B settings where the Internet is often more useful for internal and external coordination than for sales revenue generation. The additional organizational capacity derived from instantaneous global communication flattens organizational structures and speeds up real-time decision making and information flow. The results show up in profitability across the organization rather than profitability due to Internet presence, a measure not picked up in many studies."

Greg Stock, vice president of marketing for Vastera (www.vastera.com), a provider of global trade management solutions, says, "Every time I talk with prospects, especially dot.coms or those that are US-centric, they really find it a huge challenge in becoming a global company." If an e-business wants to fulfill its global customer orders, it needs to find some way to provide the functionality for automatic calculation of every aspect of the transaction.

Even e-businesses that participate in global commerce in the normal course of business, and therefore are familiar with calculating all the costs, have problems when they adopt an e-business model. Now the customer expects immediate service.

THE SMALL E-BUSINESS DILEMMA

The September 20, 2000, *New York Times* article by Barbara Whitaker entitled "The Web Makes Going Global Easy, Until You Try to Do It," cited a number of benefits and risks on globalization.

Mike Krill, a chief financial officer with Atlas Consulting, which assists emerging companies in building a commercialization strategy, stated, "The reality is, going global is difficult. What we found is it's typically something that's an undertaking for [large] ventures." But these remarks were tempered with, "I think there is a successful strategy for small businesses and that is to try and take advantage of the ecosystem around the industry."

"It's challenging for a small company to take what they have and translate it overseas," declared one small-business owner.

The last couple of years the world of e-business has been hyped as "where the e-business version of David can slay the e-business version of Goliath. The notion that the playing field is leveled is hyped and not realistic," Bob Parker, a senior analyst specializing in e-commerce at AMR Research Inc. told the *Times*. To illustrate his point, Mr. Parker referred to an advertisement featuring an Italian woman selling olive oil. In reality, he quipped, "that little old lady gets crushed."

S.V. Braun Co. (www.svbrauninc.com), which has adopted the e-business model, doesn't agree with Mr. Parker. The small e-business produces foam that, when injected into a car or truck tire, can protect a tire against going flat. Braun was sure that its product would do well in the international market, especially those with poor road conditions — but it had to get word to those distributors. International Web pages were the answer. Braun used Multimedia Marketing Group Inc., an online marketing firm, to translate a few basic Web pages that cost it less than $1,000. Thus, says a Braun spokesperson, "by people noticing the Web site overseas, they contact us and we're able to develop new contacts and accounts that would be impossible otherwise."

Fred P. Hochberg, deputy administrator with the United States Small Business Administration, also differs with Mr. Parker. He told the *Times* that the Web is fueling global opportunities for some 25 million small businesses nationwide.

All businesses large and small need to bear in mind that to participate in the international e-business arena, an e-business has to deal with extremely difficult issues — tariffs, languages and currency issues, not to mention the complication that can arise out of trying to establish effective logistics and fulfillment partnerships.

THE SERVICING (OR NON-SERVICING) OF THE GLOBAL CUSTOMER

More than 30% of online shoppers live outside North America (and the number is quickly growing). E-businesses have to learn how to sell and deliver their products to global destinations. Keep in mind that the field of competition is expanding as fast as the international online consumer market is expanding. Many of these new competitors are non-US e-businesses that know how to ship and sell internationally — they've always done it.

One way to ship to international destinations in a cost-effective acceptable manner is to partner with service vendors that can handle the "last mile" or invest in specialized systems that provide global regulatory compliance and actual landed cost calculations.

Catalog shipper L.L. Bean has expanded its international presence with a multilingual Web site. The push into world markets was launched from the shipper's existing logistics platform, affirming the view that catalogers' experience in business-to-consumer markets puts them a step ahead in the race to capture cross-border business on the Web.

"The fulfillment center we have in place has been capable of dual processing since it was conceived, so we process international orders side by side with domestic orders," says Bob Olive, L.L. Bean's senior logistics manager.

In the 1990s, L.L. Bean went after the lucrative Japanese market and in doing so managed to develop a $200 million business there. According to Olive, "that gave us a good background in the global arena." The Japan experience, coupled with a logistics infrastructure geared to e-tail demands, made L.L. Bean's transition to an e-business model relatively straightforward. Its international customer base "is growing briskly," said Olive.

"We tend to consolidate by SKU, and process all orders regardless of the destination," notes Olive. L.L. Bean's in-house fulfillment center in Freeport, Maine can process 180,000 packages a day and "the order turnaround cycle is very tightly defined." Orders are shipped from that facility within 24 hours and in-stock levels are kept at around 92%. On inventory levels, Olive comments, "we have high in-stock goals for when catalogs are shipped."

The company faced and solved many potential problems when it made its incursion into the Japanese market. Take, for instance, address labeling. L.L. Bean developed in-house software solutions to cope with the relatively complex address details that are required when delivering to destinations in Japan.

Another issue any e-business with an international customer base must address is providing adequate levels of customer service. All over the world online customers will still, from time to time, want to use the telephone for queries and this customer service issue has proved to be a 'thorn in the side' of many e-businesses. Not so with L.L. Bean, Olive states, "We are feeling comfortable within the structure we have."

In its Japanese market, L.L. Bean takes orders through its Tokyo-based call center and, because of the time difference, ships the product the same day. "So we are able to complete delivery to Tokyo in 72 hours," brags Olive. "The international customer has got the same sense that it's easy to order and to get the package quickly."

Dell Computers sells its products to the world, and other computer manufacturers are taking note. According to a Dell spokesperson, "Dell's operations in Asia, Europe, and Latin America are, for the most part, uniform. There are a few countries where we work through distributors, but the direct model has proven successful in every country into which it has been introduced."

Dell offers its international customers a menu of purchasing options, customized computer systems, phone and online technical support, and next-day, on-site product service. Like L.L. Bean, Dell understands that customer service excellence is critical when selling in an international marketplace.

Over the next couple of years, the e-business balance between the US and the rest of the world will shift. Although, all indicators point to continued growth in international e-business, there are huge problems looming in the international logistics and fulfillment area. A recent report by Forrester, entitled "Mastering Commerce Logistics," indicated that 85% of the retail and manufacturing respondents had an online presence but could not fill orders internationally because of the complexity of the international shipping process. The report stated, "of the globally incapacitated, 75% cite their systems' inability to register international addresses accurately or quote total delivered costs."

If the readers were outside the US and tried to purchase a product from many US-based e-businesses they would find disclaimers such as the ones set out below:

Amazon.com — "You may be subject to import duties and taxes, which are levied once the package reaches your country. Additional charges for customs clearance must be borne by you; we have no control over these charges and cannot predict what they may be. Customs policies vary widely from country to country; you should contact your local customs office for further information. Additionally, when ordering from Amazon.com, you are considered the importer of record and must comply with all laws and regulations of the country in which you are receiving the goods."

BarnesandNoble.com — "Customs and import duties are charged to the customer once the package reaches the destination country. These charges are the responsibility of the customer and will vary from country to country. We cannot determine what these fees will be. We recommend that our customers contact their local customs office for details on how these charges are assessed and applied."

CDnow.com — "Import duties and/or taxes may be imposed by your local government on shipments from outside your country. These charges are separate from CDNOW's charges and are beyond our control or ability to predict. These charges (if any) are made payable to your government. You are responsible for paying any taxes, duties and/or customs fees charged by your government. Please check with your local post office for more information."

Egghead.com — "All international orders, other than Canada, must be placed through our Call Center at 1-800-EGGHEAD or (360) 883-3447 x8034. International customers are responsible for any additional shipping costs. International orders may be subject to shipping delays as well as customs, duties, taxes, tariffs and other applicable charges. Orders received by phone are subject to a $7.50 handling fee."

Beyond.com — "Because Customs duties can increase the price you pay for software, we recommend you check on local import tariffs for software. In addition to the cost of your order, you are responsible for paying all import tariffs and brokerage fees."

Compusa.com — "CompUSA Net.com Inc. welcomes international customers to browse and shop on-line with certain limitations and restrictions. CompUSA Net.com Inc. doesn't collect any import taxes and or duties that your government might impose on products shipped from the United States. Please verify (in advance) what these duties might entail and make the appropriate arrangements with your local government. Additional shipping charges will also be added to your order."

Buy.com — "At this time we are unable to accept or process orders shipping outside of the United States."

To compete in the new economy, e-merchants must expand their delivery service options and capabilities to deliver reliably and economically to global destinations.

THE GLOBAL LOCALIZATION ISSUES

The simple act of translating Web content into other languages doesn't make an e-business an "international business." It takes localization efforts and cultural sensitivity.

A Jupiter WebTrack survey of the 114 leading US Web sites found that two-thirds of the sites had minimal or no globalization, such as a registered foreign domain name, translation into another language, or featured local content.

On the globalization issue, the leading question for all e-businesses should be: If an e-business's Web site is its portal to the global marketplace, how can it make the Web site a truly international presence for the e-business?

Unlike the majority of the world's populace, Americans have always conducted business in one language — English — and have little or no experience in dealing with other languages (or cultures for that matter). Yet, to stay competitive in a global marketplace, such as the e-business community, American e-businesses must learn to localize their online presence.

Lionbridge Technologies (www.lionbridge.com) is an e-business which provides "localization" and "internationalization" services to help e-businesses make their Web sites more effective in international markets.

Lionbridge's Robert Sprung gives a classic example of internationalization, a process that he defines as "designing products that are adaptable to local markets around the world" — installing a steering wheel on the right or left side of a car.

He equates a poorly implemented international site to the steering wheel of a car being on the wrong side for that particular country. It will have botched translation with bad grammar and content that can be (unintentionally) offensive.

Sprung also cited the importance of localization, which he defines as adapting a product to a given locale. Among examples Sprung notes are apparel that appeals to a specific market or providing support for multiple currencies. When going global an e-business should keep in mind that each country has its own peculiarities — local business rules, cultural issues and user interface issues — and catering to them are just as important as the proper translations.

For example, eBay stumbled when it first hit Europe because it failed to properly support European value-added taxes in currency conversions. Since it cleaned up its act, eBay has left its European competition eating its dust. "Look at eBay," said Sprung. "Because of the ease of entry onto the Web, they have strong local competition all over Europe. The acid test is that the market will give you your answer."

Cisco and IBM are Lionbridge clients. Through the implementation of localized sites they have found an added benefit: significant reduction of their customer support costs. Sprung speculates that an international e-business that channeled only 40 international calls per day from their call center to their Web site could recover the cost of producing an localized online presence. Sprung is certain that is one of the reasons Microsoft spends more than $100 million annually on localizing its Web sites.

GLOBAL LOGISTICS AND FULFILLMENT

Many e-businesses find the most expedient way to offer first-class logistics and fulfillment on a global basis is to acquire local partners on a country-by-country basis.

Forrester estimates that 85% of e-businesses can't fill international orders because of the complexities of shipping across borders. Of the 15% that can handle global orders, most are shipping to only a few countries in Europe and Asia where they can fill orders out of local warehouses. Of the "globally incapacitated," three-quarters cite basic issues such as their system's inability to register international addresses accurately or to price total delivery cost.

Firms that turn down international orders, with no prior international sales experience, cite shipping (53%) as the primary reason, and firms with international sales experience, cite channel conflict (56%) and shipping (44%) as their reasons.

To ship to international destinations — whether or not the e-business has a local presence — e-businesses can partner with service vendors to handle that last leg or invest in systems such as those provided by Syntra (now Clearcross) and/or Nextlinx (www.nextlinx.com). It's obvious that e-businesses that want to sell globally can't open warehouses in every country. However, small firms will be able to take advantage of global opportunities by using Web services to perform functions such as facilitating denied parties, calculating landed cost, and estimating arrivals. There are a variety of logistic companies, ranging from DHL to new Internet start-ups such as iLink Global, ready to help the global merchant deliver their goods.

With 30% of online consumers located outside North America and this proportion growing, e-businesses that accept only US-based orders will suffer huge opportunity losses. In order to ship to international destinations (whether or not they have a local presence), e-businesses need to partner with a business that allows them to personalize the delivery options in much the same manner as they serve up content on their Web sites. For example, From2 (www.from2.com), a logistics intelligence and service provider for global e-businesses, offers buyers a choice between Express Air, Standard Airfreight and Ocean Freight modes of transportation.

An e-business facing its global logistics and fulfillment issues head-on is Corex Technologies. In anticipation of widespread worldwide demand for its CardScan Executive and CardScan Office business card readers, it contracted with From2, to process and ship all international orders placed online at www.cardscan.com.

Henceforth, Corex can use From2's complete information, shipping and logistics solution to fulfill international online customer orders promptly, accurately and cost-effectively. "Our recent focus on forming a worldwide network of distributors, resellers and retailers has been extremely successful. Nevertheless, there are still thousands of potential customers around the globe who don't live in areas serviced by this still-expanding network," says Corex Technologies CEO and President Jonathan Stern. "For these individuals, as well as for the additional thousands of overseas customers who prefer to order via the Web, From2's expertise in global e-commerce will provide customers with a complete landed door-to-door breakdown of costs."

From2 provides Corex with its patent-pending Global Delivered Cost Calculator (GDCC), trade compliance support, customs brokerage, and international services for each targeted international market. From2's seamless technology instantly calculates freight, insurance, duties, taxes, customs clearance fees, and other import charges for products sold though Corex's Web site so its customers can determine exactly how much it will cost, in local currency, for delivery of the products prior to submitting the order.

In addition to handling trade compliance and customs brokerage for Corex, From2 will also provide comprehensive logistics services through its domestic and international facilities. These services include warehousing, fulfillment, and international door-to-door delivery, complete with on-line tracking capabilities. "Corex really fits the profile of our ideal client in that its products have just as much appeal overseas as they do here in the U.S.," stated Leon Falic, CEO and President of From2. "This, combined with the fact that the products are easy to install and easy to use, make it an excellent choice for international e-commerce, which is precisely the business we understand best."

THE GLOBAL ENABLERS

A study by Forrester shows that about 85% of American e-tailers can't fill international orders because of the complexities involved in shipping goods across borders. The barriers include local taxes, different currencies, language barriers and customs procedures.

A number of e-businesses have stopped international sales and shipment because of the associated problems, while others have instituted very specific guidelines for their international customers.

Europe presents a special challenge for Web businesses because of the complicated logistics of shipping to over 30 different countries, each with its own regulatory system. Fortunately, European logistics companies and national postal systems have developed sophisticated capabilities, and they make as good if not better partners than their US counterparts.

The answer to the US-based globalization quandary is to find a third party that can handle payment and reconciliation of customs duties, tariffs and value-added taxes, providing customers a guaranteed total-landed-costs calculation in their local currencies.

The best of these third-party expeditors will also work with customs authorities, providing shipment data in advance to expedite clearances and logistics.

With the right third-party partner, an e-business can gain access with relative ease to the large and rapidly expanding international markets without having to substantially change their existing infrastructure.

An interesting service that launched in late 2000 is Global CommerceZone (www.gczone.com). Global CommerceZone is helping e-businesses with their international logistics problems in a third-party capacity. It handles payment and reconciliation of customs duties, tariffs and value-added taxes, providing its e-business customers with a guaranteed total-landed-costs calculation in their local currencies. Global CommerceZone works with customs authorities, providing shipment data in advance to expedite clearances and logistics.

"Anyone doing business over the Internet is a global company," says Jim Treleaven, CEO of GCZ. "A number of retailers have stopped shipping overseas because of its associated problems." Speaking of the international commerce situation in the US e-business community, Treleaven explained, "It's a very uncertain proposition at this point. Some e-businesses have very specific guidelines that say they won't ship outside the US. Others figure they'll take a chance and see what happens."

This young company is focused on boxes, not pallets, and is aimed primarily at small to mid-size e-tailers that are shut out of international markets by the complexity and cost of fulfillment. Treleaven believes, "Most retailers want access to large and rapidly expanding international markets. With our service they can open up those markets without having to substantially change their existing infrastructure."

Global CommerceZone offers an e-business the ability to implement a total "click-to-door" solution, which results in a positive shopping experience for the e-business's international customers through the seamless and transparent integration of Global CommerceZone's functionality into the e-business's Web site.

Another outlet for US-based e-businesses is Overseas Brokers, Inc. (www.overseasbrokers.com). This company specializes in large and complex products that rule out a simple dock delivery by a carrier such as UPS, or that require special handling. Overseas Brokers has the means to integrate its global logistical pricing and routing matrix with an e-business's back-end. The company operates a global fulfillment network, providing shipping, customs clearance, inside delivery and installation services.

Why should US e-businesses bother with gaining and maintaining an international customer-base? The same reason they went online. It's a huge market. In another three years, online commerce will be larger than current sales in the US, especially in the e-tail sector.

Syntra is a company whose name has become synonymous with "global," in e-commerce parlance (although as previously pointed out, it is now known as ClearCross). It's the leading provider of Internet-based e-business solutions for managing the financial, logistics, and regulatory constraints associated with global procurement and fulfillment. Steve Cole, vice president of marketing for Syntra, explains "Syntra works to smooth out the rough spots and make it easy to do business across borders, by helping customers better understand how much something will cost, then generating the paperwork to complete the global transaction."

"For example, if you are deciding between two or three choices of sources, and if one or more are located outside the country, it's not merely a matter of the product's price. The cost calculation must consider the tariffs, taxes, quotas, duties, and shipping charges. In a global supply chain, the 'real cost' is much more than simply the product price." Cole adds that it's not uncommon to see examples where the real price can mean a 100% or 200% increase over the product price. People are coming to us because they see the opportunities that are being generated from their Web sites. They get international inquiries, and then don't know what to do with the order."

When e-businesses, especially the smaller ones, embark on the development of an international presence, these issues often catch them unawares. "It's hard, particularly with smaller companies," explains Cole. "They see large orders that suddenly appear like bluebirds out of the sky, and they no longer choose to say, 'Well, I'm just not going to deal with that' — they want to go global."

Many don't understand quotas and legislative controls over imports and exports. Cole comments, "the U.S. is not really a free-trading nation. There are strict controls around food, clothing, oil, and steel (to name a few) that affect how products flow in and out of this country. Smaller companies don't necessarily think about these things as they get thrust into this space."

In explaining how Syntra/ClearCross works, Cole says "We are a flavor of an ASP. We are highly specialized and provide the link to the global commerce technology." Syntra sells its services on a per-transaction basis, with no upfront investment required, making it particularly appealing for the small e-business. "The only thing that is needed is to wire our engine into their Internet site so the transaction comes to us," according to Cole. "Then we can do our thing, and get back to the client with the final details." Syntra/ClearCross's client list includes DHL, Lucent, Motorola and Fingerhut.

A recent study by Forrester found that 46% of orders coming through US e-businesses' Web sites from other countries can't be fulfilled due to the lack of the global commerce procedures to fulfill them. In some cases it's due to regulatory reasons and in others it's because e-businesses don't know how to make it easy for customers to calculate landed costs up front. "Every time I talk with prospects, especially dot.coms or those that are US-centric, they really find it a huge challenge in becoming a global company," says Greg Stock, vice president of marketing for Vastera (www.vastera.com), a provider of global trade management solutions.

If e-businesses want to do business globally over the Internet, and they have an online commerce presence, global e-commerce vendors strongly suggest providing functionality that automatically calculates every aspect of the transaction.

"If I'm a customer, I want to know the total amount of money I need to provide for things like transportation, duties, taxes, and tariffs," says Mary Lou Fox, chief operating officer for NextLinx, a single-stop solution for global e-commerce. If a customer in Paris, for example, goes to a Web site of a US-based e-business, that customer won't wait for the US e-business to get back with the total costs, he wants the information immediately. If the e-business can't automatically calculate the entire cost of the product, the customer just becomes frustrated and leaves.

"What companies are looking for is a simple way to present to their customer what the total cost is going to be," says Syntra's Cole. Though opening up your business globally can bring in more revenue, it can end up costing more as well. Vestra's Stock weighs in with, "There are cases where a company wanted to do business with another company outside the US, but the taxes were so high." The price of the product may have been a good deal, but after factoring in taxes it didn't make sense. "You have to look at what country you're doing business with regarding taxes and tariffs," continues Stock.

E-businesses seldom make the effort to follow through on every little issue when it comes to global e-commerce. In many instances, a product ordered from a US-based e-business will travel via truck, rail, ship, rail, and back to truck before it reaches its international destination. E-businesses must take the time to check each of these carriers on shipment status. In failing to do so, they ask for problems: lost shipments, delayed shipments, frustrated customers, all of which can cost them money or a loyal customer.

At Syntra/ClearCross "we set up a transportation hub. We have links to ocean carriers and rail carriers in all different countries. Because companies are operating on lean inventory, you have to know a shipment is going to be late. So visibility is important. It's part of the new economy," says Cole. Businesses are always searching for ways to lessen their financial as well as employee burdens.

NextLinx has a feature called Pipeline Visibility and Intelligent Messaging, which allows its customers to track and trace shipments and issue alerts when the status varies from plan. "We do visibility where you can ping us and ask where is this shipment, and we give you the status," says Fox.

As e-businesses go online, they become a global entity by the very nature of the Internet. The Web is accessible globally, so unless an e-business blocks sales from outside the US, it should understand that there are other international issues to be dealt with besides landed cost. An innocent order can become a hot potato. The US government prohibits US entities from conducting business with several foreign countries. E-businesses can't play dumb on these issues, the experts say. Although an e-business may be given a warning the first time, it's not uncommon for the government to levy high fines for a slip-up.

Syntra/ClearCross, in its marketing material, notes that a subsidiary of a major computer maker was fined millions of dollars for illegally exporting computers to a Russian nuclear-weapons laboratory. "Certain addresses can't receive certain goods," says Stock. "Someone just can't send a calculator to Saddam Hussein. That's a simple example, but the point is (that the restricted list) changes daily."

With companies like the ones mentioned in this section, the hassles or worries of what the costs are going to be, or where a person can sell, are taken away. The regulatory issues are particularly a concern for the buyer because, if not followed correctly, fines may result. "The (seller's) Web site has to be smart enough to recognize who can and can't be sold things," says Cole.

There is still a problem. Many e-businesses that try to fulfill international orders can't timely and reliably fulfill their international orders; therefore, the return rates on these cross-border shipments are often as high as 30 to 50 percent.

Global Challenges Hit the Stage Three LFMS

Even an e-business with a third stage LFMS will find quite a challenge when it comes to selling product to the international members within its value chain. For example, if a value chain customer clicks the buy button, the e-business systems will confirm the order in real-time and should be able to price it out in the customer's local currency along with commitment to a delivery date.

Here is where the quandary begins: the order can't be completed because it needs to be screened for compliance of export regulations and terms and conditions of sale. I'm not saying it can't be done, because it can. Global fulfillment, however means dealing with relatively unfamiliar import and export restrictions, regulatory differences, and carrying technical and process interface requirements.

Next, let's deal with collaboration among value chain members of an e-business with a Stage Three LFMS. Once again, expanding across international borders presents significant problems. For example, the transportation infrastructure must be taken into account when implementing integration or collaboration globally. The local transportation infrastructure outside of "developed" countries is uncertain, so delivery times are unpredictable. As a result, higher than normal inventory levels must be maintained on both the buy side and the sell side to buffer against transit and demand uncertainty.

TRADITIONAL CUSTOMS BROKERS

What is going to happen to the traditional customs broker with the advent of e-business? Like the majority of the business world, they will have to make peace with the new paradigm. Customs brokers have a unique advantage — their business is based largely on trust — longstanding relationships are the norm since their clients trust them to keep them out of trouble with enforcement-minded customs agencies.

However, some customs brokers are being forced to adapt by their customers. Hasbro's logistics officer, Andy Rosener, has his customs brokers log on to a Web site hosted by Cargo Systems where Hasbro's supply chain information, such as arrival times for containers, is posted.

Eventually, though, international e-businesses will move their sourcing online, and their customs brokers and transportation providers should begin taking steps in anticipation of that measure. But that isn't the only reason. These third-party enablers have a tremendous chance for growth with the advent of e-business and its global aspects.

GLOBAL VIEW

An e-business, prior to rushing into a multinational model, must rethink its corporate culture. The e-business must address the challenges of understanding the logistics and fulfillment requirements needed to deliver its product to a destination country. But it needs to also consider such matters as electrical current (if the product uses electricity) and instructions in multiple languages. Then there is the documentation needed to ensure that you get paid properly. The e-business's executives should adopt a global view and become more aware of international events, issues and cultural trends that can affect the e-business. The executives and managers also need to have knowledge of a country's history to successfully conduct business and understand the cultural priorities of that nation.

"People will go back to focusing on operational excellence and on fundamentals," states John Wilson, director of global business development for IBM's SCM group. "They often gloss over 'Why am I doing this' in the frenzy to get in on e-business. The conversation we're having today is with executives worried that they don't know what they don't know — and that there may be tons that they are missing out on," Wilson continues. "They are focusing on the wrong aspect. They are looking for the next dot.com pure market play when they should be assessing what this can mean to their company and industry across today's emerging global supply chain."

Unless an e-business can properly finance the launch of their multilingual site, it will not be able to significantly penetrate the international online market. And, in general, the first mover advantage holds. Get into your international markets quickly now...before the local competition has already won over those markets.

Conclusion

"Nothing is permanent but change."
Heraclitus, 500 BC

THE INTERNET HAS WROUGHT a revolution in business. In much the same way that the introduction of the telephone, and later the fax machine, profoundly and irreversibly changed the world of commerce, the Internet is universally transforming the economics of information and transaction.

When e-business plays a small part in an enterprise's operation, it facilitates the firm's basic functions. When the impact of e-business is greater, however, the enterprise transforms its operation, and a new way of conducting business emerges. This digitization of traditional business, engendered by the Internet and the advent of e-business methods, leads to increased productivity, faster decision making and fewer errors, along with cost-efficiencies that gladden the heart of all stockholders. New business models are emerging, and enterprises worldwide must rethink not only how they deliver products and services but also their *raison d'être*.

Logistics and fulfillment is the essential foundation of e-business. A logistics and fulfillment plan allows an e-business to blueprint its business processes to enable the planning and then the implementation of an LFMS. Such planning will initiate the control of an efficient and effective flow and storage of goods, services, and related information and financial processes, from the point of origin to delivery of the finished product.

Your customers and your competition are the major forces that will drive future changes in your e-business. Your customers expect you to deliver products and services through continuous technological innovations, with greater speed, in smaller lot sizes, with shorter lead times, and higher flexibility — with no margin for error. A competitor that has a more streamlined process for customers or suppliers to access their inventory and data has a competitive advantage over an enterprise that is warehousing tons of merchandise and using legacy enterprise-facing systems and processes.

Unfortunately, for the unprepared e-business these forces can be a double whammy that forces an e-business to squeeze product development times, shrink product life cycles, and condense production and delivery schedules, many times without the infrastructure in place to support such seismic changes in its business processes. As you read this, your savvy rivals are establishing factories with smaller inventories, real-time information flow, shorter material pipelines, and orderly material and product handling. They have realized the value of a best-of-breed LFMS.

Many e-businesses are still developmentally in Stage One, fighting an uphill battle to reach Stage Two. Determining how robust an e-business's existing LFMS is and discerning what revisions need to be made are critical. Although orders may be initiated via the Web, in many e-businesses much of that data is input manually into a variety of other systems including value chain planning and management, warehouse management, and logistics systems, etc., negating the efficiencies and cost-savings that should come with the adoption of an e-business model.

In the Internet economy, the LFMS must address content management, application development, cross-function integration, business intelligence, and mobile Internet access. At the same time, e-businesses must embrace a system that enables the entire value chain to retrieve information about the demand picture, forecasts, delivery dates, shipment tracking, and other data. A first-class LFMS should allow trading partners, suppliers, buyers, sellers, distributors, and transportation providers to tap into one central source, pull data from ERP and other back-end systems, and receive order-tracking alerts and notification of potential problems. The LFMS must also work in tandem with platforms being used for customer service management, financial management and business analysis. This is the path toward real time-saving efficiencies that bring cost reductions and profit margin growth.

However, the e-business can't rest on its laurels. Once the LFMS is in place, the value chain's members will want to pull down more and more detailed data. But, accessing that information through a PC in the office will no longer suffice — they will want the data to be fed into pagers, cell phones, PDAs, and other wireless devices, in real-time.

Nonetheless, e-businesses shouldn't plunge into technology cure-alls. Rather, they should consider alternatives such as farming out all or part of their logistics and fulfillment functions. Many e-businesses have done just that. They realize the necessity of a top notch LFMS, but they don't consider logistics and fulfillment a core competency, or they don't have the time or the cash to build out the necessary components of a viable LFMS.

Many of today's successful e-businesses spent their first few years online concentrating on their front-end (i.e., the pretty pictures) in order to attract traffic (and customers). Now, these same e-businesses need to build a loyal customer base so they will get the "bookmark" and prove they can wring profit out of their Internet venture. This profitability will ride on the shirttails of a well-tuned logistics and fulfillment management system. The winners in the e-tail arena will be the e-businesses that learn how to handle small packages and large volume quickly and cost effectively, squeezing efficiencies out of every step, while providing the level of service quality their customers expect.

All e-businesses must, over time, learn to wrench profit from their e-business model. This requires making the most of their IT infrastructure to wrest profit and value from their supply chain through efficiencies that can only be brought about through real-time collaboration and data sharing. That requires a networked value chain.

In the years to come, the focus will be more on B2B processes, whether the e-business model is e-tail or B2B, because that is where the efficiencies will be found and the most significant process improvements and savings (that make Wall Street hum) can be made. Web-to-

ERP integration, logistics, fulfillment, building the right linkages — most of that heavy lifting is still to come. Tomorrow's business leaders will be the forward-thinking women and men who have embraced and harnessed this emerging technology. These trailblazers know that e-business is where the greatest opportunities for competitive advantage will be. They realize that all enterprises will need to be in the right position if they are to capitalize on this new paradigm.

E-business is logistics.

Glossary

24 x 7 — 24 hours a day, 7 days a week.

3PL — third party logistics providers. Third-Party Logistics is basically a fulfillment or distribution center that handles all of the following functions; receiving, shipping products (by either ground — UPS, FedEx, the U.S. Post Office, etc., or by long or short haul trucking), product storage, inventory control, customer service, order tracking and handling returns.

3R's — right product at the right place at the right time.

Application Programming Interface (API) — Software that an application uses to request and carry out lower-level services performed by a computer's operation system. In short, an API is a hook into software. An API is a set of standard software interrupts, calls and data formats that applications use to initiate contact with network services, mainframe communication programs, etc. Applications use APIs to call services that transport data across a network.

Application — a software program that does some type of task. MSWord, Netscape, Winzip, anti-virus programs are some examples of an application.

Application Service Provider (ASP) — a third party that manages and distributes software-based services and solutions to its customers from a centralized server base. .

Architecture — refers to the overall organizational structure of a given system, i.e., processor architecture or proprietary architecture. Central to an architecture is the decision about the selection of structural elements and their behavior, as defined by collaborations of larger subsystems, therefore the architectural style is the definitive guide for the system. .

API — see application programming interface.

ASN (Advance Ship Notice) — a notice sent by the vendor to the customer indicating what merchandise has been shipped and may also include expected time of arrival. It enables the receiver to identify a package's contents electronically without having to open it.

ASP — see application service provider.

ATP — see available-to-promise .

Available-to-Promise (ATP) — inventory exists or is in the manufacturing process. Available-to-promise is an essential activity in many business processes within logistics — the real-time checking of available resources or status of the availability of all inventory before making a critical decision or commitment. Available-to-promise requires that each partner in a supply chain — from providers of raw materials, through manufacturing, distribution and retail — must be committed to collaboratively sharing real-time visibility into inventories for there to be near-perfect available-to-promise capability across the supply chain. Note that inventory which may still be in stock after it has been earmarked for another customer is not available-to-promise.

B2B (Business-to-Business) — an e-business model that refers to one business communicating with and/or buying/selling to another.

B2C (Business-to-Consumer) — an e-business model that refers to a business (such as a retailer) communicating with or selling to an individual consumer. B2C is the retailing part of e-commerce on the Internet.

B2E (Business-to-Employee) — an e-business model where the focus of business is the employee, rather than the consumer or other businesses. B2E can encompass everything that an e-business might do to attract and keep qualified personnel. This might include recruiting, benefits management and other human resources applications, online education, and employee empowerment strategies. B2Es are designed to increase not only employee satisfaction, but also to develop a sense of community within an enterprise. B2E can also be referred to a "B2E portal" or "people portal." B2E can encompass not only everything that an employee might hope to find on an enterprise's intranet but also any personal information and links that the employee might want (stock market information, weather, traffic, local news).

Back-end — (1) program interfaces and services relative to the initial user, which may be a human being or a program, of the interfaces/services. (2) back-end application or program serves indirectly in support of the front-end services. This is normally accomplished through its location, i.e., closer to the required resource, or perhaps due to its capability to communicate with the required resource. A back-end application can interact directly with the front-end. However, it is more likely a program that is called from an intermediate program that mediates front-end and back-end activities. (3) support components of a computer system; back-end typically refers to the database management system (DBMS), which is the storehouse for the data.

Backorder — the process used when a customer orders an item that is not in inventory; the enterprise fills the order when the item becomes available.

Bar-Code — a series of lines of various widths and spacings that can be scanned electronically to identify a carton or individual item.

Bar-Code Scanner — a device to read bar codes and communicate data to computer systems.

Bar-Coding — a method of encoding data for fast and accurate readability. See Bar-Code.

Batch Picking — the process of picking of items from storage for more than one order at a time.

Benchmarking — a management tool for comparing performance against an enterprise that is widely regarded as outstanding in one or more areas, in order to improve performance.

Best-of-Breed — the best product of its type. Enterprises often purchase software from different vendors in order to obtain the best-of-breed for each application area; for example, a human resources package from one vendor and an accounting package from another. While ERP vendors provide a wealth of applications for the enterprise and tout their integrated system as the superior solution, all modules are rarely best-of-breed. Nobody excels in every niche.

Best-of-Class — a product considered to be superior within a certain category of hardware or software. It does not mean absolute best overall; for example, the best-of-class in a low-priced category may be seriously inferior to the best product on the market, which could sell for ten times as much.

Bricks-and-Click — see click-and-mortar.

Bricks-to-Click — see click-and-mortar.

Bricks-and-Mortar — a business (manufacturer, distributor, shop, supermarket, department store, etc.) in the traditional or real world and staffed by people versus computers serviced by people.

Broker — (1) an enterprise that arranges the buying and selling of transportation, goods, or services; (2) a ship agent who acts for the ship owner or charterer in arranging charters; (3) an enterprise that owns & leases equipment.

Bulk Cargo — goods not in packages or containers.

Business Rules — a conceptual description of an organization's policies and practices enabling them to automate their polices and practices, and to increase consistency and timeliness of their business processing.

Capable-to-Promise (CTP) — the ability to check the availability of capacity at key resources throughout a supply chain. Capable-to-promise capabilities allows an enterprise to provide more accurate order promising in an assemble to order environment where resource availability is a more valid determinant of scheduled dates than material availability. Today's Just-in-Time (JIT) fulfillment e-business model requires a capable-to-promise value stream. This means an enterprise that has adopted the JIT e-business model with capable-to-promise abilities can say with confidence to its customer: "We are capable of manufacturing the product that you want and delivering it to you in four days from the day that you place an order." .

Carnet — a customs document allowing special categories of goods to cross international borders without payment of duties.

Carousel — a rotating system of layers of bins and/or drawers that can store many items (usually small) using relatively little floor space.

Cartage — (1) the charge for the pick-up and delivery of goods; (2) the movement of goods locally, i.e., short distances.

Class I Carrier — a classification of regulated carriers based upon annual operating revenues — motor carriers of property, $5 million; railroads, $50 million; motor carriers of passengers, $3 million.

Class II carrier — a classification of regulated carriers based upon annual operating revenues — motor carriers of property, $1-$5 million; railroads, $10-$50 million; motor carriers of passengers, $3 million.

Class III Carrier — a classification of regulated carriers based upon annual operating revenues — motor carriers of property, $1 million; railroads, $10 million.

Class Rate — a grouping of products, goods or commodities under one general heading. All the items in the group make up a class. The freight rate that applies to all items in the class is the class rate.

Click-to-Bricks — refers to (1) a subset or variation of the local fulfillment e-business model, but also there are aspects of the in-store e-business model. The idea is quite simple, the customers go online to find a nearby bricks-and-mortar retailer that has available for immediate pick-up the product they are seeking. The customers can then go to the specified offline store with the confidence that they can pick up what they are seeking. (2) businesses that came into existence as a Web-based enterprise and then migrated to the traditional offline business environment.

Click-and-Mortar — also called "bricks-and-click" or "bricks-to-click." The terms refer to businesses that offer online services via the Web as well as the traditional offline enterprise staffed by people. Coined in 1999 by David Pottruck, co-CEO of the Charles Schwab brokerage firm, it refers to running the two divisions in a cooperative and integrated manner where they both support and benefit from each other.

Client/Server — the client is a PC or program "served" by another networked computing device in an integrated network which provides a single system image. The server can be one or more computers with numerous storage devices.

Commerce Services Provider (CSP) — a services that supplies e-businesses with the necessary tools and services to buy and sell products/services over the Internet and/or manage their online enterprise. CSPs can provide services, such as, hardware/software, risk management, distribution control, site development and hosting, site performance monitoring.

Common Carrier — a for-hire carrier that holds itself out to serve the general public at reasonable rates and without discrimination. To operate, the carrier must secure a certificate of public convenience and necessity.

Consignee — the receiver of goods, i.e. a freight shipment, usually the buyer.

Consignment — goods shipped to an overseas agent when an actual purchase has not been made, but when the consignee agrees to sell the goods.

Consignor — the shipper of goods, or shipper of a transportation movement.

Consolidation — collecting smaller shipments to form a larger quantity in order to realize lower transportation rates.

Consolidation Point — the location where consolidation takes place.

Consolidator — an enterprise that provides services to group shipments, orders, and/or goods to facilitate movement.

Consular Declaration — a formal statement made to the consul of a country describing products, goods or commodities to be shipped to that consul's country. Approval must be obtained prior to shipment.

Consular Documents — special forms signed by the consul of a country to which cargo is destined.

Consular Invoice — a document, required by certain international governments, describing a shipment of products, goods or commodities and showing information such as the consignor, consignee, and value of the shipment. Certified by a consular official of the international government, it is used by the country's custom officials.

Continuous Replenishment (CRP) — a system used to reduce a customer's inventories and improve service; CRP is usually reserved for large customers.

Contract Carrier — a for-hire carrier that doesn't serve the general public but serves shippers with whom the carrier has a continuing contract. The contract carrier must secure a permit to operate.

Conveyor — a product handling device that moves freight from one area of a warehouse to another. Roller conveyors utilize gravity and belt conveyors use motors.

Corporate Portal — an internal Web site (intranet) that provides proprietary, enterprise-wide information to company employees as well as access to selected public Web sites and vertical-market Web sites (suppliers, vendors, etc.). It includes a search engine for internal documents as well as the ability to customize the portal page for different user groups and individuals. It is the internal equivalent of the general-purpose portal on the Web.

Cost and Freight (C&F) — the seller quotes a price that includes the cost of transportation to a specific point. The buyer assumes responsibility for loss and damage and pays for the insurance of the shipment.

Cost, Insurance and Freight (CIF) — the price quote that the seller offers to the buyer, which includes cost of the goods, insurance of the goods, and transportation charges.

Courier Service — a fast, door-to-door service for products, goods and documents; these firms usually limit service to shipments weighing fifty pounds or less.

CPFR (Collaborative Planning, Forecasting and Replenishment) — a set of industry standards; B2B Web-based communication. CPFR is a concept that allows collaborative processes across the supply chain, using a set of process and technology models. CPFR allows manufacturers, distributors, logistics providers and retailers to collaborate with their trading partners, significantly reducing inventory, increasing sales and improving service levels.

Cross-docking — the movement of goods directly from receiving dock to shipping dock to eliminate storage expense.

Cross-selling — refers to the process of increasing a customer's purchasing level by offering enhancements

or new products/services, based on that customer's current purchasing status and history.

CSP — see Commerce Service Provider.

CTP — see Capable-to-Promise.

Currency Adjustment Factor (CAF) — a surcharge imposed by a carrier on ocean freight charges to offset foreign currency fluctuations.

Customs — the authorities designated to collect duties levied by a country on imports and exports.

Customs Broker or Customhouse Broker — an individual or firm that represents importers/exporters in dealings with customs. They are responsible for obtaining and submitting all documents for clearing merchandise through customs, arranging inland transport, and paying all charges related to these functions.

Customs Clearance — the act of obtaining permission to import merchandise from another country into the importing nation.

Customs Invoice — a document that contains a declaration by the seller, the shipper, or the agent as to the value of the shipment.

Customs Value — the value of the imported goods on which duties will be assessed.

CWT — the abbreviation for hundredweight, which is the equivalent of 100 pounds.

Cyber World — the virtual world that is encompassed by the Internet.

Cyberland — see Cyber World.

DC — Distribution Center.

Declaration of Dangerous Goods — in compliance with US regulations, exporters are required to provide special notices to inland and ocean transport companies when goods are hazardous.

Declared Value for Carriage — the value of the products, goods or commodities, declared by the shipper on a bill of lading, for the purpose of determining a freight rate or the limit of the carrier's liability.

Deconsolidator — an enterprise that provides services to un-group shipments, orders, goods, etc., to facilitate distribution.

Defective Goods Inventory (DGI) — items that have been returned, have been delivered damaged and have a freight claim outstanding, or have been damaged in some way during warehouse handling.

Demand Forecast — the upper limit for accepting orders during each day and/or week is either the demand forecast or capacity, whichever is least. Suppliers build to the demand forecast. Planners and schedulers use the demand forecast to schedule new customer orders within forecasted raw material availability. The demand forecast uses factual data to project possible future demand. It gives suppliers, planners, and schedulers a tool to do their jobs better without requiring a sales forecast.

Demand-Aggregation — combines orders from multiple buyers into powerful high-volume transactions. Large transactions can increase buyer purchasing power, accelerate sales and improve a B2B marketplace liquidity.

Demurrage — a penalty assessed for exceeding free time allowed for loading/unloading under the terms of an agreement with a carrier. Note that "demurrage" is the term used in the rail and ocean industry but "detention" is the term used in the motor industry.

Detention — see Demurrage.

Devanning — the act of unloading of cargo from a container or other piece of equipment. See Stripping.

DGI — see Defective Goods Inventory.

Differential — a discount offered by a carrier that faces a service time disadvantage over a route.

Digital Marketplace — an alliance of cooperating enterprises forming a new line of business. These participating enterprises with their complementors and competitors, join together to better serve the needs of the customers and share the opportunity to lower transaction costs. Also see e-marketplace.

Direct Product Profitability (DPP) — the calculation of a net profit contribution attributable to a specific product or product line.

DNA (Distributed interNet Architecture) — Microsoft's platform for building and deploying interoperable

Web solutions. It is the precursor of Microsoft's .NET Enterprise Servers.

Document Type Definitions (DTDs) — files in which XML stores the definition tags relating to specific industries. The purpose of a DTD is to define the legal building blocks of an XML document; i.e., it defines the document structure with a list of legal elements.

Dotcom — slang for a Web-based business.

Double Bottoms — a motor carrier operation that involves one tractor pulling two trailers.

Drayage — a service offered by a motor carrier for pick-up and delivery of ocean containers or rail containers. Drayage agents handle full-load containers for ocean and rail carriers.

DTD — see Document Type Definitions.

Dual Rate System — an international water carrier pricing system in which a shipper signing an exclusive use agreement with the conference pays a rate 10 — 15% lower than non-signatory shippers do for an identical shipment.

Due Diligence — a comprehensive investigation and assessment of all attributes, issues and variables inherent in a target entity/person/product/service, which will impact upon the target's ability to achieve its strategic objectives.

E-business — the use of Web technologies and advanced networking to extend and enhance the traditional business model.

E-business Architecture — a number of modular components that together meet the overall needs of an e-business model, such as e-business rules, Web architecture, application architecture and network infrastructure. For example, one component of an e-business architecture can be the integration of an intricate set of applications in such as way that they work together to manage, organize, route and transform information.

E-business Model — the methodology enabling the conversion of activities throughout an enterprise into an electronic-based system. Such a model provides means of communication and a framework for the gathering, storing and sharing of data that facilitates an expedient and cost-effective mode for day-to-day business operations. The result of such methodology is a fully functional e-business, which provides support for physical entities such as warehouses, distribution centers, stores, transportation systems, etc.

E-commerce — buying and/or selling electronically over a telecommunications system. In doing so every facet of the business process is transformed: pre-sales, updating the catalog and prices, billing and payment processing, supplier and inventory management, and shipment. By using e-commerce a business is able to rapidly process orders, produce and deliver a product/service at a competitive price and at the same time minimize costs.

EDI (Electronic Data Interchange) — a series of standards which provide a computer-to-computer exchange of business documents between different companies' computers over the Internet (and phone lines). EDI allows for the transmission of purchase orders, shipping documents, invoices, invoice payments, etc. between a Web-based business and its trading partners. EDI standards are supported by virtually every computer company and packet switched data communications company.

EDIFACT — EDI for Administration Commerce and Transport.

EIN — see Exporter Identification Number.

E-marketplace — a neutral (as opposed to a marketplace to facilitate buy-sell interactions between the sponsor e-business and its value chain) Internet-based solution that links businesses interested in buying and selling related goods or services from one another. The e-marketplace facilitates the exchange by matching buyers and sellers while taking into account the interests of both buyers and sellers.

End User — the final buyer of an item who purchases the item for immediate use.

Entry Form — the document that must be filed with Customs to obtain the release of and to allow collection of duties and statistics on imported products, goods or commodities. Also called a Customs Entry Form or Entry.

E-prenure — slang for an entrepreneur whose activities are Internet-related.

E-procurement — the acquisition of products and services over the Internet.

ERP (Enterprise Resource Planning) — a business management system that integrates all aspects of a business, such as, product planning, manufacturing, purchasing, inventory, sales, and marketing. ERP is generally supported by multi-module application software that helps to manage the system and interact with suppliers, customer service, and shippers, etc.

E-tail — the business-to-consumer portion of e-business. An e-tail e-business model is a Web-based retailer that sells product in small quantities to its customers.

Ex Works — the price that the seller quotes that applies only at the point of origin. The buyer takes possession of the shipment at the point of origin and bears all costs and risks associated with transporting the goods to the destination.

Exception Rate — a deviation from the class rate; changes (exceptions) made to the classification.

Exclusive Patronage Agreements — a shipper agrees to use only a conference's member liner firms in return for a 10 to 15 percent rate reduction.

Exempt Carrier — a for-hire carrier that is exempt from economic regulations.

Export Broker — an enterprise that brings together buyer and seller for a fee, then eventually withdraws from the transaction.

Export Declaration — a document required by the US Treasury Department and completed by the exporter to show, for example, the value, weight, consignee, and destination pertinent to the export shipment.

Export License — a document secured from a government authorizing an exporter to export a specific quantity of a controlled commodity to a certain country. An export license is often required if a government has placed embargoes or other restrictions upon exports.

Export Management Company — a private firm that serves as the export department for several manufacturers, soliciting and transacting export business on behalf of its clients in return for a commission, salary, or a retainer plus commission.

Export Sales Contract — the initial document in any international transaction; it details the specifics of the sales agreement between the buyer and seller.

Export Trading Company — a firm that buys domestic products for sale overseas. A trading company takes title to the goods, whereas an export management company usually does not.

Exporter Identification Number (EIN) — a number required for the exporter on the Shipper's Export Declaration. An enterprise may use its Federal Employer Identification Number as issued by the IRS; an individual can use his or her Social Security Number.

Extranet — a private, TCP/IP-based network that allows qualified users from the outside to access an internal network.

FAK — see Freight-All-Kinds.

FAS — see Free Along Side.

FCL (Full Container Load) — a term used when products, goods or commodities occupy a whole container.

FEU (Forty foot Equivalent Unit) — a standard size intermodal container.

FGI — see Finished Goods Inventory.

Fill Rate — the percentage of order items that the picking operation actually found.

Finished Goods Inventory (FGI) — the products completely manufactured, packaged, stored, and ready for distribution.

Firewall — Hardware and/or software that sit between two networks, such as an internal network and an Internet service provider. It protects the network by refusing access by unauthorized users. It can even block messages to specific recipients outside the network.

Flexible-Path Equipment — handling devices that include hand trucks and forklifts.

Flow Rack — a storage method where product is presented to picking operations at one end of a rack and replenished from the opposite end.

F.O.B. (Free On-board Ship) — a term of sale defining who is to incur transportation charges for the shipment, who is to control the shipment movement, or where title to the goods passes to the buyer.

For-Hire Carrier — a carrier that provides transportation service to the public on a fee basis.

Free Along Side (FAS) — the seller agrees to deliver the products, goods or commodities to the dock alongside an overseas vessel that is to carry the shipment. The seller pays the cost of getting the shipment to the dock; the buyer contracts with the carrier, obtains documentation, and assumes all responsibility from that point forward.

Freight Alongside Ship — the point of embarkment that is chosen by the buyer and from where a carrier transports goods. The seller is obligated to pay the cost and assume all risks for transporting goods from a place of business to the FAS point.

Freight Forwarder — an individual or company that provides services to facilitate the transport of shipments. The services can include documentation preparation, space and equipment reservation, warehousing, consolidation, delivery, clearance, banking and insurance services, and agency services. The forwarder may facilitate transport by land, air, ocean, or may specialize in one mode of transport. Also known as Forwarder or Foreign Freight Forwarder.

Freight-All-Kinds (FAK) — an approach to rate making whereby the ante is based only upon the shipment weight and distance. It is widely used in TOFC service.

Front-end — (1) program interfaces and services relative to the initial user (which may be a human being or a program) of the interfaces/services. (2) a "front-end" application is an application that users interact with directly. (3) relative to the client/server computing model, the client part of the program is often called the front-end and the server part is called the back-end.

Fulfillment — the systems that provide the link between the customer experience and the actual physical delivery of goods to the customer, which include inventory management, order capture and management and reconciliation.

FTL (Full Truck Load) — a term used when product, goods or commodities occupy a whole truck.

GATT — see General Agreement on Tariffs and Trade.

General Agreement on Tariffs and Trade (GATT) — a multilateral trade agreement aimed at expanding international trade as a means of raising world welfare.

General Order (GO) — a term used in the customs arena that refers to a warehouse where product, goods or commodities not entered within five working days after the carrier's arrival is stored at the risk and expense of the importer.

General Commodities Carrier — a common motor carrier that has operating authority to transport general commodities, or all commodities not listed as special commodities.

Gondola — a railcar with a flat platform and sides three to five feet high, used for top loading long, heavy items.

GTDI — European Guidelines for Trade Data Interchange.

Harmonized Commodity Description & Coding System (Harmonized Code) — an international classification system that assigns identification numbers to specific products. The coding system ensures that all parties in international trade use a consistent classification for the purposes of documentation, statistical control, and duty assessment.

Haulage — the inland transport service that is offered by the carrier under the terms and conditions of the tariff and of the relative transport document.

HAWB — see House Air Waybill.

Hazardous Materials — materials that the Department of Transportation has determined to be a risk to health, safety, and property. Included in this classification are items such as explosives, flammable liquids (i.e., colognes, wines, liquors), poisons, corrosive liquids, and radioactive material.

Hopper Car — a railcar that permits top loading and bottom unloading of bulk commodities. Hopper cars can have permanent tops with hatches to provide protection against the elements.

Horizontal Market — refers to the entire marketplace that crosses all industry boundaries.

House Air Waybill (HAWB) — a bill of lading issued by a forwarder to a shipper as a receipt for goods that the forwarder will consolidate with cargo from other shippers for transport.

HTML (HyperText Markup Language) — used to create documents on the World Wide Web by defining the structure and layout of a Web document through the use of tags and attributes thereby determining how documents are formatted and displayed.

HTTP (HyperText Transfer Protocol) — defines how messages are formatted and transmitted throughout Cyberland and what actions Web servers and browsers should take in response to various comments.

Hundredweight (cwt) — a pricing unit used in transportation; a hundredweight is equal to 100 pounds.

ICC — the United States Interstate Commerce Commission.

Igloos — pallets and containers used in air transportation. The igloo shape fits the internal wall contours of a narrow-body airplane.

Import License — a document that is issued by a carrier and by certain governments authorizing the importation of goods into their country.

In Bond — goods are held or transported In-Bond under customs control either until import duties or other charges are paid, or to avoid paying the duties or charges until a later date.

Inland Bill of Lading — the carriage contract used in transport from a shipping point overland to the exporter's international carrier location.

Information Technology (IT) — all aspects of managing and processing information, especially within an enterprise. Can also be known as Information Services (IS) and Management Information Services (MIS).

Infrastructure — interconnecting hardware and software that supports the flow and processing of information.

Insourcing — the use of internal resources and personnel for a project.

Integrated Carrier — an airfreight company that offers a blend of transportation services such as air carriage, freight forwarding, and ground handling.

Integration — (1) a combination of units so that they work together or form a whole. (2) a process in which separately produced components or subsystems are combined and any problems due to the interaction are addressed. (3) an activity by which specialists bring different manufacturers' products together so as to form a smoothly working system. (4) products or components that are integrated and appear to share a common purpose or set of objectives or they observe the same standard or set of standard protocols or share a mediating capability. (5) products or components that were designed at the same time with a unifying purpose and/or architecture although the individual units may be sold separately even though they were designed with the same larger objectives and/or architecture, share some of the same programming code (such as special knowledge of code).

Integrator — a specialist that brings different manufacturers' products together so as to form a smoothly working system.

Intermodal Container Transfer Facility — a facility where cargo is transferred from one mode of transportation to another, usually from ship or truck to rail.

Intermodal Marketing Company (IMC) — an intermediary that sells intermodal services to shippers.

International Import Certificate — a document required by an importing country indicating that the importing country recognizes that a controlled shipment is entering their country. The importing country pledges to monitor the shipment and prevent its re-export, except in accordance with its own export control regulations.

Internet — a public global network of computers that exchange data.

Intranet — an internal TCP/IP-based network behind a firewall that allows only users within a specific enterprise to access it.

IT — see Information Technology.

Java — a high-level object-oriented programming language similar to C++ from Sun Microsystems designed primarily for writing software to leave on Web sites which is often downloadable over the Internet. Java is basically a new virtual machine and interpretive dynamic language and environment.

Just-in-Time (JIT) — originated in the manufacturing industry. Today JIT is a way to manage processes so that specific components (or services) can be made available at the appropriate times (that is, "just-in-time").

Just-In-Time Inventory Management — an inventory control system that attempts to reduce inventory levels by coordinating demand and supply to the point where the desired item arrives just in time for use.

Just-in-Time Logistics (or Quick Response) — the process of minimizing the times required to source, handle, produce, transport, and deliver products in order to meet customer requirements.

Kanban system — a just-in-time inventory system used by Japanese manufacturers.

Kitting — a process whereby individual items are grouped or packaged together to create a special single item.

Lading — the cargo carried in a transportation vehicle.

LAN (Local Area Network) — a short distance data communications network consisting of both hardware and software and typically residing inside one building or between buildings adjacent each other — thus allowing all networked devices to share each other's resources.

LASH Vessel — a ship measuring at least 820 feet long with a deck crane able to load and unload barges through a stern section that projects over the water. LASH stands for Lighter Aboard SHip.

LCL (Less than CarLoad rail service or Less than Container Load) — a term used when product, goods or commodities do not completely occupy an entire container or railcar. When more than one shipper has its merchandise in a single container, each shipper's shipment is considered to be LCL.

Legacy systems — information resources currently available to an enterprise. Legacy systems are operational mainframes, personal computers, serial terminals, networks, databases, operating systems, applications, and other forms of hardware and software that have great value to an enterprise. However, these legacy systems cannot easily or economically be extended to the Web or otherwise modified to fulfill the requirements of an e-business model.

Letter of Credit (LOC) — an instrument of payment, issued by a buyer's bank, that ensures payment to the seller.

LFMS (Logistics and Fulfillment Management System) — A collection of programs that enables an e-business to store, modify, and extract information from numerous sources within its value chain.

Lighter — a barge-type vessel used to carry cargo between shore and cargo ship. Although the terms barge and lighter are used interchangeably, a barge normally refers to a vessel used for a long haul, while a lighter normally refers to a vessel used for a short haul.

Lighterage — the cost of loading or unloading a vessel by means of barges.

Line-haul Shipment — a shipment that moves between cities and over distances more than 100 to 150 miles in length.

Liner Service — International water carriers that ply fixed routes on published schedules.

Logistics — the process of planning, implementing, and controlling the efficient, effective flow and storage of goods, services, and related information from point of origin to point of consumption for the purpose of conforming to customer requirements.

Long Ton — 2,240 pounds.

LTL (Less than Truck Load) — same as LCL, but in reference to trucks instead of containers or railcars.

LTL shipment — a less than truckload shipment, i.e., one weighing less than the minimum weight an enterprise would need to use the lower truckload rate.

Major Carrier — a for-hire certificated air carrier that has annual operating revenues of $1 billion or more and usually operates between major population centers.

Manifest — a list of all cargoes that pertain to a specific shipment, grouping of shipments, or piece of equipment. Ocean carriers will prepare a manifest will prepare a manifest per container, etc.

Master Air Waybill (MAWB) — the bill of lading issued by air carriers to their customers.

Measurement Ton — forty cubic feet; used in water transportation ratemaking.

Merge-in-Transit — a transportation provider picks up separate loads from two or more different locations, transports the loads to a location near their final destination, and then performs a "merge" operation. The merge operation can comprise just the consolidation of the loads or include value-added process, such as assembly.

Messyware — (1) the arduous process of trying to integrate a wide range of partner data, services and technology. None of which can interact with each other without the intervention of third-party applications. (2) Ravi Ganesan, chief technology officer at CheckFree Corp., coined the term "messyware" and defined it as "the sum of the institutional subject area knowledge, experienced human capital, core business practices, service, quality focus and IT assets required to run any business.".

Middleware — is used to describe separate software products that serve as the glue between two applications. This "middleware" connects two otherwise separate applications. Middleware can also be referred to as "the plumbing" because it connects two sides of an application and passes data between them.

Minimum Weight — the shipment weight the carrier's tariff specifies as the minimum weight required to use the truck load (TL) or car/container load (CL) rate; the rate discount volume.

Model — refers to the methodology that enables some kind of conversion of an organization and the results of such methodology.

Multiple-car Rate — a railroad rate that is lower for shipping more than one carload at a time.

National Carrier — a for-hire certificated air carrier that has annual operating revenues of $75 million to $1 billion and it normally operates between major population centers and areas of lesser population.

Negotiable BOL or Order BOL — provides for the delivery of goods to a named enterprise or to their order (anyone they may designate), but only upon surrender of proper endorsement and the bill of lading to the carrier or the carrier's agents.

Net Weight — the weight of the product, goods, merchandise, unpacked, exclusive of any containers.

Non Vessel Operating Common Carrier (NVOCC) — a company that offers the same services as an ocean carrier, but which does not own or operate a vessel. NVOCCs are normally the consolidator and as such accepts small shipments (LCL) and consolidates them into full container loads. NVOCCs then act as a shipper, tendering the containers to ocean common carriers and are required to file tariffs with the Federal Maritime Commission. They are subject to the same laws and statutes that apply to primary common carriers.

Non-Negotiable BOL — provides for the delivery of goods to a named

enterprise and not to any one else. This is also referred to as a straight bill of lading.

Not Otherwise Specified/Not Elsewhere Specified (NOS/NES) — used in ocean or airfreight tariffs respectively. If no rate for the specific commodity shipped appears in the tariff, then a general class rate (for example: printed matter NES) will apply. Such rates usually are higher than rates for specific commodities.

NVOCC — see Non Vessel Operating Common Carrier.

Ocean Carrier — an enterprise that offers service via ocean (water) transport.

Order Bill of Lading — see Negotiable BOL.

Order Cycle Time — refers to the time that elapses from placement of order until receipt of order. It includes time for order transmittal, processing, preparation, and shipping.

Order Cycle — refers to the time spent and the activities performed from the time an order is received to the actual delivery of the order to a customer.

Order Fill — a measure of the number of orders processed without stockouts, or the need to backorder, expressed as a percentage of all orders processed in the warehouse/distribution center or fulfillment facility.

Order Picking — the assembling of a customer's order from items in storage.

Order Processing — all of the activities associated with filling customer orders — computer related and human related.

OSD — refers to Over, Short, and Damaged.

Outsourcing — contracting with outside specialists, such as consultants, software houses, integrators or service bureaus to perform systems analysis, programming and data center operations, and other services outside the competency of the contractor.

Packing List — a document containing information about the location of each Product ID in each package. The document allows the recipient to quickly find the item being sought without a broad search of all packages. A packing list also confirms the actual shipment of goods on a line item basis.

Pallet — a platform (about four feet square) used for moving and storing products, goods and merchandise. A forklift truck is used to lift and move a loaded pallet.

PDA (Personal Digital Assistant) — a handheld device that using a stylus for input and combines computing, telephone/Internet and networking features.

Per Diem — the payment rate a railroad makes to use another railroad's cars.

Personal Discrimination — when a different rate is charged to shippers with similar transportation characteristics; or when a similar rate is charged to shippers with differing transportation characteristics.

Picking by Aisle — a method whereby pickers pick all needed items in an aisle regardless of the items' ultimate destination; the items must be sorted later.

Picking by Source — a method whereby pickers successively pick all items going to a particular destination regardless of the aisle in which each item is located.

Piggyback — a rail-truck service wherein the shipper loads a highway trailer, and a carrier drives it to a rail terminal and loads it on a rail flatcar. The railroad then moves the trailer-on-flatcar combination to the destination terminal, where the carrier offloads the trailer.

PKI (Public Key Infrastructure) — a system consisting of digital certificates, Certificate Authorities, and other registration authorities that can authenticate the validity of each party involved in an Internet transaction.

Plug-and-play — (1) the ability to add a new component and have it work without having to perform any technical analysis or procedure. (2) an Intel standard (also known as PnP) for the design of PC expansion boards to eliminate the frustration of configuring the system when adding new peripherals. Plug and Play is supported directly in Windows 95/98.

Portal — a Web site that offers a broad array of resources and services. These resources and services can be offered to the general public, to a specific authorized group, and/or maintained for an enterprise's internal organization (see Corporate Portal).

Point-of-Sale (POS) — (1) the physical location where a sales transaction takes place between a business and a customer. (2) the software that handles a sales transaction between a business and a customer. (3) a set of parameters and processes that are related to creating a record of the sale of a product/service that can flow throughout a value chain.

Pop-up Window — a second browser window that "pops up" when called by a link, a button or an action.

POS — Point of Shipment or Point-of-Sale. See Point-of-Sale.

Pro Forma Invoice — an invoice that is forwarded by the seller prior to shipment, which advises the buyer of the particulars and value of the products, goods or commodities. A pro forma invoice is usually required by the buyer in order to obtain an import permit or letter of credit.

Proportional Rate — a rate that is lower than the regular rate for shipments that have prior or subsequent moves. It is used to overcome combination rates' competitive disadvantages.

Public Warehouse Receipt — a document the public warehouse manager issues as a receipt for the products, goods or commodities an enterprise gives to the warehouse manager. Note that the receipt can be either negotiable or nonnegotiable.

Pull Ordering System — a system whereby each warehouse controls its own shipping requirements by placing individual orders for inventory with a central distribution center.

Pure-play — a "click" — an enterprise that is only Web-based; i.e, it has no bricks-and-mortar counterpart.

Push Ordering System — an enterprise makes inventory deployment decisions at the central distribution center and ships to its individual warehouses accordingly.

Real-Time — occurring immediately (as opposed to simultaneously as in real time). The data is processed the moment it enters a computer, as opposed to BATCH processing, where the information enters the system, is stored and is operated on at a later time.

Reconsignment — a service that permits a shipper to change the destination and/or consignee after the shipment has reached its originally billed destination and to still pay the through rate from origin to final destination.

Reefer — a container with a self-contained refrigeration unit that is used for the transportation of perishable cargo.

Regional Carrier — a for-hire air carrier, usually certificated, that has annual operating revenues of less than $75 million and normally operates within a specific region.

Release Approval — a document that advises products, goods or commodities are available for further movement or action.

Released-value Rates — the rates that are based upon a shipment's value. The maximum carrier liability for damage is less than the full value, and in return the carrier offers a lower rate.

Restricted Articles — an air carrier term that refers to hazardous material, as it is defined by Title 49, Code of Federal Regulations (U.S.) and Air Transport Restricted Articles Circular 6-D.

Reverse Logistics — the process of collecting, moving, and storing unwanted, used, damaged, or outdated products and/or packaging from end users.

RFP (Request for Proposal) — a document that invites a vendor to submit a bid for hardware, software and/or services.

ROI (Return on Investment) — how much "return," usually profit or cost saving, results from a particular action. ROI calculations are sometimes used along with other approaches to present a business case for a given project. The overall ROI for an enterprise is sometimes used as a way to grade how well the enterprise is managed. Many times, such as in the case of an e-business model, the enterprise has immediate objectives it wants to obtain; i.e., getting market revenue share, building infrastructure, or other objectives. In those cases, a ROI can be measured in terms of meeting one or more objectives rather than in immediate profit or cost saving.

SCM (Supply Chain Management) — the oversight of materials, information, and finances as they move in a process from supplier to manufacturer to distributor to retailer to consumer. SCM includes the coordination and integration of these flows both within and among members of the chain. The ultimate goal of an effective SCM system is to reduce inventory while still assuring that products are available when needed.

Seal Number — the identifier assigned to the tag used to secure or mark the locking mechanism on closed containers.

Service Contract — an agreement between a shipper and an ocean carrier or conference, in which the shipper makes a commitment to provide a minimum quantity of cargo over a fixed time period. The ocean carrier or conference also commits to a rate or rate schedule as well as a defined service level, such as space, transit item, port rotation, or other features.

Ship Agent — an individual or liner company or tramp ship operator representative who facilitates ship arrival, clearance, loading and unloading, and fee payment while at a specific port.

Ship Broker — an individual or company that serves as a go-between for the tramp ship owner and the chartering consignor or consignee.

Shipment Gross Weight Qualifier — a weight qualifier for the estimated gross weight of LCL and/or FCL for a booking.

Shipment Identification — unique identifier of a shipment. The shipment identification is supplied by the user and allows loads to be consolidated into shipments.

Shipper's Agent — an individual or company that primarily matches up small shipments, especially single-traffic piggyback loads, to permit shippers to use twin-trailer piggyback rates.

Short Ton — 2,000 pounds.

Short-haul Discrimination — when a shipper is charged more for a shorter haul than for a longer haul over the same route, in the same direction, and for the same commodity.

SKU — see Stock Keeping Unit.

Slip Sheet — similar to a pallet; a slip sheet is normally made of cardboard or plastic and is used to facilitate movement of unitized loads.

SMI (Supply Management Infrastructure) — an infrastructure that allows for and facilities the mutual benefit of an entire value chain through a varying sets of demand management relationships that start with the customer and end at the supply base.

Sourcing — using a specific location or enterprise from where goods will be obtained.

Special Customs Invoice — a country may require in addition to a commercial invoice, a special customs invoice designed to facilitate the clearance of goods and the assessment of customs duties in that country.

Special Commodities Carrier — a common carrier trucking company that has authority to haul a special commodity. There are 16 special commodities, which include house-

hold goods, petroleum products, and hazardous materials.

SQL (Structured Query Language) pronounced "sequel" — a database language used for creating, maintaining and viewing database data.

Startup — a new business venture.

Steamship Conference — a voluntary, collective, rate-making body representing member steamship lines.

Steamship Line — an enterprise that owns and/or operates vessels in maritime trade.

STL (Standard Two Letter) — (code designation for airlines).

Stocking Keeping Unit (SKU) — a method of identifying a product without using a full description.

Stripping — the unloading of cargo from a container or other piece of equipment. See Devanning.

Supplemental Carrier — a for-hire air carrier that does not have a time schedule or designated route, instead the carrier provides service under a charter or contract per plane per trip.

Supply Chain Management — the integration of the supplier, distributor, and customer logistics requirements into one cohesive process to include demand planning, forecasting, materials requisition, order processing, inventory allocation, order fulfillment, transportation services, receiving, invoicing, and payment.

Supply Chain — a group of physical entities such as manufacturing plants, distribution centers, conveyances, retail outlets, people and information which are linked together through processes (such as procurement and/or logistics) in an integrated fashion, to supply goods or services from source through consumption.

Switching Company — a railroad that moves railcars a short distance. A switching company connects two mainline railroads to facilitate through movement of a shipment.

Tapering Rate — a rate that increases with distance but not in direct proportion to the distance the product, goods or commodity is shipped.

Tare weight — the weight of an empty vehicle.

Tariff — the document issued by a carrier setting forth applicable rules, rates, and charges for the movement of goods. The document sets up a contract of carriage between the shipper, consignee, and carrier.

Tariff Service — the type of service required, such as dock to house, dock to pier, pier to pier, pier to house, etc.

TCP/IP (Transmission Control Protocol/Internet Protocol) — a networking protocol (the Internet's protocol) that provides communication across interconnected networks, between computers with diverse hardware architectures and various operating systems.

Terminal Delivery Allowance — the reduced rate that a carrier offers in return for the shipper or consignee delivering or picking up the freight at the carrier's terminal.

Terminal Receipt — a document that

is used to accept materials or equipment at a terminal. A terminal receipt provides the delivering carrier with proof of delivery and the terminal with a verification of receipt.

TEU (Twenty-foot Equivalent Unit) — a standard size intermodal container.

Through Bill of Lading — a single bill of lading that covers both the domestic (inland) and international carriage of an export shipment.

Time/Service Rate — a rail rate that is based upon transit time.

TOFC (Trailer On Flat Car) — see Piggyback.

Ton-mile — a freight transportation output measure that reflects the shipment's weight and the distance the carrier hauls it; a multiplication of tons hauled and distance traveled.

Tracing — determining a shipment's location during the course of a move.

Tracking — a carrier's system of recording movement intervals of a shipment from origin to destination.

Trade Lane — the combination of the origin and destination points.

Tramp — an international water carrier that has no fixed route or published schedule. A shipper might charter a tramp ship for a particular voyage or a given time period.

Transit Privilege — a carrier service that permits the shipper to stop the shipment while in transit to perform a function that changes the product's, goods' or commodity's physical characteristics. The shipper still pays the through rate.

Transmittal Letter — a document from the shipper to its agent that lists the particulars of a shipment, the documents being transmitted, and instructions for the disposition of those documents.

Transshipment — the shipment of products, goods or commodities to the point of destination in another country on more than one vessel or vehicle. The liability may pass from one carrier to the next, or it may be covered by a Through Bill of Lading issued by the first carrier.

Unitize — the consolidation of several packages into one unit whereby carriers strap, band, or otherwise attach several packages together.

Unit Load Device (ULD) — this term refers to airfreight containers and pallets.

Unit Train — an entire, uninterrupted locomotive, car, and caboose movement between an origin and destination.

Up-selling — the process of increasing a customer's purchasing level by customer to switch from one product to another through the offering of additional recommendations when the customer is browsing and/or placing an order.

Value Chain — the chain of all the companies involved in developing or delivering a particular product or solution, from raw-material supplier through final retailer and sometimes the end-user.

Valuation Charges — the transportation charges to shippers who declare a value of goods higher than the value of the carriers' limits of liability.

Value-of-Service Pricing — the practice of pricing according to the value of the product the company is transporting; third-degree price discrimination; demand-oriented pricing; charging what the traffic will bear.

VAN (Value-Added Network) — a communications network that provides services beyond normal transmission, such as automatic error detection and correction, protocol conversion and message storing and forwarding. EDI is an example of a value-added network.

Vendor — (1) software companies, (2) hardware manufacturers in the computer industry or (3) a firm or individual that supplies goods or services; the seller.

Vertical Market — refers to a particular industry such as steel, automobile manufacturing or computers.

Vertical Portal — a vertical-market Web site that provides information and services to a particular industry. It is the industry-specific equivalent of the general-purpose portal on the Web.

Vessel Manifest — a document that lists all of the cargo on a vessel.

VMI (Vendor Managed Inventory) — a customer service strategy used to manage inventory of customers to lower cost and improve service.

Vortal (Vertical pORTAL) — see Vertical Portal.

Voyage — the trip designation (trade route and origin/destination) identifier, usually numerically sequential.

VPN (Virtual Private Network) — a secure, encrypted connection between two points across the Internet. It can act as an intranet or extranet, but uses the Internet as the networking connection. Most VPNs are built and run by Internet service providers.

VSA — Vessel Sharing Agreement.

WAN (Wide Area Network) — a network that is geographically scattered with a broader structure than a LAN. It can be privately owned or leased, but the term usually implies public networks.

Waybill — a non-negotiable document prepared by or on behalf of the carrier at the point of shipment origin. The Waybill will show the point of origin, destination, route, consignor, consignee, description of shipment, and amount charged for the transport service.

Web — a subset of the Internet that in today's world is accessed via a Web browser.

Weight Break — the shipment volume at which the LTL charges equal the TL charges at the minimum weight.

Weight Unit Qualifier — the unit of measure that the user wants to see for weight.

Wharfage — the charges assessed by pier personnel for the handling of incoming or outgoing cargo.

work in process (WIP) — parts and subassemblies in the process of becoming completed assembly components. These items, no longer part of the raw materials inventory and not yet part of the finished goods inventory, may constitute a large inventory by themselves and create extra expense for an enterprise.

WPA — With Particular Average.

XML (eXtensible Markup Language) — a system for organizing and tagging elements of a document specifically designed for Web documents. It enables designers to create their own customized tags to provide functionality not available with HTML. XML also has the ability to enable the structured exchange of data between computers attached to the Web, thus allowing one Web server to talk to another Web server. This means manufacturers and merchants can begin to quickly swap data, such as pricing, stock-keeping numbers, transaction terms and product descriptions.

XSL (Extensible style language) — a companion to XML that combines the formatting advantages of HTML with object-oriented intelligence. It denotes the style sheets that work in conjunction with XML data to format the electronic information at runtime.

XHTML (eXtensible HyperText Markup Language) — a proposed XML-compliant version of HTML 4.0 to make it easier for Web pages to be displayed on handheld Internet applicances, such as PDAs, cell phones, and other outlets besides the laptop or desktop computer.

Index

APR 2 5 2001